Keeping Holy Time

STUDYING THE REVISED COMMON LECTIONARY
Year C

EDITED BY

DOUGLAS E. WINGEIER

Contributors: Terri S. Cofiell, David deSilva,
Vincent Harris, Denise Nutt-Beers,
Mary Jo Osterman, Sondra B. Willobee

ABINGDON PRESS / Nashville

KEEPING HOLY TIME
Studying the Revised Common Lectionary Year C

Library of Congress Cataloging-in-Publication Data
Keeping holy time : studying the Revised common lectionary, year C / edited by Douglas E. Wingeier; contributors, Terri S. Cofiell ... [et al.]. p. cm. ISBN 0-687-07977-2 (alk. paper) 1. Bible—Study and teaching. 2. Lectionaries. 3. Christian education of adults. I. Wingeier, Douglas E. II. Cofiell, Terri S.
BS603.K443 2003   264'.34—dc21   2003009862

ISBN 978-0-687-07977-3

This book is printed on acid-free, elemental chlorine-free paper.

Contents

Introduction

*W*ELCOME to Year C of KEEPING HOLY TIME. I trust your individual and group study of Scripture passages in the Revised Common Lectionary will be stimulating and rewarding. The advantage of Bible study based on the lectionary is that through the Christian year all the major themes of biblical faith are explored. Further, having studied the scriptural material, one is also prepared more adequately to celebrate the gospel in corporate worship. The joy of learning and celebration produces a rich harvest of spiritual growth and forming a life of Christian discipleship.

The front cover picture for year A suggested that "keeping holy time" through Scripture study is primarily a devotional exercise. Year B's cover featured an hourglass in the sunset (or sunrise), highlighting the time dimension in exploring biblical wisdom. For Year C we are emphasizing hearing the Word and worshiping God. Placing the Word at the center of our lives can add meaning to our experiences, throw light on our decisions, inform our witness, and provide a foundation for our ministry in workplace and world.

All Christians are called to ministry by our baptism, commissioned in our confirmation, and challenged to discipleship through Scripture study. Four kinds of ministry are open to us as laity, each of which can be enriched and deepened through knowledge of the Scriptures.

First, there is the ministry of *words*. Daily opportunities present themselves to speak a word of comfort, encouragement, rebuke, testimony, hope, or concern to those with whom we live and work, or merely meet in passing. The significance and impact of these words can be enhanced as they become grounded in such biblical themes as love and judgment, eternal life and hope, sin and salvation, commitment and discipleship, and the redemptive suffering of the cross.

Second, there is the ministry of concrete *aid*. Whether they ask for it or not, the persons we meet often need specific help—a loan, a ride, a meal, sharing of a burden, advice on a problem, assistance with a project, or just human companionship. When such opportunities for ministry arise, we can "just do it," or we can clothe the assistance we offer in the garments of compassion, service, or promise, as highlighted in such biblical images as foot washing, the sower and the soils, salt and leaven, the word become flesh, and the suffering servant.

A third type of lay ministry is found in *ethical decision-making*. Issues where there may be no clear right and wrong, or where we must choose between two goods or the lesser of two evils, call for much prayer, deliberation, consultation, and discernment. Biblical characters, such as Joseph who forgave his brothers, Queen Esther who came to the kingdom "for such a time as this," Jeremiah who spoke an unpopular word to the king, Zacchaeus who gave his ill-gotten gain to the poor, and Peter who overcame prejudice to welcome Gentiles into the faith community, set an example that we can emulate.

Finally, there is the ministry of the *change agent*—confronting unjust social conditions and transforming oppressive systems in light of the shalom vision and Jesus' proclamation of the reign of God. Such biblical stories as Moses liberating the Hebrew slaves, Elijah accusing Ahab over Naboth's vineyard, Nathan confronting David's sin against Bathsheba and Uriah, the council at Jerusalem deciding on just treatment of the Gentiles, and Paul and the soothsaying slave girl in Philippi provide guidance and inspiration for such approaches to ministry.

The questions for thought and discussion posed in the "Think About It" boxes and the "Study Suggestions" in this book will encourage you to probe ways of "keeping holy time" by carrying out these forms of ministry in your setting. It is hoped that as you examine biblical themes, images, characters, and stories in your study of the Year C lections, you will be both challenged and empowered to make your ministry in workplace and world more effective.

I wish also to express my gratitude to the writers who have contributed to this volume in its earlier *Linktionary* format: Terri S. Cofiell, David deSilva, Vincent Harris, Denise Nutt-Beers, Mary Jo Osterman, and Sondra B. Willobee.

Douglas E. Wingeier, editor

Resources

Harper's Bible Commentary. James L. Mays, general editor. Harper and Row, 1988.

Harper's Bible Dictionary. Paul J. Achtemeier, general editor. Harper and Row, 1985.

The Interpreter's Dictionary of the Bible, Volumes I–IV. George A. Buttrick, general editor. Abingdon Press, 1962. Supplementary Volume, edited by Keith Crim. Abingdon Press, 1976.

The Interpreter's One-Volume Commentary on the Bible. Charles M. Laymon, editor. Abingdon Press, 1971.

The New Interpreter's Bible, Volumes I–II. Leander E. Keck, convener and senior New Testament editor. Abingdon Press, 1994–2002.

ADVENT

Lections for First Sunday of Advent

Old Testament: Jeremiah 33:14-16

*T*HE Book of Jeremiah is a collection of prophetic oracles spoken by Jeremiah during his long ministry, from 627 B.C. to 587 and beyond. Early in this period, the Assyrian Empire crumbled and Judahite nationalism and confidence surged. While other prophets were proclaiming peace and promising YHWH's blessing and protection, Jeremiah proclaimed YHWH's displeasure and punishment.

Note: The most frequently used name for God in the Hebrew Bible is what scholars call "the tetragrammaton," YHWH, which appears about 6,800 times. We usually pronounce it "Yahweh," though the actual pronunciation used in biblical times is not certain. Because this name was highly revered, the title "Adonai"—Hebrew for "My Great Lord"—was increasingly used in its place. When written, the Hebrew vowels of "Adonai" were inserted with the four consonants YHWH to remind people to say "Adonai" rather than "Yahweh." The word "Jehovah" came into Christian usage in the late Middle Ages and is not correct. YHWH is usually translated "LORD" in English Bibles. Out of respect for the sanctity with which present-day Jews treat the name of God by not pronouncing it, we here will use the tetragrammaton YHWH, alternating it with "God" and "Lord."

The Promise of a King

Even as he proclaimed YHWH's judgment, Jeremiah also proclaimed YHWH's faithfulness to the promises made to David and to Levi. After the land was laid desolate, God would once again bring joy to the people. This promise of restoration focuses on a legitimate heir ("a righteous branch") from the house of David to reign over Judah. Jeremiah and his hearers would have understood this as a promise that any disaster would not be final, but that independence and good fortune would be reestablished under future Davidic kings (33:17). Jeremiah 33:18-24 speaks of a restored Levitical priesthood in a rebuilt Temple. This oracle thus looks past the coming disaster to an age of peace and security, a hope anchored in God's fidelity, and the people's return to righteous living.

The King Is Coming

This lection is read during Advent because of the early Christians' conviction that Jesus was this legitimate heir to David's kingdom, although in a realm that far transcended Jeremiah's imagining. After centuries of foreign domination and priestly corruption, such a reading of Jeremiah highlights the enduring conviction that God's promises cannot fail, even though they may not happen entirely as expected.

The Unshakable Kingdom

The central experience of God involved God's covenant loyalty and commitment to uphold righteousness (personal integrity) and justice (social morality) for God's people. As Christians who await the coming of the Messiah during Advent, this word from Jeremiah reminds us of our connection with others who have awaited their messiah—though the nature of "kingship" has been radically altered by the life, death, and resurrection of Jesus.

> **Think About It:** Jeremiah viewed God's covenants with David and Levi to be as firm and reliable as the fact that day follows night (33:19-21, 25-26). Christians ascribe the same certainty to Jesus' reign of love and justice. What are some signs in our time and lives that God remains faithful to this promise? What recent events, personal or global, may tempt us to doubt this? Where do you turn for assurance?

Psalter: Psalm 25:1-10

In a time of trouble, the psalmist looks for pillars to support him. The first is God's compassion and faithfulness toward God's covenant people. God can be trusted to rescue his own when they are in trouble. The second pillar is "getting right" with God. There is a strong emphasis on repenting of the sins that stand between us and divine favor. The juxtaposition of verses 10 and 11 points this up: Declaring that the covenant faithfulness of God is for those faithful to the Torah, the psalmist cries out for forgiveness of his own offenses.

If the train of thought in this psalm seems disjointed, it is because it is an acrostic poem. Each successive verse begins with the next letter of the Hebrew alphabet, which can lead a poet to choose words more to fit the form than the logical flow. Nevertheless, the structure of the whole is

> **Think About It:** The psalmist identifies two pillars of support: God's steadfast love and repentance and forgiveness. Where do you turn in times of distress and uncertainty? Do these two pillars work for you? What other sources of support have you found helpful?

carefully crafted. The themes of deliverance from dishonor (1-3), of God's forgiveness and favor (4-7), and of learning God's ways (8-10), are all reversed in the second half of the psalm, leaving the psalmist's cry for forgiveness standing at the center (11).

Epistle: 1 Thessalonians 3:9-13

In turning "to God from idols" (1 Thessalonians 1:9), the Christians in Thessalonica also turned away from most of their non-Christian neighbors' social and civic gatherings. Outsiders could easily come to view the Christian movement as one that turned good citizens into anti-social atheists—gathering in secret, showing no solidarity with the larger city, and looking forward to the overthrow of the Roman order (the return of the crucified revolutionary, Jesus). It should not surprise us, therefore, to find these non-Christians applying pressure on their neighbors in an attempt to bring them back into conformity with what the Greco-Roman culture would regard as an acceptable way of life.

Think About It: Paul puts the focus on seeking God's approval regardless of the reaction of unbelievers. How do you weigh the relative importance of faithfulness to God and relationships with non-Christian friends? When were some times when your doing things God's way evoked a negative response from those around you? What kept you faithful? How can we both witness for Christ and maintain relationships with persons whom we hope to influence for the good?

A Visit From Timothy

Paul sends a letter that focuses on seeking God's approval when Jesus returns and explains the insults and abuse believers endure as the natural reaction of ignorant people against the ways of God—to their detriment.

Rather than yield to society's pressures to conform, we are called to support one another in love and to maintain the distinctive way of life to which we have been called (described here with the single word, *holiness*; see 4:1-8).

Paul's thanksgiving here as elsewhere (in addition to 3:9, see 1:2-3; 2:13-15) serves to promote certain behaviors and commitments as praiseworthy in God's sight. With each thanksgiving to God, he reminds hearers Whom they must please, even if their neighbors censure them. Hope and holiness are also Advent themes. This season of preparation is viewed as a time of waiting and expectancy, a time to look inward and prepare to present ourselves as blameless before God. Paul urges the Thessalonians to make ready for the Lord's coming.

Gospel: Luke 21:25-36

The Gospel reading comes from Luke's version of Jesus' prophetic announcement of the coming of the Son of Man and the judgment in store for the Jerusalem Temple.

A Difficult Teaching

As Jesus' last teaching before his passion and death, this chapter assumes a certain solemnity. In the preceding passage (verses 20-24), Luke has interpreted Jesus' words about the "desolating sacrilege" (Mark 13:14) in light of the Roman siege of Jerusalem at the end of the Jewish War of A.D. 66–70. This is Luke's way of emphasizing for his post-70 audience that Jesus' predictions of the destruction of the Temple (Luke 21:5-6) had come true, thus underscoring the reliability of Jesus' other statements about the end and his return.

The Disrupted Cosmic Order

Most Jewish apocalypses speak of cosmic marvels and omens preceding the breaking in of God's reign, signs that are rooted in the prophecies of Isaiah and Joel. It is thus not surprising to find Jesus also referring to this expectation of the present cosmic order being thrown into an uproar as its time comes to an end (21:25-26). Precisely that which gives most human beings cause for alarm and panic should give the disciples reason for hope and confidence—these are signs of their deliverance and manifestations of the soundness of their faith.

Throughout early Christian literature, one finds church leaders pointing believers to the day of the Lord—when Christians would be vindicated by God and their detractors and antagonists exposed to fear and shame—as a means of encouraging them to remain steadfast in their hope and witness.

Israel had originally conceived of this day as the time in which oppressors would be routed and Israel, under God, would be restored, purified, and made wholly God's own. As the sins of the nation became ever more blatant, the day of the Lord came to be seen as a time of judgment against apostasy. Yet, hope remained for restoration.

The Durable Generation

Jesus' assertion that "this generation will not pass away" without seeing the fulfillment of his words has occasioned much debate. If he meant that his contemporaries would not die before his return, then Jesus' prediction was not confirmed by history, and his foreknowledge would be fallible. A frequent solu-

> **Think About It:** Jesus' final teaching ended where our Epistle also concluded—focusing the disciples' eyes on the goal of making ready for the day of the Lord by a faithful walk now. What weights, cravings, and pressures keep you from living singly and simply for God? In regard to that day, are you living now as one who is asleep in complacency, drunk with self-importance, or as one who is sensitive to signs of Christ's presence and ready to respond to his invitation?

15

tion to the problem suggests that by "all things" (verse 32) Jesus is referring only to the fate of Jerusalem in A.D. 70—which had already occurred by the time of Luke's writing.

Another solution takes *generation* in the sense of *offspring*, making this an assurance that Abraham's offspring would survive to see the end (that is, the Jewish people would not die out). However one interprets this verse, the following one stresses the certainty of the events described (Luke 21:33) in terms similar to Jeremiah 33:20-21.

Beware of Self-Deluding Pleasures

These words about the Second Coming close with an exhortation naming worldly concerns and self-deluding pleasures as the greatest threat to our eternal well-being. Whatever muddles the mind and prevents us from keeping God's judgment and our future hope in Christ clearly in view is a weight that drags us down into a trap. Here again 1 Thessalonians 5:1-8 emerges as a strong thematic parallel and can be seen as a sort of Pauline commentary on a Jesus tradition.

Study Suggestions

A. Focus on Advent

Begin by noting that this is the first Sunday of Advent. Ask: What does the word *Advent* mean? (coming, arrival, expectation) What is the significance of this season? (anticipation, preparation for the coming of Christ) What has this season meant to you in the past? What do you anticipate it will mean this year? How can we prepare ourselves spiritually for the coming of Christ?

B. Center on God, Our Hope

Invite group members into a time of silent prayer, asking God to enter their hearts, guide today's discussion, and help them devote time and energy during Advent to make themselves ready for Christmas—not only with decorated homes and yards but also with dedicated hearts and lives. Close by praying Psalm 25:1-10 together.

C. God's Faithfulness

Now ask someone to read aloud Jeremiah 33:10-21. Drawing on the commentary on pages 12–13, discuss: What does the oracle of 33:14-16 mean in its original context? What does the passage say about the reliability of God's promises in the face of human failure? Explain the use of the tetragrammaton, YHWH, and the reason for the Jews' reluctance to pronounce God's name. Ask: What can we learn about reverence from this practice? How do we express our awe and reverence for God?

Explain the promise YHWH made to Israel and Judah (verse 14; that God

16

would restore their security and well-being). Ask: What does this text bring to your understanding of Advent and the significance of Jesus' coming? How was Jesus' birth a fulfillment of this and other messianic promises? How is your faith related to these promises? Why did the Jews of Jesus' time have difficulty seeing him as the promised Messiah? How did he turn their expectations on end? How has/does his presence in your life upset your expectations?

D. Communal Responsibility

Read 1 Thessalonians 3:9-13 and the commentary on page 14. Ask: What challenges were these Christians facing? How does this passage throw light on how they might meet them? In what ways do you feel the tension between following Jesus completely and being comfortable, respected, and secure? How can we help one another live authentic Christian lives? How can we support one another (verse 12) so we can better face up to our shortcomings, deepen our faith (verse 10), "strengthen our hearts in holiness" (verse 13), and "stand firm in the Lord" (verse 8)? Also discuss the "Think About It" questions.

E. Christ Will Come Again—But How?

Read Luke 21:25-36 and the commentary on pages 15–16. Discuss: How real is this expectation for you? What gives rise to doubt? What suggests reliability and fuels assurance? Do you view Christ's coming again as a cataclysmic, end-of-the-world event or a renewing spiritual experience? Read 1 Thessalonians 5:1-8 (a Pauline parallel to this tradition), and engage the questions in the "Think About It" box. Invite participants to name the weights, cravings, and pressures that prevent them from living singly and simply for God. Consider inner desires, outer temptations, social expectations, the demands of making a living, and misfortunes. Covenant together to be an Advent support group to help one another prepare for the coming of Christ.

F. Tie It Together

Advent calls us to prepare for Christ's coming, not only as a baby (which we remember and celebrate) but as deliverer, judge, and sovereign of our lives. How does each lection contribute to this theme? Envision together Christ's coming—either in glory or as a quiet, transforming presence. What regrets, what causes for lament might you have? How is God leading you to prepare to receive him?

G. Sing in Expectation

Reflect together on what causes for joy you have as you enter the Advent season, and how those joys can focus your life. Close by singing the joyous Advent hymn, "Hail to the Lord's Anointed."

Lections for Second Sunday of Advent

Old Testament: Malachi 3:1-4

*M*ALACHI means "my messenger," and the prophet announces in this Scripture that God is about to send a messenger to prepare the way "before the great and terrible day of [YHWH]" (4:5). This messenger will bring word of YHWH's promise to fulfill the covenant. The one who "prepares the way" (3:1) is seen in Matthew 11:7-15 and Luke 1:16-17 as relating to the coming of Jesus, the Messiah.

Malachi's Message

Malachi was active in Judah after the refugees returned from Babylon and after the Temple was rebuilt (515 B.C.) but before the reforms of Ezra and Nehemiah (445 B.C.). He is interested in restoring pure worship at the Temple, castigating the priests for offering blemished animals for sacrifice, and rebuking the people for withholding the tithes needed for Temple upkeep and maintenance of the Levites (1:6–2:3; 3:8-12). The prophet also seeks to strengthen the marital bonds between Judahites, issuing one of Scripture's strongest denunciations of divorce (2:11-16). His key theme is faithfulness to God's covenant and its precepts.

God's Justice Called Into Question

This week's lection ought to be read as part of 2:17–3:5. Malachi 2:17 presents the dispute to which 3:1-5 provides God's answer. Malachi hears the question of theodicy (how God can be both all-good and all-powerful in light of the existence of evil) voiced among the people, some of whom claim it makes little difference whether one is righteous or wicked, whether one observes the law or does whatever one wishes. God appears to reward the wicked as freely as the just. This leads them to scoff, "Where is the God of justice?" (2:17; see 3:14-15).

Future Events Envisioned

Malachi looks to the future acts of God to assure Judah that there is in fact a "difference between the righteous and the wicked" (3:17-18), as well as a "God of justice" who will come "suddenly" to make that difference clear. Two future events are envisioned. The first is the coming of the messenger to cleanse the priests and restore them to the stature of Levi, the model lauded in 2:4-8. The second is the coming of YHWH in judgment against all who have lived contrary to the covenant, who have not pursued justice in their dealings with God and one another.

The Task of the Messenger

Malachi 4:4-6 adds another dimension to the work of the messenger, namely reconciling the new generation with the tradition of the old and restoring the kind of love and mutual care that must be exercised in the covenant community if the curse is to be avoided. Malachi thus turns the question around from "Where is the God of justice?" to "How shall we return?" to God and to Torah lest they find themselves on the wrong side of judgment. (Read 3:6-7; all the ethical and cultic exhortation in the book is included in this call to return to YHWH.)

> **Think About It:** In every age, the wicked seem to prosper, while the godly often suffer, leading us to ask with the people of Malachi's time, "Where is the God of justice" (2:17)? Why is this so? How does this affect your commitment to follow God? How satisfactory is Malachi's answer—a promise that one day God will make things right? But what if people get impatient and begin to chant, "We can't wait"? What response would you give? How do you sustain your faith in both God's goodness and power in the face of the cruel inequities of our time?

A New Testament Psalm: Luke 1:68-79

Luke fills his Nativity story with songs reminiscent of the Psalms and other hymns from Hebrew Scripture that celebrate the manifestations of God's faithfulness to God's promises and people.

Zechariah's psalm is a commentary on the significance of the events of Luke 1—John's birth and Jesus' conception—and the roles these two would have in fulfilling God's will for Israel. It weaves together many phrases from the Psalms (compare Luke 1:69 with Psalm 18:2; Luke 1:71 with Psalms 18:17 and 106:10) and even a line from Malachi (Luke 1:76; see Malachi 3:1; also compare Luke 1:79 with Isaiah 9:2).

The emphasis in the song, as throughout the infancy narrative, is on God's faithfulness to God's promises (notably to Abraham and to David) and especially on the coming of Jesus as fulfillment of those promises. Luke 1:74-75 is an interesting restatement of God's promise to Abraham (see Genesis 12:1-3; 15:1-7; 22:15-18). The reference to rescue from enemies is seen as a promise to be able to worship God without fear and in holiness. (See Psalm 105:8-11, 24-25 for another version of this promise.)

Epistle: Philippians 1:3-11

Paul's opening thanksgiving sections often signal major themes in his letters, and this holds true of Philippians. (Also review last week's commentary on the rhetorical effect of thanksgiving sections in Paul's letters: what Paul praises here he also promotes [page 00].) Note here the expressions of friendship (partnership) between Paul and his readers.

Friends and Partners
Friends share all things, according to the Aristotelian ideal, and Paul praises the Philippian Christians for having lived this ideal in their partnership with him. They have shared their material resources throughout his ministry. (See 2 Corinthians 11:8-9; Philippians 4:10-19.) They share his commitment to sharing the faith in their own steadfast witness to the gospel in the face of local opposition (see Philippians 1:27-30), which involves suffering for them even as it does for Paul (who is currently imprisoned; 1:7, 12-26).

Think About It: Paul valued this church's partnership in the gospel. How deep are your partnerships with fellow workers for God? How much do your church relationships reflect a vibrant, reciprocal partnership? How might you strengthen and deepen them?

They share Paul's ideals (the very core of true friendship, according to Aristotle; 3:14-20; 4:8-9). They share in mutual affection (1:7-8). Their relationship is one of "grace" (1:7), which is the basis and source of their friendship. "The good work" God will accomplish is related to the believers' partnership in the gospel. It is ultimately a community of united, faithful disciples reflecting the mind of Christ in all their dealings with one another (see 2:1-11) and with the outside world (2:12-15). They will therefore find approval at God's visitation.

Love and Insight
Verses 9-11 bring us to an Advent focus. The increase of love and insight into how to love as God loves is the path to discernment. The faithful are to deliberate and pray about what will make for a "harvest of righteousness"—a fruitful life that will result in approval when we face Christ one day. Undergirding their faithful efforts are Paul's constant prayers and unshakable confidence (1:3-6). This deep affection has sustained Paul in his ministry and in his imprisonment; now he can encourage them, even though they are apart.

20

Gospel: Luke 3:1-6

Luke's Gospel contains universal themes but he begins by grounding his account—addressed to the "most excellent Theophilus"—in particular.

Luke, the Historian

Luke grounds the sacred events of God's plan of salvation in the domain of secular history. Thus he dates the appearance of John the Baptist in a manner characteristic of secular historians. The fifteenth year of Tiberius (A.D. 28/29) becomes one of the few fixed dates for the story of Jesus and the early church. Dating a prophet's activity by reference to the reigning king also echoes the beginnings of Old Testament prophetic books (see Isaiah 1:1; Jeremiah 1:1-3). Add to this the formula "the word of God came to John," which recalls the prophetic call of many of the prophets, and one realizes that Luke wants his hearers to regard John as standing in succession to those prophets.

John, the Baptizer

Early Christians interpreted John the Baptist's significance using Isaiah 40 and Malachi 4. Malachi 4:5-6 speaks of God sending Elijah, the prophet of repentance, back to Israel to prepare the people for God's visitation, so that they would not experience the curse that befalls those who disobey the covenant (see Deuteronomy 28:15-68). This oracle became part of wide-spread expectations for the "last days," being attested by Ben Sira (see Sirach 48:10 in the Apocrypha) and presented as the consensus of the religious experts of the time (see Mark 9:11).

The common theme of the "way of the Lord" having to be "prepared" probably accounts for the linking of Malachi with Isaiah 40. So closely wedded were these texts that Mark had actually included Malachi 3:1 as part of his quotation of Isaiah 40 at the beginning of his Gospel (Mark 1:2). Luke has corrected Mark's quotation by leaving off the reference to the messenger.

The Way of the Lord

We should observe the difference between the early Christian reading of Isaiah 40 and the way Isaiah's audience heard it. For the latter, the "way of the Lord" was the path that Judah would tread back to Canaan from Babylon, at the end of their exile following the destruction of Jerusalem in 587 B.C. Here in Luke, however—influenced by Malachi 3:1-4—the "way of the Lord" ("my way") has become YHWH's covenant way for Israel, prepared by the visitation of God's end-time agents to announce the judgment and urge the people to make ready.

A Call to Repentance

Under Malachi's influence, repentance and obedience to God and the covenant have become the manner in which that "way" is formulated. John the Baptist is seen as one who sought to prepare the people for God's coming (Mark 9:11-13 identifies him as the returning Elijah), so that many would repent, return to God, and be ready. Next week's lection will provide the specifics for how, in John's preaching, one was to achieve readiness for God's visitation. Preparation and readiness are ongoing Advent themes as we await Jesus' coming.

> **Think About It:** John called people to prepare for God's coming by repenting and turning from sin toward justice—making the crooked straight. What are the paths the Spirit calls us to leave, and what new paths are we to follow?

Salvation for "All Flesh"

Mark and Matthew quote only Isaiah 40:3. Luke's quotation continues through Isaiah 40:5 as an early announcement of a major theme of Luke-Acts—the universal scope of God's salvation. God's redemption will encompass not only the Jews but "all flesh," thus fulfilling the prophecies that the Gentile nations would come to worship the one God.

Study Suggestions

A. Sing With Zechariah

Begin by reading Luke 1:68-79 antiphonally. Ask: What does the song say about God's character? How might these godly traits be important in your life? What does the song say about the significance of John and Jesus? What has God accomplished through their advent?

B. "Who Shall Endure?"

Read Malachi 2:17–3:5 and the commentary on pages 18–19. Ask: Why did the priesthood require refining? Is this needed today as well among the ordained ministry? Invite the group to skim Malachi 1:6-14 and 2:4-9 for insights. Ask: Why do you think God would take pains to restore the priesthood before executing judgment on Judah? Why does God abhor the acts targeted for judgment in 3:5? What does this say about God's heart? How does the coming of Jesus affect our view of God's judgment?

Discuss the theological problem of theodicy raised by Malachi's audience in 2:17 and 3:14-15, probing the questions in the "Think About It" box. Ask: In what ways do you sympathize with those positions? What is Malachi's answer to these issues? How satisfactory do you find this answer? What other answers have helped you deal with injustice in the world and persevere in faithfulness to God?

Listen to "Thus saith the Lord!" and "But who may abide?" from Handel's *Messiah*. What is the emotional impact of Handel's music and the performers' interpretation? What light does Handel's musical setting of the text throw on Malachi's message?

C. Partnership in the Gospel

Read Philippians 1:3-11 aloud. Then read the rest of Philippians 1 for answers to the following questions: What is Paul's situation as he writes? What hints do we have of the Philippians' situation? After reviewing the commentary on page 20, read through Philippians 1:3-11 again, inviting participants to point out signs of the relationship Paul has with that congregation. Ask: What does each party do to nurture this friendship? How have we formed partnerships with ministries and missions here and abroad? Have these included the formation of friendships and relationships of prayer, support, and mutuality? What can we do to develop more such relationships from now on?

Paul is also concerned about partnership within the church. Read Philippians 2:1-5, 14-15, and 4:2-3. Ask: What hinders a spirit of partnership? What fosters it? Where is there need in our group and church for reconciliation and rededication to Christian partnership?

D. John the Baptist

Read Luke 3:1-6. Discuss what Isaiah's prophecy meant for its first hearers and how early Christian interpretation casts a new spin on this text. Now read the commentary on pages 21–22. Discuss: How do the traditions of a returning Elijah give significance to the preaching of this desert prophet and to the one who would follow him?

E. Prepare the Way of the Lord

All four lections share the expectation that God is about to intervene in the human story in a decisive manner. All four voice the conviction that action is required for people to prepare for that encounter with God, lest it prove to be a day of judgment rather than deliverance. Invite the group to offer prayers of confession of sin in silence, using the "Think About It" prompt. Consider both individual and national behaviors calling for either repentance or affirmation. Reflect on what God may be calling you to do or to be. If you take these prophetic words and admonishments seriously, how might you be transformed?

F. Close With Assurance

Incorporate the responses to these questions in a prayer of penitence, asking for both God's forgiveness and God's guidance for next steps in this Advent journey of spiritual renewal. Read 1 John 2:1b-2, traditional words of assurance. Then sing the Advent carol, "O Come, O Come Emmanuel," as an invitation to God to accompany us on the way.

Lections for Third Sunday of Advent

Old Testament: Zephaniah 3:14-20

ZEPHANIAH prophesied during the reign of Josiah (640–609 B.C.). King Hezekiah had been the first king in Judah to attempt to reverse the tide of idolatry and neglect of God's law. After him, however, came Manasseh, the king whom the author of Second Kings held personally responsible for the destruction of Judah and Jerusalem (2 Kings 21:10-16). His successor, Amon, did nothing to help the situation. Only with Amon's son Josiah did reform take place.

Zephaniah denounced the arrogant leaders of Judah, who accommodated themselves and their people to foreign customs rather than maintaining the purity and integrity of YHWH worship and covenant righteousness. His main targets were those who had adopted idolatrous forms of worship, who sought wealth and power through exploitation, violence, and fraud, and who arrogantly carried on their business, thinking that YHWH did not care about human affairs—that "the LORD will not do good, / nor will he do harm" (1:12).

Zephaniah lamented over the corruption of Jerusalem, the predatory activity of her leaders, and the perversion of the priests. He reminded them that YHWH was holy and righteous, was deeply offended by injustice and oppression, and would act decisively against all that was unjust and unholy. "The LORD within it is righteous; / he does no wrong. /

> **Think About It:** In a city where the godless and corrupt were powerful and wealthy, Zephaniah promised that God's justice would insure that the righteous and humble would come out honored and secure. What does this contrast have to say to the situation in our country today, with the growing gap between rich and poor, corporate greed and fraud, unemployment, homelessness, and hunger? In what ways does our manner of living demonstrate trust in Zephaniah's promise? What can we do to promote God's justice in our society?

Every morning he renders his judgment, / each dawn without fail; / but the unjust knows no shame" (see 3:3-5, 8).

Good News of Deliverance

The prophecy closes, in today's lection, with the good news of God's deliverance. The haughty, godless people would be removed, and the humble and pious who seek refuge in God would enjoy a restored Zion (3:11-13). Indeed, the meek would inherit the land, while those who sought to acquire the land through scheming means would be cut off. This passage is chosen for use during Advent because Christians can interpret it as referring to the new age of joy and liberation to be inaugurated with the coming of Christ as Messiah.

Today's lection contains the prophet's invitation to the God-fearing to rejoice in what God would do for them, bringing international renown to those who were formerly nobodies. This celebration is answered by God's singing over a pious, humble, restored people. The disgrace that had befallen Israel and Judah—the scattering of the northern tribes, the blot of rapacious rulers and defiled worship—would soon be removed and turned to honor for those who do YHWH's commands (2:3).

An Old Testament Psalm: Isaiah 12:2-6

This psalm-like passage contains the song of deliverance that Judah and the remnant of Israel will sing in Isaiah's future (verse 2). It comes as the close to a set of oracles speaking about Israel's attempt, in league with Syria, to conquer Judah. This effort would be forestalled by Assyria's defeat of Syria and Israel (721 B.C.; see 2 Kings 16–17).

Isaiah assured King Ahaz and the people, however, that God would save Judah from defeat by Assyria. Isaiah spoke of a coming Davidic king who would rule as God's servant and bring God's blessings to Judah, including the gathering in of refugees from Israel, now scattered in several neighboring nations (Isaiah 11:11). This song speaks of the confidence God's people will have in YHWH's saving help, since God's anger has been turned away. The fulfillment of God's promise of salvation celebrated in these verses can also be taken as a prophecy of the inbreaking of the reign of God, which was accomplished in Christ and which we anticipate during Advent.

Epistle: Philippians 4:4-7

"Joy in the Lord" is an important motif running through Philippians. The third Sunday of Advent, known as Gaudette, reminds us of the joy that awaits the believer in Christ's appearance. Even in prison, Paul is full of this joy—a joy that does not depend on external circumstances but on the friendship of God and fellow believers.

Rejoice in the Lord

The call to "rejoice in the Lord" in Philippians 4:4 repeats 3:1, forming a pair of brackets around 3:2–4:3 (which give the sources and reasons for this joy). Rejoicing in the Lord is precisely what Paul does when he abandons attempts to build himself up on worldly credentials and leaves behind the self-centered, competitive way of life. His attention turns to seeking life as God's gift in Christ. By focusing on Christ's person and God's direction he becomes attuned to the character and will of God.

Paul encourages all his friends in Philippi to do the same. Centering on this joy provides a resource for unity and peace within the community of faith (2:1-4; 4:2-3). It is also a resource for strength in the face of hostility from outside (1:27-30), an antidote for the crushing weight of opposition. This joy enables "gentle forbearance" toward all people. Filled with joy by God, one is freed to respond with patience rather than with anger and harshness.

The Remedy for Anxiety

The Christian need not be weighed down by anxiety, whether on account of hostile opposition, congregational unrest, or personal need. The reason hinges on the nearness of the Lord. First, God's nearness means that prayer is effective (see Psalm 145:18-20). Entrusting causes of anxiety to a kind and generous God allows peace to replace anxiety, which keeps us steadfast in discipleship, whatever may beset us. Thanksgiving for God's past help also fosters this peace, witnessing to our hearts how magnificently God has cared for us.

Think About It: Paul puts forward God's nearness both now and in time to come as a ground for joy, for gentle forbearance with others, and for overcoming anxiety. How do you experience God's nearness? What effect does this have on your spirit? attitudes? behavior? relationships? commitments? How can this affirmation help us put our circumstances in perspective so we can enjoy the same benefits?

The Lord Is Near

Second, "the Lord is near" in terms of time: Christ stands ready to break into history and usher in God's reign. This is a source of confidence to the harassed Christians in Philippi. As the be-all and end-all, God is the source of lasting joy, stability, and peace. Paul's memorable words have provided a comforting benediction through the centuries: "And the peace of God, which surpasses all understanding, will guard your hearts and minds in Christ Jesus" (Philippians 4:7).

Gospel: Luke 3:7-18

Last week's Gospel lection introduced John the Baptist as the end-time messenger who called people to prepare to encounter God. Repentance and a return to God's ways was his recommended strategy for surviving "the wrath to come." Here we find John's prescriptions for preparation for "the one who is coming."

You Brood of Vipers!

John greeted the crowds unflatteringly as snakes fleeing in the face of an approaching fire. His first injunction warned them that no ritual purification would suffice to guarantee safety on the Day of Judgment. Rather, the "fruits" of a repentant heart must be clearly visible. In this John agrees with other voices of his time.

Abraham Will Not Save You

John attacked any notion that physical descent from Abraham would give one a claim on God's favor (an attack that would become characteristic of early Christian ideology, as in Galatians 3:6-18; 4:21-31; John 8:31-42). This assertion would also be at home in a Jewish context. Since the time of the prophets, many had spoken about Torah observance and piety as essential for a Jew by birth to be a part of the true Israel, the righteous remnant.

Fruits Worthy of Repentance

Nevertheless, John's message threatened the overly confident with being cut off from the lineage they so treasured. Something else was needed to avoid the "ax . . . lying at the root of the trees" (Luke 3:9)—the judgment. Lest one be "thrown into the fire" as religiously worthless, he or she must "bear fruits worthy of repentance" (3:8).

What fruits reveal a genuine repentance? The metaphor of the clearing out of unfruitful trees in 3:9 emphasizes the importance of finding fruit pleasing to God in our lives. This answer is in keeping with Luke's special emphasis on sharing possessions and using one's goods to benefit the needy.

It is astounding to the American mind to see what John considered to be "surplus" and hence available for sharing with the needy. The tangible expressions of love for neighbor, however, are essential to eschatological survival. This is certainly a theme

> **Think About It:** American culture, through advertising and emulation of the lifestyles of the "rich and famous," tells us to acquire and consume more and more; John tells us to give everything beyond the essentials to those in need. Where do you fall in this spectrum? Do you invest in the needy neighbor as fully as in yourself? How can we support one another in resisting the pressures of a greedy, affluent, wasteful society and in giving generously to meet human need?

that deeply shapes Christian ethics throughout the New Testament. (See, for example, Matthew 5:42; Luke 12:33-34; 16:19-31; Acts 4:32-35; 2 Corinthians 8:13-15; Hebrews 13:16; 1 John 3:17). To those in questionable occupations, John gives the command to act honorably—not using their jobs as opportunities to plunder their neighbors.

Prophet or Messiah?

Aware of God's Spirit behind John's call to repent, the people wondered about his role in God's plan: Was he the Messiah? John said no, he was only the forerunner of the Messiah (see John 1:19-28). The Coming One would separate out the righteous from the unrighteous.

The concept of baptism "with the Holy Spirit and with fire" has occasioned some debate. Is this a reference to judgment, to the eschatological outpouring of the Spirit (as in Joel 2, taken up in Acts 2:17-21), or to both? Certainly the following verses and the metaphor of harvesters separating wheat and chaff suggest that the deliverance of those committed to God's justice and the judgment of those who practice injustice would both receive their appropriate rewards.

Study Suggestions

A. Make Known God's Deeds

Begin by singing "There's a Song in the Air." Continue the theme of joy by reading Isaiah 12:2-6 in unison. Explain that this hymn from Isaiah invites those who have experienced God's deliverance to witness to their experience of God's grace. Point out that Paul in today's Philippians lection invites Christian prayer to take place in an atmosphere of thanksgiving for what God has done.

Then ask members to tell of ways they have experienced God's saving help. Do this in groups of three, with one person sharing, another facilitating, and the third listening supportively; then rotate roles until all have shared. Back in the total group, ask: What common themes did we hear in these experiences? How does sharing our stories help us internalize the confidence expressed in Isaiah 12:2? How can we trust more fully in God's guidance when faced with despair and loss?

B. Seek God's Joy and Peace

Next read aloud Philippians 4:4-7, and summarize the ideas in the interpretive paragraphs on pages 25–26. Ask: Why does Paul place such an emphasis on joy in the Lord in this letter? What does joy contribute to discipleship and Christian community?

Regarding Paul's prescription for peace, ask: When have you found prayer

28

or remembrance of God's help to quiet anxiety? When have you realized God's nearness, and how has that touched your life? How does the other aspect of the Lord's nearness (his coming again) affect your life? Also discuss the "Think About It" questions related to God's nearness.

C. The Removal of Reproach
Read aloud Zephaniah 3:14-20. This prophet celebrates God's removal of the blemishes that undermine the integrity and unity of the people of faith. Ask: What are some causes of reproach or shame—blemishes—in our discipleship, the life of the church, and our nation? Note those mentioned in the "Think About It" paragraph. Think together about what prevents us from tending to these blemishes and how we might overcome them.

D. The Fruits of Repentance
Read Luke 3:7-18 and the commentary on it. Ask: What are insufficient grounds for confidence in the face of the coming judgment? What is the nature of the repentance required? What are John's directions for getting ready to meet the coming One? How realistic are they in our situation? What are some first steps we might take?

Read the "Think About It" box, and use those questions to discuss the practical working out of the command to love one's neighbor as oneself. Ask: How well does our current allocation of resources between ourselves and the needy measure up to John's expectations—and Christ's? How might we covenant together to hold ourselves accountable to better stewardship of our resources?

E. Tie It Together
Today's four lections invite us to ready ourselves for salvation by humbly walking in God's ways, so we may enjoy the peace of God's presence now and the joy of his deliverance at the end. Ask: What insights have we gained today? If we were to take these to heart, what might God be calling us to be or to do differently? What will we commit to do to live out God's calling?

F. Close With Prayer
Invite members to offer brief prayers of dedication to God and responsible living in response to today's learnings, mentioning specific ways they have heard God calling them to make changes in their lives. Then use the response of Isaiah 12:2-6 as a benediction.

Lections for Fourth Sunday
of Advent

*T*Old Testament: Micah 5:2-5a

*T*HE prophet Micah (Hebrew meaning: "Who is like YHWH?") lived
and preached in the time of Isaiah of Jerusalem. Unlike his older contemporary, his origins were in the countryside. He was greatly disturbed by the sins
of city folks and deeply concerned for the poor, oppressed shepherds and
farmers whose lot he had shared as a child. Micah 1:1 indicates that his ministry took place during the reigns of Jotham (742–735 B.C.), Ahaz (735–715),
and Hezekiah (715–687). Jeremiah (26:18) identifies him as preaching during the time of Hezekiah and coming from Moresheth, a town in the hill
country southwest of Jerusalem.

Alternating Doom and Hope

The book that bears Micah's name is formed of alternating passages of
doom and hope. Chapters 1–3 predict devastation for Israel and Judah
because of their unfaithfulness. In Chapters 4–5 (which contain today's passage), the prophet proclaims that the people will eventually be restored to
YHWH's favor under a ruler coming from Bethlehem. The focus of 6:1–7:7
is YHWH's controversy with the people because of their substitution of ritual for righteousness, their unjust acts and attitudes, and their lack of gratitude and trust. The book then closes on a positive note by highlighting the
awesome glory into which a compassionate God will ultimately bring them.

Corruption, deceit, and moral decay had penetrated families, so that
"your enemies are members of your own household" (7:6). Not even the religious leaders could be trusted, as the priests and prophets were corrupt, conducted empty, meaningless ceremonies, and continued assuring people of
YHWH's blessing and guidance despite growing evidence to the contrary

(3:11-12). Lavish offerings of animals and olive oil, and even child sacrifice, could not earn God's blessing, because of the pervasive sin and hypocrisy that infected a society that was morally and spiritually bankrupt (6:6-7). What God wanted was not hollow ritual or self-righteous posturing, but "to do justice, and to love mercy, and to walk humbly with your God" (6:8).

Since such spiritual integrity was nowhere in evidence, the people would most certainly be punished—through the imminent conquest by Assyria. Beyond that judgment, however, Micah offers hopeful signs of a new day and a renewed and restored people, under the leadership of a ruler to be born in Bethlehem. God's grace and deliverance would follow calamity and dispersion. Today's lection brings this hopeful promise into focus. The agent of

> ***Think About It:*** Micah was disturbed by the injustice and hypocrisy around him. What comparable symptoms of moral and spiritual decay do we see around us? What actions can we take to "do justice, love mercy, and walk humbly with God"?

YHWH's mercy would come from Bethlehem (5:2). The long struggle would produce a restoration (verse 3). God's greatness would be manifested in tender compassion, security, and peace (verses 4-5a).

Micah's Lasting Impact

Micah's message left a lasting impact. As already noted, his warnings were cited by Jeremiah a century and a half later. His words about family enmity (7:6) were quoted by Jesus (Matthew 10:35-36). His pithy statement of God's moral and spiritual requirements (6:8) laid the groundwork for Jesus' summary of the divine law (Mark 12:29-31). And today's passage is viewed by Christians of all ages as a messianic prophecy fulfilled in the coming of Jesus.

Gospel: Luke 1:39-45

This lection sets the stage for Mary's Magnificat, which follows. After her encounter with the angel Gabriel who had announced that God had chosen her to give birth to the Messiah (1:26-38), Mary set out in a hurry to visit her cousin Elizabeth in an unnamed village in the Judean hills. As soon as the two met, Elizabeth, who was pregnant with John the Baptist, felt her baby kicking in her womb—as though to indicate a prescient recognition that this was no ordinary pregnancy and that these two little boys would be involved together in some momentous happenings in the years to come (verses 39-41).

"Blessed Are You . . ."

Then Elizabeth, overcome with emotion and possessed with profound spiritual discernment, uttered a sentence that acknowledged the special role that Mary and her baby were destined to play, a sentence that would be repeated by millions of believers for ages to come: "Blessed are you among women, and blessed is the fruit of your womb" (verse 42).

Think About It: Elizabeth wondered why God had enabled her. . . . Do you ever wonder why God has chosen you for special opportunities? What does God expect of you? How will you respond?

Elizabeth began to wonder out loud why God had enabled her to recognize that the One destined to reveal God's saving love to all humankind—and thereby to change the course of history—was present there with them in her cousin Mary's womb (verses 43-44). Finally, the Spirit used her to pronounce a blessing on Mary for accepting the role thrust upon her of becoming the mother of the long-awaited Messiah (verse 45).

New Testament Psalm: Luke 1:47-55

Clarence Jordan paraphrases Mary's Magnificat this way: "My soul exalts the Lord / And my heart exults before God my Savior. / For he has disregarded my humble origin, / And from now on the ages will honor me. / Great things the Almighty did for me, / And Holy be his name. / From generation to generation / His mercy showers those who fear him. / With his strong arm / He scatters the big boys / Who think they're somebody. / He pulls thrones

Think About It: A colossal reversal is heralded; a revolution is in the offing. Mary is the prophet of the poor. To what situations of injustice might Mary's prophecy be addressed today? Out of what *anawim* community might such a song of protest come today?

from under the royalty / And gives dignity to the lowly. / He loads the hungry with good things / But the rich he lets go with nothing at all. / Mindful of mercy, he gives a lift to his people / Just as he promised our fathers [and mothers] . . ." (Luke 1:47-55, Cotton Patch Version).

This majestic psalm of liberation has many parallels to Hannah's song (1 Samuel 1:11; 2:1-10) and probably originated among the *anawim* ("the poor"—both spiritually and materially) of the early Jewish Christian community. It praises God's deliverance and protection—of Mary and her child, of the Hebrew slaves of old, and of all in every age who suffer and are exploited by the rich and powerful.

Good News to the Poor

The central theme of good news to the poor and needy (Luke 4:18-19; see Isaiah 61:1-2), which is found throughout Luke's Gospel, is introduced and celebrated here. A colossal reversal is heralded: the mighty God stands in solidarity with the weak and marginalized; arrogant, heartless rulers will be overthrown; spiritual truth will outshine and transform present political and economic realities; God will right social wrongs and overturn the social order. Mary is the prophet of the poor. A revolution is in the offing—linked to the child she carries in her womb.

Epistle: Hebrews 10:5-10

Hebrews 10:1-10 must be considered as a unit. The writer is contending that with the coming of Christ the ritual practices prescribed in Old Testament law no longer represent true worship, but are only a pale shadow (verse 1) of what God now offers the believer. Through Christ, God offers us direct access and a close personal relationship, something animal sacrifices could not do—as the prophet Micah had long before pointed out. The sacrifices were made year after year, especially on the Day of Atonement (see Leviticus 16:1-34). They made people aware of their unworthiness but could not remove the sense of guilt and separation from God (verses 2-4). Not only do these rituals not cleanse people from sin, they actually intensify the shame and alienation.

Only the gift of God's only Son on the cross could effectively overcome the power of sin in persons' hearts and lives. To explain this truth the writer quotes the Septuagint (early Greek Old Testament, translated from the Hebrew about A.D. 270) version of Psalm 40:6-9, which substitutes the line, "but a body you have prepared for me" (verse 5b) for the Hebrew, "but you have given me an open ear." Actually, the meaning of these two translations is similar. "Given me an open ear" means "so touched me that what I hear I obey." "A body prepared for me" means "created me to do your will in and with my body." Both stress openness and responsiveness to God.

Obedience the Only True Sacrifice

The writer of Hebrews has put these words in the mouth of Jesus, showing that what God wants of us is not ritual sacrifice but the devoted commitment and sacrificial service that Jesus offered. Heartfelt obedience is the only true sacrifice.

As we have seen, Micah 6:6-8 had said essentially the same thing, as had several other Old Testament writers: "To obey is better than sacrifice" (1 Samuel 15:22). "Offer to God a sacrifice of thanksgiving" (Psalm 50:8-15). "The sacrifice acceptable to God is . . . a broken and contrite heart" (Psalm 51:16-17).

> **Think About It:** "I desire mercy, not sacrifice." Can you imagine what an adjustment it must have been for people accustomed to thinking they had met their religious obligations by paying for a goat or dove to be slaughtered to be confronted by the demand to change their whole way of life? How do we think of our religious obligations? What changes does God want in our way of life? What is the way to a personal relationship with God for us?

"I desire mercy, not sacrifice" (Hosea 6:6, NIV). "I have had enough of burnt offerings. . . . Cease to do evil, learn to do good; seek justice, rescue the oppressed" (Isaiah 1:10-20). Jesus' perfect obedience, even to death, becomes the reconciling event between God and humankind.

Self-Giving Love Our Model

The sacrifices and burnt offerings prescribed by the law (meeting legal and ritual obligations out of a sense of duty) could not open the way to a personal relationship with God based on heartfelt repentance and divine forgiveness. This was only possible through Christ, because it was only Christ who freely and fully did God's will (verses 8-9a). Jesus was the perfect sacrifice because he willingly chose to manifest God's redemptive love by resisting evil through giving himself to death on the cross. He thereby did away with the regime of ritual sacrifice and replaced it with self-giving love as a model for God's relationship with us and ours with one another (verse 9b). Through Jesus' offering of himself, the way is opened for us to be purified and dedicated to this same cruciform (cross-shaped) way of life (verse 10).

Study Suggestions

A. Highlight Christmas

On this Sunday before Christmas, begin by inviting class members to share their Christmas plans—home decorations, gift exchanges, visits with relatives, caroling parties, family customs, worship services. Ask: How will you make Christ central to your Christmas observance? Sing an Annunciation carol, such as "My Soul Gives Glory to My God" or "Lo, How a Rose E'er Blooming."

B. Revisit the Annunciation

Tell the story of the Annunciation to Mary (Luke 1:26-38), then read aloud Luke 1:39-45. Re-tell the story of Mary's visit to Elizabeth, drawing on the interpretation on pages 31–32. Discuss the "Think About It" questions regarding our being chosen for special opportunities. Ask: What opportunities for putting Christ first are being given to us this Christmas? How can we be faithful to what God expects of us, as Mary and Elizabeth sought to be faithful in the roles God was calling them to play?

C. Experience the Magnificat

Distribute paper and pens; then ask three class members to read aloud Luke 1:47-55 in three different translations, including the one from Clarence Jordan. Pause after each reading to allow persons time to jot down ideas and feelings that came to them as they listened. After the third reading and reflection time, invite members to share what they have written. Thoughts such as these may be expressed: to magnify is to praise; lowly means humble; God's mercy is continuous; God lifts the lowly and demotes the proud. Discuss the "Think About It" questions relating Mary's prophecy of reversal to conditions today.

D. Explore Micah's Impact

Drawing on the commentary on pages 30–31, review Micah's historical situation, alternating message of doom and promise, rejection of Temple sacrifices, and summary of God's expectations. Read aloud his prophecy of hope in 5:2-5a. Note his lasting influence as seen in references to his message elsewhere in the Bible. Discuss the "Think About It" questions relating his message to circumstances today. Ask: How can we give expression to Micah's emphasis on justice, compassion, and humility through our observance of Christmas and beyond?

E. Give a Word Association Test

Read out the following words, asking members to write down the first word or phrase that comes to mind in response to each: (1) *sacrifice*; (2) *offering*; (3) *ritual*; (4) *obedience*; (5) *service*.

Have members tell their responses to each word in turn. Pay attention to feeling tones. Consider: Is sacrifice something demanded or given? Is offering associated with money or service? Is ritual viewed as formal or vital? Is obedience seen as duty or dedication? Is service demeaning or fulfilling?

F. Focus on Christ's Sacrifice

Notice that the significance of Christmas is grounded in the meaning and purpose of Christ's coming. Read aloud Hebrews 10:1-10. Explain the writer's argument as developed above. Assign the several Scripture references to God's attitude toward sacrifice to different members to look up and read aloud. Relate the members' word associations to the writer of Hebrews' emphasis on the nature of Christ's sacrifice, comparing Christ's model of sacrifice to members' responses. Personalize this discussion through exploration of the "Think About It" questions.

G. Tie Things Together

Summarize by stating that to make our celebration of Christmas Christ-centered we need to: respond to God-given opportunities (Elizabeth); work with God to bring about a just reversal in the social order (Mary's Magnificat); live into the promise of God's compassion, protection, and peace (Micah); and embody Christ's model of sacrifice as compassionate self-giving (Hebrews).

Close with an extemporaneous prayer asking God for guidance and strength to make our Christmas Christ-centered in these ways.

CHRISTMAS

Lections for Christmas Day

Old Testament: Isaiah 52:7-10

*T*HE messenger is a representative of God, sent on ahead as a bearer of good tidings. The decades of exile—living an uprooted, fragile existence separated from sources of stability and hope—are coming to an end. God is promising peace (safety, serenity, well-being), good news (restoration, comfort, hope), and salvation (God's action, sovereignty, protection). The sounds of this messenger scrambling across the rocky mountain trails are music to the ears of those who have been living in anxiety, fear, and apprehension (verse 7).

Since the same four lections are used on Christmas Day in all three years of the lectionary cycle, additional exegetical helps for exploring these passages are available in Years A and B of *Keeping Holy Time*. For this year's study let us look at the imagery of this passage from Third Isaiah. We have a messenger announcing; sentinels lifting their voices; the ruins of Jerusalem singing; YHWH comforting, returning, redeeming, baring his arm; and the nations seeing God's salvation, Isaiah uses these images to speak of the wondrous hope of YHWH once again acting in history— this time to free the people from captivity and restore them to security and plenty in familiar surroundings.

The sentinels are watchmen, manning the outposts, looking for signs of danger or opportunity. They are the first to hear the messenger's hasty footsteps and joyful voice. They see not only the messenger, but following close behind the mighty YHWH himself, striding into Zion, bringing the long-awaited liberation. Overjoyed, they break into glad, lusty singing. The remnant not taken into exile, who are eking out a precarious existence in the ruined city, cannot believe their eyes. Can it really be that they are about to be reunited with their long-lost loved ones? Can they really start rebuilding a city, a temple, a life (verse 8)?

38

A Miracle in the Works

It is true! YHWH is working a miracle! The exiles are returning! The joyous singing of the watchmen now breaks into a mighty chorus that echoes off the fallen rocks and crumbling buildings. God's comfort (encouragement, support) and redemption (restoration, renewal) are bringing new hope to a forlorn and devastated people! The impossible is breaking through before their eyes! The scoffers are silenced, the despondent heartened, the lonely reunited. The rubble is stirred and begins to take shape. New life is breathed into a ravaged situation (verse 9).

YHWH is acting. His sleeves are rolled up. Divine power, which had been hidden from view, is now visible to all. A sturdy arm of holiness, justice, and compassion is revealed. The surrounding nations cannot help but take note. A people and their God are back. They can be ignored and discounted no longer. The God who cares for them cares for all. The day of salvation is here (verse 10)!

> **Think About It:** It is twenty centuries later. Sin, violence, alienation, hunger, despair—all are still with us. Can we hear the feet of the messengers? Do our sentinels lift their voices? Do we see our God engaged in the world in acts of compassion and justice? Are sounds of faith and joy echoing through the ruins of broken treaties, hopes, and relationships? Are the nations bowing in gratitude for the salvation of our God? How can we become an intentional part of this picture?

Another Liberation at Hand

Now fast-forward from the sixth century B.C. to the first century A.D. Once again the nation is occupied, the people oppressed, disconsolate—this time under the Romans. Another liberation is needed. Another messenger is sent—preaching in the river valley not the mountains. He is followed by angels on high proclaiming "Peace on earth, good will toward all." The sentinels—shepherds watching their flocks—hear the saving message and join the joyous chorus. Kings from other nations once again take note and come to worship and offer gifts. New life and hope are being offered to a needy world. Immanuel! God with us!

> **Think About It:** Is God's strong arm of justice and compassion made evident by the parties, programs, and pageants? Are our praises offered to God or only to our own self-sufficiency? Does our joyful noise carry to the ends of the earth or only until the morning after? Does the ending of the long wait of Advent bring relief that the shopping is over or confidence that God's saving providence is with us (Immanuel)?

Psalter: Psalm 98

The joy and singing of Christmas, celebrating God's saving action, continue in the psalm. This time the chorus is expanded; the sea, the floods, and the hills join the merrymaking; not only humans but the world of nature is excited (verses 7-8). The revelers are accompanied by an orchestra—lyres, trumpets, horns (verses 5-6). The nations throughout the earth are in awe (verses 2-3). We are invited, no, commanded, to join in (verse 4). We are to sing a new song (verse 1)!

And what are we celebrating? God has once again bared his arm for action. A wondrous work of God has taken place. Vindication is accomplished. The power of evil is vanquished, and people of good will are justified (verses 2-3). God is faithful; God remembers us; God loves us (verse 3). The Messiah is come! Immanuel! God with us!

Epistle: Hebrews 1:1-4 (5-12)

Verses 1-4 are a prose prologue to a theological treatise by an anonymous author whose purpose is to emphasize the reliability of salvation in Christ. In the past God had tried to reach humanity in a variety of ways—laws, covenants, oracles, mighty works (verse 1). Each effort was rejected by a rebellious people. So now God has sent the Son to bring the message of love and redemption.

He was the One designated to rule over all creation, the agent of God's creative power (verse 2). He is the revelation of God's greatness, the image of God's loving nature, the One whose cosmic energy is at the heart of ongoing creation (verse 3a). His redemptive act has overcome the power of sin, and he now governs the universe in the company of God, with a position superior to the lesser ranks of heavenly beings (verse 4b). Clearly, the author of Hebrews intends to exalt the stature and importance of Christ to his Jewish Christian readers who may have been tempted to return to reliance on traditional rituals for their religious assurance.

Think About It: God in Christ our caring companion! Do we find him amongst the Christmas merrymaking? Do we unwrap him amongst the gifts? Do we "receive him in our hearts by faith with thanksgiving"? Do we have a heartfelt experience of Immanuel, God with us?

Praise to the Reigning Christ

The psalm of praise that follows the prologue lauds the reigning Christ in poetic verse. Not only human beings but also the angels are commanded to serve this Son of God, whose reign is both just and enduring (verses 6-8), for they cannot claim a direct kinship with God (verse 5). Because he has upheld goodness and struggled against evil he has been blessed with a special measure of joy (verse 9). Though the works of creation are temporal and will perish, his reign is everlasting (verse 10).

Like the prologue to John's Gospel, which we examine next, this passage points up the cosmic and eternal significance of Christmas. The almost unnoticed birth in a remote corner of the world has become a pivot of history. The God who created has now redeemed. The reign of emperors is replaced by the reign of a Savior. The Almighty has entered the earthly arena to show compassion and incarnate love, to become a caring companion. Immanuel! God with us!

Gospel: John 1:1-14

Another prologue, another take on the significance of Christ, another way of talking about Immanuel, God with us. The author of the Fourth Gospel tells the story from a different perspective than those of the other Gospel writers. The story reflects on what it all means—for the writer, for his contemporaries, and for all time.

The Word (Greek *logos*)—God speaking, acting, creating, from the beginning onward—had actually incarnated the man Jesus—with whom the writer had walked, joked, and eaten. In the cosmos, as the *Logos*, he had brought the worlds into being; on earth, as the man called Jesus, he had brought life, light, love, and hope to poor Galileans who were suffering under a dark, evil, unjust system (verses 1-5).

Think About It: The Creator God incarnated the man Jesus. How do you understand the relationship between Jesus and God? How did Jesus participate in the Creation? Is Jesus God? the Son of God? a human with godlike qualities? part of the Trinity? Do you pray to Jesus or to God? The Christmas stories in Matthew and Luke depict him as a baby conceived and born in a special way whom God sent to save his people from their sins. John presents him as the only begotten Son of God taking on human form to empower persons to be born again. How do you experience Jesus? How do you introduce him to your friends?

Pointing to the Light

Another John—the Baptizer—was the first to call this Jesus to people's attention. God had sent him as a messenger, a sentinel, a witness to the good news that light was about to penetrate their darkness and extinguish the shadows forever. His message enlightened them, but he was not the source of illumination. He only pointed them to the light. Jesus was coming, sent by God to banish the shade and invite everyone to live in the sunlight of God's love, to bring radical change into their lives (verses 6-9).

He was there in plain sight, but the darkness of evil had prevented people from recognizing him for who he really was—the agent of One who had brought the worlds into existence. Even his own countrymen, neighbors, family—those who knew him best—had not accepted him. Others, however—Gentiles, foreigners, the lame, halt, and blind, those not deemed worthy to associate with "good people"—did see in him the God of compassion

Think About It: Immanuel. God with us. How do we experience the presence of God in our lives? As "high and lifted up," remote, distant, austere? Or as our constant companion, guide, support? What are the shadows that obscure our vision of God and Jesus? How does belief in God help us believe in ourselves? Does the busyness and business of Christmas illuminate or impede our awareness of both the majesty and the intimacy of the God experience? How can we become like John the Baptist—pointing the way into the light of God's love?

and thus in themselves the dignity of a child of God. They—and we, who likewise believe—are not mere creatures of flesh but are infused with the Spirit of God (verses 10-13).

The Word Made Flesh

So, this *Logos* of God, this divine energy that authored the universe, had actually been embodied in a human being named Jesus. John and the others had known him as a builder, a friend, a companion, a prophet—but also as someone special. They had sensed the aura of God upon him. He had manifested divine goodness, he had spoken the truth that confronted and compelled them. To be with him was like being in the presence of God (verse 14). He was Immanuel, God with us!

Study Suggestions

A. Celebrate Christmas

Create a celebrative atmosphere through singing the first stanzas of several Christmas carols. End with all verses of "Angels from the Realms of Glory." Ask: How are you feeling this Christmas Day? Repeat each feeling expressed for all to hear. Write the feeling words all over the chalkboard or on a large piece of paper in crazy-quilt fashion. Comment that this complex of feelings names who we are and what we bring to church as a diverse people of God.

B. Study the Scriptures

Form four groups, assigning each to study one of the four lections, using these questions and directions: What feelings does this passage evoke? What is its central theme? How is it related to Christmas? Summarize its message in one sentence. If we were to take this message seriously, how would it change our Christmas observance? our lives in general? Ask each group to select someone to report its ideas to the larger group.

C. Report Back

Reassemble to hear the reports. Compare and contrast the feelings evoked by Scripture with those expressed in response to the carol singing. Write the four one-sentence summaries for everyone to see. Identify common themes in the reports. These might include joy, singing, God's action, messengers, salvation, hope, God with us. Discuss the connections between these Scriptures and

Christmas as we observe it. Explore the changes suggested by Scripture in our Christmas observances and in our everyday lives. Ask: How prepared are we to make them? How can we support each other in making our Christmas and our lives more Christ-centered?

D. Seek Commentary Help

Now go to the commentary on pages 38–42. Summarize the explanations of each passage. Ask: How do our ideas compare with those of the commentary? In what ways does the commentary broaden, contrast with, or illumine our reading of the lections? How does the recurring refrain of "Immanuel! God with us!" affect us? How can we become more aware of and responsive to the presence of God in our lives?

E. Think About It

Return to the commentaries, and discuss the "Think About It" questions. Support members as they struggle with the questions of what we see and hear and how we are to be involved as posed by the Isaiah passage; the purpose of Christmas celebration raised by Psalm 98; the question of whether we find Christ in the midst of the Christmas festivities that confront us in Hebrews; the mystery of the relation between Jesus and God in the Gospel lection; and the matters of the shadows that obscure, belief in ourselves, and pointing the way mentioned at the end of that reflection. Encourage members to be honest in expressing what they really think by respectfully accepting every comment as worthy of consideration.

F. Create a Worship Experience

Close with a spontaneous worship response. As a call to worship, read out the feeling words named earlier in response to carols and Scripture. For the Scripture reading, repeat the summary statements developed from the four lections. For hymns, sing the first stanza of a carol or two. For the affirmation of faith name the common themes running through the lections. For the prayer time, invite sentence prayers from group members expressing how this session has changed their understanding of Christmas. For the meditation, summarize learnings from the discussion of the "Think About It" questions. For the offering, ask members to name changes they hope to make in their lives. For the benediction, repeat together the refrain, "Immanuel! God with Us."

Lections for First Sunday After Christmas Day

H Old Testament: 1 Samuel 2:18-20, 26

*H*ERE we meet young Samuel, who would grow up to be a maker of kings. Samuel's mother, Hannah, had been unable to have children, which was a great disgrace to her. She is one among several barren women in the Bible—Sarai, Rebecca, Rachel, the wife of Manoah, and Elizabeth—to whom God granted a special child.

A Special Child

Praying at Shiloh (then the central Israelite shrine), Hannah vowed that if YHWH would give her a son, she would dedicate him to God's service. Samuel was thus set apart for God from birth, growing up in the temple as a servant of Eli, the chief priest. Today's verses focus on aspects of the story that are picked up in Luke's narrative of Jesus' youth. The similarity between verse 26 and Luke 2:52 is striking. Just as Samuel developed physically (in stature), spiritually (in favor with the Lord), and socially (with the people), so did Jesus develop in these dimensions—with the addition of the intellectual aspect (wisdom). Both men of God were outstanding, well-rounded, well-thought-of religious leaders, and showed early signs of special future potential.

> **Think About It:** Both Samuel and Jesus showed signs of special potential. Are there young people in your congregation who show signs of future religious leadership? What are you doing to cultivate their spiritual growth and to nurture and guide them toward church vocations?

In terms of the story in Second Samuel, Samuel appears in stark contrast to the sons of Eli, Hophni and Phineas (see 2:12-17, 22-25). These two young men abused their priestly office, using it for self-gratification. Their self-serving behavior came at the expense of honoring God and at the expense of the people whom they were supposed to serve, not exploit. Their dishonor was evident in the handling of sacrificial meats and in their sexual exploitation of the female servants in the temple.

An Abuse of the Sacrifices

The way in which a sacrifice was performed in ancient cultures was a reflection of the social hierarchy. First the god would get the deity's portion, then the priests, and finally the worshipers would receive theirs. Hophni and Phineas violated this order, demanding raw meat even before the fat was offered up to God.

For placing their own bellies ahead of God's honor as represented in the procedure of sacrifice, the brothers would be punished. Both died in a single day.

> *Think About It:* How do your patterns of giving, spending, and working reflect your honor for God, God's "firstness" in your life?

Psalter: Psalm 148

This is one of the most expansive psalms, in that the writer invites the celestial realms and their angelic inhabitants to join in the praise of God with all terrestrial creation. All that has been created by God is included in this invitation: the stars, mountains, and animals are all called to worship. Even the meteorological phenomena of hail, snow, and wind are incorporated. (These have been shown in other biblical narratives to do God's bidding, such as in Exodus and Revelation.)

There are similar scenes of worship in Revelation 4–5 and Philippians 2:9-11, where earthly and heavenly voices are united and vast distances bridged in the worship of God and God's Anointed. Universal in scope, the psalm also speaks of the covenanted relationship between the Lord and Israel.

> *Think About It:* The psalm reflects a contrast between the universal and the national. How does your worship balance praise of the God of all peoples and the universe with attention to national and local concerns? Do you allow the God of all creation to be part of your particular life as well?

Epistle: Colossians 3:12-17

Clothing is an important metaphor for identity and character. Early Christian authors make much use of this metaphor, especially to emphasize the leaving behind of one set of values and behaviors and embracing a new life—as one removes one garment and puts on another.

Put Off the Old; Put on the New

The clothing metaphor complements the image of dying to (leaving) one lifestyle and rising to (taking on) a new dimension of living (see 3:3-5). Baptismal rites in the early church dramatized this transition, not only by means of the death/life imagery of immersion in water but also as initiates took off their clothes at the edge of the pool, were baptized naked, and were clothed in new, white garments. Both metaphors were powerfully present in this dramatic rite, making clear that a radical change was taking place from one way of life to another.

Verses 5-9 speaks of the disciple's rejecting and "putting to death" specific sinful behaviors and attitudes inconsistent with being a child of God and recipient of God's grace. Verse 10 adds the image of "putting on" new clothing (claiming a new being), that is, being made to look more like the God who fashions the person. This new identity overcomes religious, ethnic, and class divisions and unites all newborn creatures in Christ (verse 11). Persons claimed by God replace the sinful traits of past life with loving, modest, upright virtues (verse 12).

This motif of the transformed life continues in verse 13, with an emphasis on forgiveness within the faith community (see also Matthew 6:12, 14-15; 18:23-35). Imitation of the love and compassion of God in Jesus constitutes a central theme in Christian ethical instruction.

Chosen Ones

The author addresses the Colossian Christians, including Gentiles, with language reserved for ethnic Jews in the Hebrew Bible: They are "God's chosen ones, holy and beloved" (verse 12). Their chosenness is a natural result of the conviction expressed in verse 11 that "there is no longer Greek and Jew" in the renewed community. (See also Galatians 3:28.) What counts now is learning about God and reflecting God's character.

Marks of the Godly Life

The description that follows tells us as much about the Christian concept of God as it prescribes Christian conduct. "Clothe yourselves with compassion, kindness, humility, meekness, and patience" (verse 12). Compassion signifies feeling deeply for the need and well-being of one's neighbor, and acting upon it. It is a connectedness with the neighbor that makes her or his pain one's own. Kindness is evident when one uses one's power to build up another person, coming alongside as a helper rather than a judge. Humility, recognizing the worth of others as equal to one's own, is the glue that binds Christians in community. Bearing with (accepting) and forgiving one other (verse 13), as dimensions of Christian love, are the sash that holds all the garments together.

Work for Perfect Harmony

In this new life, a person is to be guided by Christ's gift of peace (both inner serenity and harmony with others), rather than one's inner drives or the approval

46

of worldly voices. This is also the goal of the community's life together. The author lifts up a model of Christian community in verses 15-17, in which believers edify (build up) one another with words informed by the Lord (see 1 Peter 4:11). The faithful are urged to keep the worship of God central, with gratitude for God's goodness a dominant theme. The final instruction (Colossians 3:17) calls us to increase Jesus' good repute in the world through words and deeds that identify him as Lord of our lives.

> **Think About It:** We are to clothe ourselves with garments of virtue that lead to peace and harmony. What attitudes and behaviors do we need to discard or take on in order to become better reflections of Christ?

Gospel: Luke 2:41-52

Noncanonical writings seek to fill out the picture of Jesus' childhood with all manner of fanciful tales. These were attempts to answer questions like: How did the child Jesus use his divine powers? and how did he come to understand and use them in a mature manner? An example is the *Protoevangelion* that shows Mary healing neighbor children who bathed in Baby Jesus' bath water. They also recount less favorable reports of Jesus retaliating cruelly to injuries inflicted by playmates, including Judas. (No wonder this isn't included in the New Testament canon!)

The Young Jesus

Luke provides us with the only canonical portrait of the youthful Jesus. The passage echoes 1 Samuel 2, that earlier narrative of another special child set apart for God from an early age. Like Samuel, Jesus' youth is summarized (Luke 2:52) as growing in bodily stature and in divine and human recognition of his worth and character. In both passages, the parents come to the Temple to meet their son, though there is a striking difference in their encounters.

Elkanah and Hannah knew their son was "lent to the Lord" for life. But Mary and Joseph were only beginning to discover the truth about Jesus. His comment, "Did you not know that I must be in my Father's house?" (verse 49) carries a weightier meaning than his need to be educated in the Hebrew tradition. Though they did not fully understand (2:50), Mary and Joseph would soon come to realize what the angel's words really meant—that Jesus belonged ultimately to God. They must acknowledge the call placed on him, free him to pursue it, and not allow this to lead to alienation but to a new grasp of their relationship, one that would make room for God's sovereignty.

Model Parents, Model Jews

Joseph and Mary are shown to be model Jews, observant of God's Torah, making the journey to Jerusalem for Passover. Though Luke makes the most universalistic claims for the gospel, he also shows that John and Jesus both grew up in pious Jewish families. Jesus is depicted as standing on the threshold of adulthood, which is acknowledged at the age of thirteen in Jewish culture.

A Serious Student

Where one might expect to find a twelve-year-old playing with his friends in the caravan of pilgrims, Jesus showed an unusual seriousness about his vocation and the way he would take part in adult society. Thus he remained in Jerusalem, staying for days in the Temple engaged with rabbinic study groups. Asking penetrating questions could reveal insight into the Torah. The paintings of Jesus sitting with the rabbis "teaching" them are an exaggeration. It was enough for him to be an advanced student, whose attention to Scripture and meditation on its meaning was already bearing fruit in a growing understanding.

> **Think About It:** What were the defining moments as you came to discover your identity and calling? How did loved ones react? How have you responded when those close to you (siblings, children, friends) grew in self-understanding or felt called to God's business? How can we better discern signs and be supportive of choices in our own and others' spiritual and vocational journeys?

Mary and Joseph found and scolded him. His answer was not one of disrespect, but a serious inquiry: had they not observed who their son was becoming (verses 48-49)? This did not entail a break in the relationship, and Jesus continued to be the model son of Deuteronomy, honoring and obeying his parents. Nevertheless, this gentle confrontation led them to part with any expectations they might have for their son and to recognize that God was guiding his steps in a special way.

Study Suggestions

A. Acknowledge the Season

Begin by making an emotional transition between festive gaiety and the "ongoingness" of life. Invite reporting of last week's activities and coming expectations. The successive stanzas of the hymn, "We Would See Jesus," make a good transition from Jesus' birth to his life and ministry, and then to his call to discipleship. After singing it, offer a prayer asking God to help us make this transition in our lives as well.

B. Join in Creation's Hymn

Read in unison Psalm 148. Invite members to share experiences of worship that were bigger than they. Ask: When have you felt—like the psalmist—this deep connection with all creation, praising the Maker? How have such experiences affected you and your relationship with God?

C. Making Room for God's Call

Read aloud Luke 2:41-52, then summarize the commentary (page 47–48). Discuss: What led Jesus to stay behind? Why was he surprised that his parents did not know where he was? What does Jesus' response tell them about their son? How must they adapt to make room for his call? When have you had to adapt in order to let a loved one pursue God's call? How was the relationship affected? Did this change make room for God in the relationship? Discuss the "Think About It" questions.

D. Honoring God First

Review 1 Samuel 1 as background. Then read 2:18-26 and the commentary on pages 44–45. Ask: How did Samuel come to be in the Shiloh temple? What was special about his birth? In what way did God reward Hannah and Elkanah for their first son? When have you experienced God's favor where you have "lent" to the Lord (time, talents, even loved ones)? How do Hophni and Phineas contrast with Hannah and Samuel? Discuss the questions in both "Think About It" boxes.

E. Check Your Wardrobe

Read Colossians 3:5-17 (to get the flavor of the metaphors of clothing and of dying and rising). Review the commentary on pages 45–47. Ask: What does the metaphor of dying and rising communicate to you? that of clothing? What is the nature of the old way of dressing—the way we presented ourselves to the world? What new garments (attitudes, behavior) does a Christian put on? What are the benefits and handicaps of this new "uniform"? What are the motivations for such a change of attire? What do we need to put off and put on (or die to and rise to) in order to reflect Christ more clearly and completely?

Focus on verses 12-17, and ask: What is the author's vision for Christian community? Does this require speaking the name, or is "name" more of a symbol for one's identity or spirit?

F. Affirm Yourself as Beloved

Examine what it means to be "God's chosen ones, holy and beloved" (Colossians 3:12). Ask: Do you think of yourself this way? What words would you use to describe your relationship with God? What does this passage suggest about how we are to manifest this relationship? Is being chosen and blessed by God primarily a privilege or a responsibility?

G. Godly Resolutions

New Year's is the traditional time for examining one's life and pondering how to amend it, to deepen our discipleship. The New Year's resolution is often only a weak stab at cleaning out the old wardrobe and putting on a new self—mostly because we think we can do it under our own steam without relying on God's forgiveness and strength.

Summon members into a time of reflection by stating: "As these lections have led you to consider your response to God's call, and whether you are rightly dressed for the work, what is God leading you to focus on at the start of a new year?"

EPIPHANY

Lections for the Epiphany of the Lord

Old Testament: Isaiah 60:1-6

*T*HE Book of Isaiah is a compilation of prophecies. It does not present a sequential story or even an orderly set of oracles; rather, it is a collection of items from various periods addressing different situations and composed by writers living in different centuries. It includes brief public statements noted down at the time by disciples, visions or spiritual experiences, sermon notes, and some biographical and historical features. Three parts of the book have been identified—First Isaiah (Chapters 1–39) who prophesied 740–701 B.C. about the divine punishment Judah was soon to receive, Second Isaiah (Chapters 40–55) who proclaimed in Babylon in the 540s B.C. that the punishment was almost over, and Third Isaiah (Chapters 56–66) who preached to a postexilic community that had been liberated by Cyrus of Persia to return and begin re-forming a nation and rebuilding their city and Temple (516–444 B.C.).

This lection is from Third Isaiah and is set in the Palestine of Malachi's time (see lection for the second Sunday of Advent). The overall mood of these chapters is one of melancholy, which is not surprising since the people were still vassals of Persia, harassed by enemies, living in a ruined city, and facing harsh economic conditions. Many of the oracles offer them hope and encouragement, however; this one is a prime example.

Light in the Darkness

Their deliverance from Babylon had restored light to their lives; God's presence (glory) had returned to their midst; they were called to respond with brightened countenance and renewed hope (verse 1). To be sure, their hearts and lives had been enveloped in gloom and despair, but YHWH would penetrate the grim circumstances and manifest himself in radiant, hopeful ways (verse 2). This restored divine brilliance would illuminate the path and prospect not only of the Jews but, through them, all nations and rulers, who had been dwelling in the dark of evil and ignorance as well (verse 3).

So, the prophet urged, open your eyes and look around. The situation is not as bad as you feared. Your scattered people are coming in from hither and yon. Long-lost relatives will be reunited. Grandchildren you have never seen—born to sons and daughters from whom you were forcibly separated—will be restored to loving arms (verse 4). Economic prospects are looking up. Fishermen will go to sea again and bring in plentiful catches. Traders will venture forth and return bearing consumer goods to restore comfort and elegance to their lives (verse 5). Camel car-

> ***Think About It:*** God's restored blessing is equated (or symbolized) by the prophet with family reunion and material abundance. Are comfortable life and family harmony signs of God's favor? How does this relate to the theodictic question raised by the Malachi passage on the second Sunday of Advent? How do we explain that sometimes it is the wicked who prosper while the righteous suffer? Can we experience God's blessing even in the midst of suffering and misfortune? What does Jesus' teaching about taking up our cross to follow him say to all of this?

avans will set out across the deserts and bring them wealth and affluence. And for all this the praise will go to YHWH. For the promised restoration will be due to YHWH and to YHWH alone (verse 6).

Epiphany Is Manifestation

This passage is read on Epiphany (the celebration of God's manifestation through Christ to the world) because it speaks of God's coming to a beleaguered people to bring light and life and hope. It calls us to take heart because the glorious grace of the Almighty has come to dispel the darkness of sin and despair by performing a saving work. We are urged to rise up, catch the vision of a new day, and embark on the path to restoration and wholeness. It is not by accident that the Feast of Epiphany is set on January 6, just as the days are beginning to lengthen and—even though weeks of cold winter remain—a hopeful glimmer of spring is in the air.

Psalter: Psalm 72:1-7, 10-14

This is a royal psalm, written by court poets for use on the occasion of the accession to the throne of a crown prince or on the anniversary of the coronation. Kings in the ancient Near East were viewed as their god's adopted son and divinely appointed representative. Through him, the god's blessing was bestowed on the people. Whatever fortune befell him also affected them, and he was considered responsible for it. The king's two main roles were seen as attributes of God—upholding the covenant and its laws and rituals, and protecting the nation against enemies.

These qualities are readily apparent in this psalm. YHWH is implored to bestow a sense of rightness and morality on the king so he will rule justly, treat the poor with fairness and compassion, rescue the needy from poverty and oppression, and punish those who are exploiting them. An equitable distribution of wealth among both those who tend flocks in the hills and those who till the soil in the valleys will bring abundance to all (verses 1-4).

The psalmist prays that the king will have long life (verse 5), that he will be a blessing to his people (verse 6), and that his reign will foster virtue, honor, and peace throughout the realm (verse 7). The prayer goes on to ask YHWH to give the ruler power to extend the nation's borders (verse 8), conquer his enemies (verse 9), bring in tribute and bounty (verse 10), and make the rulers of surrounding nations his vassals (verse 11). This power is not to be used for self-aggrandizement, however; for the king is to care for the needs of the poor and helpless, show compassion on the weak and marginalized, and protect the victims of injustice and brutality (verses 12-14).

These godly standards for royal conduct were applied not only to reigning kings but also to the expected messiah and were fully manifested, though in unexpected ways, in the life and ministry of Jesus.

Epistle: Ephesians 3:1-12

Another dimension of the Epiphany (revelation) of God through Christ is presented in the Epistle. Paul has been the recipient of a special vision into the mysteries of God's plan of salvation for all. It was not previously understood that not only the Jews were to benefit from God's grace but the Gentiles as well—that is, all peoples on earth. This truth the Holy Spirit had revealed to Paul and other apostles, and he (or someone writing in his name) now made it plain to all. God bestowed on you Gentiles the same gifts, incorporating them into the same community of faith and promising them the same assurance of salvation provided to the Jews. It was Paul's special charge to broadcast this message, even when he was persecuted for it and imprisoned (verses 1-6).

Think About It: The purpose of the Epiphany is not to awe but to invite. Do you think of God as an awesome being, far-removed, distant, unapproachable? or as a welcoming, caring presence? How has Jesus brought God closer to you? What epiphanies (disclosures) of God have addressed your life? How have you responded?

The Mystery Is Revealed

Though Paul humbly considers himself in the lower ranks of God's servants, he is nevertheless confident that God's grace and power have called him to make known to the Gentiles that God loves them too and has rich blessings awaiting them if they believe the good news. This has been God's plan from the beginning, but only now has the time become ripe for this mystery to be fully revealed. Christ has come; the Epiphany has happened; and the church has the task of sharing the richness of God's wisdom, not only with the common people but also with persons of power in high places. The Christ who was present with God from creation has now, through his incarnation and manifestation on earth, made possible a direct, personal relationship with God to all who come to God in faith. The Epiphany has a purpose—not to awe or impress, but to invite us into God's loving presence (verses 7-12).

Gospel: Matthew 2:1-12

In the church year, Epiphany is associated with the visit of the wise men, to whom their Eastern wisdom and the brightly shining star had made known the true identity and startling significance of the Babe born in Bethlehem. The fact that Herod commanded that all children under two be killed in order to remove any possible threat to his rule, suggests that Jesus could have been as old as two when the magi arrived to pay homage. These men were astrologers, who related the movements of the stars and planets to human events and future predictions. The theological significance attached by Matthew to their visit is that it symbolized that Jesus' coming was part of God's cosmic plan—not only for humble shepherds or the inhabitants of this remote province, but for the wise and mighty and for all people on earth.

This earth-shaking, history-changing event took place during the despotic reign of Herod the Great (37–4 B.C.), whose marriage to Mariamne, a member of the royal Hasmonean family, gave him some legitimacy in Jewish eyes. He was a crafty, vicious ruler, who murdered both enemies and family members to stay in power, but also carried out some momentous building projects, including improvements to the Temple in Jerusalem. The slaughter of the children fits his ruthless reputation and is recorded nowhere except in Matthew.

A Fulfillment of Prophecy

The location of Jesus' birth in Bethlehem is viewed as fulfillment of the prophecy in Micah 5:2, which is also referred to in John 7:42. Bethlehem was home territory for David; so this ties Jesus to David geographically, as the genealogy in Matthew 1:6 does historically—further substantiating messianic claims.

Unlike Luke, who has Joseph and

Think About It: Matthew and Luke offer very different accounts of Jesus' birth. Mark, John, and Paul do not mention it at all. How do you account for these differences? Why was it important to shape the accounts to fit Old Testament prophecies of the Messiah's coming?

Mary coming to Bethlehem solely for census registration and being temporarily housed in a stable or cave, Matthew suggests that they were actually living there and that the magi visited the baby in their home. It was only to avoid the violence of Herod's son Archelaus that they later moved to Nazareth in Galilee, which was ruled by Antipas, another of Herod's sons. This also fulfilled a messianic prophecy (Matthew 2:22-23).

When they first reached the area, the wise men paid a courtesy call on Herod; and he pried out of them information about the star and the child with deceptive claims of wanting to go pay his respects. So they followed the star, found the place, entered and worshiped, and presented their gifts. Later interpreters have related the gold to Jesus' royalty and the frankincense to his divinity (since it was used in worship). Because myrrh was used for embalming, this gift foretold his death.

> ***Think About It:*** God is not mentioned but was working in the wings. How do we discern God at work in our lives? How can we test the spirits to make sure it is God who is doing or saying what we see and hear? (Consider comparing the message with Scripture, church teaching, rational criteria, and the voice of experience—our own and that of trusted friends.) Must God-talk be used to make clear that God is present and active? When is it appropriate and helpful and when not?

God at Work in the Wings

Although the magi had at first believed Herod, once they were warned in a dream of his true intent, they decided not to report back to him. Instead they headed home by a different route. This is one of six references to dreams in Matthew (1:20; 2:12, 13, 19, 22; 27:19), a motif that suggests that God (who is not directly mentioned in this story) was at work in the wings to carry out the divine plan and purpose.

Study Suggestions

A. Draw on Other Resources

Keep in mind that these same four lections are used in all three lectionary cycles for Epiphany, so refer back to Years A and B of *Keeping Holy Time* for additional background material and study ideas.

B. Explain Epiphany

Begin by noting that today is the Feast of the Epiphany (manifestation, revelation), commemorating the making known to the world of God's plan of salvation through Christ. It is associated in the Western church calendar with the visit of the wise men and in the Eastern Orthodox church with Jesus' baptism. It falls on January 6, just after the winter equinox, when the days begin to lengthen and hope is stirring that the buds of spring will before long throw off the cold of winter.

C. Examine the Contexts

Drawing on the interpretive comments on pages 52–56, note the situations to which the lections are addressed. Third Isaiah was preaching to a people who had just returned from a trying half century in captivity and a rough journey through the wilderness, only to find a ruined city, a barren land, and hostile neighbors. The psalmist is speaking to a crown prince about to ascend the throne, reminding him of the divine mandate to deal justly and compassionately with the poor. The writer of Ephesians is addressing his Gentile hearers with the good news that they are no longer to be written off as ineligible for God's saving grace, but instead are welcome in God's presence on equal status with the Jews. In the magi story, Matthew is saying that the birth of a baby in an out-of-the way corner of the Empire has cosmic significance. Discuss: What are today's circumstances that cry out for such hope and assurance? How can we be vehicles for sharing this good news?

D. Compare the Epiphanies

The passages show different but complementary facets of God's revelation. Isaiah speaks of God's blessing on a deprived and oppressed people in terms of material abundance. The psalmist sees God acting through a righteous, caring ruler. Ephesians breaks open God's eternal, mysterious plan of salvation through the gift of a savior. Matthew calls on astrology, dreams, and the fulfillment of prophecy to illuminate the significance of the Messiah's birth. Discuss: What means does God use today to communicate this grace to us? What commitments can we make at the start of a new year to be such avenues ourselves?

E. Seek New Epiphanies

Form small groups for a sharing time. Invite members to tell stories of how God has been made known to them. Conversion experiences, times of pain and loss, dreams and visions, loving relationships, worship and prayer, the beauties of nature, Scripture study, group sharing, struggling with hard questions—all are possibilities. Ask each group, after all have shared, to identify points of similarity and difference. When the group reassembles, have someone from each small group report these common themes and write them on chalkboard or a large sheet of paper.

F. Blend Sharing With Worship

Build these shared themes into a litany of gratitude. Read them one at a time, with the group responding after each with words of thanksgiving. For example:

Leader: For showing us your love through illness and grief,

Group: We give you thanks, O God.

End the litany with the Lord's Prayer; then sing "O Love That Wilt Not Let Me Go."

Lections for Baptism of the Lord
(First Sunday After the Epiphany)

Old Testament: Isaiah 43:1-7

*C*HAPTERS 40–55 of the Book of Isaiah were preached in Babylon by an unknown prophet whom we call Second Isaiah. He prophesied in the 540s B.C. to the people exiled from Judah that a leader would soon come to liberate them from captivity and lead them home. He also extended God's salvation beyond Judah to all the nations. Many of his oracles, such as today's lection, are seen retrospectively as referring to the redemption to be brought by Christ, God's promised Messiah.

Amid Spiritual Crisis, Hope

Second Isaiah preached to the social and political elite of Judah who had been living in Babylon for half a century. Although they enjoyed some political and religious freedom, they felt guilty and pessimistic. Many must have mourned like the exiled prophet Ezekiel: "We have sinned. Our bones are dried up. Our hope is lost. How can we go on living?" (See Ezekiel 33:10; 37:11.) Or they lamented with an exiled poet: "We have transgressed. God has not forgiven. No one comforts us." (See Lamentations 1:16-17; 3:42-45.) The exiles thought God had deserted them—and perhaps had even disappeared from history. They were experiencing a spiritual crisis, comprising guilt over their rebellion and apostasy and despair over their dismal plight and bleak prospects.

In the midst of this gloom, Second Isaiah saw hope in the person of King Cyrus of Persia, who was about to overthrow Babylon. Cyrus would become God's agent to restore the exiled peoples (see Isaiah 45:1-4). Thus, Second Isaiah preached a persuasive dual message to the exile community: YHWH, the sovereign God of the heavens and of history, has not abandoned you, but still has compassion for you; and, the changing political events in Babylon are being directed by YHWH—through Cyrus your return to Jerusalem is imminent.

Beyond Punishment, Compassion

Our verses are from a larger unit in Isaiah (42:14–43:13). The passage first summarizes why the people are in exile: they were supposed to be God's servant and messenger, but had failed to obey God's law and glorify God's teachings among the nations. Verse 43:1 is the turning point—from despair to hope: "But now thus says the LORD, . . . Do not fear, for I have redeemed you."

In 43:1-7, Second Isaiah prophesies that God would again call Israel by name (indicating a renewed intimate relationship with a God who had not forgotten them after all) and would protect them through the dangers (water and fire) that they would face in a return journey across the desert. YHWH would redeem them by giving Egypt, Ethiopia, and Seba in Arabia as ransom and would gather the scattered exiles from across the earth. (Also see Isaiah 45:14, which says that these nations would pay tribute to Israel and acknowledge YHWH as the only God.)

Notice the powerful imagery with which the promise is offered: In the midst of fear, rescue and personal recognition (verse 1). In flood and fire, protection (verse 2). Power over enemy nations (verse 3). An esteem and compassion that reclaims them (verse 4). Presence, preservation, and restoration from all points to which they have been scattered (verses 5-6). A reminder that they have been lovingly and personally shaped and named (verse 7).

> **Think About It:** The exiles were in a spiritual crisis, experiencing guilt and despair. God, through a prophet, offered them comfort and hope. When have you experienced similar feelings? Where did you turn for succor? Who served as a "prophet" to you? What did this person (or these persons) say or do to comfort or assist you? What words or gestures touched you? How can you be a "prophet" and offer hope to persons now facing crisis?

Psalter: Psalm 29

Our January psalms are part of two collections of Davidic psalms (2–41 and 51–72) that form the bulk of Books I and II of the Psalms. With Book III they move from the establishment of a covenant between YHWH and the Davidic king (Psalm 2) to the failure of that Davidic covenant and the mournful cries of the Davidic descendants (Psalm 89, Book III). Ancient Israel believed that the Davidic monarchy embodied God's purposes (see Psalm 72) and that the king was God's adopted son (Psalm 27). The failure of that monarchy created the theological crisis for the exiles who searched for a new understanding of God and their relationship with God. Thus, while various psalms may reflect individuals' experiences, the Book of Psalms must be read in light of Israel's corporate crisis of faith.

Psalm 29, one of the oldest psalms, has an archaic repetition pattern. It was probably adapted from an ancient hymn to Ba'al, a local deity who was lord of the land. YHWH's power and glory are revealed as a thunderstorm that rises over the Mediterranean Sea, moves inland to devastate the forests of the Lebanon mountain, then subsides in the Syrian desert (verses 3-9). The entire heavenly court of Canaanite gods is called to acknowledge YHWH as the ruler of the universe who surpasses and dethrones all other powers. Only YHWH, says the psalmist, can grant strength and peace (verses 10-11).

Epistle: Acts 8:14-17

A single writer is the author of both the Gospel of Luke and the Book of Acts. Addressed to Theophilus, the books are similar in language and style. Together they tell a continuous story.

Christianity Expands

The Philip in our verses is not one of the Twelve; rather he is one of the seven deacons chosen to assist the Twelve by distributing food to the neglected Hellenist widows (see Acts 6:5). Hellenists were Greek-speaking Jewish Christians who probably interpreted the Torah less stringently than the "Hebrews," who were Aramaic-speaking Jewish Christians in the Jerusalem church. The appointment of Philip thus represents the earliest expansion of Christianity into the Greek-speaking world, although he was still in Jerusalem and among Jews.

Think About It: Philip went to Samaria to preach the good news even though antagonism had long existed between Samaritans and Jews. What hostile situations exist today in your community or denomination? What biases or barriers separate people? How might you bridge these barriers and overcome these antagonosims? With whom might you share the good news of God's love in Christ?

Taking Good News to Enemies

Besides distributing food, Philip traveled north to Samaria on an evangelistic mission. Animosity had long existed between Jews and Samaritans. They shared a common heritage through Jacob but differed radically in their respective commitments to Jerusalem and Mount Gerizim as sanctuaries and in their laws and purity codes. The Jews considered the Samaritans to be lax in their religious observances. Jews and Samaritans avoided contact, as Jesus' parable of the good Samaritan demonstrates (Luke 10:29-37). Luke indicates that the people of Samaria were not at all receptive to the Jewish Jesus (9:52-56).

For Luke, Jesus' ministry moved from Galilee (north of Samaria) toward Jerusalem in the south; then Christianity later moved outward from Jerusalem. Thus, Philip's outreach into Samaria signifies the expansion of Christianity beyond Jerusalem and Judea. Philip's work in Samaria fulfilled part of the prophecy that Luke reports in Acts 1:8.

Gospel: Luke 3:15-17, 21-22

In 1000 B.C.—a millennium before John the Baptist—David became king over Judah and also Israel. God promised that his descendants would reign forever (2 Samuel 7:16). Yet after David's son Solomon died (about 922 B.C.), Israel rejected a Judahite as their king and chose their own king. Israel was conquered by Nineveh in 722 B.C.; and Judah fell to Babylon in 587.

The Coming One

The Jews, however, remembered YHWH's promise to David and looked for a descendant of David to rise as an anointed king or messiah, reunite the scattered peoples, and establish God's reign of peace and prosperity (see Isaiah 9:7; 65:17-25; Jeremiah 4:1-2; Ezekiel 37:15-26). In Luke 3:15-17, the crowds who came to hear John preach and to be baptized wondered if he were that messiah. John said he was not, but that another was coming who would "baptize . . . with the Holy Spirit and fire" (verse 16).

Baptizing With Spirit and Fire

Scholars have interpreted John's reference to Spirit and fire in at least five different ways: "(1) fire describes the inflaming, purifying work of the Spirit; (2) the repentant will receive the Spirit, while the unrepentant will experience the judgment of fire; (3) . . . Jesus' baptism will bring the judgment of a mighty wind and fire; (4) . . . 'Spirit' or 'wind' and 'fire' reflect the Christian interpretation of the Pentecost experience; or (5) John saw in Spirit and fire the means of eschatological purification: the refiner's fire for the repentant and destruction for the unrepentant" (*The New Interpreter's Bible*, Vol. IX, Abingdon, 1995; pages 85–86).

> ***Think About It:*** Before reading any further, ponder which of these interpretations of Spirit and fire make the most sense to you. Why?

Since John immediately followed his statement with a description of a farmer gathering the grain and burning the chaff, he seems to mean some version of interpretations (2) or (5). For him, Spirit and fire were a baptism of judgment (see Luke 3:9, 17). In Acts, however, when tongues of fire fell on the disciples at Pentecost and the Holy Spirit filled them, they were gifts and signs of promise, not of judgment (see Acts 2:1-4, 38-39).

Jesus and the Spirit

Each of the Synoptic Gospels treats Jesus' baptism differently. Luke says only that "Jesus also had been baptized." His focus is on what happened afterward: Jesus prayed; the heavens opened; the Spirit descended "in bodily form like a dove"; a heavenly voice called Jesus "my Son, the Beloved" and said, "With you I am well pleased."

Rabbis taught that when the last of the prophets of Israel departed, so did the Spirit; but that occasionally God caused a "daughter voice" to speak from heaven. After Jesus' baptism, the voice identified Jesus as "my son," thus connecting him with Israel's past when Isaac was the child of God's promise to Abraham. Israel's king was called the son of God; and Israel itself was later called God's son. Thus, identifying Jesus as God's son not only points to his special relationship with God but also connects him with his people's messianic tradition.

Jesus as the Beloved Child

The voice also identified God as a beloved parent who blesses and affirms the child. Here, stripped of sophisticated theological language, is the essence of the relationship between God and Jesus—the love that blesses and unites. God accepts, blesses, and affirms God's children, and we are called to do the same.

Think About It: God said to Jesus, "You are my Son, the Beloved; with you I am well pleased." Can you hear God saying this to you? To whom would you give a blessing, and what would you say?

Luke's description of Jesus' baptism thus acknowledges that he could not have done what he did apart from God's empowerment and blessing. Coming after Luke's report that John is imprisoned, the baptism signals the beginning of Jesus' public ministry.

Study Suggestions

A. Experience Ancient Beliefs

Read together the Psalm 29 background material (pages 59–60). Then read Psalm 29 responsively, alternating every half verse, to experience its ancient pattern. Discuss: How might the psalm also speak to exiled Judahites? What does this psalm say to us? (Could the "strength" in verse 11 include our scientific and technological capabilities, so that any advances are God's gifts, not merely the results of our own efforts?) What does this view of God's sovereignty say about the ecological and economic areas of our lives?

B. Judgment and Compassion

Read Isaiah 43:1-7, and review the commentary on pages 58–59. Ask: Who was this Isaiah? To whom was he speaking? What is he specifically saying to the exiles? How does this passage express Second Isaiah's dual message? (Verses 1-3a, 4-5a, 7—God has not abandoned the exiles; verses 3b and 5b-6—God directs historical events.) What does this passage mean for us today? (Possibilities: God's judgment is never final; God has compassion on us; God seeks to reconcile with us.)

C. Examine Jesus' Baptism

Read Luke 3:15-17, 21-22; and review the background material on pages 61–62. Ask: For whom were the Jews looking? What did they think he would do? Why did Jesus fail to meet this expectation? Which of the five interpretations of Spirit and fire do you think John meant? Why? What role do judgment and promise play in your faith life?

D. Christianity's Expansion

Read Acts 8:14-17. Ask: Who was Philip? Why was he significant to the early church? (Review Acts 6:1-6 and the commentary on pages 60–61.) As Philip exemplified, all followers of Christ are called to share the good news through both word and deed. Ask: How does Philip help fulfill Acts 1:8? Point out on a map the locations of Jerusalem, Judea and Samaria, and the extension of the gospel throughout the Mediterranean world.

E. Make Connections

Ask: What connections do you see among today's four lections? (Possibility: The psalm and Isaiah 43 declare the cosmic context: God, who reigns universally and seeks us out to bless, affirm, protect, and bring peace. Luke announces that Jesus embodies God's reign and love; the heavenly voice after Jesus' baptism affirms it. In Acts, Jesus' followers experience the baptism of Spirit and fire that John predicted. Then, like Philip, Jesus' followers share this baptism, embodying God's ever-seeking reconciliation, with all humanity.)

F. Sing and Pray

Sing "When Jesus Came to Jordan" or a hymn about mission extension. Close with a prayer asking God to fill us with the Spirit and empower us to share the good news with those about us.

Lections for Second Sunday After the Epiphany

Old Testament: Isaiah 62:1-5

*S*OME scholars assume that Second Isaiah returned with the exiles to Jerusalem and that Chapters 56–66 are a continuation of this prophet's work. Others identify these chapters as Third Isaiah, another unknown prophet who was perhaps a disciple of Second Isaiah.

A Harsh Reality

As previously mentioned, Third Isaiah prophesied in Jerusalem after 539 B.C. when the Persian king Cyrus (who conquered Babylon) allowed the exiles to return to rebuild Jerusalem. This Isaiah preached to a mix of the previously exiled Judahite elite and the poor who had remained behind during the Exile. (See 2 Kings 24:10-16; 25:12; 2 Chronicles 36:19-21; Ezra 1:1-4.)

The exodus from Babylon was not nearly as glorious as Second Isaiah had predicted in last week's lection. Life was harsh economically. Canaanite rituals and beliefs were being blended with Jewish practices. Intermarriages had occurred. Third Isaiah preached against idolatry, pagan worship, and failure to observe the law (Chapters 56–59 and 63–66).

A Glorious Vision

In Chapters 60–62, Third Isaiah moves away from the practical problems of restoring a devastated land and a disobedient people. In Chapter 60, he offers a grand vision of God's glorious restoration of the ruined city. It will receive a new name, Zion. It will be delivered from oppressors and esteemed by all the nations. Peace and prosperity will abound. All the exiles will return. In Chapter 61, he describes a prophet (anointed one) who will bring liberation to the poor.

In Chapter 62—this week's lection—the prophet announces that he will not cease praying until God's full vindication of Jerusalem occurs (verses 1-2). By vindication he means a restoration to normal life and honored status after their humiliation at the hands of the Babylonian conquerors. The Hebrew word for "vindication" is rendered as "righteousness" by the NIV. Its translation of verses 1b-2a is as follows: ". . . till her righteousness shines out like the dawn, / her salvation like a blazing torch. / The nations will see your righteousness, / and all kings your glory." This puts the onus on Judah to shape up and manifest themselves as a just and moral community, rather than on the nations to accord them due recognition— an inner rather than an outer modification. In either case, though, it is God who must initiate the change.

> **Think About It:** The same Hebrew word means both "vindication" and "righteousness." We think of the former as coming from others, the latter from within ourselves. How are we vindicated or made righteous by a power beyond ourselves or by our own efforts?

The writer describes the glorious restoration of Jerusalem as a jeweled crown and a no-longer-abandoned wife (verses 3-5). YHWH will be as attentive as a new bridegroom is to his bride.

Third Isaiah typically does not distinguish sharply between the outer physical city of Jerusalem and its inner spirit. Sometimes Third Isaiah's description of Zion is seen, not as an actual physical restoration, but as an eschatological vision of a transformed city to be established by God at the end of time.

Exilic and postexilic writers (Daniel, Ezekiel, Third Isaiah) may have introduced utopian and apocalyptic thought (possibly influenced by Babylonian apocalyptic ideas) because they had lost hope of God ever re-establishing a unified Israel by historical, political means. Or perhaps they objected to the narrow, sectarian reforms initiated by Ezra and Nehemiah (whose reforms we will study in our next session).

> **Think About It:** Third Isaiah anticipated that God would restore and vindicate (make righteous) the ruined city of Jerusalem. Would this come about through a mighty divine act or by means of painstaking human effort? How do you perceive God acting in history? How do human and divine initiatives combine to create change?

Psalter: Psalm 36:5-10

The psalmist acknowledges the reality of evil in the threats and deeds of the wicked and arrogant (verses 1-4, 12), but proclaims a different, more profound reality—God's steadfast love (Hebrew *Hesed*).

A Cosmic Hierarchy

Verses 5-6 profess an understanding of God's character by using ancient Near Eastern cosmological terms in descending order: (1) God's steadfast love is like the heavens above all; (2) God's faithfulness is like the clouds; (3) God's righteousness (the ability to set things right) is like the mighty mountains—that anchor the dry land, hold up the sky, and restrain the waters; and (4) God's justice is like the power of the deep oceans. The psalmist says that the world depends on God's righteousness as the earth depends on the mountains and that God's justice is as deep and powerful as the sea.

> **Think About It:** This psalm draws a sharp distinction between the upright and the wicked, with only the former being sustained by God's *hesed*. Do you experience people as being either all good or all bad? Or do you see degrees of good and bad in everybody, so that all are in need of God's grace, and God's steadfast love is available to all?

Taking Refuge

The psalmist takes refuge under God's wings and in God's house, depending on God—in contrast to the wicked who assert their self-sufficiency. Life and nourishment are acknowledged as gifts from God; in fact God—portrayed as light—is the source of life (verses 7-9). However, since this gift of life is experienced in the midst of opposition and evil, the psalmist prays for God to continue loving steadfastly, righteously, and justly (verses 10-11).

Epistle: 1 Corinthians 12:1-11

Prior to Chapter 11, Paul addresses issues in Corinth that arose because the Corinthians, who belonged to an end-time community, still had to interact with the unbelieving culture around them. In Chapters 11–14, he turns to divisive issues within the believing community itself—head coverings, abuses at the Lord's Supper, taking Communion unworthily, ecstatic speech, disorderly worship—and practical advice is given to restore unity and build community.

Many Gifts, One Spirit

Paul proclaims that no one becomes a believer and professes "Jesus is Lord" unless graced by the Spirit. Furthermore, every believer receives some kind of spiritual gift—all from the same Spirit. These diverse gifts are given for the benefit of all and are to be used to build up the community. Members of the body come from a variety of backgrounds and classes (Jew and Gentile, slave and free), but all belong together and are affirmed equally

> **Think About It:** All belonged together and were affirmed as equals. Is your church inclusive of groups that are rejected in society at large? How can you become more accepting of all?

because all are baptized by the same Spirit into one community (verses 12-13). This radical assertion, and the way it was lived out in love by the early church, was a direct challenge to the deeply divided Greco-Roman society and a prime reason the church rapidly—especially among groups at the margins.

Paul's Beliefs

Paul wasn't stating a systematic theology; he was responding to the specific problems of a particular group of believers. Despite his mention in 12:4-6 of the "same Spirit," the "same Lord," and the "same God," there is no trinitarian formula here. It was passages such as these that necessitated the creation of trinitarian dogma in later centuries. Paul did, however, associate the Spirit with God and with the founding of the believing community. Paul was convinced that the Spirit graced believers with gifts for the continued building up of the body of Christ in faith, hope, and love (see 1 Corinthians 13:13).

> ***Think About It:*** Paul believed that the Spirit gives believers diverse gifts. What different gifts have you and members of your church received? How can you better recognize, affirm, and use these gifts for the benefit of all?

Gospel: John 2:1-11

John's story of Jesus is different from that of the other three Gospels. To understand what John is saying about the heavenly Father and Jesus, we must look carefully at his basic assumptions. The writer of John assumes *incarnation*: Jesus is the Word of God transformed into human flesh (1:1, 14). He further assumes that the incarnated God brought—and brings—the world to a moment of crisis and decision *now*, not later. God's full glory and eternal life are both available *now* by faith. John does not assume (as the Synoptic Gospels and Paul do) that God will judge the world someday when Christ returns to resurrect the dead and usher in God's new creation. John assumes that the world is judged now by Jesus' "hour" (his death, resurrection, and ascension). These assumptions underlie the miracle at Cana.

Miracle—and More

The setting, characters, and crisis in the story of Jesus turning water into wine at the wedding in Cana (found only in John) are quickly established. Jesus' interaction with his mother in 2:4 is blunt but not hostile or disrespectful; it distances Jesus from the traditional type of familial relationship and signals the incarnated Word's freedom from human expectation and control. While it is clear from Jesus' disengaging language that his mother can make no claim on his power, Mary gives instructions anyway, trusting in Jesus' ability.

Everything about this miracle story is overdrawn. Jesus, the incarnate Word, reveals God through extraordinary signs. The six stone jars (probably used ritually to purify hands at meals) are filled, and Jesus gives instructions to take the new wine to the steward. The miracle itself is not described—only what happens before and after it. Unlike the clay, stone would be free from ritual impurity. Reference to Jesus' "hour" ties the story to the end of Jesus' life and the dawning of a new era. People must decide *now* to believe or not.

Different Responses

A divine sign, or revelatory event, shatters our conventional explanations of why and how things happen. Some, like the steward who was perplexed by the sudden appearance of more wine, try to reshape the event to fit our categories of reality. We attempt to explain the event by conventional reasoning: "The bridegroom must have saved the best wine for last."

Others, like the disciples, allow our conventional expectations to be shattered and reshaped by the extraordinary transformation of water into wine. We allow for the possibility that God could break into our world with something new and unexpected. Like the disciples, we see God revealed in the abundance of good wine, recognize Jesus as the one who brought it, and respond by believing in Jesus as the revealer of God. "Jesus did this, the first of his signs, in Cana of Galilee, and revealed his glory; and his disciples believed in him" (John 2:11). The signs disclose God at work and lead to faith.

We may be tempted to focus on the physical changes or how water got turned into wine. But if we try to reshape this event to fit conventional thinking, we miss John's point. This is a story of the abundance, extravagance, transformation, and new possibilities that God offers. It suggests that Jesus' ministry began with an extraordinary gift of grace, and it anticipates the even more extravagant gift of new life that Jesus' "hour" would bring. For John, this story is a sign of God at work within human history. We have only to observe and respond.

> *Think About It:* The disciples allowed for the possibility of God breaking into their conventional world in extraordinary ways. How do you allow for such a possibility in your world? How do you respond?

Study Suggestions

A. Illustrate a Psalm

Read Psalm 36:5-10 and the commentary on pages 65–66. Divide large sheets of paper in half. On the left, sketch the ancient cosmology levels and label them with attributes of God as the psalmist does. On the right, draw your twenty-first-century understanding of the cosmos and label it with attributes of God. Compare your drawings. How do they help you understand how God orders creation?

Discuss: How do we generally view life in our consumer-oriented culture?

(as a challenge to be self-sufficient and gain status? as a reward earned by hard work? as a "rat race" with no time to rest and reflect?) How might the psalmist's view re-order our perspective on life?

B. Study Third Isaiah's Vision

Read Isaiah 62:1-5. Drawing on the commentary on pages 64–65 and those of the previous two sessions, review which Isaiah was preaching, to whom, and what his message was. Ask: How might Isaiah's message have been heard by those struggling to rebuild Jerusalem? What do the two metaphors for Jerusalem (a jeweled crown and a no-longer-forsaken bride) convey about God's relationship with the city? What relevance does this vision of Zion have for Christians today? How might it be understood as the promise of God's just and peaceful society on earth?

Based on your understandings of who God is and how God relates to humanity, imagine an ideal "city of God" for the twenty-first century. Discuss this in small groups, then read Isaiah 60:11-22 aloud. How are your ideal "cities of God" similar to or different from Isaiah's vision of Zion? Given the unrest in the Middle East, what hopes do you have that this vision will ever literally come to pass?

C. Examine Spiritual Gifts

Read 1 Corinthians 12:1-11, and review the commentary on pages 66–67. Discuss: What problems is Paul addressing? What are the various spiritual gifts Paul identifies? (See 12:8-10. "Faith" means a special ability to do extraordinary things, not the fundamental faithfulness of Christian life. "Discernment of spirits" means the ability to distinguish between true and false prophecy. "Tongues" refers to unintelligible utterances.) What gifts does Paul say are more important? How can we cultivate, affirm, draw out, and use the gifts of *all* our members?

D. Explore John

Read John 2:1-11, review the commentary on pages 67–68, and discuss: How do John's assumptions about Jesus as the incarnate Word influence the point of this miracle story? What is the principal difference between the steward's response to the event and the disciples' response? What does this story say about our assumptions of reality and how it is ordered and controlled? How do personal beliefs about incarnation, miracles, resurrection, and endtimes affect the interpretation of the story?

E. Make Connections

All four lections describe in some way who God is and how God relates to us. What similarities and differences do you see? What claim do these passages make on your faith and life of discipleship?

F. Sing and Pray

Sing "Many Gifts, One Spirit." Close with a prayer affirming the gifts of each class member and asking God to bless and use them for the upbuilding of the whole church.

Lections for Third Sunday After the Epiphany

T Old Testament: Nehemiah 8:1-3, 5-6, 8-10

*T*HE books of Ezra and Nehemiah bear the names of two well-known Jewish leaders of the early postexilic period of Judah's history. Ezra, a priest, and Nehemiah, a governor, both lived in Jerusalem in the 400's B.C. The two books continue directly from the end of Second Chronicles. Traditionally, authorship has been attributed to the same person—a Palestinian often called the Chronicler who lived in Jerusalem in the 300's B.C. The Ezra-Nehemiah story focuses on recreating a distinct Jewish identity and religious and ethnic purity.

When the Persian king Cyrus conquered Babylonia in 539 B.C., he decreed that Judahite exiles could return to Jerusalem and rebuild the Temple (2 Chronicles 36:22-23; Ezra 1:1-11). Many exiles returned, among them Third Isaiah, who envisioned a magnificent restoration. However, the actual rebuilding of Jerusalem was a lengthy and difficult process. Life was hard. Tensions erupted between the returning exiles and those who had remained on the land. Reconstruction of the Temple was delayed, and it was not completed until 515 B.C. (Ezra 6:15)—nearly a quarter century after it was begun.

The Law

About sixty years later, in 458 B.C., the priest Ezra was commissioned by the Persian king Artaxerxes I to establish the law of Moses as state law in Judah and to regulate Temple worship (Ezra 7). In September of that year Ezra read the Torah to the people at the Festival of Booths (Nehemiah 8). From December 458 until the spring of 457, Ezra continued an inquiry into mixed marriages. All Judahites who were married to Gentiles were required to divorce their wives or leave Jerusalem (Ezra 9–10).

Proper Repentance

When Ezra read the law to the returned exiles in Jerusalem, they wept and mourned in repentance because they had not been observing it faithfully. However, Ezra urged them to celebrate their new-moon festival as they had planned—and to keep the law by sharing their bounty with the poor and foreigners (Deuteronomy 14:29; 26:12-13).

The Wall

A decade later, in 445 B.C., Nehemiah, a cupbearer to King Artaxerxes, was appointed governor of Judah and charged with rebuilding the wall of Jerusalem (Nehemiah 2; 5:14; 6:15). The wall would enhance Jerusalem's status and security. After the wall was completed, Nehemiah enlarged the city's population by resettling Judahite villagers inside the wall. It separated Judahites from Gentiles. Nehemiah, like Ezra, also instituted religious reforms, purging the Jerusalem community of all foreign things—more exclusionary tactics aimed at rebuilding a distinctive identity and guarding ethnic purity (Nehemiah 13:4-31).

> **Think About It:** Ezra sought to protect the people's identity by forbidding intermarriage. What factors do you think best insure a group's identity? How is Christian identity formed and preserved? (Consider: strong relationships, mutual respect, shared goals and customs, common beliefs and values, formative education, a common heritage.)

> **Think About It:** Ezra discouraged an emotional display of repentance, urging the people to keep the law through ritualized celebration and sharing. When have you been tempted to emote about your wrongdoing rather than taking action as a proper repentance? Why is it easier to express emotional remorse than practice amendment of life?

Psalter: Psalm 19

The psalter was ultimately edited after the Exile to serve as an instruction manual, as the first two psalms imply. These psalms introduce God's instruction to humanity about salvation and faithful living. Together they propose that faithful persons will know (1) that their lives depend on God alone and (2) that God reigns supreme.

Psalm 19 further orients readers of the Psalms to the importance of God's instruction. In verses 1-6, the psalmist first proclaims the glory of God's wordless instruction that comes through creation, especially through the sun. (This psalm may have been composed to counter ancient worship of the sun god and other astral deities. It claims that YHWH created the sun; the sun is not a god.)

In verses 7-10, the psalmist proclaims that YHWH the cosmic creator offers a personal word of instruction through the Torah. God's word in the law is perfect, clear, reliable, and truthful; one is righteous (happy) if one lives by Torah. However, even God's personal word is not sufficient to keep one completely in harmony with God. Human errors, faults, and presumptuous behavior will emerge; therefore, one needs God's forgiveness and grace that is freely given. In response, one dedicates oneself to depend entirely on God (verses 11-14).

Epistle: 1 Corinthians 12:12-31a

Continuing to address issues about spiritual gifts in the Corinthian community, Paul here compares the believing community to a human body where unity and diversity are both compatible and necessary.

An Ancient Metaphor

The "members" of a body are interdependent parts of the organic whole, and diversity is what enables the unified body to function properly. Since this body metaphor was often used in ancient Greek and Roman literature, especially to describe political matters, the Corinthians would have been familiar with it.

Believers as a Body

Paul applied this familiar body metaphor theologically to the Corinthians' own situation. As believers they were baptized into the one "body of Christ" and drank of the one Spirit. Baptism provided them with a new shared identity in Christ, even as they retained their individuality. For their community to function properly, God graced individual members of the one body with different gifts and roles.

Think About It: Paul compares the believing community to a human body, unified yet diverse, and calls believers to strive to build up the community. How do we help build up (or break down) the whole body of the church today?

Furthermore, God arranges the body so that the weaker or inferior members, who are indispensable, are given greater honor. In this way, members of the body are united in caring for one another in the midst of both suffering and rejoicing. With this image of a supportive, interdependent community, Paul departs from the ancient Greek and Roman ideal of dispassionate self-sufficiency.

When Paul reminds the Corinthians that they are individual members of "the body of Christ" (verse 27), he is simply asking believers to consider how their life together resembles a body.

Later New Testament writings declared that Christ was "the head of the body, the church" (see Colossians 1:18; 2:19; Ephesians 4:15-16). But for Paul, believers were not "under Christ" in the sense that the head has "power over" others (see Ephesians 5:23-24). Rather, believers were "in Christ"— implying God's loving, saving power. For Paul, that saving love was revealed in the cross.

Gospel: Luke 4:14-21

According to Luke, after Jesus' baptism and temptation, he returned immediately to Galilee to begin his ministry. In verses 14 and 15, Luke quickly sets the stage: Jesus' work is teaching; the source of Jesus' power is the Spirit; a common setting for teaching is the synagogue; the response to Jesus' teaching is universal praise; Jesus' work is intended for all. The rest of Luke 4 describes Jesus' ministry in two villages: Nazareth (verses 16-30) and Capernaum (verses 31-41)—two paradigms for Jesus' ministry. What he proclaimed in Nazareth, he demonstrated in Capernaum. Through these two stories, Luke summarizes Jesus' ministry as one of both word and deed.

Fulfilling Scripture

In the course of his Galilean ministry, Jesus stopped in Nazareth where he grew up. As a practicing Jew, he went to the synagogue on the sabbath and participated (as all male members were allowed to do) in reading and commenting on the Scripture. As was customary, he stood to read (from Third Isaiah), returned the scroll, and sat down to comment.

> **Think About It:** Jesus returned to his hometown synagogue and proclaimed that he was fulfilling God's promises of deliverance. What might you think if someone you had grown up with made a similar claim? Does familiarity often breed contempt?

Third Isaiah's message of deliverance by one who was anointed by the Spirit was originally meant for those who had returned from exile to a destroyed Jerusalem more than five hundred years earlier. Ever since the Exile, Jews—remembering God's promise to David of an everlasting dynasty—had looked for an anointed king or messiah to unite Judah with tribes of Israel and establish God's peace, justice, and prosperity among the nations.

Earlier in Luke, the crowds who heard John the Baptist preach thought that he might be that messiah; but John said no, another was coming. Now, in Chapter 4, Luke reports that Jesus claimed to be that Spirit-anointed one who would bring deliverance and blessing.

Bringing Deliverance

Luke seems to have intentionally modified Isaiah (by combining 58:6 with 61:1-2, changing a verb form, and omitting the line about the brokenhearted). In doing so, he provides a succinct summary of Jesus' ministry. Deliverance encompasses bringing good news to the poor, releasing prisoners (probably debtors), restoring sight to the blind, liberating the oppressed, and announcing the year of jubilee.

In his ministry, Jesus brought such deliverance. He moved among the poor and outcast, pronouncing God's blessing on them and criticizing the rich and powerful. He healed the lame, cast out demons, and forgave sins—all forms of release from bondage. He restored physical sight to the blind and symbolically became "a light for the nations." He proclaimed that the time for liberation of the oppressed was *now*, thus fulfilling the ideal of social and economic liberation promised in the jubilee year (see Leviticus 25:8-17, 23-55; 27:16-25). Significantly, Jesus did not quote Isaiah 61:2 about the day of God's vengeance. (That day was when God would vindicate the righteous who had suffered because of their loyalty to God.)

Identity and Purpose

Jesus' one comment about the Scripture he read summarized both who he was and what his ministry was all about. "The Spirit of the Lord is upon me, because he has anointed me to bring good news. . . . Today this scripture has been fulfilled in your hearing" (verses 18-21). Through this brief story Luke proclaimed that Jesus was the fulfillment of Jewish Scripture; he was the hoped-for Messiah who would deliver them. But, as we will see in next week's lection, what Jesus understood by deliverance and what his Jewish listeners understood were quite different.

Study Suggestions

A. Hear the Law

Invite group members to get comfortable for a guided visualization of Ezra reading the law. Say, "Imagine you are living in a devastated Jerusalem in 458 B.C.—about eighty years after the first exiles were allowed to return. . . . You are gathered outside the Temple area . . . waiting for Ezra, the priest who has come from Babylon to reestablish the law of Moses in Judah. . . . There he is, climbing the wooden platform. . . . Listen: "You shall have no other gods. . . . You shall not murder . . . not steal . . . not covet . . . not make false report. . . . You may eat any clean birds but not unclean animals or certain fish. . . . You shall forgive debts . . . give your tithe to the priests, the aliens, the orphans, the widows . . . observe these statutes." With each law that is read, you weep a little louder, thinking. . . ." [Pause for 30 seconds of complete silence.]

Discuss: What did Ezra say to their weeping? What other steps did Ezra and Nehemiah take to reestablish a strong Jewish identity? (See Nehemiah 8:9b-10; the covenant in Nehemiah 10:28-39; and the commentary on pages 70–71.) Why was this expression of loyalty to God achieved by exclusion? Was Ezra's position the only viewpoint held in Judah?

B. Examine a Radical Way

Assign Psalm 19:1-6; 19:7-10; and 19:11-14 to three groups. Read the psalm aloud. Ask: What does it claim? (Consult the commentary on pages 71–72. God created the cosmos; God is supreme. Human life is adequately understood only in relationship to God. To be faithful, one must depend entirely on God.) How does this view of life compare to our cultural view today?

C. Explore a Metaphor

Read 1 Corinthians 12:12-31a. Share insights from the commentary (page 72). Ask: What was Paul's main point? Is his body metaphor helpful in understanding the nature of the church? How or how not? What other metaphors might be used to describe our modern Christian communities? If time permits, form small groups to create modern metaphors of both actual and ideal communities. Use an artistic medium (paints, clay, dance) to portray those metaphors; then, explain them.

D. Discuss a Proclamation

Before the session, invite someone to portray Jesus (perhaps in costume). Prepare a scroll with the quotation from Luke 4:18-19. Prepare the group to become synagogue worshipers in Jesus' time. Review the "Fulfilling Scripture" section in the commentary. Choose someone to hand the scroll to "Jesus." Invite everyone to be silent and get into character. Then ask "Jesus" to stand, receive the scroll, read it, return it, sit down, and make the comment in verse 21.

Ask: What do you think Jesus meant in saying, "Today this scripture has been fulfilled in your hearing"? As twenty-first–century Christians, what significance does this Scripture have for you?

E. Make Connections

What connections do you see among today's four lections? (One possibility: All four call believers to embrace similar God-centered, God-dependent assumptions and lifestyles.) What might God be calling you to do differently or to be if you allow these Scriptures to claim your life and attention?

F. Sing Your Praise

Sing either "Cantemos al Señor" ("Let's Sing unto the Lord"), which is based on Psalm 19, or "Christ, from Whom All Blessings Flow," based on 1 Corinthians 12:4-31.

Lections for Fourth Sunday After the Epiphany

J Old Testament: Jeremiah 1:4-10

JEREMIAH came from the village of Anathoth in the hill country of Benjamin two miles northeast of Jerusalem, an area often controlled by Judah. His name means "YHWH exalts." He may have been a descendant of Abiathar, one of King David's two chief priests who vied for control of the royal shrine in Jerusalem. Abiathar was banished by Solomon for supporting Adonijah as David's successor (1 Kings 1:5-8; 2:26-27). This history of priestly rivalry and royal expulsion (as well as his Benjaminite heritage) certainly influenced Jeremiah's criticism of the house of David and the Jerusalem Temple.

Jeremiah's Call

Our lection is Jeremiah's call to be a prophet of YHWH. Call narratives, common throughout the ancient world, verified that an encounter with a deity had occurred and legitimized the prophet's authority every time a message from the god was delivered. Jeremiah's call narrative describes such a dialogue that moves from YHWH's commissioning him (verses 4-5), to Jeremiah's objection (verse 6), to YHWH's reassurance (verses 7-8), to the offering of a sign of YHWH's support and presence (verses 9-10). This pattern is similar to the commissioning of Moses (Exodus 3), Gideon (Judges 6:11-24), and Isaiah (Isaiah 6), and links Jeremiah to these great leaders from the past.

In these verses, "word of the LORD" (verse 4) makes clear that his message comes from God; "knew" (verse 5) suggests intimate relationship; "only a boy" (verse 6) implies inexperience, which God's power will overcome; and "touched my mouth" (verse 9) denotes God's direct inspiration of his prophetic ministry.

Jeremiah's Ministry

Jeremiah's prophetic activity spanned a very volatile political time in Judah's existence (627–587 B.C.). He began during King Josiah's reign when Judah, a vassal nation of a weakening Assyrian empire, attempted to reestablish its independence. He continued as Assyria fell and the Babylonians conquered Jerusalem and deported Judahites. Through it all, he preached that YHWH's judgment was occurring through political events. When Jerusalem fell, he told survivors that God wanted them to stay on the land, accept their punishment, and not flee to Egypt. Tradition says that some of his followers, fearing reprisals, carried him to Egypt against his will.

Later Interpretations

Although Jeremiah's prophecies were to Judah, he was also appointed a prophet "to the nations" (verse 5). These references probably represent a later interpretation by the postexilic preservers of Jeremiah's material. Since Jeremiah prophesied during such volatile international times and had such strong opinions about Assyrian, Egyptian, and Babylonian influences in Judah's life, as well as about the expected duration of YHWH's punishment, exiled Judahites might well have concluded that his original call included international responsibilities to address a wider audience.

Similarly, although Jeremiah preached destruction and judgment, his call says he was also "to build and to plant"—which refers to the restoration of Jerusalem after the Exile. Verse 10 is connected with the oracles of salvation in Chapters 30–31. Some scholars believe the restoration theme in these oracles came from Jeremiah; others say it was added by exilic preservers who reshaped Jeremiah's material to explain their situation. Whichever it was, the result is a book containing both dire predictions and hopeful promises.

> **Think About It:** YHWH called Jeremiah "to pluck up and to pull down, and to destroy and to overthrow, to build and to plant." To what historical events do these verbal metaphors refer? What word from God by prophets is appropriate for our time and situation? What needs judging and what needs supporting?

Psalter: Psalm 71:1-6

The arrangement of this psalm (a plea for YHWH's help) is unique, moving three times from pleas to trust/praise. Our reading involves the first plea for help (verses 1-4) and part of the first statement of trust (verses 5-8). The pattern continues: second plea (verses 9-13), followed by trust (verses 14-17); third plea (verse 18), followed by praise (verses 19-24). Overall, this alternating pattern radiates tremendous assurance.

In verse 1, to "take refuge" in God may imply that the psalmist has sought asylum in the Temple from persecutors or accusers. The reference to past youth and present old age in verses 5 and 6 (and elsewhere in the psalm) may indicate that the psalmist is old and ill. Or both images (refuge and advancing old age) may be metaphorical. Either way, the psalmist lived with adversity yet depended utterly on God—from birth and regardless of life's circumstances. The psalmist lived not from a stance of self-confidence, but in a state of hope that resulted in praise of God (see verse 14). Like the psalmist, Christians during the season of Epiphany remember their baptisms and profess God's claim on us from birth and our trust in God. In our self-oriented and achievement-centered culture, such faith is radical!

Epistle: 1 Corinthians 13:1-13

This famous love chapter is part of Paul's larger discussion about knowledge and spiritual gifts.

A Caution

Paul opposed some Corinthians' claims that because they *knew about* the one God, they could eat meat from pagan rituals. He told them that having knowledge only inflated their egos; they must *love* God and thus *be known by* God (Chapter 8). Paul also admonished some Corinthians not to think they were superior because they spoke in ecstatic speech. He told them that all members are created by God and are equally important to the unity of the believing community, which is like a body that is fit, whose members are appropriately interdependent (Chapter 12).

The More Excellent Way

Ironically, even though he had just claimed that all members are equal, Paul introduced this love statement by urging the Corinthians to "strive for the greater gifts" (12:31a). Slyly, since that is what they are doing, he got their attention and then immediately shifted their focus to a "more excellent way" (12:31b). They can exhibit any number of spiritual gifts—but if they do not have *agape* (self-giving, other-regarding love), they have nothing and are nothing.

Agape—love that is selfless, whole, and encompassing—builds up the whole believing community. *Agape* is nothing less than the unmerited, compassionate, enduring love of God. The Corinthians were to be agents of that love in their relationships with each other (13:4-7). God's love toward humankind is patient, kind, self-giving, generous, encouraging, and truthful; the faith community is called to exhibit this same love to the best of their ability, since it is an excellent way.

Limitations and Expectations

Paul concluded that prophecies, tongues, and knowledge (about which the Corinthians had been making inflated claims) are limited, partial, and childish; what is permanent is love. He shifted the Corinthians' focus from the spiritual gift of knowledge that some of them had received to the more profound and universal *knowing of God in relationship*. Even this knowing is incomplete and immature during our lifetime—like seeing a dim, distorted image in the mirrors of polished bronze or silver that were made in Corinth. However, a radically complete, mature, and perfect kind of *knowing* will occur in the age to come when we will see God "face to face."

> ***Think About It:*** Paul cautioned the Corinthians not to rank spiritual gifts and inflate themselves but rather to manifest God's love in their relationships. How well do we manifest God's *agape*? What do we need to work on in order to be more loving?

Gospel: Luke 4:21-30

Our story continues from the last session. Jesus read portions of the Isaiah scroll in the synagogue in Nazareth where he had grown up. He commented, "Today this scripture has been fulfilled in your hearing" (4:21).

Nazareth Rejects Hometown Boy

What must the people have thought! Israel had been waiting for centuries for the scriptural promise of an Anointed One who would bring peace, prosperity, and justice. At first they praised Jesus, just as did people from other parts of Galilee (see 4:15). They marveled that Joseph's boy had become a prophet! They might have thought that Jesus would favor his hometown with his mightiest works and that they would share in his fame. No longer could people say (however wrongly) that no prophet ever came from Galilee [see John 7:52 and 2 Kings 14:25]. The Pharisees considered Galileans unlearned and misguided.) Jesus, they conjectured, would bless them and his hometown.

Jesus responded to the people's expectations rather harshly by quoting two proverbs. The first ("Physician, cure yourself!") expressed the people's criticism that he had not performed miracles for them. The second ("No prophet is accepted. . . .") is Jesus' own response that a prophet is not acceptable at home. He then referred to Elijah and Elisha, two of ancient Israel's prophets who took God's blessings to non-Jews. This reference enraged the people, who drove him out of town. They meant to do him physical harm, but Jesus evaded them and continued on his way. Luke's point here is Jesus remained in control of his life and refused to die in obscurity.

Different Understandings

The religious identity of the people of Nazareth was founded on the belief that they were God's special people. Expectations of privilege were ingrained in them: Surely Jesus would bless hometown folks in greater abundance than others; certainly he meant that God would bless Jews, not Gentiles. Nazareth was surrounded by Gentile neighbors With great effort, Jews sought to maintain their identity. Was Jesus suggesting this was wasted effort?

God would bless *all* the poor, *all* the captives, *all* the blind, *all* the oppressed—Gentiles as well as Jews. This claim was similar to the claims of other prophets, as Jesus' references to Elijah and Elisha would have reminded them. This indictment from their own Scripture was simply too much for Nazareth. Jesus was saying that God's blessing would not fall on them alone or even on all Israel but also on Gentiles. This, in fact, came true. At the end of Jesus' life, his "home country" (Galilee) rejected him just as his hometown folks had done. Furthermore, as Luke's story continues in Acts, Peter, Paul, and others turned to Gentiles to share God's inclusive love and grace.

Exclusion Excludes the Excluder

The people of Nazareth heard Jesus' explanation of Scripture as God's exclusive covenant with them. God would deliver *them* from their oppressors and shower *them* with blessings. However, Jesus promised a radically inclusive deliverance of all peoples everywhere—not an exclusive deliverance based on nationality, ethnicity, or religion. (Today we might add disability, gender, criminality, and other characteristics that we use to exclude from acceptance.)

Think About It: The people of Nazareth expected God's blessings to be exclusively for them; Jesus proclaimed God's grace for all. Do you feel entitled to special benefits from God because of your Christian faith? How do we exclude persons God includes? How does excluding others result in our own exclusion?

Many people still do not fathom the all-inclusiveness of God's grace—and missing the point has serious consequences. As one commentator notes: "Those who would exclude others thereby exclude themselves" (*The New Interpreter's Bible,* Vol. IX; Abingdon Press, page 108).

Study Suggestions

A. Explore "Calls"

Read Jeremiah 1:1-10 and the commentary on pages 76–77. Discuss: What are the four main elements of Jeremiah's call? What was Jeremiah called to do? Was Jeremiah really a prophet to the nations? Explore the "Think About It" questions.

Read Exodus 3:1-10; Judges 6:11-24; 1 Samuel 3; Isaiah 6. What elements in these call narratives are similar to Jeremiah's call? What is different or unique about the various calls? Discuss: What do we mean today when we say that someone has been "called to ministry"?

B. Illustrate a Psalm

Before the session, prepare a large strip of paper as a banner. Print on it the words of Psalm 71:1a, 5, and 6 (the last line only). Provide colored markers or crayons. Invite group members to illustrate the banner while you read the whole psalm aloud. Encourage illustration of dependence on God and trust and praise of God. Discuss the commentary (pages 77–78). Hang the banner in the room for closing worship.

C. Examine *Agape Love*

Assign 1 Corinthians 13:1-3; 13:4-7; 13:8-12 to be read by three groups. Read the entire chapter aloud, with everyone reading verse 13 in unison. Ask: What are the spiritual gifts the Corinthians could exhibit and still have nothing? Are our gifts eternal? Discuss the "Think About It" questions.

Make two lists of how love acts (see verses 4-7). In one column, list the two things that love *is* and the five ways that love *acts*. In a second column, list the eight things that love *is not*. Discuss: What does this contrasting description say about love-in-action in our Christian communities? How well do we manifest the positive things in our local church or denomination? How are the negative things sometimes demonstrated in our churches and denomination? How can we address this so that love is truly expressed in our relationships?

D. Reflect on Inclusion/Exclusion

Read Luke 4:21-30 and the interpretation on pages 79–80. What beliefs in Christianity are exclusive? Have you ever excluded a person or group only to discover later that you have excluded yourself from some larger blessing? Also examine the questions in the "Think About It" box.

E. Make Connections

Discuss: How is Jesus' radical message of God's inclusiveness related to Paul's "more excellent way"? How do Jeremiah's call and the psalmist's plea relate to Luke's and Paul's messages? One possible relationship: God's inclusiveness (see Luke 4) is manifested in *agape* love (see 1 Corinthians 13), which is God's response to the realities of human life (see Psalm 71). Humanity is called to love God and each other (see Jeremiah 1).

F. Close With Praise and Prayer

Read the psalm banner together (see Activity B). Close with the prayer hymn "Help Us Accept Each Other" and a prayer asking God help us extend *agape* love to *all* God's people.

Lections for Fifth Sunday After the Epiphany

O Old Testament: Isaiah 6:1-8 (9-13)

NE of the best-known passages from the prophet, Isaiah 6 offers the reader a glimpse of what it might be like to come face to face, or rather, face to hem of garment, with the Lord. The text is rich in imagery, enticing all the senses with details of Isaiah's vision.

In the Temple

Set in approximately 736/35 B.C., the year of King Uzziah's death, the reader finds Isaiah in the Temple. He is there, perhaps, to gather strength, to pray for the people upon whose deaf ears the word of God has been falling. Will they ever listen to God? Will they ever turn from their evil ways? Is there any way to make them understand the covenant with YHWH and how to fulfill their part of the covenant?

> **Think About It:** Isaiah was confessing not only his own personal unworthiness but also the transgressions of his people. In our individualistic culture, do we take responsibility for the evil and injustice in our society in which we are implicated? Do we blame injustice on others and protest our own innocence? What can we learn from Isaiah?

Smoke and Sin

In the Temple, frustrated and alone, Isaiah received a vision. He saw "the Lord sitting on a throne, high and lofty; and the hem of his robe filled the temple" (6:1). Surrounding God were singing seraphs, lifting glory and praise. As suddenly as the presence of God appeared, the Temple foundations began to shake; and smoke rolled in on the waves of the seraphs' songs.

When faced with the pure holiness and boundless love of God, humans become sharply aware of their own sinfulness.

Confronted with the sanctity of God, Isaiah at once began to confess not only his own unworthiness but also the disrepute of his people, crying, "Woe is me! I am lost, for I am a man of unclean lips, and I live among a people of unclean lips" (6:5).

Coals and Call

As the declaration of guilt left his lips, one of the singing seraphs flew to the altar retrieving from there one of the hot coals. Touching Isaiah's lips with the purifying fire, the seraph declared, "Now that this has touched your lips, your guilt has departed and your sin is blotted out" (6:7).

What a spectacle to behold! A throne, the hem of God's garment, singing seraphs, smoke and hot coals, the shaking of the Temple foundations, indeed, the very voice of God: "Whom shall I send, and who will go for us?" (6:8).

> ***Think About It:*** After what must have been a surreal experience, Isaiah answered the call of God to go to the people of God. How has God made you aware of the sinfulness of our culture? How do you seek to be a witness to God in the midst of a secular and ungodly society?

To the twenty-first–century reader, the vision of Isaiah may seem surreal, other worldly, a Hollywood creation complete with special effects, perhaps even a practical joke to provoke the witnesses' reaction for a (candid?) camera. To trust such a vision, even one that touched all the human senses, would require tremendous faith.

Send Me!

Isaiah, purified by holy fire, stood strong and answered God's call, "Here am I; send me!" Isaiah was given the words to say—with a caveat: The people would hear, but would not heed. Their hearts would be hardened, leaving them open to judgment. So why go? Because God required the purification of the people as well. Isaiah's lips were cleansed with fire, and Judah would also be "cleansed" (6:11-12).

Psalter: Psalm 138

In concert with the other lectionary readings, Psalm 138 describes the giving of the psalmist's "whole heart" to God, as well as trusting in God to deliver him from strife. Believers are reassured that God is ever-present and everlasting. Even surrounded by trouble and wrath, the psalmist writes of the Lord: "You stretch out your hand, / and your right hand delivers me" (verse 7).

Verse 3, when read in the NIV, states, "When I called, you answered me; / you made me bold and stouthearted." To encounter God, as with

Isaiah and Paul, is to be forever changed. To the lowly, the people of unclean lips, the unworthy, God comes, offering "steadfast love and . . . faithfulness" (138:2). Touched by this great God, humanity is transformed, even "all the kings of the earth shall praise [God]" (verse 4). The promises of the Lord are resolute. Although troubles come, the assurance of God never wavers.

Epistle: 1 Corinthians 15:1-11

On occasion, it seems to us that Paul's letters to the church at Corinth are written for our specific congregations. Lax faith, ties to the world, and petty disagreements are part and parcel of the church of the present day. However, even the early church did not escape intermittent argument or controversy. It was Paul, after all, who founded the Corinthian church and then spent much time attempting to keep the members in harmonious relation with one another and faithful to high moral standards.

Witnesses and Visions

The fifteenth chapter of Paul's first letter to the Corinthians reminds Christians of the centrality of the resurrection of Christ, stating, "For I handed on to you as of first importance what I in turn had received: that Christ died for our sins . . . and that he was raised on the third day" and appeared to numerous witnesses (15:3-4).

Think About It: "I proclaimed [the good news] to you, which you in turn received . . . through which also you are being saved . . . unless you have come to believe in vain" (15:1-2). What are examples of "vain belief" in the church today? How might the world see the Christian faith as "vain belief" in regard to the discrepancy between what we say we believe and how we live out that belief?

As proof, and in the tradition of Isaiah, Paul listed those to whom the risen Christ appeared: Cephas, the Twelve (one wonders at the omission of Christ's appearance to the women at the tomb), more than 500 brothers and sisters, James, all the apostles, and then to Paul himself.

Again, like Isaiah, Paul's vision of the risen Christ revealed to him his own sinfulness while simultaneously making plain to him God's forgiveness and call upon his life. He, too, answered that call and "worked harder than any of them" to proclaim the gospel (15:10). Lest he appear immodest, Paul quickly referred the credit for his endeavors to God and turned again to the point: sharing the good news with others.

Paul recognized that because of his persecution of the church prior to his conversion, he felt himself to be an unfit choice to spread the gospel. Yet through God's grace, even he was entrusted with this precious gift.

Vitalizing Vain Belief

Perhaps the Corinthian church denied the Resurrection. Perhaps they relaxed their main beliefs to conform to the world around them. Perhaps they began to "believe in vain," as Paul states in verse 2. Perhaps their faith was only superficial, not stable. Whatever the reason, Paul deemed a restatement of the Resurrection, the core of the gospel, as necessary to bolster the faith of his readers.

Today's church might need this reminder all the more. For when is it as real to us as it was to those one or two generations from the physical resurrection? Paul's words speak not only to the particular church at Corinth but also to churches through all time—even ours.

Gospel: Luke 5:1-11

Here Luke gives readers another story of call and response. In fact, the call of Peter in Luke, of Paul in Acts (recalled in First Corinthians), and of Isaiah closely mirror one another.

Extraordinarily Ordinary

We find Jesus beside the lake of Gennesaret, encircled by the usual crowds who followed him wherever he journeyed. This setting was a natural amphitheater; nevertheless, hearing all that Jesus spoke could have been difficult. In efforts to hang onto his every word, the crowds pressed in on Jesus from every side.

For the people fishing on the lake, that day was no different than any other—except, perhaps, for the fact that they had worked all night and caught nothing. Tired, disgruntled, finishing up by cleaning his nets in the morning sun as he had done hundreds of times, Simon was about to find his life changed dramatically.

A young teacher approached him, the one who drew those swarms of people. Could Simon take him out on the water a little way so the sound of his voice might travel more powerfully? Simon complied, possibly eyeing the crowd as it drew nearer and nearer to Jesus.

From offshore, Jesus sat in the boat and taught the people. Finishing, he turned to Simon and said, "Put out into the deep water and let down your nets for a catch" (5:4). Imagine Simon's feeling of contempt and his tired sigh: "Well, I've *been* doing that all night. I *am* a fisherman; but if you say so, here goes." Picture Simon's look of amazement when the nets came back full to near breaking. Imagine the first awakenings of the first disciple as it dawned on him *who this must be.*

A Day Like No Other

Forgetting the tasks concerning the fish, Simon, on this ordinary fishing morning, one like every other of his life, one that would become completely different than any other in his life, turned to Jesus and fell on his knees.

Isaiah, Moses, Jeremiah, and scores of people before Simon gave him voice on that day: "Go away from me, Lord, for I am a sinful man!" (5:8). Confronted with the holiness of God as seen in the piercing, caring eyes of Jesus, Simon's first response was to confess his own sinfulness; for what other reaction could one have, standing in the presence of the Lord? Like his ancestors before him, Simon, going about his daily routine, stinking of work and the sea, tousled by the wind, bleary-eyed with lack of sleep, was about to be invited to help change the world!

Simon Who?

Readers of the story of the call of Simon and his partners, James and John, are told nothing about their character, their qualifications, their merit. Were they scholars? Probably not, if they fished for a living. Particularly righteous? Perhaps not, given Simon's immediate confession. Successful? Not at the moment, given that they had caught nothing that night. They were ordinary men, at an ordinary place, doing ordinary things on an ordinary day. But then. . . .

> ***Think About It:*** Ordinary fishermen were tending their boats and nets when Jesus called them to service and to salvation. When, where, and how have you experienced God's salvation and call in the ordinariness of daily life? When have you been surprised—and challenged—by God? What did God call you to do? How did you respond? Or is Jesus calling you now?

Simon Peter, That's Who

To Simon and the others, Jesus said, "Do not be afraid; from now on you will be catching people" (5:10). They went ashore, walked away from their ordinary lives, and followed Jesus into the extraordinary salvation history we call the gospel. This is not the only time that Luke reports on a follower leaving everything for the awesome gift of salvation. Levi (5:28), would-be followers (9:57-62; 14:33), and the rich ruler (18:22-23) were all awed or struck with fear at their invitation. No wonder Jesus began with, "Do not be afraid."

Study Suggestions

A. Experience the Psalm

Begin by standing and reading Psalm 138 antiphonally (one side of the room reading the first half of each verse, the others responding with the second part). Share the background on the psalm (pages 83–84). Point out that worship resources like this were in the consciousness of people like Isaiah, Paul, and Peter and laid the foundation for their responses to the call of God as described in today's other three lections.

B. Study the Call Experiences

Form three groups, assigning one of the three lections—Isaiah 6:1-8, 1 Corinthians 15:1-11, Luke 5:1-11—to each. Write these questions on chalkboard or poster paper for each group to discuss after reading its passage and the commentary on it: What do you think is the context of this passage in the experience of its principal characters? What was the nature of the call/message/challenge addressed to them? Put this into a single sentence.

Then bring the groups back together, call for reports, and write the single-sentence summaries on chalkboard or poster paper.

C. Dramatize the Stories

Reassemble the three groups, asking each to work up a skit dramatizing the scenes depicted in their lections. For the Corinthians passage, the group could show the persons named in verses 5-8 testifying to how Christ had appeared to and called them. After a brief time of preparation, have the skits presented. Then discuss: What are the common themes in these call experiences? How do they differ? What do they model for us?

D. Review the Three Lections

Summarize the three passages in turn. Mention important insights from the background material (pages 82–86). In the Isaiah experience, note the progression from adoration to confession to forgiveness to challenge to response—a pattern often followed in Sunday worship in our churches. In the Corinthians passage, emphasize the significance of firsthand experience with Christ as basis for belief in the Resurrection. In the Luke story of Peter's call, Jesus came to Peter's turf and entered his reality to issue the invitation. Note that a sense of unworthiness is voiced in all three call narratives. Also discuss the questions in each of the "Think About It" boxes.

E. Make It Relevant and Personal

Ask: How does all this relate to us? Is it only religious professionals (pastors, missionaries) that are called? How is God calling us? What must be we leave behind? What obstacles do we face that were not present for the people in these texts? How can we support one another in responding to and living out our call?

F. Close With Worship

Sing together either "Here I Am, Lord," or "Lord, You Have Come to the Lakeshore." Observe a brief time of reflective silence in which group members contemplate the ways in which God is calling them. Pray for the ability to discern the call of God, the courage to receive it without fear, and the power to respond in faith and discipleship.

Lections for Sixth Sunday After the Epiphany

T Old Testament: Jeremiah 17:5-10

HE old folk tune "I Shall Not Be Moved" teaches hearers not only about the lectionary reading from Jeremiah but also about the psalm for this Sunday. According to the song, no matter what happens, from the valleys to the mountaintops, from rocking churches to happy souls, like trees on the banks of the water, we "shall not be moved."

The prophet Jeremiah was born into the priestly family of Hilkiah in the territory of Benjamin (Jeremiah 1:1-2). His career spanned several decades, beginning in the reign of King Josiah (640–609 B.C.) through the reigns of Jehoiakim (609–598/7) and Jehoiachin (598–597) and ending during the reign of Zedekiah (597–587). Speaking to Judah, around 609 B.C., when Jehoiakim was king, Jeremiah warned the people of the catastrophe about to befall them.

Dire Consequences of Idolatry

The people had indulged in idolatry (worshiping at the "altars and sacred poles" of the Canaanite ba'als, 17:2), and dire consequences would result. YHWH would dispose of their treasure, their land, and their heritage (17:3-4). Conquest and exile are just around the corner if they do not repent and change their ways.

The lections this week contain various curses and blessings. Jeremiah began with those who relied upon "mere mortals" for their strength and wisdom, for this short-sighted policy would deprive them of resources and blind them to the offer of divine assistance (17:5-6). Turning their back on the teachings and guidance of God would place them in a desolate wilderness—both spiritually and literally (17:6). How easy it is to rely on our own human wisdom and the advice and example of others who appear strong and successful—and how perilous!

Water and Shade

Water and shade, precious resources in the land of Judah, offer succulent images for a life lived in the arms of God (17:8). Unlike a mirage, however, God's truth is sure and fast. Blossoming with green leaves, deeply rooted beside the stream of life, those who trust in God have no fear of the heat of the noonday sun. Persons who walk by faith receive nourishment to sustain them in hard times.

The Devious Heart

Jeremiah reminded the people that their perverse hearts were leading them astray. God knew what was in their hearts, even when they might try to pretend otherwise (17:9). Try though they might, humans are abysmal failures at understanding one another. God alone, Jeremiah said, "search[es] the heart and examine[s] the mind" (17:10, NIV). The image folks present to the world and the truth of their hearts can be completely contradictory. Jeremiah prophesied that God, however, could see into the hearts of humanity and discern the truth that no pretty church clothes and winning smiles can hide.

Given this, only God is able to make judgments concerning humankind. God will treat us according to the true intent of our hearts and how this is expressed in our lives (17:10). Unless we change our ways, God will look into our hearts and dispense justice according to what we truly deserve: the sure and certain destruction of our nation and way of life.

> **Think About It:** Does your life feel more like a barren land or a lush tree planted by the water? What does God see in your heart? How does this compare with the image we try to project? What would we get if God were to treat us as we really deserve? Can we depend on God's grace to save us if we don't try to live a life consistent with our profession?

Psalter: Psalm 1

This psalm speaks of two paths. The path of the righteous is walked by those who reject sinful ways and instead submit their lives to the guidance and instruction of God (the law), who study and reflect on it, who sink their roots into it, and whose lives are nourished and directed by it. Only this path of life brings blessing and happiness (abundance, steadfastness, productivity, endurance; verses 1-3).

In contrast, the wicked (self-centered, unfaithful, violent, corrupt) do not trust

> **Think About It:** The NRSV translates the reward of the righteous life as "happiness," the NIV as "blessing." Are these the same or different in meaning? How would you define each? The former word is more current, but runs the risk of superficiality. The latter is more "religious," but may not communicate well to the modern generation. Which do you prefer and why?

in God or value divine guidance. As a result, when hard times come, they become weak, unstable, and unreliable; they cannot measure up to the standards or endurance of the faithful in the congregation (verses 4-6).

In twenty-first–century America we tend to view happiness (not just its pursuit) as a right to be claimed not a result or benefit of faithful living as the psalmist suggests. To be happy, we think, means having personal fulfillment, individual contentment, prosperity, and good health. The psalmist tells us, happiness (blessing) is to pursue God's will rather than one's own and to be devoted only to the Lord.

Epistle: 1 Corinthians 15:12-20

In 1 Corinthians 15:1-11, Paul proclaims the centrality of the Resurrection to our faith. In view of the fact that Paul forcefully reminded them of the basic tenets of faith, the Corinthian church evidently had doubts, faced opposition or dissension, and therefore engaged in theological dialogue just as we do in the church today.

Resurrection Is the Key

To the questioners he asserted: "Now if the rising of Christ from the dead is the very heart of our message, how can some of you deny that there is any resurrection? For if there is no such thing as the resurrection of the dead, then Christ was never raised. And if Christ was not raised then neither our preaching nor your faith has any meaning at all" (verses 12-14, JBP).

> **Think About It:** What does the Resurrection mean to you? How does faith in the Resurrection enable you to make the difficult choices requird to live in the kingdom of God? How does Jesus' resurrection reveal who God is for us?

Clearly, for Paul, belief in the Resurrection was the linchpin of Christian faith. Without it, the gospel was gutted, faith was hollow, and preaching lost its point. If Christ is not raised, then humanity is still in bondage to sin and death. If humanity is still in bondage, there is neither forgiveness nor salvation. If there is no forgiveness or salvation, then life on earth is all there is and nothing has changed through Christ. If that be the case, says Paul, "we are of all people most to be pitied" (verse 19).

> **Think About It:** How does your belief in the resurrection of Christ affect your belief in life after death? Is resurrection from the dead the same as or different from going to heaven when we die?

Resurrection and Eternal Life

Because God was faithful to Jesus, Jesus was raised from the dead to vindicate his life and mission and to demonstrate that in him God's righteousness was fully revealed. The promise to us is that the God and Father of our Lord Jesus Christ, who was faithful to him, will also remain faithful to all who trust in his mighty acts accomplished in Jesus Christ. Death is conquered; those who have received new life through his grace will live in his loving presence forever.

Gospel: Luke 6:17-26

This discourse is sometimes called the "Sermon on the Plain" (in contrast to Matthew's "Sermon on the Mount") because Jesus came down and "stood on a level place" (verse 17). A more important difference, though, is that Matthew (5:1-12) speaks only of blessings, while Luke pronounces woes as well. The scene recalls the gathering of the people in the plain between Mount Gerizim (Mount of Blessing) and Mount Ebal (Mount of Cursing) presented in Deuteronomy 11:29 and Joshua 8:30-35. The differences in interpretation between the two accounts are also significant.

Blessings

Matthew tends to spiritualize; Luke is more straightforward and literal. Blessings are offered to the poor (literally, not the humble of spirit of Matthew); the hungry (literally, not those who yearn for righteousness); the disconsolate (who weep real tears because they suffer, not those who are sorry for their sins); and those who are despised, rejected, berated, maligned because of their association with Jesus (similar to Matthew's "persecuted for righteousness' sake," but more specific). The friends of Jesus receive the same treatment as did the prophets of old, and for that they can rejoice and will be rewarded (Luke 6:20-23).

To call the poor blessed may seem absurd to us; it was a scandal in the first century. Poverty was considered a punishment for sin. While this beatitude does not say that one must be poor to be part of the kingdom of God, it does emphasize that God's reign will not resemble earthly kingdoms. In God's realm, the least will become the greatest; the poor will be honored; the hungry will be fed; the weeping will become glad; those hated on account of Jesus will be vindicated. In short, it will be "fruit basket turnover."

The Poor

The poor in Jesus' time had little value in society; their condition was thought to be the result of laziness or stupidity (sound familiar?). The well-fed wealthy wanted nothing to do with them. The poor were dirty, diseased, helpless outsiders. Nevertheless, the law was clear about the obligation to care for them. This duty was constant, as Jesus would point out (see Deuteronomy 15:11; Mark 14:7; Luke 12:33).

Woes

The flip side is reserved for the enemies of God—those who have been doing the persecuting, exploiting, rejecting, castigating of the poor and outcast whom Jesus came to save. The rich are living it up now; their reward is in the present. The future judgment is another matter, which they ought to consider. Those who have plenty to eat now—at the expense of those they are oppressing—will soon have empty plates. Those who laugh now—whether of decadent pleasure or derisive scorn—will sober up soon enough and regret their wasteful, heartless lifestyle. The solid citizens of good repute on the outside, but whose hearts are barren and callous on the inside, are riding high but are headed toward a fall. Again a comparison is made with the "false prophets" of times like Jeremiah's, who enjoyed the temporary confidence and splendor of nobility, but whose prestige was shaky and would crumble sooner than they thought.

Think About It: What does this passage say to our twenty-first–century affluence? about our extravagant comforts and toys? to churches with elegant sanctuaries, highly paid staffs, high-tech equipment, and costly programs? What would it mean for us to "become poor" so we might receive the kingdom of God? In what ways might (or do) you and your church identify with and serve the poor and hungry whom Jesus affirms in this passage?

The rich and famous, according to Luke, are soothed by the illusion that what they have on earth is evidence of God's favor and will ensure their place in heaven. Engaged in acquiring and caring for their possessions and wealth, they are too preoccupied to hear the call of God to be humble, generous, and just. As Luke repeatedly emphasizes, they must repent, not just in wordy prayers, but by giving up their wealth because it is an obstacle to wholehearted reliance on God (see 18:22; 21:1-4) and then make restitution for their unfair profits (19:8).

Study Suggestions

A. Open With Prayer and Singing

Begin with a brief time of meditation. Ask members to think of the dry, parched places in their lives, the places in which they feel poor in spirit, the places full of mourning. Invite them to bring these needs to God. Read or sing the first three stanzas of the hymn "How Firm a Foundation."

B. Dry as the Desert; Wet as Water

Read Jeremiah 17:7-8. Ask members to share stories about favorite lakes or other bodies of water and the beauty of the vegetation along the shore. How is God's love and word like the water that nourishes our spirits and gives us (the trees) a firm foundation for the life of faith? Now think about this metaphor in terms of the crisis of the people of Judah. (See Jeremiah 15:1-4.) The prophet was not talking about the weather and nature. Ask: What was the context for these images? Why were they so powerful for them? How do they speak to us today?

C. Blessings and Woes Today

Read Luke 6:20-26, Psalm 1, and the interpretations on pages 89–90, 91–92. Also read Matthew 5:1-12. Ask: Which set of words best describes us and our church—poor, hungry, weeping, hated, excluded, reviled, defamed? Or, rich, full, laughing, well-thought-of? Ask: For which of these descriptions do we tend to strive? Which does Jesus affirm, and which does he censure? What does his reversal of values say to our priorities? Why is it important to be reminded of blessings and cursings? Also discuss the "Think About It" questions.

D. Share in Pairs

Discuss the following in pairs: Is your awareness of and need for God more keen when life is difficult? At what times do God's blessings seem more (or less) accessible to you? When the group reconvenes, ask: What came out of your sharing that all would benefit from hearing?

E. Consider Eternal Blessings

The beatitudes of Luke, Jeremiah, and Psalm 1 certainly carry expectations of righteous behavior and belief in the here and now; but they have eternal dimensions as well. Read 1 Corinthians 15:12-20 and the commentary on pages 90–91. Ask: What is the blessing or promise affirmed in this passage? What is the eternal dimension to it? What kind of power or authority does Paul's proclamation hold for you? Is his argument compelling? Discuss the questions about the Resurrection in the "Think About It" box. Ask: How does this passage (along with the other lections) address issues in your faith and life that call for change or growth? How can we in this group support one another in these struggles?

F. Close With Prayer and Singing

Invite participants to lift up with one word (such as health, finances, marriage, work) the places in their lives that need to be nourished by the water of God's love. After each need is named, have them respond with, "Lord, hear our prayer." Then ask the group to mention places in the church, community, and world that also need to be rooted in the firm foundation of God's healing love. Again respond to each with, "Lord, hear our prayer." Close by singing the last two stanzas of "How Firm a Foundation."

Lections for Seventh Sunday After the Epiphany

M Old Testament: Genesis 45:3-11, 15

UCH had transpired in Joseph's life before the story in this lection. Joseph was a favored son of his father, Jacob (37:1-4). He dreamed many dreams that indicated his family would one day bow to him (37:5-11). Angry and jealous, his brothers conspired to kill him.

Instead, they sold him to a passing caravan of Ishmaelites (or Midianites) and told their father he was dead (37:12-28). Joseph ended up as a slave in Egypt (39:1-23), where he eventually found favor with the pharaoh, rising to a position of great power under him. In his interpretation of the pharaoh's dream, Joseph foresaw seven years of abundance followed by seven years of famine. Egypt prepared during years of plenty (40:1–41:57). Thus, when surrounding lands turned barren, Egypt had food. Joseph's brothers went from Canaan to Egypt to buy food (42:1-25). After many comings and goings, Joseph finally revealed to them that he, the one in charge of the grain of Egypt, was their brother (42:26–44:34).

Family Reunion

The drama of Joseph and his brothers teaches some significant life lessons on forgiveness and trusting God's will. At no time in the story does Joseph ask for repentance from his brothers. At no time does he ridicule or blame them for their crime, although he did let them twist in fear and uncertainty for a while not knowing who he was. Instead he saw that they were distressed, frightened, and traumatized.

For all they knew, Joseph was Zaphenath-paneah, an Egyptian second only to Pharaoh (41:41-45). When he revealed himself as Joseph, their brother, whom they had done in and thought was long since dead, they no doubt feared he would seek revenge. But Joseph told them not to worry or blame themselves for their treachery, because God had a purpose in it that had transformed an evil intent into benefit for many ("God sent me before you to preserve life," 45:5). Their actions notwithstanding, God had brought about blessing for the people of Egypt, their entire extended family, and their descendants for many generations to come. After the brothers were reconciled, Joseph made provision for all of them to live in prosperity in the land of Goshen, the fertile region in Egypt's eastern Nile delta (45:9-11, 15).

In this instance, the writer of Genesis suggests that Joseph believed that God's actions and will had prevailed throughout. Joseph's brothers did not intend their actions for good nor did they seek to do God's will. They were jealous and wanted to get rid of Joseph. Though their purpose was not of God, God overruled their actions to counter famine, save lives, and reconcile a family. God put the actions of the brothers into a larger context and used not only their evil intent but also the actions of Pharaoh to ensure the survival of the Egyptian populace, reunite a divided family, and guarantee the continuation of the line established by Abraham and Sarah (50:20).

> **Think About It:** God transformed evil into benefit. One must be cautious here when attempting to discern God's will. Did God use the brothers as puppets or pawns to implement the divine plan? Did God mean to test Joseph's faithfulness by allowing his enslavement? Is God the only one acting in the story? What is the interaction of the human and divine wills in the happenings of life? Which has the stronger influence: our freedom and initiative, divine providence, or divine predestination?

> **Think About It:** When has an action that you beieved to be evil paved the way for blessing in your life? When has God brought life out of the ashes of death? In the communty and world, how have you seen God bring blessing out of tragedy? Does it require the eyes of faith to see this?

Psalter: Psalm 37:1-11, 39-40

Why does God let bad things happen to good people? Or good things to bad people? This is the theoditic problem we encountered in a couple of previous sessions. Psalm 37 is a response to the same vexing question.

Throughout this psalm we are encouraged to "not fret, . . . refrain from anger, and forsake wrath . . . ; be still . . . wait"—all of which seem diametrically opposed to how folks want to deal with wicked enemies or unjust, unexplainable circumstances (verses 1, 7, 8). How can one hope to remain confident or come out the victor with such strategy as this?

Should believers wait upon the Lord without resentment, God promises to "make your vindication shine like the light, / and the justice of your cause like the noonday. . . . / The meek shall inherit the land, / and delight themselves in abundant prosperity" (verses 6, 11).

Such a trust in God—a trust that, despite adversity and malevolent antagonists, God will provide—is as heartening as it is rare. Such trust empowers us to continue to "do good." Such trust, even as one encounters wrongdoers, helps us "delight in the LORD" so we can "live in the land, and enjoy security," and receive the "desires of your heart" (verses 3-4).

Our faith tells us that, ultimately, good will prevail over evil. But until that time, we can find peace by learning to live with our circumstances while relying on the promises of God and living securely in the light of God's love.

Epistle: 1 Corinthians 15:35-38, 42-50

The entirety of 1 Corinthians 15 dwells on the Resurrection and questions surrounding it. Paul first reminded the church that the Resurrection is central to the gospel message. Next, he taught them about the resurrection of the dead. In the lection today, we meet the inquisitiveness of the Corinthians. In spite of all they were taught, they still asked—"How?" (15:35).

But How?

Thinking Christians struggle with a variety of "how" questions. How did God make the earth? How did Cain and Abel get wives? How did Jesus walk on water? How did Jesus make the blind to see? How will we look in heaven?

It may be frustrating, but we must be willing to accept "I don't know" as the only answer to many of our questions. We do not know the "how" of some things, but we can rely on the "what" God has done. Just so, we see that Paul did not have an answer to the question "How are the dead raised?" Although he could not answer that question, he had confidence in the God who raised Jesus from the dead. Paul's lengthy explanation basically came down to: "We will look however God wants us to look, and how God chooses to do that is God's business." God "gives it a body as he has determined" (15:38, NIV). A new, heavenly body will be received. We trust the grace of Christ for salvation and know that God will look after the details.

> **Think About It:** Recall situations in which difficult "how" questions troubled you. How did you deal with them? What resources did you draw on? How do you handle similar questions when you share your faith with others? Are you willing to accept some mystery in your journey? When does faith suffice as we face the unanswered "hows"?

Before and After Pictures

Paul used an agricultural analogy to speak of resurrection. When a seed is sown in the soil, the seed disappears and is replaced by a plant. A seed is not a plant and a plant is not a seed; yet, each seed produces a plant after its own kind. So the resurrection is not the resurrection of the human corpse, but the resurrected spiritual body does have some continuity with the person who dies. Like the plant from the seed, resurrection is to a related, yet new existence.

How that will happen and what we will look like remain a mystery. What is revealed and clear to us is the life and ministry of Jesus. All believers need, in actuality, is the confidence that they, like Christ, are heirs to life eternal. Therein lies the Christian hope.

> *Think About It:* From whence does your belief in eternal life come—knowledge or faith?

Gospel: Luke 6:27-38

Jesus' disciples, who were to turn the world upside down (Acts 17:6), continued to hear from Jesus an astonishing message that reversed all their conventional wisdom. Still reeling from the news that the poor would inherit the Kingdom, they are further shocked to hear Jesus tell them they must love their enemies and do good to those who hurt them.

Whom Do You Love?

We are usually comfortable loving friends and family. When we are loved, it is easy to love back. But, says Jesus, "even sinners do the same" (6:33). There is no place here for retaliation or revenge. Indeed, Jesus says, "Love your enemies, deal kindly with those who hate you, give your blessings to those who give you their cursing, pray for those insulting you" (6:27-28, Cotton Patch Version).

These teachings may seem contradictory to the Jewish tradition and normal custom. As far back as Moses, the law was structured in "if-then" type statements such as, "Whoever curses father or mother shall be put to death" (Exodus 21:17). If a sin is committed then appropriate restitution is expected. The "eye for an eye" legal concept was rooted in a justice system that mitigated against unbridled revenge or excessive retaliation. It left the appropriate punishment up to God. But Jesus spoke of a different kind of justice—not of retribution but of reconciliation; not of getting even but of turning the other cheek; not of an eye for an eye, but of offering the thief or oppressor one's shirt as one's coat is being stolen or taken as security. Love your enemies. Expect nothing in return for good deeds. Love. Just love.

Mother Said

How many times have we heard, "Treat others like you want them to treat you," or other variations on the Golden Rule? But Mother didn't always explain what Jesus meant. The Golden Rule goes beyond "do unto others as you would have them do to you," and adds: "regardless of their actions." So often we are *reactive* rather than *proactive*. We treat another not as we *want* to be treated but as we *have been* treated.

Here Jesus makes a radical, counter-cultural departure from the norm. Love your enemies because God loves them, regardless of their actions. But loving and forgiving does not mean becoming a victim. Forgiveness does not mean continuing an abusive relationship. In repeating the Great Commandment, Jesus reminds us to "love your neighbor *as yourself*" (Matthew 22:39, italics added). We must maintain our self-respect; we can forgive without being victimized again.

Idealistic Maybe, Risky Probably, Faithful Yes

Jesus then advises: "Don't blame, and you won't be blamed. Don't run others down, and they won't run you down. Free others, and you shall be freed; give, and it shall be given you. . . . For it will be measured out to you in your own measuring basket" (Luke 6:37-38, Cotton Patch Version). Take the first step toward understanding and reconciliation. Love and good will evoke a like response. We must not be passive, allowing evil to run amok. Rather, we are to resist evil non-violently, not with bloodshed, but with *agape* (self-giving, other-regarding love).

Think About It: "Love your enemies, do good to those who hate you, bless those who curse you, pray for those who abuse you." How would our life, church, community, and world be different if we treated each other this way? Who in our world is hard to love and forgive? What would it take for us to love, bless, and pray for them? to break the cycle of enmity, violence, and retribution? What reasons do we give for perpetuating the alienation? How can we support one another to begin a cycle of acceptance, respect, and good will?

In a society in which children are murdered for their designer clothes, in which deadly violence enters our schools, in which bombs go off under daycare centers to make political statements, in which airplanes are used as deadly missiles, these words of Jesus may seem as idealistic and impractical today as they did to those who first heard them. But they are the standards of Christian discipleship. If the world is to be turned upside down, we must take the risk of trying to live by the hard sayings of Jesus.

Study Suggestions

A. Open With Prayer and Singing

Ask members to list on paper their "enemies" or those who are hard for them to accept or love. Then lead the group in silent prayer for God's love and mercy to surround them. Sing the hymn, "We'll Understand It Better By and By."

B. Healing Relationships

Read Genesis 45:3-11,15, and review the commentary on pages 94–95. Either give an overview of the entire Joseph story as found in Genesis 37–45, or assign the seven Scripture references in the introductory paragraphs of the commentary to different persons or small groups to read and summarize.

Discuss the challenge of forgiving someone when there has been a breach in the relationship. Ask: Did Joseph's brothers repent before he forgave them? Must those who have wronged us apologize before we will forgive? Also discuss the "Think About It" questions.

C. Living Reconciliation

Read Psalm 37:1-11, 39-40; Luke 6:27-38; and the commentaries on pages 95–96, 97–98. What do these passages tell us about the nature of God and the relationship God wants us to have with others?

Ask: How often do we treat these admonitions from the psalm and from the Sermon on the Plain as mere pious platitudes?

Consider how these teachings compare to the messages of today's society. Make two lists: one of these guidelines of Jesus, the other of contemporary "wisdom" regarding relationships and conflicts. Ask: What similarities and differences do we discover? What pressures are we under to conform to one or the other?

D. Resurrection Faith

Review 1 Corinthians 15:35-38, 42-50, and the commentary on pages 96–97. List Paul's "if-then" arguments. Examine how his line of reasoning unfolds. Ask: How do you understand the links in Paul's chain of logic? If any of these links break, how are we "misrepresenting God"? What is the basis for our belief in the Resurrection? Also explore the "Think About It" questions.

E. Close With Worship

Ask members to review their list of "enemies" (Activity A). After silent prayer, have them rip up the lists and leave the pieces on the altar to symbolize giving them over to God. (Be sure to discard these after the session.) Sing "Forgive Our Sins as We Forgive," then pray the Lord's Prayer together. As a benediction, repeat the line, "Forgive us our sins as we forgive those who sin against us. Amen."

Lections for Eighth Sunday After the Epiphany

Old Testament: Isaiah 55:10-13

*W*RITTEN in the sixth century B.C. near the end of the Babylonian Exile, Chapters 40–55 of Isaiah are a collection of prophecies about the deliverance and restoration of the people of Judah. The words, "comfort my people," which begin this section (Second Isaiah), offer hope and promise to a hurting people (Isaiah 40:1).

Isaiah 55:10-13 is just one portion of a much-longer passage of consolation that urges the faithful to "seek the LORD while he may be found" (55:6), so they may avail themselves of God's wisdom and pardon. The thoughts and ways of YHWH are far and above those of mere mortals; they have a power and insight that humankind needs and yearns for. And he promises to send the people a leader (messiah) who will not only liberate Judah but also draw other nations to him to give him honor and glory (55:2-5).

God's Word Brings Results

The efficacy of God's word and deeds is described through natural images—water, food, and drink. Water, a powerful and essential resource, evokes images of life and death to people living in a desert culture. The word of the Lord is like "rain and the snow [that] come down from heaven" and water the earth, nourishing the soil to produce first seed, then grain, flour, and bread to feed a hungry people (verse 10). That is, the activity of God is as reliable in history as in the world of nature. Thus, God's word (Torah, law, covenant) can be depended on to nourish the people—forming, feeding, redeeming, leading them, and acting in history on their behalf. As in the Creation story (see references to "and God said . . ." in Genesis, chapter 1), God's word brings results; it is not a mere empty echo, but a source of power to accomplish the divine purpose for humanity and all creation (verse 11).

Humans and Nature Join in Joy and Praise

Sustained by God's word, the people will joyfully return to a fertile land full of fruit-bearing trees and life-sustaining vegetation. Their coming life will be blissful, fruitful, and flourishing. To persons hoping to find sustenance in a semi-arid land, this is heartening news.

Joy and praise are themes found throughout this week's readings. Despite darkness, sin, death, and evil, God will prevail. The people will rejoice. God will act in saving ways. Indeed, the mountains, hills, and trees—symbolic of the world of nature—will join the happy chorus. It is not only human beings that will be made happy by God's redemptive acts. All of creation will benefit and will offer praise to the Almighty One (verse 12).

Joyful Singing Heralds God's Reign

The weeds and briars will no longer choke out fruitful life; instead the beauty of God's creation will be manifest in the hanging cypress and the flowering myrtle. Joy, peace, singing, clapping of hands, flowering shrub—these are the signs of the breaking in of the everlasting reign of God (verse 13). The time of loneliness and exile in Babylon is coming to an end. The people have endured suffering long enough. God has heard their prayers and will act to redeem them. History will soon take a turn for the better. God's word and power will be made known to the nations.

> **Think About It:** God's word "waters." God's purposes, expressed in his word, will blossom, grow, and bear fruit. When in your life have you felt yourself in "exile," needing to be nourished by the living water of God's world? How do you experience God's sustaining presence?

Psalter: Psalm 92:1-4, 12-15

This song of personal gratitude was likely sung in the Temple while presenting a thank offering to YHWH. It beautifully but naively assumes that God will cause the righteous to prosper and will bring calamity on the wicked. There is no theoditic speculation here: good comes to the good and evil comes to the evil.

The psalmist declares that it is good to give God thanks and praise and does so twice a day—morning and evening. He is thankful for the certainty of God's loving nature, which he experiences in four ways—God's name (presence and power), steadfast love (*hesed*), faithfulness (unchanging dependability), and works (saving deeds by which God becomes known in human affairs) (verses 1-4).

Not all have reason or inclination to praise God, however. The simpletons are too dense to realize that their life and their good fortune come from God. The corrupt are living it up now, but will shrivel like grass under the heat of God's judgment. Those who flout God's law or deny God's power will soon come to regret it (verses 5-9).

Part of the psalmist's joy comes from the prospect of punishment coming to evildoers, who are his foes as well as God's. He may be hurting now, while his adversaries are having their day. But he is rubbing his hands together at the prospect of his elevation and their undoing (verses 10-11).

The psalmist is but one of a host of righteous people whose faithfulness to YHWH will be rewarded with good fortune, longevity, and zestful energy. This is not their accomplishment, however; it is the gift of God (verses 12-14). For it is only God who is truly good and faithful; human righteousness emanates from God; and on that we can depend (verse 15).

Epistle: 1 Corinthians 15:51-58

In the final verses of 1 Corinthians 15, Paul reaches the climax of his resurrection teaching, which we have been studying in recent weeks.

A Mystery

"Listen," says Paul, "I will tell you a mystery" (verse 51). Mystery and intrigue—phenomena causing sharp gasps, sending shivers down the spine, compelling the listener to lean close to hear. What could it be? Would the secrets of life beyond the grave, the afterlife, be revealed? What truth will Paul unveil?

Ah, listen, in the twinkling of an eye, in the last days when the great trumpet sounds, "we will not all die, but we will all be changed" (verse 51). No longer will humanity inhabit mortal bodies. At the end of time, human beings become imperishable and death will be no more. Jesus will take away the sting of death. This implies that at this time of writing (A.D. 54 or 55) Paul believed that some still living would not die before seeing Christ come in glory. It also suggests a distinction between resurrection (transformation of the body) and immortality (continuous, eternal existence of the soul).

Through the resurrection of Jesus, sin and death are wiped out. The immortal words ring out—"Where, O death, is your victory? / Where, O death, is your sting?" (verse 55).

Think About It: Paul wrote: "We will not die, we will all be changed." What do you understand this change to be? Do you think we go directly to heaven at death, or do we sleep in death until we are raised at the last day "when the great trumpet sounds"? What would happen to Paul's faith (and that of the early Christians) when Jesus does not come as soon as expected?

102

Your Labor Is Not in Vain

Until then, the Corinthian believers must be the church. In praise and thanksgiving, they (we) must proclaim the risen Christ, offering God's salvation to a dying world. Unified and strong, they (we) must be the body of Christ until the end. Passed on to us, this admonition still rings true. We are called to "be steadfast, immovable, always excelling in the work of the Lord"; for through the promise of the Resurrection's transforming power, "your labor is not in vain" (verse 58).

Gospel: Luke 6:39-49

The Sermon on the Plain culminates in this third and final section. Already instructed in blessings and woes, love, judgment, and forgiveness, the disciples and other listeners learn how to live as followers of Jesus. Luke presents Jesus as using numerous metaphors and analogies (leaping from one to the next) to make his points.

Pits, Logs, and Specks

Unfortunately, readers of the parables and analogies found in these verses often use them defensively. Phrases such as, "Far be it from me to judge, but . . ." and "he better get his own house in order before he starts talking about mine . . ." do not reflect Jesus' meaning.

While people do make judgments, moral and otherwise, Jesus reminded the disciples that judging people for their faults and frailties was not of God. We have the capacity for making judgments not to criticize others but to understand how we need to live our own lives. We are to judge ourselves and live in such a way that it is safe for others to follow us. How can one safely lead someone who cannot see if blinded oneself? How can one help another with a minor fault, when exhibiting a major defect in oneself (verses 39-42)? Followers of Christ do not make themselves better by disparaging the brokenness of others. Putting another down to build oneself up only reveals one's own weakness. Christians have a concern to help one another live righteously and faithfully.

First Things First

We must deal with our own problems first before trying to correct others. This is like the flight attendant's instruction to parents to don their own oxygen masks before giving masks to their children. If the adults have insufficient oxygen and lose consciousness, how can they aid their children? In the same way, only when we first address our own faults and needs are we able to be helpful to others.

Brambles, Grapes, and Figs

The next parable (verses 43-45) tackles the matter of consistency. "Figs are not gathered from thorns, nor grapes picked from a bramble bush" (6:44). It is not enough to *do* good things; we must *be* good as well. What we say and do reflects who we are inside. An impure heart cannot produce good thoughts and deeds. Likewise, evil does not issue from a heart of integrity. The fruit produced by a person reflects his or her true inner being (verses 43-44). Jesus also uses the metaphor of "treasure" (6:45) to make the same point: good begets good; evil produces evil. The adequacy of any belief or faith claim may be determined by results or outcomes.

The House That Went "Smash"!

Prior to telling the last parable in this lection, Jesus asked the disciples, Why do you claim to believe but not live by my words? Why is there no real change in your lives? Some theologians refer to this as the contrast between orthodoxy (right belief) and orthopraxy (right practice). We talk the talk, but don't walk the walk. Jesus then told them a story. One man built his house on a good, solid rock foundation (a wise builder). Another built his house on the bare ground (a poor plan). Suddenly, disaster! Devastating floodwaters crashed against the house on the rock, which was able to withstand the catastrophe. However, the house built with no foundation collapsed and was demolished (verses 46-49). Inadequate beliefs seem as strong as true faith in fair weather; but a driving storm reveals true faith. Sadly, the house without foundation will collapse at the worst possible moment.

> **Think About It:** Jesus chastised blind guides and hypocrites, challenged them to look first to their own faults, and called for a life consistent with one's profession of faith. As we examine our hearts and lives, do we judge others more severely than ourselves? How do our words and actions reflect the inner state of our souls? Do we practice what we preach? Will our integrity stand the test of outer pressure and persecution?

Study Suggestions

A. Celebrate in Prayer and Song

Open by reading Psalm 92:1-4, 12-15 antiphonally, with the women reading the first line of each verse and the men responding with the second. Then ask each member to share in a word or phrase a celebration or blessing. Next sing or read together the first two stanzas of the hymn, "My Hope Is Built."

B. Study the Psalm

Review the psalm in light of the commentary (pages 101–102). Discuss: Why does the lection omit verses 5-11? Could you pray these words? How can we be thankful even when we are hurting and the undeserving seem to prosper?

C. Explore the Meaning of God's "Word"

Read Isaiah 55:6-13 and the interpretation on pages 100–101. Savor the grand image of God's word and influence being as expansive as the heavens (55:8-9). Ask: How does this majesty and grandeur affect you? your image of God? your relationship with God? Is it God in the earthquake, wind, and fire, or in the still small voice that most moves you (see 1 Kings 19:11-12)? Why?

Weigh the profound influence of God's word (expression, law, covenant—verses 10-11). Ask: What does it mean that God's word will not "return empty" but will accomplish whatever God desires? Also discuss the "Think About It" issues.

D. More on the Resurrection

Read 1 Corinthians 15:51-58, and review the Resurrection teaching in the first 50 verses of the chapter, as well as the commentary on pages 102–103. Discuss the "Think About It" questions, including those about Paul's expectation of Christ's early coming and the distinction between immortality and resurrection. Ask: What is the relationship between a transformed life now and a transformed body in the resurrection?

E. Discuss Practical Problems

Read Luke 6:39-49 and the commentary (pages 103–104). Form three groups, assigning one group to study each of the following verses: 39-42, 43-45, 46-49, using the following questions: (1) What problem do these verses address? (2) What is the message (put in a single sentence) that Jesus addresses to this problem? (3) How would our lives be different if we took this message to heart and lived it out? (4) Develop a roleplay of a situation in everyday life that illustrates the problem and the way Jesus says to deal with it. (One way to do this is to roleplay two approaches to the situation—one illustrating the problem and the other the attitude Jesus suggests.)

Return to the total group, share results of the discussions, write up the one-sentence summaries, and perform the roleplays. After each, debrief with the following questions: How did you feel in your role? Did the Jesus way seem natural? helpful? effective? right? What help do we need to live this way on a regular basis? Comment that the Jesus who lays these expectations on us also provides the grace and strength to fulfill them.

G. Close With Prayer and Song

Sing the last two stanzas of "My Hope Is Built," then pray for guidance and strength to live the Jesus way, and for forgiveness when we stumble.

Lections for Transfiguration Sunday

Old Testament: Exodus 34:29-35

*T*HIS is the Sunday in the church year when we remember the experience
of Jesus on the Mount of Transfiguration. All four lections are chosen with
that in mind. This passage from Exodus relates a similar experience in the life
of Moses, the Second Corinthians selection refers to the Moses event, and the
psalm addresses an awesome God who is worshiped at a holy mountain.
Thus, all speak of "mountaintop" experiences that are unusual, inspiring,
life-changing.

In this passage Moses has just come down the mountain from receiving the
covenant from YHWH (Exodus 33:7–34:28). He has seen God's glory, heard
God's commandments (both moral and ritual), and been given the covenant
that will bind his people to YHWH. Interestingly, the commands listed in
Exodus 34:12-26 are different from the list in Exodus 20 and Deuteronomy
5. The words that Moses wrote on the tablets were the terms of the covenant
as stipulated by YHWH. Israel was to obey the terms of the covenant
because God had driven out her enemies and given the land to his people.
They could live in the land that belonged to God only on the basis of being
faithful to the covenant.

The experience with God transfigured Moses. There was an aura of
holiness about him showing that he had been with God. The writer represents this in terms of his face being radiant with a reflection of God's glory
(splendor, brilliance, luster, majesty). Aaron and the people were so
stunned by this sight that they were afraid to come near Moses. There is
something awesome and forbidding about a person who exhibits signs of
a special relationship with the Almighty. They don't quite know what to
make of it.

So Moses made the first move. He beckoned them to come near, told them
all that transpired in his meeting with God, and gave them the command-

ments that they must henceforth observe. Then he put a veil over his face. (See 2 Corinthians 3:7-18, where Paul interprets this.)

The veil was likely a ritual mask, made of burnished metal, decorated with symbolic ornaments, and used in liturgical rites to give the priest or prophet personal anonymity while emphasizing his sacred, ceremonial role. Here, it softened or hid the luminescent glare coming from the skin of Moses' face, thereby enabling the people to focus on his words and the solemn covenant into which they were about to enter.

Apparently, from these verses, this happened several times. Moses would go into the tent of meeting outside the camp to meet with YHWH, come out with his face glowing, put on the veil or mask, report to the people, then go in again for more. Each time he emerged the holy aura of divine presence enveloped him, and each time he would don the veil to shield the people from its brilliance to let them better contemplate the awesome, life-changing step they were taking.

> **Think About It:** Moses' face shone with reflected glory from being in God's presence. The fearful people needed protection from this awesome radiance so they could consider carefully the covenant demands. The text suggests that humans can be altered because they have been in the presence of God. How does our worship of God transform our appearance? Can worship create a face of kindness, gentleness, and love so that others who see us know God is with us? Does our awareness of the glory of God create reverence and obedience to God in our lives?

Psalter: Psalm 99

This psalm is an enthronement hymn used during the royal coronation ceremony and at the annual celebration of the king's reign. The distance separating the majestic king—and the God he represented—from the people, is emphasized by the song's refrain in verses 3, 5, and 9—"Holy is he!" People shiver and the ground shakes in the presence of the Almighty One. Their only appropriate response is to bow in praise. His might is not used merely to coerce his subjects into submission; rather, it is expressed in a rule of righteousness (personal integrity) and justice (fair, equitable treatment of all). Worshipers are therefore summoned to bow down and glorify the just and mighty YHWH (verses 1-5).

> **Think About It:** The psalmist and his people were awed by God's splendor and felt his distance, yet were reminded of his presence by the pillar of cloud. What symbols in our sanctuaries speak to us of God's presence and power? How do we keep in balance our awe at God's majesty and our intimacy with the Abba of which Jesus spoke?

The justice of YHWH is best seen in the covenant, of which Moses, Aaron, and Samuel were mediators, representing God and the divine commandments to the people. On their journey in the desert, YHWH's presence had been indicated by the pillar of cloud (by day) and the pillar of fire (by night), hovering over the tabernacle, reminding them of his guidance and blessing. A box (ark) containing tablets on which God's covenant was written was carried from place to place and eventually was brought to Jerusalem (verses 6-9). The ark reminded God's people of his saving mercy that brought them into the Promised Land and of their obligation to remain faithful to God's commands (verse 8).

Epistle: 2 Corinthians 3:12–4:2

This reading must begin with 3:4, where Paul opens his argument contrasting the old covenant of Moses with the new one in the Spirit of Christ. Paul is a minister of the new covenant, which is not based not on lifeless commandments chiseled in stone, which are inevitably disobeyed, resulting in punishment and spiritual death. Rather, our spirits are quickened by Christ's Spirit, bringing life and hope (verse 6). Moses hid his face behind a veil when he introduced this covenant, Paul believes, because he feared it would lead to condemnation and would have to be replaced by a better one. The glory of the law is illusory, while the glory of redemption in Christ is sure and lasting (verses 7-11).

This gives us confidence to proclaim the gospel openly, whereas Moses had to obscure his message that could not endure. And, sure enough, the veil concealing true access to God is still in place by those who reject the Messiah who has opened the way. Only when we seek God through Christ can the veil be torn away (verses 12-16). Only the Spirit of God brings freedom from the limitations and the judgment of the law. Once the veil of ignorance and disobedience is removed, we enter the presence of Christ and begin a step-by-step transformative process of spiritual growth, moving ever closer to embodying the image of God. The source of this growth in grace is none other than the Spirit of God. The separation of the veil and the distance from the throne are bridged by the Spirit who enters our hearts (verses 12-18).

Think About It: Paul completely reverses the meaning of the veil—from symbolizing God's grandeur to obscuring God's grace. Can religious practice obscure God's graces? How can the church reveal God's glory that shines through Christ?

Because Paul had experienced this himself, he knew it to be true, so he had no need to try to trick people into believing through manipulation or false argument (as his adversaries in the Corinthian church contended). He could be completely open, under God, in presenting himself and the message of salvation to the conscience of his hearers. Paul had no need or use for the veil of Moses.

108

Gospel: Luke 9:28-36 (37-43)

The word *transfiguration* is a translation of the Greek *metamorphoo,* meaning a change of form. Unlike Matthew (17:2) and Mark (9:2), however, Luke does not use this word, choosing rather the phrase *egeneto heteron,* meaning simply "changed" (Luke 9:29). The difference, to us, is slight and subtle; but the former term could have suggested to Gentiles the stories of frequent metamorphoses of heathen gods from one form to another in Greek and Roman mythology.

It is significant that this event took place just a week after Peter's recognition of Jesus as the Messiah, in contrast to the view of crowds that he was merely another prophet (9:18-20). Jesus then confided in the disciples that, because the resistance to his message was building up among powerful figures, he would soon be put to death. If they were to continue following him the cost could be high. If they chose to be safe they would have to leave or deny him and thus risk losing their souls. If they were willing to suffer and maybe die with him, however, their eternal salvation would be assured. If they were ashamed or afraid to stand with him now, they could not count on him to defend them later (9:21-27). So they knew he was the Messiah, they knew he would be rejected and persecuted for making this claim, and they knew they had a choice to make.

> **Think About It:** They knew they had a hard choice to make. What does "taking up the cross" mean for you? What issue or situation are you facing that may make your discipleship costly? Would a time of prayer help you make such a choice and prepare you to assume such a cost?

Jesus asked the three who had been closest to him to go with him up a mountain to pray. This could have been either Mount Carmel, Mount Hermon, or Mount Tabor (the traditional site). Perhaps he hoped that the prayer experience would help them make that choice and steel them for the trials to come. Perhaps he thought the encounter with God would further convince them of his true identity. Perhaps he just wanted company. While there an epiphany (manifestation) occurred. (This is the last Sunday in the season after Epiphany.) They saw God's glory in the face of Jesus and realized his connection with Moses (the Torah tradition) and Elijah (the prophetic tradition). The luminescence of Jesus' face was obscured by a cloud (veil?), and a voice confirmed what Peter had confessed—Jesus was God's chosen one. This was an awesome event, and they wanted to commemorate it by building a

> **Think About It:** Spiritual inspiration did not bring spiritual power. Do mountaintop experiences have value in and of themselves? Or must their efficacy be demonstrated in deeds of compassion? How do you respond to the sign over some church doors, "Enter to worship, depart to serve"? How have your mountaintop experiences changed your life?

shrine. But instead they just kept quiet. Perhaps they realized that no material structure could do justice to such a revelation, and no words could adequately describe the experience they had (9:28-36).

Jesus was transfigured, but the disciples—in spite of their mountaintop experience—remained pretty much the same. Coming down the mountain, they had opportunity to perform an act of mercy with a boy suffering from epilepsy, but were powerless to do so. Jesus rebuked them fiercely, then healed the boy himself (verses 37-43). Spiritual inspiration had somehow not been translated into spiritual power.

Study Suggestions

A. Explain Transfiguration

Drawing on the commentary on pages 106–110, explain the significance of Transfiguration Sunday in the church year, the meaning of the word *transfiguration*, and the connection of today's four lections.

B. Experience Awe

If possible, go into the nave, sit quietly, and let the atmosphere—altar, windows, candles, vaulted ceilings, and maybe organ music—settle in on you. Have two members read Psalm 99 antiphonally, from pulpit and lectern or the back of the church. File out silently and return to your meeting room.

Reflecting on this experience, ask: What feelings did you have in the nave? How did the words of the psalm affect you? How do you relate to a God of majesty and grandeur? Summarize the interpretation of Psalm 99 on pages 107–108. Discuss the "Think About It" questions about the balance between majesty and intimacy.

C. Interpret the "Veil"

Read aloud Exodus 35:29-35 and 2 Corinthians 3:12-4:2 one after the other. Explain the meaning of each based on the comments (pages 106–107, 108). Be sure to read or summarize the context in the verses mentioned above that precede these verses. Explore the contrast between the two interpretations of the veil over Moses' face. Discuss the questions in the "Think About It" boxes. Also ask: Why do you think the Exodus writer had Moses donning the veil? Was it a carryover from pagan worship custom? a symbol of God's awesome presence and power? a recognition of the inadequacy of the covenant? How does Christ cause the church to have a different understanding of the Hebrew Scriptures than the synagogue?

D. Explore Mountaintop Experiences

Read Luke 9:28-36, summarize the events preceding and following this account of the Transfiguration, and present the ideas in the commentary on pages 109–110. Invite members to share revelatory events they have had. These might include worship services, prayer times, camps and conferences, sharing in fellowship groups, and encounters in the world of nature. Ask them: How was God present, how did it change you, and what effect did it have on your life afterward? Then compare these experiences with the Transfiguration and its aftermath in the disciples' lives. Discuss the "Think About It" questions. Ask: How can we support one another in translating our spiritual high moments into more faithful discipleship and more effective service in Christ's name?

E. Paint a Transfiguration

Distribute paper and crayons or felt pens, and invite members to draw their impression of a transfiguration experience—either that of Moses, Jesus, themselves, or of what they think one should be like. Then post these on the walls around the room, and invite members to walk around and view them without comment. After they return to their seats, ask for one-word responses to what they have drawn and seen, and write these on the board in crazy-quilt fashion.

F. Close in Worship

Sing the hymn based on 1 Corinthians 3:4–4:6, "Spirit of Faith Come Down." Pray this prayer in unison: "Holy God, upon the mountain you revealed our Messiah, / who by his death and resurrection / would fulfill both the law and the prophets. / By his transfiguration enlighten our path / that we may dare to suffer with him in the service of humanity / and so share in the everlasting glory of him / who lives and reigns with you and the Holy Spirit, / One God, for ever. Amen" (written by Lawrence Hull Stookey; from *The United Methodist Hymnal*; © 1989 The United Methodist Publishing House. Used by permission).

LENT

Lections for First Sunday in Lent

Old Testament: Deuteronomy 26:1-11

*B*IBLICAL scholar Gerhard von Rad suggests that this passage contains one of the most ancient creeds of the Hebrew faith. Other scholars say the creed was composed to sound ancient by writers much later in Jewish history who sought to bolster faith shaken by the destruction of Jerusalem and exile in Babylon.

The language of the creed in verses 5-9, with its stately rhythm, poetic repetition, and historical detail, certainly sounds archaic and liturgical, suited to the solemn act of ritual sacrifice it was intended to accompany. That the creed closes a section of law code in Chapters 12–26, becoming the climactic chapter of what the writer presents as Moses' address to the Israelites as they were about to enter Canaan, only gives it further authority.

God Acts Mightily

The creed rehearses the formative event of Hebrew history, the Exodus, when YHWH acted mightily to deliver the Hebrew people from slavery in Egypt. By reciting the creed, worshipers claimed the old story as a new one, becoming one with the ancestors whom God had saved, as shown by the shift of pronouns from "he" to "us" (26:5-6).

Tithes

Every year at the beginning of the various harvest festivals, Israelites were required to bring their "first fruits" to the central sanctuary, a token portion of the produce of their land—grain, wine, oil, sheep, and cattle (see 26:1-4). "First" could mean either "earliest" or "choicest." The token represented a pledge of

Think About It: Tithes were not seen as voluntary. How does the Deuteronomic understanding of *tithe* contrast with the practice of paying income taxes to support human services? What does Jesus teach about giving beyond what is required?

114

full payment of the required tithe and afforded an opportunity for family celebration (14:22-23). Agricultural tithes were not seen as optional; they provided support for the priests, widows, orphans, and aliens (14:28-29). Tithes were a public expression of the worshiper's intention to live an upright life, obeying the law in full.

The Festival of Booths

The festival of booths (or tabernacles, or ingathering), which celebrates the fruit harvest, came to be associated with the wilderness wandering after the Exodus. It was one of three annual pilgrimage festivals. The other two included Passover, celebrating release from Egyptian slavery with the spring barley harvest; and the festival of weeks, celebrating the covenant at Sinai at the time of the summer wheat harvest.

Verse 5 reflects a people's transition from a nomadic (herding) to a settled (agricultural) existence, even though they received harsh treatment in Egypt as slaves. The phrase "wandering Aramean" recalls Abraham's North Syrian nomadic ancestry (Genesis 20:13) and suggests Jacob's settlement in Egypt (47:27) so crucial to Hebrew identity. Because they had known what it was like to be homeless and without resources, they were to care for the needy out of their newfound affluence. The phrase, "land flowing with milk and honey" (verse 9) suggests that life in Canaan, both before and after they arrived, included both herding (milk) and food gathering (honey). The final verse of the passage calls for an inclusive meal in which the worshiper's whole family, "together with the Levites [priests] and the [resident] aliens," all feast in gratitude for God's bounty (verse 11). A diet of milk and honey is adequate but not luxurious.

Psalter: Psalm 91:1-2, 9-16

This psalm of trust expresses confidence in God's ability to protect the believer in all circumstances of danger and difficulty. The first thirteen verses of the psalm, addressed to an individual believer ("you"), promise that those who have made God their "refuge" (a frequent image in the psalms) will be protected from all manner of ills: evil (malicious acts from demonic or human enemies, verse 10), disease (verse 10), injury (verse 12), and wild animals (verse 13). Verses 11-12 are quoted by Jesus (Matthew 4:6; Luke 4:10-11) during his temptation experience, as we shall soon see.

Verses 14-16 are spoken directly by God, promising that those who love and know God's name will be delivered. In Hebrew, to know someone's name implied close association. These verses are a divine oracle of assurance, uttered in a Temple ritual by a priest or prophet. The names used for YHWH in this psalm—"Most High" (*Elyon*) and "Almighty" (*El Shaddai*)—are ancient names for God from the time of the patriarchs, recalling how YHWH had protected the families of Abraham, Isaac, Jacob, and their descendants. The psalm's promise of deliverance echoes the Exodus story of call and rescue. "The Israelites groaned under their slavery, and cried out. . . . God heard their groaning" (Exodus 2:23-24).

Scholars have imagined a variety of settings for Psalm 91, suggesting that it might have been created by someone who had sought sanctuary in the Temple ("the shelter of the Most High," verse 1), or have been recited by kings before battle (see verses 4-7). The various situations implied by this psalm, along with the echo of earlier biblical stories, suggest that there is no circumstance beyond God's power.

Epistle: Romans 10:8b-13

In this portion of Romans, Paul asserts a basic credo of the gospel: If you profess faith in Christ, you will be saved. In previous chapters he argued that true righteousness comes not from "works" (rigorous obedience to the Torah) but through faith in Christ (9:30–10:13). The credo is shaped by Paul's rendering of Deuteronomy 30:12-14 (Romans 10:6-8) in which he personifies righteousness; that is, he gives it a voice. "Righteousness" tells the believer not to look for a messiah whose coming down from heaven could be hastened by obedience to the law, as some Jews believed (10:6), or for a savior who would come up from the underworld as many Gentiles thought (10:7). Rather, Christ is ever near us, through the gospel ("the word of faith") that Paul proclaims.

One Act of Faith

The dual phrase from Deuteronomy 30:14, "in your mouth and in your heart," provides the structure for Romans 10:9-10. Confession with the lips and belief in the heart are not two separate processes; they are part of the same act of faith in which one is set right with God (justification) and saved from God's wrath in the Final Judgment (salvation).

Paul may be echoing a formula recited during baptism. "Jesus is Lord" was one of the oldest expressions of Christian belief. A Christian who made this confession of faith also courted martyrdom, for "Jesus is Lord" asserted the kingship of Christ over the Roman emperor who claimed to be divine.

Think About It: "Jesus is Lord" is one of the oldest expressions of Christian belief. Does it give full and adequate expression to your faith? What present-day counterparts to Caesar might be threatened by our living out of this affirmation?

Saved by Faith

Paul here cites two other Scriptures—Isaiah 28:16 (in Romans 10:11) and Joel 2:32 (in Romans 10:13)—to bolster his argument that all (both Jew and Greek) can be saved by faith. The citation from Joel also figures promi-

116

nently in Luke's story of the first converts at Pentecost (Acts 2). Thus, this basic credo became the watchword of a Christian faith that pushed beyond ethnic identity and regional boundaries to spread throughout the world.

Gospel: Luke 4:1-13

Jesus is the Son of God, and this is confirmed by the Holy Spirit (4:1). But what does it mean to be the Son of God?

Luke used the titles "Son of God" and "Messiah," interchangeably. Many expected the Messiah to be a powerful political leader, restoring the Davidic monarchy. Some expected him to be a priestly figure, purifying the nation with high standards of ritual holiness. These external expectations combined with the inner temptation for Jesus to use his power to meet his own needs. What would he do?

The Temptations

The temptation scene in this lection and the synagogue scene that follows (verses 14-30) show what Jesus rejected and what he accepted for his vocation as the Son of God. During this sojourn in the wilderness, he struggled with several personal and political options for his mission.

Jesus was hungry after a forty-day fast. The devil said that if he was the Son of God he would turn a stone into bread. The temptation was that he had to prove his sonship rather than believe the word God had spoken to him in his baptism (Luke 3:22). The devil used the same phrase to introduce the first and third temptations: "If you are the Son of God" (Luke 4:3, 9). The "if/then" construction has two meanings: "if," meaning something yet to be proved, or "since," which assumed the validity of the statement and sought to clarify its implications.

Next, Jesus was offered authority over worldly kingdoms, political power to accomplish any end. But Jesus knew he could not serve two masters (Luke 4:5-8; see Deuteronomy 6:13). Power corrupts, and should he become enamored with realms and armies, he would be diverted from his primary calling: sharing the love of God. Foiled thus far, the devil mimicked Jesus' use of Scripture, quoting Psalm 91:11-12 (see page 115), which promises that God will protect the faithful with special power (Luke 4:9-11). The temptation is to be invulnerable. Jesus replied that he could not test God this way (Luke 4:12; see Deuteronomy 6:16).

Think About It: Psalm 91:11-12 promises that God will protect the faithful with special power. When is it appropriate to ask God for protection? How might our longing to be invulnerable interfere with doing God's will? How did Jesus use his special power? What does his call to "take up the cross" imply about the place of protection and vulnerability in Christian discipleship?

Jewish Heritage

The Scriptures Jesus used come from a key section of Deuteronomy (Chapter 6), the Shema, thus lodging his ministry squarely within his Jewish heritage. His obedience contrasted with the behavior of his forebears, whose complaints, testing, and idolatry grieved God during their forty years in the wilderness. The temptation scene shows him to be a prophet like Moses (Exodus 34:28) and Elijah (1 Kings 19:8), who also fasted and prayed for forty days in the wilderness. Right after the temptation, Jesus cited Isaiah 61:1-2 in the synagogue at Nazareth to clarify what he had come to do—"bring good news to the poor."

Victory Over Evil

This opening personal struggle with the devil prefigures Jesus' ongoing battle with the realm of evil throughout his ministry. These temptations foreshadow Jesus' final temptation on the cross. One criminal echoed the devil's words, "Are you not the Messiah? Save yourself and us!" (Luke 23:39). Neither a political messiah nor an inviolate priest, the Son of God did not invoke special powers or perform mighty works (to save himself); instead he was obedient unto death (to save others). His dying overcame evil and made possible the living of all in the Resurrection.

Study Suggestions

A. Introduce Lent

Begin by noting that this is the first Sunday in Lent and referring to whatever observance of Ash Wednesday was held in your church. Explain that in the early church this forty-day period—based on Jesus' experience of fasting and searching in the wilderness—was a time of preparation for baptism. In medieval times it became a season of public penitence so that persons who had committed egregious sins could be restored to communion in the church. Now it is used by believers for deepening faith and strengthening belief through devotional preparation for Holy Week and Easter. Discuss how this group will observe Lent this year.

B. Recite a Creed

Confession of faith is a recurring theme in today's lections. Lead the group in reciting the Apostles' Creed or the Nicene Creed. What is the importance of corporate tradition and individual freedom in the church?

C. Consider the Festivals

Read Deuteronomy 26:1-11 and the commentary on pages 114–15. Ask: What tithes were levied in Judah and Israel? What did the tithes support? How do we support these needs and purposes today? What are the major Christian festivals in our liturgical year? How do they help us understand and relate better to God?

D. Confess Faith

Read aloud Romans 10:8b-13, and review the commentary on pages 116–17. Write out verse 9 on poster paper. Ask: What does it mean for you to confess Jesus as Lord? What are you saved from or for? Discuss the "Think About It" questions. Recite Romans 10:9 aloud together.

E. Chart Christianity

Bring a world map or globe to class. Print "Jesus is Lord" on small sticky notes. Have group members affix the notes in places over the world where Christianity is practiced. (Note especially the location of missionaries or projects that your congregation supports.) Remind the group how Christianity has "pushed beyond ethnic identity and regional boundaries to spread throughout the world."

F. Examine the Psalm

Read Psalm 91 and the exposition on pages 115–16. List all the names and images for God in this psalm. Ask: Which names or images best express for you who God is? Why? Discuss: When have you experienced God's protection? When did you wish for it but not receive it? If persons do suffer illness, injury, or attack, does that mean God has chosen not to protect them?

G. Study Jesus' Temptations

Read Luke 4:1-13 and the commentary on pages 117–18. Form three groups. Assign each group one of Jesus' temptations. Ask each group: What did the devil offer Jesus? How would you express the substance of this temptation in today's language? How would the offer have diverted Jesus from his true mission? How did Jesus respond? What spiritual resources do you rely on to resist temptation?

Return to the total group, and hear the groups report. Ask: What do the three temptations have in common? What does the devil represent in the story? What held Jesus firm to his purpose? What is the significance of the place, the forty days, and the use of Scripture?

Comment that some Christians practice fasting or give up something during Lent as a spiritual discipline to help them keep their focus on discerning and following God's will. Have you found this practice meaningful to you? Would you like to experience it this year during Lent? How can the group support one another in carrying out a fasting discipline?

H. Close With Hymn, Creed, and Prayer

Sing the hymn, "Lord, Who Throughout These Forty Days." Recite Romans 10:9 as a confession of faith. Close with a prayer asking God to lead us into a deeper spiritual walk during this Lenten season.

119

Lections for Second Sunday in Lent

T   Old Testament: Genesis 15:1-12, 17-18

HIS is the one of several seminal passages in Genesis describing God's covenant with Abram, the ancestor of Israel. Repeating the promise of land and descendants first made in Genesis 12:1-2, this passage sharpens the issue because, though Abram had traveled to Canaan as commanded, he still had no son.

Complaining to God

The conversation between Abram and God took place during a night vision (15:1). God promised Abram a great reward (15:1), a reference generally to the spoils of war. Abram complained that, since he was still childless, what good was a reward? A household slave stood to be his heir (15:2-3). (Slaves in this ancient Near East society were sometimes adopted by a childless couple to receive the estate and insure proper burial for their "parents.") God reassured Abram that his own biological child would be his heir. "Count the stars, if you are able," God said. "So shall your descendants be" (15:5). God also promised Abram long life and a peaceful death (15:15)—both signs of divine blessing in traditional societies.

How Will I Know?

Abram apparently was convinced about the promise of an heir but remained unconvinced about the land, asking, "How will I know this?" (15:6-8). Though some people say it is wrong to question God, the pointed dialogue between God and Abram typifies "call" scenes in the Old Testament, wherein humans talk back to God with no apparent repercussions.

When YHWH told Moses to lead the Hebrew people out of slavery, Moses raised several objections—he was a nobody, he didn't know the name of God, they might not listen to him, he was tongue-tied (Exodus 3). The warrior Gideon, called to battle, likewise demurred—he was least in his family, he needed a sign (Judges 6:11-27). The prophet Isaiah, too, was reluctant to accept God's call—"I am a man of unclean lips" (Isaiah 6:5).

God's Answer to Abram

In each case, YHWH answered their objections and provided a sign to assure them that he would be with them and would fulfill the promises made. YHWH's answer to Abram came during a covenant-making ritual. "A smoking fire pot and a flaming torch" passed between the halves of the animals Abram had prepared (Genesis 15:17).

An Ancient Ritual

According to ancient practice, participants who "cut a covenant" walked between divided animals, calling death upon themselves if they broke the terms of the covenant (see Jeremiah 34:18-20). Here, the brazier and torch were signs that God would keep this promise to Abram. (See Exodus 1:7 and 1 Kings 4:21 for ways in which the promises were fulfilled.)

A Prototype for Believers

In this passage, Abram is the prototype for all who believe God's promises but still need reassurance. The statement by the narrator in 15:6 that Abram believed God and God "reckoned it to him as righteousness" became a key part of the arguments of the apostle Paul and the author of the Letter to the Hebrews. To be righteous means to be faithful to the relationships in which one stands. God's faithfulness preceded and made possible Abram's faith, and Abram's faith became a model for generations to come. God's favor was to be granted, not as payment for keeping the law (works), but as a gift for faith.

> **Think About It:** To be righteous means to be faithful to one's relationships—with God and with other persons. What do we usually understand *righteousness* to mean? What is the difference between being good and being faithful? How does God's faithfulness to us make possible our faithfulness in our relationships?

Psalter: Psalm 27

Psalm 27 divides neatly into two parts, the first expressing trust in God's protection (verses 1-6) and the second pleading to God for deliverance from enemies (verses 7-14). The psalmist compares God's saving presence to light. He wants to be so close to God as to live in the Temple (verse 4). The Temple was sometimes used as a sanctuary for refugees, perhaps explaining the reference to shelter and concealment in verse 5.

Verses 7-14 plead for help with a series of positive and negative imperatives, such as "hear," "teach," "do not turn away," and "do not cast me off." Believing that God's goodness can be experienced in this life, the speaker exhorts others also to "wait for the LORD" (verses 13-14).

Though most modern scholars believe David did not write all the psalms attributed to him, some details of Psalm 27 do coincide with David's life—his success on the battlefield (verses 2-3) and his procession of praise (verse 6). The psalmist's bravado (verses 1-2), joy (verse 6), guilty pleading (verses 7-9), and quiet trust (verses 13-14) also match David's volatile temperament. Penned by David or not, the psalm voices the situation of all believers who look to God in trust and hope.

Epistle: Philippians 3:17–4:1

Taken alone, this verse may seem arrogant: "Brothers and sisters, join in imitating me" (3:17). Is Paul an egomaniac wanting to create little clones of himself? In the context of the preceding chapters, however, in which Paul describes the humility and suffering of Christ (2:5-8) and alludes to his own suffering (1:12-13), this statement reads differently. Afraid that the Philippians might be misled by false teachers, Paul offered himself and other leaders as role models (3:17), while also pointing to the true model, Jesus.

Enemies of the Cross

Who are these false teachers, these "enemies of the cross" (3:18)? If they are the same opponents described in 3:2-4, they were teachers who argued that Gentiles needed to be circumcised. As Jews, then they could be Christians. This would make Christianity a sect within Jewish tradition. The words "their god is the belly" could refer to the observance of Jewish dietary laws, and "their glory is in their shame" to the rite of circumcision. However, Paul might also have been countering a group of libertines who believed that their salvation by Christ allowed them great liberty of lifestyle. In this case, "belly" and "shame" could refer to gluttony and sexual promiscuity. Paul stated that it is suffering for Christ, not circumcision, that marks the true Christian. Self-denial, not license, characterizes the Christian life.

> **Think About It:** Naming Christ as "Savior" is a direct challenge to the claims of empire. What "empires" compete for your allegiance—government? work? military? consumerism? business? school? How are you faithful to Christ by living as a responsible member of society?

Citizens of Heaven

Paul told the Philippians that their true citizenship was in heaven, from which their Savior would return (3:20). "Citizenship" and "Savior" would have been powerful words to his hearers, for Philippi was a Roman colony. Any who were Roman citizens enjoyed legal, economic, and property rights denied noncitizens. However, they would have been expected to observe the cult of the emperor, who was hailed as a divine "savior." Naming Christ as Savior was a direct challenge to the claims of the Empire and led to the persecution of Christians.

Infused With Joy

Besides countering false teachers, Paul wrote to reassure the Philippians about his imprisonment (1:12-18; see also Acts 28:16, 30-31); to thank them for a gift (Philippians 4:10-13); and to commend a fellow-worker, Epaphroditus (2:25-30). Though Paul spoke of humility and suffering, the letter is infused with joy (see 1:3-4, 18; 4:4, 10). Comforted in prison by their prayers (1:18), Paul rejoiced in the affection of the Philippians and returned it wholeheartedly (4:1).

Gospel: Luke 13:31-35

This short lection is crammed full, containing a death threat (13:31), a prediction (13:32-33), a lament (13:34), and a judgment (13:35). The scene pulses with suspense, urgency, and emotional tension. Are the Pharisees trying to help or hurt Jesus? What will happen to him?

The Pharisees' Warning

Just before this passage, Jesus had been teaching in towns and villages on the way to Jerusalem, warning that not everyone would be invited to God's feast at the end of the age (13:22-30). "At that very hour" some Pharisees told Jesus that King Herod wanted to kill him (13:31).

Jesus and the Pharisees had argued throughout this Gospel, Jesus calling them greedy fools and hypocrites and comparing them with "unmarked graves" (11:37-44). They responded with hostility and stealth, "lying in wait for him" (11:53-54). It is hard to interpret their warning here. They may truly have cared about his welfare as a fellow Jew, or they may have wanted to frighten him into silence. The connecting phrase, "at that very hour" (13:31), suggests that it was these same Pharisees who would be excluded from the heavenly banquet.

A Deadly Enemy

Herod was a deadly enemy. Herod Antipas, son of Herod the Great, desired his father's title, "King of the Jews"; but the Romans had not bestowed it on him. Uneasy in his power, Herod presided over a court rife with corruption and deadly intrigue.

Rebuked by John the Baptist for taking Herodias, his brother's wife, in a political marriage, Herod had John imprisoned (3:19-20) and later beheaded (9:7-9). Some were saying John had been raised from the dead and reappeared in Jesus (9:7). Others had suggested that either Elijah or another of the prophets had returned in the person of Jesus. Perplexed, Herod "tried to see him" (9:9b).

No Fear

Jesus refused to be cowed by Herod's reputation. Calling Herod a "fox" (a dangerous insult, since foxes were considered creatures of low cunning), Jesus said calmly that he would continue to teach and heal for three days until he arrived in Jerusalem. The phrase, "on the third day I finish my work," may allude to the Resurrection, which Jesus had predicted in 9:22 (see also 18:33; 24:7, 21, 46). Jesus "must" (13:33) go to Jerusalem, the imperative conveying a sense of urgency to be faithful to God's purpose for his life.

Judgment on Jerusalem

The sense of impending crisis was heightened, however, when Jesus reminded his hearers that he had predicted Jerusalem to be the place of his death (13:33). "Jerusalem" had killed other prophets, notably Zechariah (2 Chronicles 24:20-22) and Uriah (not Bathsheba's husband, see Jeremiah 26:20-23). Because Jerusalem had failed to recognize its "time of visitation" by God (see Luke 19:44), it would be destroyed—"Your house is left to you [desolate]" (13:35; Matthew 23:38). Jesus' oracle of judgment echoed the words of Jeremiah 22:5.

Jesus' Tears

Jesus lamented the fate he foresaw for Jerusalem, wishing they had allowed him to lovingly gather them "as a hen gathers her brood under her wings" (Luke 13:34). The tender, maternal imagery comes from Wisdom Literature, such as Psalms 36:7 and 91:4, recalling the feminine figure of divine Wisdom (an image of God), who offered herself and was rejected (Proverbs 1:24-28). Jesus' lament expressed the grief of a God who was constantly reaching out to a resistant people. Some day they would suffer the consequences of their failure to welcome him (Luke 13:35). Jesus' tears were not for himself but for his people.

> **Think About It:** "Divine Wisdom . . . offered herself and was rejected." When have you reached out to someone and been rebuffed? What did that experience suggest to you about God's reaction to human rejection?

Study Suggestions

A. Open With Praise

Sing a hymn of praise, such as "From All That Dwell Below the Skies." Then form two groups and recite responsively Psalm 27, with the groups alternating half-verses. Summarize the commentary (pages 121–22) to put the words in context.

B. Dramatize the Dialogue

Ask three persons to assume the parts in Genesis 15:1-12, 17-18: narrator, Abram, and God. Have them briefly review the Scripture to determine which voice speaks in each verse; then read the dialogue aloud with appropriate emphasis. Discuss: What were Abram's concerns? Were they legitimate? How did God answer them?

C. Trace Interpretation

Review the commentary on the Genesis passage (pages 120–21), then focus on verse 6. Form three groups and assign each group a passage: Galatians 3:6-9; Romans 4:1-3, 20-24; and Hebrews 11:8-12. Ask: How does Paul interpret Genesis 15:6 in each case? How does the author of the Letter to the Hebrews apply the same verse? Report your findings.

D. Name Role Models

Read Philippians 3:17–4:1 aloud, and review the interpretation (pages 122–23). What did Paul want the Philippians to do (3:17)? Invite members to name persons who have been role models for them. Ask: Why were these persons important to you? What qualities of theirs did you try to emulate? How did your relationship with these persons help you grow? For whom might you serve as such an example? Also discuss the "Think About It" questions related to conflicting loyalties.

E. Pray the Psalm

Review Psalm 27:7-12. List the imperatives in this portion of the psalm. What did the psalmist want God to do?

F. Note Predictions

Read aloud Luke 13:31-35, and review the commentary on pages 123-24. Ask: What fate did Jesus predict for himself (13:32-33)? for Jerusalem (13:35)? Why would Jesus be killed? Why would Jerusalem be destroyed? How will God bring good out of each disaster? When have you experienced God bringing good out of calamity in your life? Briefly talk about these experiences.

G. Consider Christ's Care

In Luke 13:34, Jesus compared himself to a mother hen gathering chicks under her wing. Invite members to close their eyes; recall a time when they were held in a warm, protective embrace; then imagine it is Christ who is gathering them in his arms. Ask: How do you feel? How can we help draw others into Christ's embrace? Discuss the "Think About It" questions. Close by reading Psalm 27:13-14 aloud together as a benediction.

Lections for Third Sunday in Lent

Old Testament: Isaiah 55:1-9

*T*HE prophet, Second Isaiah, opens this oracle by mimicking the cries of the vendors in the marketplace: "Ho, . . . come, buy and eat!" (55:1). Their loud calls could be heard in any Near Eastern market, competing with one another hawking their wares. (A remnant of that practice remains in modern North America in the cries of food vendors at sporting events.)

The prophet gained his hearers' attention with this vivid beginning, then suggested a metaphor: What he offers is not simply bread, wine, or milk, but abundant life from God, the "rich food" (55:2b) of God's wisdom and salvation. God's salvation is about to be realized; now is the time to come to God.

Think About It: The prophet asked, Why do you spend money and labor for what does not satisfy? Why did Isaiah consider buying and consuming a waste of time? How do you feel after a shopping spree? When is enough enough? What do you think about the contemporary phenomena of credit card debt and the increase in bankruptcies? Why is milk cheaper than soda pop and yet children are drinking less milk? Is our society really "eating what is good"? To what end do you work? What gives you true satisfaction?

A Great Feast

Another image behind this passage might be that of the coronation banquet provided by a king at the beginning of his reign. In Proverbs 9:5, the figure of divine Wisdom invites people to such a feast: "Come, eat of my bread / and drink of the wine I have mixed." (Christians might also see an allusion to the Last Supper, or to the great eschatological banquet in the world to come.) God is the host at an abundant table to which all are invited.

Labor That Does Not Satisfy

In verse 2 the prophet suggests that the people have been spending their resources on

126

"that which does not satisfy" (Isaiah 55:2a). They toil and fret, falling into frustration and despair. Their condition was aptly described by the English poet William Wordsworth, who wrote, "Getting and spending, we lay waste our powers."

Promise for Exiles

Isaiah 40–55 is addressed to the exiles in Babylon who believed that God had earlier forsaken them when Judah was defeated by the Babylonians in 587 B.C. The prophet promised that God would act soon to liberate the exiles from captivity and return them to their place of origin. The second exodus will be more glorious than the first as they return to a land "flowing with milk and honey" (Exodus 3:8, 17). Salvation and material well-being intertwine. Their privation during exile will be over, and they will once again enjoy bountiful prosperity, free for all.

> *Think About It:* Salvation and material well-being intertwine. Has this been your experience? Does our faith assure us a prosperous future?

Repentance and Restoration

There is a price to be paid in one sense, however; the people are urged to "seek the LORD while he may be found" and return to God to find mercy and pardon (55:6-7), thereby renewing their faith and trust in God. Though God's ways seem lofty and inscrutable to finite, sinful humans (55:8-9), if they repent, God will bring them back into right relationship. Indeed, God will take the "sure" covenant once made with David (55:3b) and extend it to the whole people.

The faith of the people will be a "witness" to other nations about God's saving grace, just as David's leadership and authority testified to God's glory and protective power (55:4b). Moreover, just as David and Solomon received tribute from other nations, the postexilic Judah will draw foreigners who want to attach themselves to the restored nation under the protection of the mighty YHWH.

Psalter: Psalm 63:1-8

Vivid imagery opens this psalm. The speaker longs for God like a thirsty person gasps for water in the desert. Water, precious in the arid climate of Palestine, is also the key image in Psalm 42:1 and Isaiah 44:3: "As a deer longs for flowing streams, / so my soul longs for you, O God." John (4:10) describes Jesus as "living water," a symbol of accepting grace offered freely to the woman at the well. The rite of baptism echoes this yoking of water with God's gift of new life in the Spirit.

The psalmist alludes to an experience of God's power and glory in the sanctuary, similar to the vision of the prophet Isaiah that propelled him into ministry: "I saw the Lord sitting on a throne, high and lofty; and the hem of his robe filled the temple" (Isaiah 6:1; see lection for the fifth Sunday after the Epiphany). Worship can slake our spiritual thirst, prompt our praise, and send us out to witness and serve (Psalm 63:3-4).

Ascribed by later editors to David "when he was in the Wilderness of Judah" (1 Samuel 23:14-15), this psalm expresses the people's longing for God's presence during their "wilderness" experiences (doubt, fear, illness, oppression). The lifted hands in verse 4 refer to the posture of prayer. God's steadfast love (Isaiah 63:3) will uphold the believer in all times and places.

Epistle: 1 Corinthians 10:1-13

Falsely secure in their own knowledge and Eucharistic religion (8:1-2), some Corinthian Christians had eaten food sacrificed to idols, which unsettled weaker believers (8:1-13). Some had committed fornication (5:1-2; 6:12-20); others fomented division (1:10-13). It seems they believed that the sacraments of baptism and Holy Communion would magically protect them from punishment for sin.

If they are so proud, Paul warned them, they should take heed of what happened to their Jewish ancestors (10:1-4), onto whose tree they have been grafted (Romans 11:17-22). The Hebrews, who had received a kind of baptism when they passed through the Reed Sea (1 Corinthians 10:1-2), and who had received a kind of communion when YHWH provided them manna and water (10:3-4), nonetheless had committed grave sins and had to be punished.

Similar Sins

The Israelites had committed idolatry by sacrificing to the golden calf (Exodus 32:6) and later by worshiping Canaanite ba'als. Paul likely equated these with the idolatrous feasts attended by the Corinthians. The Hebrews had sexual relations with the women of Moab, which was punished by a plague killing 23,000 (24,000 per Numbers 25:1-9). For their complaints and rebellion, they were visited by poisonous serpents (1 Corinthians 10:9; Numbers 21:1-9) and the same avenging angel of God that killed the Egyptians (1 Corinthians 10:10; Exodus 12:23). If God did not spare the Hebrew children from the punishing effects of their sin, God would not spare others who were likewise idolatrous and immoral.

Future Endurance

Even if they felt secure, Paul said, they should beware: They have thus far escaped the persecutions endured by other believers. The Corinthians thought they were strong even though they had not been tested and been proven faithful, but harder trials and persecutions may well come. In that case, God will strengthen them and provide the means to endure (10:13). Such testing will reveal their true character and the depth of their commitment (Deuteronomy 8:2).

> **Think About It:** Testing can reveal true character and commitment. What tests have you endured in your life? How did this affect your character and commitment?

Christ the Rock

In his description of the "baptism" and "communion" experienced by the Israelites, Paul stated that the "spiritual rock" following and sustaining them "was Christ" (1 Corinthians 10:4). There was a rabbinic legend based on Exodus 17:1-7 and Numbers 20:2-13 that a rock followed the Israelites on their wilderness journey, giving water as they needed it. Paul is thus suggesting that the pre-incarnate Christ was present with his Hebrew ancestors in the desert (1 Corinthians 10:1-4).

Gospel: Luke 13:1-9

This passage contains a commentary on current events and a parable of warning. Concluding a long discourse en route to Jerusalem (12:1–13:9), Jesus used the occasion to drive home his message: Repent before it is too late.

A Horrific Story

Someone in the crowd repeated the horrific story of how Pilate, the Roman governor of Judea, slaughtered a group of Galileans who were offering sacrifices in the Temple. Human and animal blood intermingled on the floor. Pilate's harsh treatment of the Jews, killing large numbers who protested his siphoning of funds from the Temple treasury, is well attested to by ancient sources. The Galileans described in 13:1-9 may have been zealots, Jewish revolutionaries who had a stronghold in the hill country.

Challenging the Crowd

Declining either to praise or condemn the Galileans, Jesus instead turned on the crowd, asking if the men were killed because they were worse sinners than other Galileans. It was a rhetorical question. It was common wisdom that people who suffered were being punished for their own or their parents' sins, while the righteous were rewarded (see John 9:2). "No, I tell you," Jesus said, strongly repudiating common belief (Luke 13:3). Jesus challenged the idea that God is the immediate cause of every event, thereby leaving room for human freedom.

Lest his hearers become complacent, however, Jesus added quickly: "Unless you repent, you will all perish as they did." Citing his own example from another recent incident, when a tower in the city wall fell on eighteen persons in south Jerusalem, Jesus repeated the same hard sequence: rhetorical question, repudiation, and call to repent.

Vulnerable Before God

If people could no longer assume their good fortune was a result of their own righteousness, and if they, too, could die at any time, they were utterly vulnerable before God. Repentance is the only way, Jesus said. Conduct your affairs so that you are not afraid to stand before God when judgment comes. With quick speech and strong words Jesus sought to overcome the deep resistance in his hearers to challenge and change.

A Barren Tree

Jesus followed these challenges with a parable that compared the people of Judea to a barren fig tree. The owner of the vineyard told the gardener to cut it down, but the gardener asked for one more year in which to aerate and fertilize the soil. Old Testament prophets often used the fig tree as a metaphor for the people of God (Jeremiah 8:13; Hosea 9:10; Micah 7:1). John the Baptist, whose preaching preceded Jesus, also warned that "the ax is lying at the root of the trees; every tree . . . that does not bear good fruit is cut down and thrown into the fire" (Luke 3:9).

Time to Repent

Jesus stood with these other prophets but with an important difference: he said that there was time ("one year"—verses 8-9) in which to repent, perhaps referring to the span of his own ministry. In mercy and patience, God would grant an additional period for the people to repent. Luke's version of this parable (compared to Matthew 21:18-19 and Mark 11:12-24) balances a harsh call to repentance with a note of patient grace.

Think About It: Conduct your affairs so that you are not afraid to stand before God. If you knew you were going to die tomorrow, would you do anything differenctly today? Is fear of judgment the primary incentive for living faithfully? What motivates you?

Both Jesus and John specified one of the "fruits worthy of repentance" (Luke 3:8): to share food and clothing with those in need (3:11; 6:30; 12:33). They demanded repentance not only from their own followers but from the whole populace. Nearing his own time of testing in Jerusalem, Jesus tried to prepare those who would follow him for the hard demands of discipleship.

Study Suggestions

A. Open With Prayer

Recite Psalm 63:1-4 as an opening prayer. Share the background (pages 127–28) to put this psalm in perspective.

B. Hear the Prophet

Read aloud Isaiah 55:1-9, and review the commentary on pages 126–27. Ask: How does the prophet get his hearers' attention in the opening verse? What is he offering to the people? What might Isaiah say in the aisles of our grocery stores? at the mall? on Wall Street?

The imagery of the great feast suggests a vision of abundant life. Have two people read Luke 6:21a and John 10:10b. Ask: What does Jesus want us to have? What is abundant life? Does God care about our material well-being? Discuss the "Think About It" questions about consumerism and affluence..

In Isaiah 55:3c-5, the prophet applies the covenant made with David to the whole people of Israel. Read 2 Samuel 7:8-17 for background. Discuss: How did Isaiah reclaim the covenant with David for his people in his time? In what ways are we heirs of God's promises to David?

C. Meditate on God

Read Psalm 63:5-8 aloud. Ask members to recall a time they were awake in the night. Were they troubled? Did they pray? Memorize Psalm 63:5-7 phrase by phrase to use as a prayer for sleepless times.

D. Study Paul's Counsel

Read 1 Corinthians 10:1-13, and summarize the commentary on pages 128–29. Identify the problems Paul was facing in the Corinthian church. Ask: How did he address these problems? Discuss: Do Christians today practice idolatry, commit sexual immorality, or complain? How would you apply Paul's counsel to them?

E. Consider Sin and Suffering

Read Luke 13:1-9 and the commentary on pages 129–30. Ask: What did people believe about the cause for suffering in Jesus' time? What explanations do we have for suffering today? (Some are: to test our faith; the consequence of choices we make; to build character; life would be boring if everything were pleasant; punishment for sin; sometimes chosen to benefit others or heal a situation; reveals a loving God who shares the struggle and suffering with us.) What did Jesus say about the relationship between sin and suffering? What did he want his hearers to do in this situation?

Lent is a time for reflection and penitence, for turning from our own self-centered ways to seek God (repentance). Invite members to spend time in quiet reflection on these questions: What sinful behavior hurts me? others? God? How might I live differently? How might I demonstrate a renewed commitment to God?

F. Close With a Hymn and Benediction

Sing or read the hymn, "Seek the Lord," which is based on Isaiah 55:6-11, then repeat Isaiah 55:6-7 as a benediction.

Lections for Fourth Sunday in Lent

Old Testament: Joshua 5:9-12

*T*HIS brief passage describes the first Passover feast celebrated in the land of Canaan, looking back to the Exodus from Egypt (5:9) and looking forward to the renewal Passover that King Josiah would keep (2 Kings 23:21-23). The feast followed a mass circumcision of the male children born in the wilderness.

Gilgal

The Passover feast was held at Gilgal, one of the ancient shrines of the tribal confederacy, along with Shechem, Shiloh, and Bethel. At Gilgal the prophet Samuel anointed Saul as king. Verse 9 explains the origin of the name "Gilgal" as the place where God "rolled away . . . the disgrace of Egypt." "Gilgal" is related to the Hebrew word, *galal,* meaning "to roll." However, exactly what was "rolled" that day is unclear. The area does have many boulders that look like large balls and may be the origin of the name.

Think About It: The pile of stones was a memorial reminding them of God's delivery and guidance. What symbols do we use in our churches to remind us of God's presence and activity in our lives? How do we use these to tell others our stories of faith?

After they crossed the Jordan River at Gilgal, Joshua told the elders to bring twelve stones from the bed of the river and erect a memorial to remind everyone of their safe crossing over the Jordan, which was similar to their miraculous delivery from the Egyptians at the Sea of Reeds (Joshua 4:19-24). It was fitting, then, to celebrate a Passover feast as they recalled the first Exodus and YHWH's guidance through the years of wandering and the day of crossing.

Passover

The word *Passover* first referred to the evening feast on the fourteenth day of the first month of the Jewish year during which a lamb was slaughtered and eaten whole before morning. The seven-day feast of unleavened bread followed. During this time, no leavened grain was eaten (Leviticus 23:6), reminiscent of the first Passover in which the meal was eaten in haste as they prepared to depart.

Passover later came to refer to the whole range of observances related to the season. The slaughter of the lamb appears to have originated in a nomadic shepherds' rite that celebrated the move to new pastures in the spring during the full moon. The feast was held outside the sanctuary "on the plains of Jericho" (Joshua 5:10). Modern-day Samaritans still keep Passover on top of Mount Gerizim, strictly following all the Leviticus prescriptions. A Canaanite agricultural festival may lie behind the Feast of Unleavened Bread. However, in this passage, both traditions are claimed as a remembrance of the Exodus and associated with their entry into Canaan.

Time of Transition

Verse 12 notes that "the manna ceased on the day they ate the produce of the land." Thus, the Passover Feast marked a time of transition for the Hebrew people, from one period of sacred history to the next. They went from being wilderness wanderers dependent on daily manna to a people poised on the edge of settlement in a new land. In earlier days, YHWH had provided manna. Now they would gradually shift from a nomadic to a settled agricultural way of life, in which they could grow their own food. The Passover Feast provided a ritual passage to their new life lifestyle. The sacred meal allowed them to recognize YHWH's faithful care in changing circumstances.

> **Think About It:** The Passover Feast provided a ritual passage to the Israelites' new way of life. What rituals mark life changes in our culture and faith? (Baptism? graduation? marriage?) How do such rituals help us recognize God's faithful care and guidance?

Psalter: Psalm 32

The first half of this psalm expresses the joy of having received forgiveness. Unconfessed sin had made the speaker miserable (verses 3-4). After acknowledging the sin, the psalmist experienced relief. The transgression was forgiven, the sin covered (verse 1), the iniquity exonerated, the deceit revealed (verse 2), the guilt forgiven. Transgression, sin, iniquity, deceit, and guilt, used as parallel terms in the poetic structure of the psalm, convey the whole web of behaviors in which sinful humans entangle themselves. Forgiveness frees us from all of this.

The second part of the psalm tells what the forgiven person is empowered to do: offer faithful prayer (verse 6), receive God's protection (verse 7), offer instruction to others (verses 8-9), and rejoice in God's love (verses 10-11). Verses 8-9 sound like portions of Proverbs in which the speaker tries to persuade another person to accept moral instruction (Proverbs 2:1-5). The promise of blessing to the faithful and the sharp contrast between the wicked and righteous also place this psalm firmly in the Wisdom tradition.

The apostle Paul quotes Psalm 32:1-2 in Romans 4:7-8 in making his argument about justification by faith. As one of seven penitential psalms in early Christianity, Psalm 32 reflects the experience of centuries of believers who have been restored to right relationship with God and others by the power of forgiveness.

Epistle: 2 Corinthians 5:16-21

Paul regarded the Crucifixion as the central event of history. Everything was changed by the death and resurrection of Christ. He described the change as no less than a "new creation" (5:17), echoing the cosmic vision of transformation heralded by the prophet of the Exile (Isaiah 43:18-19; 65:17).

A New Creation

Though Paul's scope was cosmic, his application was intensely personal. Each Christian, too, is a new creation; therefore, we should judge no one from a "human point of view." The Greek phrase is *kata sarka,* "according to the flesh." By this Paul meant judging according to outward appearance or worldly position (see Galatians 3:28, which stresses the unity and equality in Christ across ethnic, ideological, class, and gender boundaries). We should instead look to others' hearts, remembering that Christ died for them and set them right with God (2 Corinthians 5:18a). Before his conversion, Paul had regarded Christ by human standards, zealously persecuting his followers as defilers of Judaism (Acts 8:3; 9:1). Christ had changed all of that—for him and for all time.

Human Standards

In writing about the new creation, Paul also hoped the Corinthians would regard him differently. Too often they had judged him by human standards, saying "his bodily presence is weak, and his speech contemptible" (2 Corinthians 10:10). Paul wanted them to be reconciled to God, thereby recognizing his apostolic authority and treating one another more charitably. He called himself (and them) "ambassadors for Christ." Since ambassadors were seen as personal representatives of the emperor, Paul claimed a high authority for all of Christ's followers. Yet he stressed that the initiative for transformation always comes from God through the sacrifice of Christ (5:21).

Made to Be Sin

"[God] made [Christ] to be sin who knew no sin." This verse can be interpreted in several ways: (1) that Christ assumed the form of sinful beings, as in Romans 8:3; (2) that God treated the sinless Jesus as a sinner on the cross, as in Galatians 3:13; or (3) that Jesus was a sacrificial offering for sin, as the servant in Isaiah 53:10. Paul may have intended any or all of these meanings, the outcome being most important—that "we might become the righteousness of God" (verse 21).

Gospel: Luke 15:1-3, 11b-32

Verses 1-3 set the context for Luke's beloved parable about the prodigal and his brother. Jesus' ministry to the "lost sheep of Israel" (19:10) was a smashing success. Outcasts pressed to be near him, and he ate with them (verses 1-2). However, some of Jesus' tablemates were notorious sinners, who did not observe the traditions. Others, such as tax collectors who routinely ate with Gentiles, engaged in occupations that made them ritually unclean. Observant Jews believed that by keeping the laws of ritual cleanliness, they showed respect for God and hastened the coming of the Messiah.

Jesus' acceptance of sinners seemed to convey a laxity about obedience to God's laws. So the Pharisees and scribes "grumbled" about him. Their phrase, "this fellow," succinctly conveyed their distance and distaste.

Lost and Found

Jesus responded to their criticism with three parables: the lost sheep, the lost coin, and the prodigal and his brother. In each parable, something lost is found; and the return of the lost thing is cause for great celebration. Jesus clearly intended the lost item in each parable to represent sinners who repent, the outcast and rejected ones who are welcomed into the heart of God (verses 7, 10).

Great Storytelling

The vivid characters, dramatic action, and careful details all invited Jesus' hearers to identify with the story of the prodigal and his brother. His depiction of the sibling rivalry between the two sons would have rung true to his hearers who knew the stories of Cain and Abel, Jacob and Esau, and Joseph and his brothers. Faithful to the gritty dynamics of family life, the parable's open ending forced Jesus' listeners to consider how the story applied to them.

The Prodigals

The sinners and ritually unclean pressing around Jesus would have seen themselves in the younger brother. The parable called them to come to themselves (verse 17), to recognize how they had squandered God's gifts (verse 13), to repent and seek God's forgiveness (verse 18), assured that a joyous welcome would await them (verses 20-24). That the prodigal was feeding pigs showed how far he had fallen: Jews considered pigs unclean. The prodigal's first step was to come back as a hired hand, not a son. Yet, the father told everyone in no uncertain terms that "this son of mine" (verse 24) is home.

The Older Brothers

The parable cast the scribes and the Pharisees in the role of the elder brother sulking outside the party. God told them in the words of the story that "you are always with me" and "all that is mine is yours." They had "never disobeyed [God's] command"; but instead of rejoicing in their status as beloved sons, they saw themselves as dutiful slaves (verse 29). They begrudged the "party for sinners" that Jesus' ministry had been. In the parable, the father attempted to bridge the distance implied by the elder brother's words, calling him "son" (verse 31) and describing the prodigal as "this brother of yours" (verse 32).

> **Think About It:** The parable's open ending forced Jesus' listeners to consider how the story applied to them. With whom do you identify most in the story? Why? Is there any person or group whom you regard with distance or distaste? How can you be restored to right relationship with them? How can we claim our true status as children of God?

The Rest of the Story

The parable leaves the elder brother fuming outside the party. What will he do? The remainder of the Gospel provides the ending for the parable. Far from rejoicing at the return of Israel's "lost sheep" who have gathered around Jesus, the scribes and the Pharisees conspired to have Jesus killed. Yet, God had the "last laugh" and the great celebration. Like the prodigal, Jesus "who was dead" came to life again (verse 32); and those he came to save have found new acceptance and status in God's loving presence.

Study Suggestions

A. Open With Singing

Begin by singing a hymn of forgiveness and new life such as "Where Shall My Wandering Soul Begin," "Freely, Freely," or "This Is a Day of New Beginnings."

B. Hear the Story

Read the commentary on the Old Testament lection, then ask the group to summarize the events leading up to and including the one described in Joshua 5:9-12. Ask: What did the Israelites do here? Why did they do it? What was the significance of the memorial of stones and this Passover Feast? Also explore the "Think About It" questions.

C. Contrast Humanity and God

Read 2 Corinthians 5:16-21 and the commentary on pages 134–35. Ask group members to describe a public figure as she or he might be known from "a human point of view"—appearance, wardrobe, house, car, job, credentials, status. Now describe the same person as she or he might appear to Christ. Ask: How might our assessment of persons become more closely shaped by Christ's view?

D. Experience Forgiveness

Read aloud Psalm 32:1-7, then invite participants into a time of guided meditation. Ask the following questions and provide moments of silence after each: What unconfessed sins are making you miserable? . . . Silently confess these to God. . . . Imagine your sins being like a pile of dust whirled away by the wind. . . . Imagine Christ embracing you with open arms . . . and a party being thrown in your honor! . . .

End with a prayer thanking God for forgiveness.

E. Claim the Parable

Assign four persons to read the parts in Luke 15:1-3, 11b-32: narrator, younger son, father, and older son. Invite the group to listen carefully as the parable unfolds, trying to hear things they have never heard before and to decide with which character they most closely identify.

After the reading, ask the group to make up an ending to the story from the point of view of the character with whom they most identified.

Review the commentary on pages 135–36. Name persons who are "lost" or rejected in our society. (Examples: the homeless, ex-offenders, welfare mothers, prostitutes, persons of another race, immigrants and refugees, the working poor.) Ask: What is God doing to seek and find them? What are we doing? Select one of these groups and develop a roleplay illustrating ways of fostering reconciliation.

F. Close With Prayer

Review the "lost persons" from Activity E. Assign these persons to group members. Ask them to speak their person aloud during a time of intercessory prayer using this format: "Let us pray for [insert name of "lost person"]. Lord, in your mercy, hear our prayer." Close with a prayer for each group member as well.

Lections for Fifth Sunday in Lent

Old Testament: Isaiah 43:16-21

*T*HIS lection is taken from that portion of Isaiah that is often called "The Book of Consolation," since the tone changes markedly at Isaiah 40:1 from the material that has preceded it. The situation presupposed by the prophet is the Babylonian Exile, which lasted from 597 B.C. (the first deportation of Judah's elites to Babylon, prior to the major deportations of 587 B.C. until about 539 B.C., when they began to return.

It is a matter of debate among scholars whether Isaiah of Jerusalem, the eighth-century prophet, would have been given oracles pertaining to a period centuries removed from his own time. Many scholars now favor the view that the "Book of Consolation" was actually written by an unknown prophet in Babylon, usually called Second Isaiah, near the end of the Exile, who sought to encourage his people that God would soon be moving again on their behalf.

The End of Exile

Whatever one's conclusion about authorship, there is no doubt that the oracle speaks of God's determination to end the exile of the people in Babylon and to liberate them from captivity to return to Canaan. The means by which God would accomplish this is the growing superpower of Persia, led by Cyrus the Great, who is even called God's "anointed" in this section of Isaiah (45:1; see also 44:28; 45:13).

Cyrus would indeed conquer Babylonia in 539 B.C., acting as God's arm to "break down all the bars" and turn the Chaldeans' "shouting ... to lamentation" (43:14). The Baby-

> **Think About It:** Cyrus is called God's "anointed." Does God use agents outside the faith community to accomplish the divine purpose in history, even without their knowledge or assent? Other than Cyrus, what other instances of this can you cite?

lonian kings had implemented a policy of relocating conquered peoples, shifting huge populations so as to destroy any sense of nationalism or unity that might lead to rebellion. Cyrus, however, adopted the practice of repatriation, allowing those who had been relocated to return to their native lands. The Judahites were among the first to benefit from this new policy.

A New Exodus

This return is described using the original Exodus from Egypt as a precedent. God had shattered the "chariot and horse, army and warrior" of Pharaoh (43:17) and made a path for the people through waters and deserts where previously none had existed. Once again God would make a way for his people across the river Euphrates and the desert (see Isaiah 40:3; 35) to bring them back to the land from which their forebears had been driven a half century before. God's provision of water in the desert (43:20-21) continues to recall the Exodus story, even as it announces new acts of God.

> **Think About It:** The prophet invited the congregation to find hope for God's acts in the future by contemplating God's acts in the past. Why would he have done this? What wuld it accomplish? When has a reference to the past helped you ind hope for the future? What "new thing" do you expect God to do in your life?

Former Things and a New Thing

The "former things" are God's acts in the Exodus. The prophet specifically recalled the contours of these "former things" so as to paint a picture of the "new thing" that God would do. "I am about to do a new thing; / now it springs forth, do you not perceive it?" (43:19). With these memorable words the prophet pointed to the certainty of God's imminent action in history. It would be like the Exodus, but so much grander and more wonderful that the Exodus event would be eclipsed in their memory.

Psalter: Psalm 126

Although some translations express verses 1-3 in the future tense in order to harmonize with verses 4-6, there is no reason to ignore the Hebrew grammar and adjust the tenses in this manner. Part of the power of this psalm is the awareness that God brought Judah back from the Babylonian Exile and that Zion was restored. It recalls the joy and celebration that came with the rebuilding of the Temple and restoration of worship.

The first three verses exist in tension with the concluding three verses. Just as God had been faithful to his people in the past and renewed their life, so God would be faithful to Judah in the midst of their present difficulty and would bring about restoration and health. The psalm expresses the reality that hope is not based on wishful thinking; hope is based on the character of God. Through God's saving acts in the past, the divine character is revealed. Knowing who God is for us, we can have hope toward the future.

The brief petition (verse 4) is followed by an assurance that God will answer, drawn from the metaphor of sowing and harvesting. Pagan agricultural myths and rites (with which the Hebrews were familiar) regarded sowing as a time of entering the ground to die and harvesting as a time of rebirth from the dead.

The annual cycle of sowing and reaping was thus a natural rhythm that served as an annual reminder of the hope and conviction that joy followed sorrow, life came from death. The psalmist uses this commonplace image as a means of reinforcing the specific hope that God would hear the prayer and, indeed, bring laughter to replace sorrow, hope to supplant despair.

Epistle: Philippians 3:4b-14

The Christians at Philippi were Paul's special partners in the Lord, working together with him through material support and prayer. This letter is, in fact, first of all a "thank you note" for a gift sent by them to sustain Paul in his imprisonment (4:10-20).

A Desire for Solidarity

Paul's principal concern, however, was to give the church guidance in resolving some internal squabbles (see 2:1-4; 4:2-3)—all the more as they needed to be in solidarity if they were to resist society's erosive pressures (1:27-30). This theme dominates the letter, and Paul offers his own example here in 3:4b-14 as part of the remedy for the causes of division and disharmony.

Impressive Credentials, But . . .

Paul listed the credentials that gave him status in Jewish circles and that he had previously used as a basis for self-confidence and for his claim on God's favor. These are also the distinguishing marks that created division, separating Torah-observant Jews from the Gentiles and others who might be regarded as "sinners," with the resulting devaluation of the latter. It was an egotistical confidence, since at its peak it brought Paul into conflict with God's vision for humanity. Paul realized that what he had been doing in God's name was actually contrary to God's purpose revealed in the cross.

Think About It: Paul's example teaches that one cannot continue in the old ways and discover the riches of new life in Christ at the same time. On what do you ground your self-esteem? What old attitudes and traits continue to plague your relationships and witness? How can these be changed?

140

The Real Prize Is in Christ

Having begun to taste the goodness of the Lord Jesus, Paul cast aside those claims and achievements as weights and impediments in his race toward Jesus' full embrace. Paul set the past (shortcomings and successes alike) behind him and attuned his whole being to gaining the prize through being made like Jesus in self-giving love and service. This is growing "maturity" in Christ (3:15).

Those who adopt this mindset no longer need to build themselves up (too often by tearing others down) and need not use their deeds of service as a claim on recognition and influence in the church. Instead, they take on a shared vision, one that calls each into relationship with the One who gave himself for others and sought only God's approval.

Gospel: John 12:1-8

This passage is one of the relatively rare instances where John includes material that parallels two of the Synoptic Gospels. In Mark (14:3-9) and Matthew (26:6-13), an unnamed woman anointed Jesus' head just prior to his Passion, an act symbolic of preparation for either coronation or interment. Both Synoptic writers made a point of saying that "wherever the/this good news is proclaimed in the whole world, what she has done will be told in remembrance of her" (Mark 14:9; Matthew 26:13). And it has been.

In Luke (7:36-40), a penitent woman washed and anointed Jesus' feet in gratitude, presumably stemming from some unnarrated act or word of Jesus prior to that evening. The two stories probably reflect different events, with some cross-pollination of details as the stories were passed down.

An Extravagant Gift

John's distinctive touches give the story a measure of irony. Here, it is Lazarus who gives a dinner party for Jesus upon his return to the region of Jerusalem (see 11:53-57). The one who was recently raised from the dead sits next to the one who is about to lay down his life and who is being anointed as if for burial. Mary's act of devotion was indeed extravagant, since the perfumed ointment was valued at a year's salary at minimum wage (if you will).

Since the episode follows so closely upon the raising of Lazarus (11:1-44), however, it is hard for the reader to escape the feeling that this lavish act of devotion, respect, and hospitality was being offered as the only suitable display of gratitude for Jesus' recent, compassionate gift to this family.

An Objection

In Mark, the disciples objected to this extravagance. Perhaps they are not greatly to be blamed, for surely they were among the poor, living on donated funds, depending on hospitality and support. In John's account it was Judas, for whom the Fourth Evangelist has no good word, who alone voiced disapproval.

Jesus' answer asserted that the right gift was made at the right time, thus affirming the nobility of Mary's action. There is a time for charity—indeed, most of the time! But there is also a place for Mary's use of these resources for no other purpose than to express her love for Jesus and to show him a kindness while there was still time.

It is difficult to apply Jesus' saying to expenditures made in later centuries. We should be wary of lavishly adorning our churches "for love of Jesus" while others starve. Extravagant acts of devotion and love in our time might be best accomplished by showing them to "the least of Jesus' sisters and brothers," which Jesus would accept as given to him (Matthew 25:31-46).

> **Think About It:** Mary's extravagance stemmed from her appreciation of Jesus' benevolent favor and kindness toward her and her family. When have you been filled with a similar feeling of gratitude? What was your response? When have you tried, like Judas, to restrain another's generosity, possibly from selfish motives? What is the appropriate balance in our giving between maintaining buildings and meeting human need?

The Coming Passion

It was Jesus who related the anointing to his forthcoming passion. Mary might also have understood this as she selected this particular venue for displaying her gratitude, all the more as she appears in Luke to have had "ears to hear" what Jesus taught (see Luke 10:39). The fact that people were aware of the Sanhedrin's determination to remove Jesus renders this plausible, at least in the world of the narrative John has woven together (John 11:55-57). What was happening inside the house took on a singular propriety in light of what was happening outside the house (11:55-57 and 12:9-11).

Study Suggestions

> **Note** that traditionally this is Laetori Sunday; the vestments are rose. Even in Lent, Laetori points to the joy of the coming Resurrection.

A. Looking for Restoration

Begin by reading Psalm 126 responsively, then singing "Great Is Thy Faithfulness." In an urbanized, commercialized culture, what images might we substitute for sowing and reaping to symbolize restoration? (Possibilities: recycling, remarriage after divorce, organ transplants.) What past movement of God in your life gives you hope for God's action in your present situation? How do you visualize God's response taking shape?

B. A New Thing

Invite someone to read aloud Isaiah 43:16-21. Ask: What are the parallels with the Exodus story? Why would the prophet speak of God's coming help by calling to mind past mercies? Set the passage in its historical context by sharing the commentary information (pages 138-39). Discuss the "Think About It" questions concerning Cyrus as God's agent.

Comment that in the New Testament Christians are sometimes referred to as "exiles," "aliens," or "foreigners" in the world (see Hebrews 11:13-16; 1 Peter 1:1; 2:11-12), because of the hope of a future repatriation in God's kingdom. Recall the gospel song, "This world is not my home; I'm just a-passing through." Ask: How real is the identity of an "exile" to you? What are the comparative risks of separating ourselves from the world and of identifying too closely with the world? To the extent you feel like an exile, how do these words of hope from Isaiah speak to you? What might change in your life if you took this "exile" identity seriously?

C. Losing Life to Find It

Invite members to name the credentials and accomplishments by which we tend to be known and evaluated in the "world" (education, wealth, profession, position). Ask: How important are these things for your sense of worth? How can we overcome the barriers created by distinctions?

Read aloud Philippians 3:4b-14 and the commentary notes on pages 140–41. Ask: What is so valuable about knowing Christ and sharing in his sufferings? Why did Paul choose between his worldly credentials and seeking a deeper relationship with Christ? What is the appropriate role for status, hierarchy, and recognition of achievement in the church? How do you appraise the worth of persons?

D. Extravagant Gratitude

Conduct a dramatic reading of John 12:1-8. Assign persons to take the roles of narrator, Jesus, and Judas. Look at the broader context of John 11:1–12:11. How does this context affect how we understand the story? Read or review the commentary on pages 141–42. What is the meaning of this act for Mary? for Jesus? Ask the "Think About It" questions. Discuss: How can we best show Jesus gratitude for what he has done for us?

E. Tie It Together

Discuss how the theme of God's extravagant deliverance that turns mourning into laughter (Psalm 126), the extravagant promise of "a new thing" (Isaiah 43), the extravagant riches of knowing Christ (Philippians 3), and the extravagant responses evoked by God's grace in Christ (John 12) bind today's lections together around the Laetori theme of joy.

Close with prayer expressing gratitude for God's extravagance, asking for God's grace to touch points of need in the group or congregation, and invoking the Spirit to move each person to a suitable response.

Lections for Passion/Palm Sunday

Old Testament: Isaiah 50:4-9a

*T*HIS passage is the third of four "servant songs" found in Isaiah's Book of Consolation (Isaiah 40–55; the four are 42:1-4; 49:1-6; 50:4-11; 52:13–53:12).

The Servant

There is sharp debate among scholars concerning the identity of this "servant," whether it be the prophet himself, Israel as a whole, or some future individual. Each interpretation can claim strong support from the text, and it may be best not to force an either/or decision on this point. The prophet himself acts on behalf of Israel and is in a direct sense God's servant. But ancient Israel as a whole, even though some rejected God and the prophet's message, was God's servant as well. There may be a sense that, as the prophet was faithful to his vocation as servant, he sought to help the Diaspora of Judah and Israel claim this identity as well.

> **Think About It:** Some would contend that the special blessing of this servant identity extends to the modern state of Israel. What do you think? Does the modern state of Israel manifest a servant identity and the other messianic qualities exhibited by Jesus?

The Servant's Life

Three key aspects of the servant's life are thrust to the fore in this song. First, the servant listened to God, morning by morning (verse 4). The servant's message to, and actions in, the world gained their bearings from God each new day. Second, nothing made the servant turn back from obedience to God's voice (verse 5). The servant showed boldness in the face of all opposition. He sustained the people, regardless of "insults and spitting," particularly vulgar behaviors (verse 6). He was willing to endure persecution in the faithful pursuit of his prophetic calling.

Third, the servant had absolute confidence in God's justice and in God's commitment to vindicate God's servant. Using legal language, the servant issued his own challenge to the Israelites with God as the vindicator. The servant did not seek the approval of others, but sought only God's favor (verses 7-8). He was confident that, while his adversaries would fall by the wayside in time, God would sustain and justify him and his mission (verse 9).

> **Think About It:** How were these three aspects of the servant's example, prayer, commitment, and trust, manifested in the life of Jesus? How are they expressed in your life? What prevents you from a deeper prayer life, stronger commitment, and more complete trust in God? How might the servant's example—and that of Jesus as well—embolden and strengthen your own service to God?

Jesus as the Servant

This passage is read on Palm Sunday, of course, because the church has identified Jesus as the Servant of God par excellence, whose attentiveness to God's heart, obedience to God, and endurance of suffering fulfilled this description of the servant in a whole new way. Jesus set his face "like flint" to go to Jerusalem (Luke 9:51); and the scene of false arrest, flogging, torture, and insult in verse 6 is a remarkable parallel and apt summary of a large portion of the Passion story.

Seen in this light, this servant song speaks of Jesus' absolute commitment to obedience and his assurance that God would vindicate him rather than allow disgrace and shame to be the final word. Because of these factors, the servant is able to pour himself out to the utmost, reserving nothing, in service to God and commitment to his prophetic ministry.

A Model for Disciples

It is clear from Paul's variations on the theme of Isaiah 50:8-9a in Romans 8:31-39 (compare especially Isaiah 50:9a with Romans 8:33-34) that he believed that the disciples of the servant could have the same confidence. Thus they can be free to follow God through any circumstances.

Psalter: Psalm 31:9-16

This is a psalm of lament or personal complaint. These psalms were used as a part of a liturgy when one was accused of a crime. When charges were brought and there was insufficient evidence to convict but not enough evidence to exonerate, the accused could only bring the case to the sanctuary and ask God to serve as judge and bring vindication. The psalm contains a word of salvation given by the priest to the supplicant assuring the supplicant that God will vindicate the innocent.

The choice of this psalm for Passion/Palm Sunday is especially appropriate, though the segmenting of it is not so apt. Verse 5 of the psalm is placed on Jesus' lips by Luke (23:46) as his last word from the cross. This is a calmer expression of confidence and trust than the single word from the cross, "Why have you forsaken me?" (Psalm 22:1, also a psalm of lament), preserved by Matthew (27:46) and Mark (15:34). Jesus' ability to commit himself into God's hands in the midst of a dreadful ordeal should help his disciples also to commit themselves to a faithful God in any adversity (see 1 Peter 2:213; 4:19).

The emphasis on disgrace and mocking, the element of conspiracy, the psalmist's description of himself as a horrifying spectacle, and the hope of God's vindication of the righteous one from all such human jeers and plots, are also singularly appropriate as a prayer for the Crucified. It is small wonder that the early church found in the Psalms many "prophecies" concerning Jesus and his passion.

Epistle: Philippians 2:5-11

Many scholars regard this passage, woven into this Espistle, as one of the earliest hymns of the church. Others maintain that Paul, who was certainly capable of using lofty, poetic prose (see Romans 11:33-36), authored this passage himself for this occasion. Either way, the meaning remains unchanged: Disciples are to reflect the mind and character of their master.

Honor and Emptying
The hymn presents a contrast between clinging to the honor that one might rightfully deserve and emptying oneself of all such claims for the sake of obedience to God. The one who had the ultimate claim to honor—equality with God by virtue of existing "in the form of God"—chose to set aside his claims and their legitimate enjoyment in order to serve God's will. Thus Christ voluntarily took on "the form of a slave" (verse 7), humbling himself in service to others even to the point of a cruel death by crucifixion (verse 8). The result, however, is even greater honor, as all beings, wherever they exist, would come to confess his honor and thus the nobility of his sacrificial example (verse 10).

Serve One Another
The hymn must be heard in connection with 2:1-4, where Paul called his friends in Philippi to set aside ambition and conceit and choose to serve one another and regard the other as completely worthy of this service. The pattern of Jesus is offered as grounds for this charge. If the one who was equal with God could give himself in loving compassion and service, how much more should we who follow him?!

By following Jesus' pattern, a church can achieve that unity of spirit and love that makes it strong to do God's work, and Jesus' pattern assures the disciples that honor is not lost but only increased in the end. The examples of Timothy (2:19-21), Epaphroditus (2:25, 29-30), and Paul himself (see last week's lection) provide further examples of how one can "have this mind" in oneself.

> **Think About It:** When has conceit or pride prevented you from manifesting the mind of Christ? When have you allowed Christ's mind to shape your actions and relationships?

Gospel: Luke 22:14–23:56

The Passion stories of the first three Gospels are read every year in a three-year rotation. We will examine this lengthy passage by considering some of Luke's distinctive features.

Who's First?

Luke places the disciples' dispute about who should have preeminence, and Jesus' response to this argument, within the celebration of the Last Supper rather than before the entry into Jerusalem (see Mark 9:33-35; 10:35-45). Mentioning this conversation on the very eve of the Crucifixion highlights all the more how foreign such disputes about rank and "pecking order" should be to the followers of the Crucified, the one who serves.

Satan

Satan is given an explicit role in this story, both with regard to Judas's betrayal and to Peter's denial (22:3-4, 31-34). This adds to the dimension of cosmic struggle that lurks in the background of the story of Jesus and that of the early church (see Ephesians 6:10-12; 1 Peter 5:8-9), reminding us that an expedient soft-pedaling of our commitment to Jesus might, in another realm, be a victory for God's enemy. We also see Jesus in his role as intercessor (22:31-32), loving Peter even as he foresees his denial and praying for his disciple's eventual empowerment.

Take Up Your Sword

Luke includes the strange episode of Jesus urging his disciples to acquire swords for the confrontation with the authorities, specifically in order that Isaiah 53:12 might be fulfilled in his arrest (22:35-38). All the Evangelists take great pains to link specific details of Jesus' life—and especially his passion—with the plan of God.

The Servant's Ear

Only in Luke does Jesus actually heal the ear of the high priest's servant, cut off by one of the more eager disciples (22:51), showing his compassion even while being arrested.

147

A Telling Glance

Luke includes the small but compelling detail that, after Peter's third denial, Jesus looked at Peter from across the courtyard (22:61), a meeting of the eyes that brought home to Peter his utter failure to live up to his brave words. How would such a look affect you?

The Weeping Women

On the road to Calvary, Jesus addressed the women weeping beside the road. Luke was especially aware of the calamitous siege of Jerusalem in A.D. 70, and 23:27-31 would be heard as another prediction of that event.

Last Words

All three words from the cross (23:34, 43, 46) are distinctive to Luke. The first two show that Jesus retained a supremely generous, noble spirit even in the agonies of crucifixion. The final cry before his death (Psalm 31:5 as replacement for Psalm 22:1; see Mark 15:34) seems to Luke more appropriate for the Son of God who voluntarily laid down his life. The words set the scene for viewing the Resurrection as Jesus' vindication.

> **Think About It:** One of the powerful aspects of this story is its broad array of characters. With whom do you most easily identify? Do you see yourself in the disciples' jockeying for top position? in a disciple's angry swordplay? in Peter's denial? in Pilate's passing the buck? in the mute, helpless bystanders? Of course, the primary character is Jesus. What do you learn about him as you encounter this story again? How does his death speak to your questions about your own death?

The Centurion

The centurion makes a rather more modest confession after witnessing Jesus' death, namely that "this man was innocent" or "just" (Luke 23:47; see Mark 15:39). Throughout Luke and Acts, Luke is at pains to show that there is no legal basis for opposition or persecution of Jesus or his followers.

Study Suggestions

A. Begin With Prayer

Begin by noting that today's lections are selected to relate specifically to the themes of Passion/Palm Sunday. Then invite the group to pray Psalm 31:9-16 responsively. Ask: How does this connect with Jesus' passion? Might he have prayed this psalm during that trying week? When have you felt this way? What weighs down your soul, and what help would you seek from God? Pray specifically for any concerns in the group, then read Psalm 31:19-24 together. Help the group relate the psalm to the day's theme, using the explanatory material on pages 145–46.

B. Consider the Servant

Invite someone to read aloud Isaiah 50:4-9a. Ask: Who is the speaker? What does the servant do? What challenges does he face? What resources does he have? Read or summarize the first four paragraphs of the commentary on pages 144–45. Discuss the "Think About It" questions. Ask: What is your pattern of listening to God? How does your life move out from those times of listening? How have you responded to opposition when seeking to be faithful? Now read the two paragraphs on "Jesus as the Servant." Ask: How does Jesus' example embolden us for faithful witness and service?

C. The Mind of Christ

Read aloud together Philippians 2:5-11. Explain that this likely was an early hymn or creed. Ask: What do his actual choices tell us about his character? How does Jesus' servanthood reveal to us the nature of God?

Look at Philippians 2:1-4; 4:2-3. Ask: What is Paul hoping the Christians in Philippi will do? What does he mean by the mind of Christ? Could there be a difference between being of the same mind and having the mind of Christ? How do we discern the mind of Christ in a given situation?

Now apply this to your congregation. Ask: When have you been more intent on getting your way or getting recognition than in looking out for the interests of others? When have you sought to discern and follow the mind of Christ? What obstacles do we face in trying to do this?

D. The Passion Story

Form eight buzz groups, and assign one of the eight paragraphs in the Gospel commentary (pages 147–48, beginning with "Who's First?") to each. Ask each group to read its section and the biblical references it mentions. Then have each group in turn present and discuss how its distinctive aspects of Luke's version add depth and texture to understanding what happened in the Passion. Summarize and synthesize your discussion of the Passion narrative by responding to the "Think About It" questions.

E. Tie It Together

The three main texts speak of willingness to endure difficulties out of one's trust and commitment to God and in hope of vindication. How does Christ's example assist us to steadfast allegiance?

F. Close With Song and Prayer

Sing "All Praise to Thee, for Thou, O King Divine," a hymn that paraphrases the Epistle lesson. Ask: What light has our discussion of the Passion Sunday lections thrown on our understanding of the events of Holy Week? How will this affect our participation in services this week? Pray together that these learnings will bear fruit in the days and weeks to come.

EASTER

Lections for Easter Day

First Lesson: Acts 10:34-43

*T*HIS sermon, placed on Peter's lips by the author of Acts, was delivered in the house of a Roman centurion named Cornelius. Along with his household, Cornelius was a "God-fearer," that is, a Gentile worshiper of the God of Israel. Although the opening sentence (10:34-35) is really the point of the passage, the lesson is chosen for Easter because it speaks of the death, Resurrection, and Resurrection appearances of Jesus in a compact way.

A Turning Point

Chapters 10–11 provide a critical turning point in Acts. Here Peter learns, and then confirms for the body of apostles, that God's plan for salvation extends beyond Israel to all the nations. According to Matthew 15:24, Jesus himself had "been sent only to the lost sheep of the house of Israel" and had sent his disciples to Jewish communities to preach the good news. He had traveled in Gentile territory (Mark 7:31), however. His encounters with the Syrophoenician woman (Mark 7:24-30) and the Samaritan woman at the well (John 4:7-42) suggest that he would honor faith wherever he found it.

Now that the church had grown throughout Judea, Samaria, and Galilee (see Acts 9:31), God was raising the sights of the fledgling Jesus movement. God initiated this new openness by instructing Cornelius to send to Joppa for Peter, thus preparing Peter for overturning old definitions of Gentiles as "unclean" through a divine act of cleansing (see 10:11-15, 28-29).

God Shows No Partiality

The sermon expresses what God's lack of partiality really meant. Jews had always confessed that God did not regard the face but the heart (see 1 Samuel 16:7). But they had not yet brought this insight into full conversation with the narrow, conflicting conviction that God had chosen the Jewish people and excluded the Gentiles.

Paul argued that God's impartiality meant that the Jew did not have a better claim on God's favor simply on account of being born a Jew (see Romans 2). Election of Israel, a frequent theme in Scripture, was not overthrown; rather, it was not permitted to be used as a claim to be "on the inside" with God and automatically included within God's favor. Several Jewish reform groups would have agreed with this part of the claim, including the Essene community at Qumran. But they would not have agreed with the implications drawn;

> **Think About It:** God's impartiality accepts everyone who trusts, honors, and lives a life pleasing to God. How would the early church react to this startling new dedication? Does the church today practice this kind of radical impartiality? What groups do we tend to exclude as the Jewish Christians of Peter's time did the Gentiles?

namely that the Gentiles were acceptable in God's sight simply on the basis of "fearing God and doing what is right" (Acts 10:35) and without being circumcised and becoming observant Jews.

The lection encapsulates several key Lucan themes: Jesus as "benefactor" (The specific verb for *doing good* is based on the same roots that go together to form the noun *benefactor*.), God's vindication of Jesus in the Resurrection (an act that gives the world God's perspective on Jesus; see 5:30-31), and the motif of "witnesses." (The disciples' acquaintance with Jesus before his resurrection is a critical element in their testimony afterward; see 1:21-22.)

Psalter: Psalm 118:1-2, 14-24

Originally a psalm in which the king celebrated victory over his enemies, this became one of the "Hallel Psalms"—those sung by pilgrims on the way to Jerusalem for one of the three annual festivals. It is exceptionally well suited to such a use, since it begins with the worshipers outside the city gates (verses 19-20) and concludes by sending them on to the altar (verses 26-27).

As a Hallel psalm, it was probably sung by Jesus and the crowds on the way to Jerusalem before the final Passover. Several of its verses figure prominently in Jesus' triumphal entry and his reflection on his own significance. (Compare verses 22-23 with Matthew 21:42-44, and verse 26a with Matthew 21:9 and 23:39.)

This psalm would continue to be an important resource for the early church as a means of making sense of the world's low esteem for the One whom they held in highest regard. It would also give them assurance that they, too, were held dear by God, even while the unbelieving society dishonored them (see 1 Peter 2:4-10).

Epistle: 1 Corinthians 15:19-26

This lesson is a fragment of Paul's refutation of the idea that there is no resurrection from the dead (15:12-34; also see the Epistle lections for the fifth through the eighth Sundays after the Epiphany), an idea that was being promoted within the Corinthian churches.

Rejection

Some Christians were rejecting the notion of a future resurrection for human beings, perhaps because the Greco-Roman ideal was immortality of the soul—liberation from the "prison" of the "body" rather than having the soul burdened with the body after death as it had been in life. There was a connection, however, between the devaluation of the mortal body (as something not intimately connected with our eternal state) and the ethical lapses that were so prominent in Corinth (a connection Paul himself made in 15:32b-34).

> **Think About It:** Paul contrasts the resurrection of the body with the Greco-Roman ideal of the immortality of the soul. How is resurrection different from immortality? Why has the church retained "resurrection of the body" in its creeds?

Paul refuted the thesis "there is no resurrection from the dead" by citing the precedent of Christ (15:12). Paul regarded the hundreds of witnesses to the risen Jesus (15:3-8) as the basic foundation of the gospel's proclamation. He went so far as to say that, if Christ were not raised from the dead, the whole company of apostles would be a bunch of liars and the Corinthians would still be mired in their sins (15:12-18).

First Corinthians 15:19 closes this section of the rebuttal this way: Seen from only its benefits for this life, the Christian faith makes people's this-worldly lot worse and even pitiable, especially for the missionaries who risk great danger to bring this message to others. It would be better to indulge in the pleasures of this world, however illusory, than to be the loser in both worlds (see 15:30-32).

Death, Thou Shalt Die . . .

The fact of Easter, however, shows that this sad scenario is far from true. The resurrection of Jesus provides the proof for the general resurrection of all who are in him. Paul saw a fitting correspondence between the fact that one man brought death to all (Adam) and now one man (Christ) brings life to all. A human society based on selfishness and greed from time immemorial, now, through Christ's resurrection, is offered the opportunity to live another way—a way of love and justice.

Paul then used agricultural imagery to connect the resurrection of Jesus as the first fruits with the resurrection of all as the full and final harvest (15:23). After Christ's triumph over every power (see Psalm 110:1, which lies behind

1 Corinthians 15:25), he restored all rule to God, at which point, to borrow John Donne's immortal words, "Death, Thou shalt die."

Gospel: John 20:1-18

The Gospel lesson has two scenes: the mystery of the empty tomb (20:1-10) and the resolution of this mystery in Jesus' first Resurrection appearance (20:11-18).

Scene One

The first scene shows that an empty tomb is not sufficient to give rise to Christian faith. It is too susceptible to misunderstanding. Here, Mary assumes, and Peter and John come to believe, that someone has removed Jesus' body. Grave-robbing was quite common in the ancient world, although usually the robbers were looking for jewelry and other adornments buried with the deceased. Malicious vandalism, however, might well have been on Mary's mind, since Jesus had just been exposed to public disgrace and execution.

Some commentators contend that the "beloved disciple" had already arrived at an Easter faith on the basis of seeing the empty tomb. While it is true that the verb *believe* is a highly loaded term, it is unlikely that it would already carry its full weight in 20:8, so soon after the Crucifixion. The disciple may merely have "believed" Mary's report about the grave robbery at this point.

Grasping the Truth of Resurrection

John 20:9 merits closer consideration, since it invites us into the early Christian reading of the Jewish Scriptures. It is not that the disciples at this point distrusted the prophecies that could be interpreted to speak of the resurrection of Jesus. Rather, they simply lacked any clear grasp of this aspect of Scripture's message at all. No Jewish group prior to the early church had seen in Scripture any suggestion of a crucified and resurrected messiah. It was only after their encounter with the risen Jesus that they could begin to read their Scriptures in this new light.

Having encountered God's resurrected and vindicated Messiah, they were able to see reflections of the Passion, death, and Resurrection of the Messiah wherever they looked in the Psalms and Prophets. (See Luke 24:44-47; Acts 2:24-36; 4:25-28 for examples.) We need

> **Think About It:** A new concept derived from experience. How have your faith understandings been influenced by fresh circumstances? When have previous assumptions been challenged by new experiences? Could God be at work in such encounters fostering new growth?

to bear in mind, however, that this was a wholly new messianic concept and one that derived solely from their experience of the risen Lord. The Hebrew Scriptures found a totally new interpretation in Christian experience (Luke 24:27).

Moreover, if we were to blame the non-Christian Jews of the time for failing to recognize Jesus as the Messiah foretold by their Scriptures, we would be guilty of a gross anachronism. Prior to Jesus' resurrection, such a belief simply did not exist.

Scene Two

In the second scene, we find Mary still looking for a corpse and unable to recognize Jesus at first. There are signs of progress, however, as two angels appeared, conspicuously at the two ends of the slab where Jesus' grave cloths had been laid out, hinting to the reader that God, not people, was behind the absence of the body (20:12). It is only when Jesus called her by name that she recognized him.

The command against touching or holding onto him (20:17) is an admonishment that Jesus' physical availability is fleeting. The Resurrection occurred not merely to restore a friend's physical presence but to inaugurate the return to God's heavenly presence and the beginning of a universal mission. Mary was thus not permitted to hold her friend, but was given instead a message to proclaim: "I have seen the Lord."

> **Think About It:** "I have seen the Lord." How have you encountered the living Jesus? How has this changed your life? your understanding of Scripture? your sense of purpose and mission?

Study Suggestions

A. Begin With Greeting and Song

Begin by reciting in unison Psalm 118:24. Then introduce to the group the early Christian greeting, whereby one person says, "Christ is risen," and the other responds, "He is risen indeed." Have members move about the room greeting one another in this fashion. Then reassemble and sing one of the group's favorite Easter hymns (or one not likely to be used in your worship service, such as "O Sons and Daughters, Let Us Sing").

B. Tell the Gospel Story

Read aloud John 20:1-18, asking two persons to read the voices of Jesus and Mary. Ask: What does Mary think happened to the body? Where does the text suggest that to you? Next, review the commentary on this passage (pages 155–56). Ask: What finally awakened an Easter faith in Mary? What do we mean by an "Easter faith"? How does this differ from other kinds of faith? What impact has this awakening had on your life and sense of mission?

C. Read Scripture Anew

Invite the group to read Psalm 118:1-2, 14-24 antiphonally (two halves of the group reading alternate verses). This will be an exercise in a post-Easter interpretation of the Old Testament. Ask: Who is the psalm talking about? Look especially at verses 22-23. Compare these with Matthew 21:42-44. Ask: Where do you see Jesus' story in this psalm? How would this psalm have been understood before Jesus' earthly ministry? Use thoughts from the commentary on page 153 to inform this discussion. Ask: What difference does your understanding of Jesus as Messiah make in your interpretation of passages such as this one?

D. Consider the Scope of Christ's Triumph

Read 1 Corinthians 15:12-26. Set the passage in its historical and literary context by reading or summarizing the commentary on pages 154–55. Ask: Why would the idea of resurrection from the dead be difficult for some Corinthians to accept? What, for Paul, was at stake in the affirmation of the resurrection of the body?

Discuss: What evidence does Paul offer of Jesus' resurrection? How real to you is the hope of the resurrection from the dead? How does it affect how you live life and face death?

E. Consider the Scope of God's Mission

Read Acts 10:34-43, and the review the commentary on pages 152-53. Ask: What is revolutionary about Peter's statement in 10:34-35? What are the implications of God's impartiality for Jewish doctrines of election? How do we as Christians seek to be inclusive of all persons?

Examine the message by asking: To whom would God have the message of repentance and of hope in the Resurrection preached? Discuss the "Think About It" questions having to do with contemporary groups we exclude and how the "God shows no partiality" statement addresses this. Ask: Whom do we exclude, functionally if not consciously? What barriers do we need to cross in order to manifest genuine acceptance and community? Unless congregations have plans and programs to be inclusive, how will greater inclusion be achieved?

F. Tie It Together

Resurrection . . . new life . . . rejoicing in God's steadfast love . . . new understandings of old words and truths . . . a fresh vision of inclusiveness . . . new understandings of old truths—these are the themes of today's Easter lections. Ask: How has our discussion today enhanced your appreciation of the significance of Jesus' resurrection? What new understandings of old truths have occurred to you? In what ways do you see new life bursting forth within and around you? How might God be calling you to participate? Close with a prayer of thanksgiving for the Resurrection.

Lections for Second Sunday of Easter

First Lesson: Acts 5:27-32

ONCE again the lectionary provides only a brief excerpt from a well-developed episode in Acts. Tension between the apostles and the Temple authorities had been increasing from the beginning of Acts. The authorities finally made their move, imprisoning the apostles. An angel (whether a supernatural power or a human accomplice we do not know) freed them from prison and sent them back to preaching. When the priests sent for the apostles, the prison was found empty; and the apostles were brought in again from the court. The high priest was amazed that his authority had been so openly flouted, but Peter spoke what our lesson from Revelation will also proclaim—it is God who demands our first and complete allegiance. If ever this conflicts with human authority, the person of faith must remain constant and be willing to endure the anger and persecution of worldly authorities.

Peter concluded by boldly proclaiming his message even to the Sanhedrin!

"This Man's Blood"

The high priest was concerned that the apostles sought to bring Jesus' blood on them (5:28). The priest was aware that, by decrying injustice and publicly exposing a legalized murder on trumped-up charges, the apostles were provoking unseen powers or the wrath of a fickle populace to bring retribution down on the guilty ones.

This is another motif shared by Acts and Revelation (see Revelation 6:9-11; 18:21-24). John would not be silent about Rome's violent,

> **Think About It:** The apostles understood that they must obey God rather than people. When have you been confronted with the choice between serving God's purpose and fulfilling human expectations? How did you respond? What were the results?

repressive bloodletting, all in the name of "peace," "order," and "national security." In his eschatological vision, John was sure that the martyrs and the angelic witnesses would continue to cry out until the blood of the dead was visited upon the guilty perpetrators.

Oppressive regimes depend on the silence and collusion of their frightened people and their apathetic neighbors. One remembers the horrifying situations of Nazi Germany, apartheid South Africa, East Timor, Sierra Leone, Guatemala, and Serbia. Silence is not, however, the way of the Jewish and Christian prophets. The same powers that protect themselves by killing dissidents will also try to silence the prophets. The call of God, however, is to speak up for spilled blood, to keep crying for justice.

> **Think About It:** The authorities feared that the apostolic "whistleblowers" would provoke judgment on them for their crimes perpetrated in the name of "peace, order, and security." What present-day perpetrators of human rights violation, labor abuses, and crimes against humanity might have the same fear? What is our responsibility as Christians to be "whistleblowers" in relation to such abuses?

Psalter: Psalm 150

The conclusion to the Psalter as a whole, this psalm calls upon every living creature to honor God in worship. While not explicated, the rationale for the invitation in verse 6 is provided by what was common knowledge in the ancient world: the affirmation that life itself was the gift of God (or the gods, in non-Israelite religions). Honoring God was thus a primary obligation of "everything that breathes" (verse 6).

God's mighty works, though not specified, and God's power (verse 2) are also named as grounds for worship. The psalm's inventory of musical instruments gives some insight into the constitution of the "praise band" employed in the Temple on festive occasions.

Epistle: Revelation 1:4-8

John of Patmos addressed the Book of Revelation to diverse congregations facing very different circumstances. Christians in Smyrna (2:8-9) and Philadelphia (3:7-11) suffered slander from non-Christian Jews, and the former might face imprisonment. One man had died for his faith in Pergamum (2:12-13). There were also churches, however, who were living quite comfortably and innocuously alongside the pagan society (Sardis and Laodicea; 3:1-5, 14-16) and tempted to participate in the larger culture with its idols (those in Pergamum and Thyatira who accept the Nicolaitans' message; 2:14-15, 18-28).

The persecution John foresaw was imminent. The picture he painted of enmity between empire and church was in fact part of his strategy for reinforcing the church's boundaries, for making it clear that there could be no compatibility between confessing Jesus' lordship and buying into Roman ideology and popular idolatry.

Christ as Judge

Revelation 1:4-8 establishes, first, the centrality of the coming of Christ in judgment of the world. First, John refers to God as the One "who is and who was, and who is to come" (1:4, 8) as a modification of the Greek designation of Zeus as "the one who is and who was and who is to come." The third phrase ("is to come") is changed from a statement about Zeus's ongoing existence to one about God's imminent coming to the world in judgment (see 14:6-7).

Verse 7 tells us that every eye will see Christ coming and introduces quotations from Daniel and Zechariah to expand this picture. John set before his hearers a vision of an awesome happening, when all the world would be held to account and when people would grieve at their rejection of this Messiah and their lack of preparedness for his coming.

This strong emphasis on the imminent coming of Christ is part of John's strategy for helping these congregations make faithful choices in their varied circumstances. He first set before them the crisis of God's judgment of the world through Christ and then called them so to weigh all their options and make their choices that they would not be found among those who wail on that day.

The Character and Work of Jesus

The second contribution of this lection concerns the character and work of Jesus. First, strong political claims are made about Jesus. He is named the ruler of secular kings: the latter would be made accountable to him. Christians are emboldened to resist the tyranny of a worldly ruler where yielding would compromise their commitment to the one God, knowing that the Christian and the tyrant would both stand before Christ to make answer.

Think About It: Revelation calls Chrisitans to live fully and faithfully in the light of Christ's coming. How real is that expectation to you? Visualize Christ coming as described in verse 7. How do you anticipate Christ's manifestation? What do you regret as you face him? What in your lifestyle and circumstances would make you sorrowful on that day? What words of praise would you utter?

Moreover, Jesus has fulfilled God's promise by bringing together a kingdom for God, people set apart for God as priests (consecrated for God's service; see Exodus 19:6; Isaiah 61:6; 1 Peter 2:5, 9). Christians are thus reminded that they do not belong to the secular order but are citizens of God's realm. John calls them throughout Revelation to manifest boldly their first allegiance in their daily lives.

Jesus is also their model. As the "faithful witness," he calls his followers to bear witness to the truth of God's reign and Rome's oppression rather than acquiesce to the fictions about the emperor as the channel of divine favor and Rome as the gods' instrument for peace and security.

Gospel: John 20:19-31

Prior to his passion, Jesus had told his disciples that he would be removed from them for a while.

A Hopeful Prediction

They would see him again, however (John 16:16-19); and their mourning would be turned into rejoicing (16:20-22). Jesus specifically told his friends ahead of time about his absence and restoration to them, so that, after the events transpired as Jesus predicted, their faith in him would be the stronger (14:28-29). In today's lection, we find these words of Jesus being fulfilled. Jesus had been taken from their sight by death; but now, on the evening of that first Easter Day, he appeared to the disciples.

No Phantom

The story suggests that a resurrected body is quite different from a merely resuscitated body. The doors were locked against the perceived threats to the disciples' well-being. (Since the priests had done away with the master, they would surely hunt down the followers in the inner circle.) But Jesus appeared in their midst with a blessing of peace (verse 19). This is not, however, because he was a phantom or a product of a collective hallucination. John leaves us in no doubt about the physicality of Jesus' resurrected body; it was not only visible but tangible (verse 20, 27). (It is instructive to read 1 Corinthians 15:35-49 on the "otherness" of the resurrection body.)

Holy Boldness

Seeing Jesus alive again began the process of turning these timid disciples into the fearless witnesses of the Resurrection that we encounter in Acts. The process would not be completed, however, until the Holy Spirit was poured out on them at Pentecost, an event that Jesus anticipated symbolically by breathing upon them (verse 22). The Spirit would not come, even in Johannine theology, until after Jesus' departure from the earthly sphere (see 15:26-27; 16:7, 12-15). Nevertheless, Jesus incorporated the Spirit symbolically into his commissioning of the disciples in verses 21-23. As Jesus was the "Sent One," so the disciples are now "sent ones," commissioned as he had been to bear witness to the light. Just as one's encounter with, and response to, Jesus meant either salvation or condemnation (3:17-21, 36), so now the encounter with the disciples will have the same potential (verse 23).

Thomas's Confession

Thomas had missed the first appearance of Jesus, and the testimony of his friends had not been enough to persuade him that Jesus was indeed alive again (verses 24-25). He would not believe just on their say-so, but demanded the same opportunity to see Jesus and especially to inspect his wounds.

> **Think About It:** Thomas moved from doubt to faith to witness. What doubts have you had about the faith claims of the Christian gospel? How have these been resolved? How is believing different than knowing something on the basis of observation?

Jesus appeared a week later to offer Thomas this opportunity. He urged the startled Thomas not to be distrustful (*doubting* is a weak translation) but to believe the truth (verses 26-27) and so be equipped for the work to which he was called as well. Without actually needing to touch Jesus, Thomas made the climactic confession of the gospel, acclaiming Jesus as "my Lord and my God" (20:28). In so doing, he accepted the truth of Jesus' claim to be one with the Father.

This confession had political overtones for the first readers of the Gospel, for at the end of the first century the emperor Domitian was frequently addressed as "our lord and god," according to the historian Suetonius. Hence, John was reminding his readers in this way that only One has the power over life, death, and life beyond death; and it is not Domitian. Thomas's story was thus an important conclusion to this Gospel, the aim of which was to inculcate and reinforce belief and trust in the hearts of the readers who were seen to stand among those blessed by Jesus' closing words of promise (verse 31).

Study Suggestions

A. Praise the Lord!

Open by reading Psalm 150 worshipfully together in unison. Then sing the hymn, "Praise to the Lord, the Almighty." Ask: What about God's character moves you to praise?

B. Encounter Jesus

Read aloud John 20:19-31, assigning the roles of Jesus, a group of disciples, Thomas, and a narrator. Ask: Why was it important for the disciples and Thomas to inspect Jesus' wounds? What would that prove?

Read John 16:16-22, and ask: How are Jesus' words there fulfilled in 20:19-23? How would the fact that John has Jesus predicting his death and resurrection affect the disciples' faith? Ask: What does Thomas's skepticism do for your faith? Explore the "Think About It" questions related to doubt as a bridge between the struggles of group members and the Gospel story.

C. Consider Your Loyalties

Read Acts 5:17-32, inviting people to read the parts of the angel, the Temple police, the messenger (5:25), Peter and the apostles, the high priest, and a narrator. Ask: What emboldened the apostles to disobey Judea's highest Jewish authority? Respond to the "Think About It" questions for more discussion and application.

Review the commentary on the Acts passage (pages 158–59). Bring in recent newspapers and magazines, and invite members to select headlines or stories about injustice in the social, business, political, and/or religious arenas. Ask: About whose spilled blood are we currently being silent? On what issues or for what oppressed group might we become "whistleblowers" out of our Christian, moral convictions?

D. Look to the Final Scene

Read Revelation 1:4-8, and reflect on what the passage says about Jesus and about Christian identity. Ask: What does it mean to be made a kingdom of priests for God? How might that affect our orientation to the world around us? How does the description of Jesus in verse 5 invite us to live out our identity as people of faith?

After reviewing the commentary on pages 159–61, ask: Why does John focus the churches on Christ's coming? Use the "Think About It" questions to help the group enter into John's vision, and let it interpret their lives. Ask: As you think about encountering Christ in judgment, what do you need to change in your life?

E. Tie It Together

The themes of trust in Jesus and of navigating life based on loyalty to him run throughout the readings from John, Acts, and Revelation. Discuss: How is faith described in each of these lections? What does each have to say about living out our faith in our setting? How can we be supportive of one another as we seek to be faithful?

F. Close With Worship

Sing "O Young and Fearless Prophet," pausing after each stanza to allow members to voice sentence prayers asking God to do for us what that stanza and today's lections call us to do. Send the group forth with the simple benediction, "Go in peace."

Lections for Third Sunday of Easter

First Lesson: Acts 9:1-6 (7-20)

*P*AUL entered the stage of Acts as an antagonist of the church, standing prominently on the scene of the stoning of Stephen, initiating a persecution of Jewish Christians in Jerusalem, and finally requesting official authorization to root out the Christian movement in Damascus, the chief city of Syria. Indeed, this accords very well with Paul's own recollection of his earlier life. (Compare Galatians 1:11-24 with Acts 8:1-3; 9:1-6.)

Many Jews had both an Aramaic name and a Greek or Roman name, the latter being an accommodation to the dominant culture. Thus the same person was known as Saul (going by his Hebrew name, *Shaul*) and Paul (going by his Roman name, *Paulus*).

A Man of Zeal

Saul was not, however, an otherwise accommodating person. His zeal for Torah was so consuming, so absolute, that he felt himself compelled to apply pressure by any means necessary upon his fellow Jews whom he regarded to be in danger of violating that covenant (see Philippians 3:6). Proclaiming as God's Messiah a man condemned by the Temple leadership for misleading the people was, to him, a clear and present danger and a serious offense.

Jesus might well have been seen by Paul as a sabbath-breaker, a flagrant violator of purity and dietary laws, and an opponent of the Temple and established leadership. Those who followed him were also likely to be multiplying transgressions within Israel, creating a public disturbance, and endangering the people with a visitation of God's wrath.

A New Orientation

In spite of his zeal, however, when encountered by the risen Christ, Saul learned in a single, shattering moment how completely wrong was his grasp

164

of God's priorities and plan. In his most ardent, zealous attempts to reinforce Torah-observance and the authority of the Temple hierarchy, Saul suddenly found himself to be God's enemy.

The scene in Chapter 9 develops providentially, with God preparing both Ananias and Saul for their mutual encounter, showing the reader how important a step this was in the unfolding plan of God. Drastically disrupting the direction of Saul's life, God had set him apart to take the good news of the year of God's favor to non-Jews throughout the Roman Empire.

Ananias had to shift his prejudices and priorities as well. He was justifiably confused and nervous about having any dealings with a man whose persecutions were well-known. Thus, Saul was not the only one making a huge attitude adjustment, as Ananias was led by God to become his bridge to a relationship with the disciples and future ministry in the Christian movement.

As Paul looked back on these experiences (see his firsthand account in Galatians 1:13-24), he acknowledged his commission as well. He understood from that experience that the walls of Torah he sought to preserve around Israel were to be smashed as Jew and Gentile came together in Christ to worship the one God and serve the same Savior.

> **Think About It:** The lives of both Saul and Ananias were radically changed. When has an encounter with God shown you the inadequacies of your concept of God and the mistaken direction of your life? How did that encounter help you grow both in your understanding of God and in your commission to serve God?

Psalter: Psalm 30

This is a psalm of thanksgiving, extolling God for a specific act of deliverance (verses 1-5), a recollection of distress and a cry for help (6-10), a return to confessing God's response to that cry (11-12a), and a final promise of ongoing gratitude (12b). The theme of the psalm is God's dramatic reversal of the dire circumstances that had distressed the psalmist, such that, metaphorically speaking, the psalmist has been restored from death to life. Many psalms use the image of being trapped by death's grip then freed by God, as a metaphor for deliverance. This made it possible for the early church to look back on these psalms and see intimations of Jesus' resurrection as the hope of resurrection for all.

The psalm's superscription suggests that it was used at the feast of dedication (Hanukkah). Though originally an individual thanksgiving, it does resonate well with the national reversal experienced in 175–164 B.C. In the midst of prosperity, the Jerusalem leadership attempted to abrogate the claims of Torah and become a Greek city. God's favor turned to wrath for several years, bringing on harsh oppression by the Syrian king. With the resurgence of zeal for Torah and the military successes of the Maccabean revolt, however, there was a deep sense that God's favor had returned to Judah as her national fortunes were turned around.

Epistle: Revelation 5:11-14

This lection presents the climax of John of Patmos's depiction of the heavenly scene of the adoration of God and of the Lamb.

The Heavenly Host

In Chapter 4, John painted a picture of concentric circles of beings (the four cherubim, the seven angels of the Presence, the twenty-four angelic elders) surrounding God's throne and offering honor for God's creation and cosmic rule. In Chapter 5, he introduces the Lamb, the heavenly representation of Christ, with the singular distinction of being the only being "worthy" to take the scroll from God's hand and open it. It is thus Jesus who is singled out as the master of the unfolding judgment, whose unique authority over the end sets him above all earthly kings and rulers (see 6:12-17).

Behold the Lamb

The heavenly liturgy continues with an acclamation of the Lamb, whose source of honor or worthiness is his ransoming of a people for God, to be God's own kingdom (5:9-10, recalling 1:5-6 and Exodus 19:6). The phrase "from every tribe and language and people and nation" will recur throughout Revelation and shows the Lamb and the beast, Christ and the emperor, to be in competition for sovereignty and for people's loyalties (see 13:6-8; 14:6-7).

In that time, especially in Asia Minor, loyalty was expressed through worship, including the cult of the Roman emperors. The scene concludes as numberless angelic armies are joined by all creation in acclaiming God and the Lamb (5:13-14).

Petty Idolatries

> **Think About It:** Christians focused on the true center of cosmic worship. Around what center does your life revolve? How do these words remind you of the preface that is said before singing or saying the Sanctus in the liturgy of Holy Communion?

This scene of majestic, orderly worship, all focused on the true center of the universe, sets up a contrast with all the little, idolatrous centers of worship encountered throughout Revelation (see 9:20-21; 13:11-18; 14:9-11). In painting this picture, John constructs a very different interpretation of life in Asia Minor. Now Christians could look at the majority population, who worshiped idols and the emperor, as in fact the deviant minority. The vision affirmed their own commitment to worship only God and the Lamb. They could see that they were the real center of cosmic worship and that the Christians were in line with the divine order as they worshiped God and avoided idols.

Gospel: John 21:1-19

It is very likely that John's Gospel originally ended at 20:31, with this story about a Resurrection appearance being added after the death of the beloved disciple.

Epilogue

The authenticity of the story is not called into question, however. Just like the story of the woman caught in the act of adultery (John 7:53–8:11), there were many free-floating pieces of apostolic tradition used in the teaching and edification of the church. Some of these were eventually worked into John's Gospel so that they would not be lost but would remain a permanent part of the Fourth Evangelist's testimony.

An Amazing Fish Story

This Resurrection appearance takes place in Galilee (see the expectation of Mark 16:7), near the location of the feeding of the five thousand (John 6:1), another meal of bread and fish surrounded by mystery. The first scene (21:4-8) is typically read as a moral tale. The message is that fishing (perhaps as a symbol for missionary work) on one's own is fruitless, whereas fishing as Jesus directs yields bountiful results (see John 15:5). The number of the fish, and the fact that the nets were not broken, are also read symbolically as indications of the success that the Christian mission would have, and the capacity of the church to contain all who entered.

Such a reading is worth contemplating, but one should also bear in mind the main point of the story. It is a sign that points to the identity of the doer. (This identity is a little murky so early in the morning and in a resurrected state, as in 20:13-15). The beloved disciple was the first to comprehend the sign: "It is the Lord."

A Sustaining and Restoring Meal

Landing their boats with their huge catch, the disciples found that Jesus already had bread and fish on the fire. As in the feeding of the five thousand, Jesus' ability to provide sustenance for his disciples was again demonstrated through the narrative. This meal became an occasion for Jesus to restore Peter. There is a significant parallel between the threefold confession of love and the earlier threefold denial of fellowship (see 18:15-18, 25-27). The detail of a charcoal fire is also common to both, helping the reader link the scenes by smell as well as literary pattern.

167

Peter Is Recommissioned

This almost ritual reenactment of the earlier failure, giving Peter the opportunity of a "repeat" in the context of his Lord's forgiveness, was aimed at recommissioning Peter for the task he was to perform for Jesus. Peter was to look after Jesus' flock (a prominent image for the church in John; see 10:1-18), to nurture them with teaching and pastoral oversight. He would also have the opportunity in his old age to live up to the boast he had made in his prime (see 13:36-38), accepting a martyr's death with courage (21:18-19). According to tradition, he insisted on being crucified head down because he was not worthy to die in the same manner as his Lord.

> **Think About It:** Jesus is a Lord of second chances. When have you failed to live out your Christian commitment as you would have wished? What does Peter's restoration tell you about the possibility of restoration for you?

The second half of this reading very much shows us a Lord of second chances, who patiently and skillfully restores the fallen and provides new opportunities for them for both fruitful service and living up to their own best intentions. Simon Peter was invited not once, but three times, to confess his love of Jesus and to nurture the faithful ("feed the sheep"); a task that he took on with great vigor. The Book of Acts portrays a more mature Peter, preaching, leading, defying authorities for the sake of God, even going to the Gentiles. The third-century *Acts of Peter*, in fact, shows Peter using the memory of his own denial and restoration to encourage lapsed Christians to return to the fold.

Study Suggestions

A. Begin With Prayer

Invite the group to reflect briefly on a time of need when they persisted in prayer and found resolution. Explain that this was the experience of the writer of today's psalm. Then read Psalm 30 responsively. Ask if there are concerns today, and pray for each other and for the guidance of the Spirit in today's study and discussion.

B. Center on the Lamb

Play a recording of "Worthy Is the Lamb" and the "Amen" chorus from Handel's *Messiah*. Help the group visualize the whole picture of heavenly worship in Revelation 4:2-11; 5:8-14; and ask them to hold this image in their minds as they hear the music.

Read aloud Revelation 5:11-14. Set it in context by summarizing the commentary on pages 166–67. Ask: How would this vision lead the early Christians to interpret the involvement of their neighbors in worshiping the emperor and the Roman gods? How would it help them feel like less of a minority? How would it strengthen them to withstand the pressure to conform to an idolatrous culture? To personalize this vision, discuss the "Think About It" questions.

Read Revelation 5:1-10. Jesus enjoys a singular distinction, an awesome authority. Ask: What is different about Jesus' "rise to power" compared to the careers of most temporal leaders? What does Jesus' ultimate authority mean for our lives under political and business leaders? How do we respond when the expectations of these secular authorities (such as to fight in an unjust war, to falsify accounts, to advertise unhealthy products, or to put winning above sportsmanship) conflict with what Jesus would have us do? Where can we gain the strength and courage to resist these pressures?

C. Have Breakfast With Jesus

Review the commentary on the Gospel lection (pages 167–68), then read John 21:1-19, assigning readers for the roles of narrator, Peter, the beloved disciple, the disciples as a group, and Jesus. Then ask: What details in this story are reminiscent of other stories in John? Since Jesus did not need the disciples to catch fish for their breakfast, what are other possible meanings of this story of the miraculous catch of fish? Why was it important for Peter to have Jesus ask him if he loved him (verses 15-17)? Consider the personal implications of this event by discussing the "Think About It" questions.

D. Turn From Misguided Zeal

Read Acts 9:1-20, then have volunteers present the event in three brief scenes: Saul's encounters with the risen Jesus (verses 1-9), with Ananias (verses 10-19a), and with the Christians in Damascus (verses 19b-25). Ask: What do you think really happened on the Damascus road? How do you account for such a sudden, drastic change in Paul? Why did this encounter change his mind about the new Jewish sect he had been opposing? What other ways does God use to guide us?

Now read Paul's own testimony in Galatians 1:13-24 and 1 Corinthians 15:8-10. Ask: How did Paul understand the revelation he had? What did that event teach him about God's grace? Use the "Think About It" questions to relate Paul's experience to that of group members.

E. Get Back on the Horse

The readings from John and Acts speak of two men who disappointed God for a time: Peter by denying Jesus and Saul by persecuting Christians. Ask: Do you identify with either of them? Why? Both were later commissioned to play a central role in expanding and strengthening the church. Ask: How have you been restored by God after a failure or misguided venture? How can we support and hold one another accountable to fulfilling God's purpose? How can the lections from Revelation and Psalms assist us to fulfill our commission faithfully?

F. Close With Worship

Sing or read the hymn, "See the Morning Sun Ascending" (based on Revelation 5:11-14). Pray for forgiveness for times we have disappointed God and for strength to be faithful to the end.

Lections for Fourth Sunday of Easter

First Lesson: Acts 9:36-43

*T*HE Book of Acts is the only book of the New Testament that contains stories of the early church. It signifies that the church, the body of Christ, is a continuation of the Incarnation—the embodiment of the redeeming love of God for the salvation of the world.

A Story of Good News

The opening words of Acts indicate that it is a companion book to the Gospel of Luke. Although neither book actually identifies its author, both books are traditionally attributed to Luke, the physician who was Paul's traveling companion. This anonymous author of Luke/Acts, a well-educated Gentile Christian, was familiar with the Jewish Scriptures translated into Greek and called the Septuagint. He most likely intended his two-part story to be read as a continuation of the Old Testament story. His Gospel offered more good news about God's generous gift of salvation through Jesus. His Acts of the Apostles narrated the exciting story of the spread of that good news to the world beyond Jerusalem and even beyond Palestine.

In the first part of Chapter 9, Luke describes Paul's conversion and prophetic ministry north of Jerusalem in Damascus and Tarsus (9:1-30). In today's lection, Luke tells a parallel story of Peter's prophetic ministry to the northwest of Jerusalem toward the Mediterranean coast. Both stories document the early spread of Christianity.

Peter's Ministry

In his travels, Peter first healed a bedridden man in Lydda (9:32-35), which caused many residents of Lydda (and the fertile seacoast plain of Sharon on which Lydda was situated) to believe in Jesus. Peter then traveled to Joppa, an important harbor in ancient Palestine (today a suburb of Tel Aviv), where a disciple named Tabitha (Greek: *Dorcas*; English: *gazelle*) had just died (9:37). Tabitha, who was known for her generous acts of charity, had been washed and laid out in an upstairs room where the widows were mourning her, as was the ancient custom. The widows showed Peter tunics and other clothes she had made (9:39). Making and distributing clothes to the needy was one of the special tasks assigned to widows in the early church. Peter sent them away, then prayed beside her, and said "Tabitha, get up" (9:40). She opened her eyes and sat up. When they saw her alive, many in Joppa also believed in Christ.

Significance of Peter's Acts

These two stories of Peter's ministry are significant in four ways. First, both of Peter's acts testify to the continuing work of Jesus through the apostles. Peter's power is evident in the fact that people "turned to the Lord" (Jesus). Conversion takes place through "acts" of the apostles rather than by words. The "acts" of God are part and parcel of the mission of the church. Second, these stories are similar to Old Testament stories of Elijah raising the widow's son (1 Kings 17:17-24) and Elisha raising the Shunammite woman's son (2 Kings 4:18-37). Luke firmly connects Peter to Jewish sacred history in order to indicate the authenticity of Jesus' ministry.

Third, these two stories are unusual in that Luke lifts up real people with names and particular situations. Finally, through these stories of the spread of the gospel, Luke prepares his readers for the story of Cornelius, who sends for Peter in Joppa (10:1–11:18). Cornelius becomes the first Gentile to be converted to the Christian "way" by the "acts" of God and an apostle.

> *Think About It:* Many in Lydda and Joppa believed in Christ because of the healing "acts" of Peter. What is it that Christian leaders do or say today that causes (or helps) us to believe more firmly in Christ? How do you assess the relative importance of deeds and words in leading persons to faith in Christ?

Psalter: Psalm 23

This familiar psalm is usually read at funerals, and it certainly is an appropriate word of comfort in the midst of death. However, Psalm 23 is more about living than about dying. In the ancient world, kings were often portrayed as good shepherds or hosts to their people; but the psalmist here declares that *God* is his shepherd. God provides "green pastures" (food), "still waters" (drink), "right paths" (shelter and protection from danger). God "restores his soul" (keeps him alive). God is also a good host, providing food, drink, and shelter for guests just as the shepherd does for the sheep. The psalmist proclaims loyalty to God and an intention to live within God's reign.

Verse 4 (which connects the shepherd and host images) and verse 6 provide the theological content of this psalm. God is with us. God actively pursues us. God provides our ultimate sustenance, protection, and security. If we place our trust in God, we will dwell in God's house. We ordinarily hear this psalm in very personal terms. Yet it has a strong communal dimension: God's household includes us all, perhaps even our enemies!

Epistle: Revelation 7:9-17

Revelation is an apocalyptic account of John's vision of heaven and God's plan of judgment for the world, which sharply distinguishes between the present evil time and a future blessed age. Conflict between a righteous minority and a wicked majority is identified as a clash between God and Satan. God would decisively intervene in history to vindicate God's people, punish their persecutors, and usher in a "new heaven and a new earth."

A Continuing Vision

John's revelation began with a vision of the Son of Man (Chapter 1; see Second Sunday of Easter), who gave him messages to seven churches. It continued with a vision of the slaughtered Lamb who is worthy to open the scroll sealed with seven seals (5:1-14; see Third Sunday of Easter). The Lamb opened the first four seals and unleashed the four horsemen who would bring war, famine, and death to the world. When the fifth seal was opened, John saw the souls of those who had been martyred for their faithfulness. They cried out for God's vengeance but were given white robes and told to wait (6:1-11).

Think About It: In John's vision he saw a multitude who had come through a great ordeal and had "washed their robes." What do you think this means? accepted Christ as savior and Lord? cleansed through baptism? purified through faithful witness, suffering, martyrdm? resisted the temptation to deny their faith or conform to the secular culture? How do you "wash your robe" as an expression of your faith? What discrimination have you faced because of it?

The Sealed and the Multitude

In Revelation 7 John heard that 144,000 persons from the twelve tribes of Israel would be marked with God's seal to protect them from the coming torment of the locusts (see 9:4). These were men who had not "defiled themselves with women" (14:1-5), which was John's way of saying that they were pure enough to fight with God in a holy war against the power of evil.

Then John saw a multitude who had come through a time of suffering that would inaugurate the messianic age. These could refer to a group faithful in their martyrdom but not a part of the "sealed" 144,000, who had been persecuted by the dominant culture (called the beast or Babylon). The multitude had "washed [their] robes" and now worshiped before God (7:14). They were seen by the world as troublemakers because they challenged the dominant violent and oppressive culture.

Refusing to conform, they offered an alternate way of manifesting God's love, peace, and inclusion. Whitening one's robes means being prepared (as Jesus was) to face rejection and death for the sake of faithful witness to God's word and grace. God will shelter this multitude and bless them in the age to come (7:15-17). But without the seal, they apparently are not protected as are the 144,000 martyrs.

Gospel: John 10:22-30

This passage is part of the closing of the second cycle of Jesus' public ministry as told by John (6:1–10:42). Jesus engaged for the last time with "the Jews" (the religious establishment in Jerusalem) who had been constantly challenging him.

John wrote during the latter part of the first century (A.D. 85–100) after the destruction of the Temple in Jerusalem and during a time when early Jewish Christians were being persecuted as a religious minority. Some were being expelled from synagogues because of their faith in Jesus. Thus, John's first readers were extremely interested in what he had to say about Jesus and the Jewish authorities.

Who Are You?

The Jewish authorities pressed Jesus: "How long will you keep us in suspense? If you are the messiah, tell us plainly" (10:24). The ancient Greek contains a difficult idiom. In modern Greek it means, "How long will you continue to *annoy* us?" Thus, some scholars believe that the question reflected irritation and hostility rather than suspense and a genuine desire to know the identity of Jesus.

My Works Testify to Me

The Jewish authorities wanted Jesus to tell them plainly who he was. Jesus' response serves as John's theological conclusion about Jesus' public ministry. Jesus responded to the authorities: "I have told you, and you do not believe. The works that I do in my Father's name testify to me" (10:25-26). While Jesus' "works" include the signs, they are not restricted to these. John is clear that Jesus' ministry was to do *all* the works that revealed who God is.

My Sheep Know Me

Jesus also responded to the authorities that they did not believe because they did not belong to his sheep—that is, his followers, whom he knows personally, who hear and believe in him, whom God has drawn to him, who will be kept faithful, and who will live with him eternally (10:27-29). This is a summary statement of John's paradox between *faith* and *election*. One who believes belongs to those who hear Jesus' voice; they receive eternal life. But a person will not hear Jesus' voice unless that person is "elected" by God to believe. The authorities, said John, do not know Jesus because they are not among the elected believers whom God has given to Jesus.

> **Think About It:** John says that God elects some people to believe in Jesus and not others. Do you believe that God chooses some and denies others an opportunity to believe? Why or why not? Have you been elected to believe, or is this a choice you have made?

The Greek in verse 29a is ambiguous. The NRSV translation suggests that the believing *community* is "greater than all else." The NIV translates it that *God* who has given the sheep (the believing community) to Jesus is the greatest. Both meanings are possible; but in light of verses 29b and 30, an emphasis on the greatness of God is more likely.

God and I Are One

Jesus concludes that the Father and he "are one." This is not a reference to the Trinitarian doctrine of God. That concept emerged out of a Christological controversy between the second and fourth centuries. Rather, Jesus makes a plain response to the authorities' request. He summarizes: the Son and the Father are united in the *work* they do. Works is a consistent theme in John, though the authorities had trouble believing what they heard and saw (10:25-26, 31-33, 38). God judges, and Jesus judges; God gives life, and Jesus gives life. Jesus' response indicates that the *works* of the Father and the *works* of the Son are one and the same.

Study Suggestions

A. Sing a Psalm

Look in the Scripture index of your hymnal to identify a hymn based on Psalm 23 ("The Lord's My Shepherd, I'll Not Want" or "The King of Love My Shepherd Is," for example). Sing or read the hymn, then discuss: What does the text say about our relationship with God? (If we trust God, God will provide; we are like children at home with God.) Why is it a radical notion today to give one's loyalty to God and to believe that God will provide? (Could it be that it is because we are so focused on our own self-sufficiency?) Is it realistic to live this way? What does it mean that God prepares a table in the midst of our enemies? (See commentary on pages 171–72.) Do you think this psalm is primarily meant to be personal or communal? Might God's household include your enemies? Why or why not?

B. Examine John's Claims

Read John 10:22-30 aloud. Ask: Why do Jesus' sheep know him and believe but the Jewish authorities do not? Review the explanation on pages 173–74. Discuss the paradox of faith and election in this passage, as posed by the questions in the "Think About It" box. Invite members to share their perceptions of their own experience of coming to belief, in terms of whether it has been their choice or God's.

Ask: What does Jesus mean that he and the Father "are one?" How do you understand Jesus' statement that he and the Father are one? Relate this to John 3:16.

C. Share Good News

Read Acts 9:36-43, and review the commentary on pages 170-71. Discuss: How did Peter spread the gospel? How did people respond? Why was Peter's ministry important? How do his "healing works" relate to Jesus' works and to the "good news"?

Involve the group in writing a summary of the good news of the gospel. Discuss: Which is more important in sharing this with others, words or deeds? Which is more effective? Can one stand on its own without the other?

D. Revelation

Read Revelation 7:9-17, and review the commentary on pages 172–73. Ask: Who is "the multitude" in John's vision? What was their "ordeal"? What are they doing now? What does whitening or "washing their robes" mean? Also discuss the "Think About It" questions.

E. Connecting Images

Who is the shepherd in Psalm 23? Who is the "Good Shepherd"? (See John 10:1-21.) Why does Revelation emphasize "the Lamb" instead of the shepherd? (It reflects the crucified and risen Jesus.) What are the Gospel of John and Revelation saying about "sheep" (John 10:26)? "other sheep" (John 10:16)? the "sealed" (Revelation 7:3-8)? "the multitude" (Revelation 7:9, 14b)? (Possibility: Together they make up the larger household of God's faithful from every tribe, nation, and religion.)

F. Close With Song and Prayer

Sing "He Leadeth Me: O Blessed Thought" or "Savior, Like a Shepherd Lead Us." Pray for faith and trust in God. Pray for courage to "whiten our robes" in the midst of our modern church and society, which are sometimes unjust, prejudicial, and violent. Pray for God's household of the faithful wherever they are undergoing persecution.

Lections for Fifth Sunday of Easter

*I*N Acts 10–11, Luke introduces Cornelius as a pious Gentile centurion

First Lesson: Acts 11:1-18

who had a vision from God telling him to send for Peter who could offer a message that would save him and his whole household. (The first part of this story was told in the lection for Easter Day.)

Call No One Profane

Peter was also having a vision. A large sheet full of all kinds of creatures, reptiles, and birds was lowered from heaven. A voice said, "Eat"; but Peter said to the Lord that he had never eaten anything that was "profane or unclean." The voice persisted, "What God has made clean, you must not call profane" (Acts 10:14-16). As Peter puzzled over this vision, Cornelius's messengers arrived. Peter went to see Cornelius and his family and close friends. Peter related to Cornelius that, while Jewish law forbade him from associating with Gentiles, he had just received a new insight from God that such distinctions were no longer valid (10:28).

Peter was here exaggerating a bit. Jewish law did not prohibit all interaction with Gentiles; and, on a practical level, Galilee was essentially Gentile territory. As Jews had been exiled and fled persecution throughout the Greco-Roman world, no doubt they had extensive contact with Gentiles. But the point was still dramatic—a new day was dawning in which Jews and Gentiles would become one in a common faith and mission!

Preach an Inclusive Gospel

Peter then shared the good news with all who were gathered: God shows no partiality but accepts anyone in any place who honors God and does what is right. God sent Jesus to proclaim reconciliation to a limited audience—the people of Israel—but now, through Peter, God is saying that *all* who believe

176

in Jesus can be forgiven (10:34-43). While Peter was speaking, the Holy Spirit fell on those who heard the word, and they began uttering ecstatic speech. This astounded the circumcised (Jewish) believers who had accompanied Peter. Peter concluded that they could no longer refuse to baptize Gentiles, since they could receive the gift of the Holy Spirit just as the apostles had at Pentecost.

Peter did an unheard of thing! He socialized with "unclean" or "profane" people (Gentiles). He ate with them. He baptized them in the name of Christ! The "circumcised believers" in Jerusalem (who had given sanctions for other Gentile contact; see 8:14) questioned Peter: Why did you do this? Peter explained and then reminded them of the promise that Jesus would baptize with the Holy Spirit (see Luke 3:16). Peter concluded that God had given to Gentiles the repentance that leads to life (11:18). The early church ultimately concluded (at the Council of Jerusalem, Acts 15) that Gentiles did not need to be circumcised as Jews to become Christian, even though they needed to observe the moral laws.

> *Think About It:* As a faithful Jew Peter assumed he should not associate with people considered "unclean," "impure," or "uncircumcised." How do we as Christians sometimes avoid or reject people who do not fit our understanding of who is faithful or acceptable? What insight does this sory give us? What groups do we exclude? How do we rationalize this? Who are the Peters of our day through whom God may be calling us to become more accepting?

The irony of this story is that today Christianity is a Gentile religion. The excluded minority has become a dominant majority. And the tragedy is that we Christians often discriminate not only against Jews but also against many others who do not fit our understanding of who is acceptable. Christians often ignore this story's message that *all* whom God has created are acceptable to God; *all* are eligible to receive God's grace and to be embraced as God's children.

Psalter: Psalm 148

The last five psalms (146–150) are hymns of praise. They summarize much of the message of the Psalms: Trust God, not mortals; God is a God of justice for the oppressed; God acts through creation; God also acts in history to deliver God's people; praise God.

As one of these five psalms, Psalm 148 calls on creation to praise God. First, the heavens are invited to praise God's "name" (God's essential character and purpose as revealed in God's creative actions). Then, the earth (world of nature) is invited to praise God, followed by praise from humankind. In inviting humanity to praise God, the psalmist emphasizes that even those whom people consider sovereign (kings, princes, rulers) are to recognize God's ultimate sovereignty. The psalm concludes by noting that God's divine purpose is being fulfilled specifically through God's people. God has "raised up a horn" (protected or strengthened) the people, who are summoned to offer their praises to God.

The list of beings, objects, and elements on earth that are to praise God is reminiscent of the story of God creating earth and giving humanity "dominion" over it (Genesis 1). But this psalm challenges us to understand *dominion* not only as "stewards of" creation but also as "partners with" creation. Francis of Assisi, who called the sun, wind, and fire his brother, the moon and waters his sister, and the earth his mother, understood that we are called to exercise dominion in a God-ordained way—as a servant and partner!

Epistle: Revelation 21:1-6

Most of Revelation is concerned with John's vision of God's plan for judgment of the earth. However, in Chapter 21, the vision turns to what will happen *after* God's judgment.

John is shown a "new heaven and a new earth." This vision would not have been amazing to first-century Jewish Christians, for it echoes the final chapters of Isaiah (see Isaiah 65:17 and 66:22). Five hundred to six hundred years before John wrote, Third Isaiah described a new heaven and earth related to the return of the exiled Judahites from Babylon to Jerusalem. For John, the new heaven and earth would come from God after a last judgment of earth. First-century Christians generally believed this would happen soon, perhaps even in their lifetime.

A New Heaven

Revelation, written in the late first century, assumes a three-deck universe: heavens, firmament (a firmament separating the heavens from earth), earth, and a region below. God presided on a throne in a majestic chamber in the heavens (see Revelation 4). These assumptions make John's vision quite radical! God would move from the heavenly throne to dwell among mortals (21:3). Some Christians refer to this as "God's kingdom on earth." Others prefer to replace this hierarchical ruler image with "God's "kingdom" on earth," implying a relational commonwealth. Either way, the image is one of God "tabernacling" or dwelling with all peoples on earth.

> **Think About It:** Revelation predicts massive destruction and death before God's new earth arrives for the faithful. What is your vision of God's "commonwealth on earth"? How do you think it will arrive?

178

A New Earth Promise

The New Testament is full of images of a godly commonwealth. Jesus ushered it in, but it is not yet complete. It is the "already-here, not-yet-fully come" new earth of God. When God dwells with the people in the new earth, sadness, pain, injustice, and death will cease. The thirsty (needy) will drink (benefit) from the water (grace-filled sustenance) of life (21:4, 6b). Peace, justice and love will reign.

The One seated on the throne of heaven—the Alpha and Omega, the beginning and the end—says: "See, I am making all things new" (21:5a). Yet, lest we forget, John's vision of a new earth (embodying God's grace and peace) comes only after horrible destruction (God's judgment).

Gospel: John 13:31-35

Prior to Chapter 13, John leads readers to anticipate Jesus' "hour" (his crucifixion, resurrection, and ascension; see John 2:4; 7:30; 8:20). In John 13, John signals that Jesus' hour had arrived. During a final meal with his followers, Jesus instructed his followers about the meaning of being disciples. He washed their feet, symbolically embodying what it means to be in relationship with him and modeling the life of servanthood. He instructed them directly: they are to imitate him in communal service.

Mutual Glorification

In our passage, John uses the verb "to glorify," shifting from past to present to future tense and causing some confusion as we try to interpret. However, if we remember what John believed, the purpose of shifting verb tenses becomes clear. John believed that the mutual glorification of the Father and the Son *began* in the past with the Incarnation (see John 1:14) and that it *continued* in Jesus' words and works during the course of his life (see John 2:11; 7:18; 8:54; 11:4). John also believed that this mutual glorification of the Father and of the Son was *only fully revealed* in Jesus' death, resurrection, and ascension (see John 17:1). Thus, in our passage, John underscores that the mutual glorification was a reality-in-progress *even as* Jesus spoke to his disciples during their final meal.

Called to Love

Having reminded his disciples that he came from God and would return to God where they could not immediately follow, Jesus gave them a new commandment: Love one another, as I have loved you, so that everyone will know that you are my disciples.

In the Gospel of John, this is the only explicit commandment that Jesus gave—and he gave it not to the multitudes but to his followers. The command was not a surprise. Jewish Christians would recognize in the Torah the

Think About It: Rather than "giving up" his life on the cross, Jesus "gave away" his life out of the fullness of his love and commitment. What do you make of this distinction? What do you believe about the cross? Do you live a life of sacrifice or of grace? Why?

divine injunction to love of community. What was new was that Jesus rooted it in his incarnation.

But loving each other within the Christian community is no easy task! It may be easier to love our neighbors; but just because it seems more difficult to love one's enemies, one must not imagine that loving one's own community is without its challenges. It was in anticipation of his betrayal, arrest, and death that Jesus instructed his *community* to love one another as he had loved them.

Giving Life Up—or Giving It Away?

We often interpret Jesus' death on the cross as a *giving up* of his life. Another way to think about this is that Jesus *gave away* his life for his followers. The difference is crucial: Jesus' love for his disciples was not a denial of his life for their sake, but an expression of the fullness of his relationship and love for them. Jesus remained committed to his values and beliefs and followed his vocation where it led him. He lived a life of grace, not sacrifice; and for this he was killed. In the end, his love and commitment had no limits; it led him to the cross.

Martin Luther King, Jr. knew the difference between "giving up" and "giving away" one's life. So did Archbishop Oscar Romero of El Salvador. Neither lived a life of denial and sacrifice; both lived grace-filled lives of justice-love and were assassinated as a result. Thousands of nameless Christians across the centuries have given away their lives for this radical love. Having received salvation through divine grace, we too are called to live out our lives with grace and justice-love. In the process, we not only are to love our enemies and our neighbors; we are to love each other.

Study Suggestions

A. Praise God's Past Actions

Divide into two groups. Have Group 1 read aloud Psalm 148:1-6 and Group 2 read verses 7-13; together read verse 14. Discuss: Who is to praise God? (Consult the commentary on pages 177–78.) What does the vast inclusivity of Psalm 148 say to us? (It emphasizes that theology and ecology are inseparable.) What does this say about our human vocation of "dominion over" the earth as stated in Genesis 1:26, 28? (Again review the commentary regarding humanity's partnership with creation.)

B. Explore God's Inclusiveness

Print this sentence in advance on posterboard or chalkboard: "God has given to _____ (group or class of people) the repentance that leads to life even without asking them to _____ (specific belief or behavior)."

Read Acts 11:1-18, and review the commentary on pages 176–77. For emphasis, reread verses 17 and 18. Ask the group to complete the above sentence in as many ways as they can. If Peter and the other apostles were here today, who might they say had received God's grace and salvation even though they did not meet the church's understanding of who is acceptable?

C. Hear Jesus' Command

Read John 13:31-35, and review the commentary on pages 179–80. Discuss "mutual glorification": What do you think John means in verses 31 and 32? What does the concept of a preexistent Christ mean for your faith? How does this image relate to the Son's return to the Father? How does the return and gift of the Spirit make us children of God and all siblings together?

Discuss Jesus' command: What is your experience of trying to "love one another" within the Christian community? Do you think this is an "easier" or a "harder" commandment to follow than Jesus' command to love our neighbors (Mark 12:31) or his command to love our enemies (Luke 6:27-38)?

D. Reflect on God's Future Actions

Read Revelation 21:1-6, and review the commentary on pages 178–79. Compare John's statement about the new heaven and earth with Third Isaiah's view in Isaiah 65:17 and 66:22. Ask: How are these two visions similar and different?

Sing or read: "O Holy City, Seen of John." Provide paper and colored markers. Ask each person to sketch quickly what "a new heaven and a new earth" look like to them personally. Invite members to display their pictures. Ask: What is the core truth of John's vision even if we disregard his layered universe assumptions of "up there and down here"? What do you believe God's future actions will be and why?

E. Sing and Pray

Sing: "They'll Know We Are Christians by Our Love." Close with prayers for courage to live our lives fully in love in response to Jesus' call to discipleship.

Lections for Sixth Sunday of Easter

First Lesson: Acts 16:9-15

*I*N Acts 13, Luke's story of the spread of the gospel shifts from Peter and the other apostles to Paul. On his first mission, Paul preached both to Jewish Christians and to Gentile audiences (Acts 13–14). Positive responses to the gospel by Gentiles in Antioch and negative responses from Jewish Christians ultimately led to a major council meeting in Jerusalem.

An Old Conflict Resolved

The issue before the Jerusalem Council was the status of new Gentile Christians. Were they equal to Jewish Christians? Did they have to follow Jewish law? The Council heard Peter recall how the Holy Spirit had come to the Gentile Cornelius (see Acts 10; lections for Easter Day and Fifth Sunday of Easter). They also heard Barnabas and Paul's stories of the many signs and wonders that God had done among the Gentiles (Acts 15:6-12). Then James, the brother of Jesus, reminded the gathered leaders that the inclusion of Gentiles had long been part of God's plan. James proposed that Jewish Christian leaders not bother Gentile believers with requirements for following Jewish law, but ask them only to observe four purity regulations that had long governed strangers who lived in Israel (Acts 15:13-21). The Council agreed and sent this word back to Antioch.

Journey Into Europe

With a sticky issue resolved, Paul embarked on a second mission, this time with Silas. First he revisited his mission churches and shared the decision from Jerusalem, thus alerting them that the Jerusalem decision was not meant for Antioch alone and that the way was open for full acceptance of Gentiles into the church in their own right. Then he attempted to continue his travel plans, but was thwarted by divine intervention. Finally, he had a

182

vision of a man in Macedonia who pleaded for him to come to Europe. Luke thus emphasizes that the mission into Europe was God's will, not merely the plan of Paul (Acts 16:1-9).

Lydia's Conversion

Paul and Silas quickly went to Philippi, a thoroughly Gentile city in Macedonia. The Greek word translated "place of prayer" (16:13) could also mean "synagogue." However, at the edge of ancient Philippi there was a Roman arch that may have indicated the area from which the worship of non-Roman gods was banned. There, near a bend in the river, the bank forms a natural amphitheater; this would have been a likely spot where this event took place.

Among the women gathered was Lydia, a merchant of purple cloth (for which her home city of Thyatira was noted) and a Gentile worshiper of the God of the Jews. Lydia responded positively to Paul's sharing of the gospel, and she and her household were baptized. Reference to her "household" suggests that she was either unmarried or a widow of considerable social status. She was accompanied into the faith by her relatives and slaves, since in that culture the decision of a head of household was binding on all its members. She showed the depth of her new faith—as well as of her heart and her purse—by hosting Paul and Silas during their extended visit in her Gentile city (16:15, 40).

Luke's story of Lydia's conversion is a female parallel to his earlier story of Cornelius's conversion. While Cornelius was the first official Gentile convert to Christianity, Lydia was the first European convert and the first named woman.

Think About It: Lydia demonstrated her new faith by publicly supporting Paul and Silas in her city. What kind of response do you think she received from her neighbors and fellow merchants? What might we do to publicly demonstrate our faith in a non-Christian situation? What might be the "cost"?

Psalter: Psalm 67

This psalm has an interesting pattern. Verse 4 is the core, asserting God as sovereign. Surrounding that claim are verses of praise (3 and 5). Finally, verses 1-2 and 6-7 ask for God's blessing on his people in order that all the earth, all the nations, may come to praise the sovereign God.

Together the seven verses form a communal song of thanksgiving. The psalm may have been used during ancient harvest festivals (see verse 6) or at an annual celebration of God's "enthronement." In traditional Jewish practice, it is recited at the end of every sabbath. Christians have used it as a benediction prayer or song.

The call for God's blessing in this psalm reminds us of the promise of blessing to Abraham and Sarah in Genesis 12:3. In that story God promises that a blessing bestowed on one couple and their descendants will expand outward to "all the families of the earth." The message of this psalm is critical in a world full of injustices and divisions—and in a church that often seeks to limit who is acceptable to God. As John 3:16 also proclaims, God's blessings are not just for some, but are extended to all the peoples of the earth.

Epistle: Revelation 21:10, 22–22:5

John's vision of God's future plan for the world comes to a magnificent close in Chapters 21 and 22. John saw a new earth and a New Jerusalem, where God would dwell among the people.

The Old Jerusalem

Around 1000 B.C., King David captured Jerusalem and made it the political and religious center of his reign. He planned also to build a temple, but was instructed by God to leave that project for his heir. Solomon built the Temple (as well as numerous shrines to foreign gods) and expanded the city's international importance. However, as the city became more cosmopolitan and pagan, the symbolism of God's reign was eroded.

After Solomon's death in 922 B.C., the monarchy broke up; and Israel was conquered in 722. In 587 B.C., Babylonia invaded Judah and plundered Jerusalem, destroyed the Temple, and exiled its rulers. In 538, King Cyrus of Persia, who had conquered Babylonia, allowed the Judahites to return to Judah. A few returned and rebuilt a much smaller Temple. Over the centuries, different factions struggled to control Jerusalem. Rome conquered it in 63 B.C. and ruled during Jesus' life. In A.D. 70, Roman legions destroyed both the city and the second Temple, which had been extensively refurbished by Herod.

The New Jerusalem

Having lost faith in the ability of earthly leaders to unite them under God's reign, the Jews looked to the future. From the third century B.C. on, prophets wrote of visions of a transition from the present age to a glorious new age when God would reign on earth. Revelation, written in the late first century A.D., is one such vision.

According to Revelation, the physical features of the New Jerusalem would be large, radiant, and made of pure gold and rare jewels (21:11-21). There would be no need for a temple because God would be totally present among the people. The river of the water of life (God's grace) would flow directly from the throne into the heart of the city, as a sign of its utter purity.

The tree of life, reminding us of the garden of paradise, would grow beside that river. God would serve as the city's light, which would illuminate the path of all nations. The gates of the New Jerusalem would never be closed to the people, although nothing that was tainted by—and no one who colluded with—Babylon (a symbol for Rome or "evil empire") would be able to enter the city. Heaven

> **Think About It:** John has a magnificent vision of God coming to reign on earth in a "new Jerusalem." How do you envision God's rule on earth—in both present and future?

would be found on earth. People would share God's character because they would share God's name (identity, purpose) and see God's face (be in God's presence).

Gospel: John 14:23-29

Our Gospel lection is from Jesus' "farewell speech." In the ancient world, a farewell speech of a well-known person was a common form of literature. In the Bible, besides Jesus' farewell, we have representations of such by Jacob (Genesis 49), Joshua (Joshua 23–24), Moses (entire Book of Deuteronomy), David (1 Chronicles 28–29), and Paul (Acts 20:17-38). This literary type typically included these aspects: a gathering of followers or family; an announcement of imminent departure or death; a review of the person's life; the naming of a successor; prophecies, promises, blessings; final instructions; and prayer. Jesus' farewell (John 14:1–16:33) includes all these elements.

Jesus' Farewell Message

In our passage, Jesus assures the disciples that he will reveal himself to them and leave them a helper. A counselor or advocate—the Spirit of Truth, or Holy Spirit—will succeed him. The function of the Spirit is to "teach you all things, and remind you of everything I have said to you" (14:26, NIV). The disciples would often need this assurance and remembrance as they taught, healed, and spoke in Jesus' name.

This promise was a gift, not something the disciples could achieve; however, they could forfeit Jesus' gift if they did not follow his injunction to love one another as he loved them. Philip (14:8) apparently was looking for a public messianic sign

> **Think About It:** The Spirit would help the disciples remember and act on Jesus' teachings. When have you felt the Spirit guiding you to express the right word or deed? How do you distinguish between the Spirit and other voices or influences in your life?

and did not understand Jesus' point about his self-revelation. Jesus spoke of a spiritual revelation and presence that was contingent on the disciples' expression of love for the Son and the Father. Having clarified this point, Jesus then blessed his followers as he was about to leave them. This was not the peace of the world (a mere absence of conflict), but God's peace (Hebrew: *shalom*; Greek: *eirene*), a characteristic of the realm of God involving wholeness, justice, harmony, well-being, and right relationships.

Levels of Meaning

Jesus' farewell functions on several levels just as Moses' farewell did in Deuteronomy. On one level Moses spoke to the Hebrews as they were about to enter the land of Canaan. However, Deuteronomy was written centuries after Moses' death for people who had long occupied this land. Thus, on another level, the Deuteronomist used the voice of Moses to sanction a much later understanding of Israel's experiences. The writers spoke through Moses' farewell to invite later generations of Israelites to see themselves as ones also about to enter a new land.

Likewise, on one level Jesus spoke to his followers during his last meal with them. However, on another level John spoke through Jesus' voice to encourage late first-century Christians to realize that Jesus' promises, blessings, and commands were meant for them too. John used the voice of the victorious risen Christ to convey his own post-Resurrection understandings of Jesus' departure from his followers, the meaning of the cross, and the future of the community of believers. By using the voice of the risen Christ, John effectively communicated that God's new age was shaping both the disciples' lives before Jesus' death and the lives of late first-century Christians' as well (14:29-31). John was assuring his early Christian readers that Jesus had not left *them* orphaned, that the Spirit was with *them*, that God loved *them*—if only they would respond with love for one another.

Jesus' farewell also functions on a third level, because John also speaks to us. Through Jesus' voice John assures us that the future we look for is already unfolding. We, like the disciples and the first-century Christians, also live in the "already-here-but-not-yet" new earth of God. We too are promised the peace that comes with God's new age.

Study Suggestions

A. Praise God

Read Psalm 67 responsively. Drawing on the commentary (pages 183–84), explain the pattern of this psalm. Ask: What is its message? What inequities might God address today (see verse 4)? How might we become the voice and hands of God to confront these injustices?

B. Sing John's Vision

Sing "O Holy City, Seen of John." Read aloud Revelation 21:10, 22–22:5, and summarize insights from the commentary on pages 184–85. Ask: What are the key elements of John's vision of the New Jerusalem? How does it differ from the realities of the historical Jerusalem in Jesus' day? in our day? What does John's vision mean for us as twenty-first–century Christians? What is our vision for the future? How can we cooperate with God in bringing this to fruition?

C. Listen to Jesus

Read aloud John 14:23-29, and review the commentary (pages 185–86). Look up the other farewell speeches mentioned, and compare them with this one of Jesus. Ask: What did Jesus charge his followers to do? What would be different in our lives, church, and world, if modern Christians observed this directive? List steps you and your church might take to follow this command.

D. Travel With Paul

Read aloud Acts 16:9-15, and review the commentary on pages 182–83. Using a map of Bible lands, trace the journey from Phrygia to Philippi (see also Acts 16:6-11). Then, look up "Macedonia" or "Philippi" in a Bible dictionary.

Consider Lydia. Ask: Why do you think her conversion was important enough to be included in Acts? What did Lydia risk to welcome these missionaries into her own home? What level of risk are we willing to assume to act out our faith and take part in spreading the gospel?

E. Love Like Jesus Loved

Review the command Jesus gave his followers (John 13:34; 14:23). Ask: What does it mean to "love one another . . . as I [Jesus] have loved you"? How did Jesus express his love for others? What does this imply for our relationships within and beyond the church? Jesus said also, "Those who love me will keep my word." What does it mean to keep Jesus' word? (To memorize it? treasure it? proclaim it? live by it?)

Review your discussion of John's vision of a New Jerusalem. What is Revelation's point of "a New Jerusalem" without a temple? (The reconciled community would be so steeped in God's love that their entire lives would be an expression of worship; thus there would be no need for a temple or specified place of worship. They would have embraced and demonstrated Jesus' love of God, self, and neighbor.)

F. Close With Prayer

Invite members to offer sentence prayers expressing gratitude for insights gained through today's study. Then pray together: "O God, be gracious to us. Bless us. Shine your face on us that the earth and all its peoples may know your way and your saving power. We praise you, Sovereign God! Let all the peoples of the earth praise you. Bless us all. Amen." (Based on Psalm 67.)

Lections for the Ascension
of the Lord

The four lections selected for Ascension Day are all related to the theme of God's sovereignty over all of creation and all of history. Since they are read each year on this day, the commentaries on them in Years A and B of *Keeping Holy Time* may also be consulted for insights as to their significance and interpretation. This year we depart from the usual order of the lections in order to discuss them in chronological order.

Psalter: Psalm 47

*T*HIS is the first of a group of "enthronement psalms" (The others are Psalms 68, 93, 97, 98, and 99), which were used in ancient Israel in a yearly ceremony initiating the New Year by proclaiming YHWH anew as king over this people and all people. God is conceived as sitting on a heavenly throne surrounded by the angelic hosts, reigning over the universe and receiving homage and praise from all creatures. Scholars have found evidence of a similar rite in ancient Babylon, in which the god Marduk was similarly enthroned in a New Year festival, with use of the exclamation, "Marduk is become king" (compare 47:7).

As a group, the enthronement psalms make mention of the trumpet blast, this enthronement cry, and the joyous praise of the Temple congregation, all Zion, the nations, and the world of nature. With shouts, hand clapping, instrument playing, and singing, the worshipers call upon all other gods, rulers, and the elements to bow down in fear and trembling before the mighty YHWH who has come to rule and judge the world.

Psalm 47 begins with a summons to the nations to join in clapping, shouting, and crying out in praise of the almighty sovereign YHWH, who inspires awe, rules over all peoples, and assures his beloved people their heritage (verses 1-4).

Following this attention-getting call to worship, the enthronement ceremony begins with the holy procession of YHWH the king. The priests carry the ark of YHWH, the symbol of his presence among the people, up to the

Temple (see 1 Kings 8:3), accompanied by his subjects, the worshipers. "Gone up" in verse 5 refers to this procession. The people shout, the trumpet (*shofar,* ram's horn) is blown, and the congregation is commanded to sing a song of spiritual power in praise to YHWH who once again "is become" king over all creation (verses 5-7). Again another year YHWH is established on the throne of power and acclaimed as sovereign of the nations (verse 8).

In the psalmist's vision and the liturgy of the occasion, all rulers of surrounding nations gather with the children of Abraham at the throne of YHWH as vassals of the mightiest of gods, who is lifted up and celebrated on this awesome occasion (verse 9). The ascension of YHWH, sovereign over all, is complete.

> **Think About It:** Once a year the people of Israel engaged, with shouts and singing, in a ritual act celebrating the sovereignty of their God. Once a year we observe Ascension Sunday. How does our celebration compare with the one described in Psalm 47?

Gospel: Luke 24:44-53

We now fast-forward to Luke's account of the post-Resurrection appearances of Jesus. Fear-stricken women had been confronted at the empty tomb by "two men in dazzling clothes" who announced to them, "He is not here, but has risen." When they returned and reported this to the disciples, their witness was discounted. When Peter ran to the tomb to check, he found only graveclothes lying on the ground and went home amazed (24:1-12).

Then Cleopas and another disciple, leaving the city bereft and despondent, met a stranger on the road to Emmaus, invited him in for supper, recognized Jesus in the sacramental act of breaking bread, and were suddenly left alone to ponder the stunning and mysterious news of the risen Christ. Returning at once to Jerusalem, they rejoined the other disciples and shared the joyous words of faith, "The Lord has risen indeed" (24:13-35)! Suddenly, there in their midst was Jesus himself, announcing, "Peace be with you," and assuaging their fear and astonishment by showing his wounds and eating a plate of fish (24:36-43).

Imagine how stunned, almost shell-shocked, they must have been! Their emotions must have been on a yo-yo. In seventy-two hours, they had gone from fearful avoidance of arrest, to painful witnessing of the brutal execution of their best friend, to abject disappointment at the death of a beautiful dream, to despondent dispersal of a close-knit community, to the astonishing reappearance of the one they had followed and loved.

And what does he tell them when he rejoins them? First, according to Luke, he claims his messianic identity by declaring that the references to the

Messiah in the three parts of the Hebrew Scriptures—Torah (law of Moses), Prophets, and Wisdom Literature (psalms) were to be brought to fruition in him (verses 44-45). Specifically, he cites Hosea 6:2 as an allusion to his death and resurrection (verse 46) and the many prophecies of proclaiming God's glory to the nations (Psalm 96:3; Isaiah 49:6, 66:19; Ezekiel 39:21) and their ultimate coming to God (Psalm 67:4; Isaiah 2:2; Isaiah 60:3, 66:18; Jeremiah 27:7; Ezekiel 36:23; Joel 3:2; Malachi 3:12) as forming a mandate for the apostles to begin spreading the good news from Jerusalem outward (verses 47-48). Third, lest they embark on this daunting mission naked and unprepared, he suggests that they stay right where they are for a while until they are garbed and empowered for the task by the cloak of God's Spirit (verse 49).

Finally, after leading them out of the city, down through the garden of Gethsemane, up and over the Mount of Olives, and into the vicinity of the suburb of Bethany—no doubt commanding, explaining, reassuring, and comforting all the way—he raised his hands and gave them a blessing. This may have been some familiar words of Scripture, like: "The LORD watch between you and me when we are absent one from another" (Genesis 31:49); or, "The LORD bless you and keep you; the LORD make his face to shine upon you, and be gracious to you; the LORD lift up his countenance upon you, and give you peace" (Numbers 6:24-26).

Or, it may have been some much needed words of encouragement, like: "May the God of hope fill you with all joy and peace in believing, so that you may abound in hope by the power of the Holy Spirit" (Romans 15:13); or, "Cheer up, you can do it, I'll be with you every step of the way." Or, it may have been a stern challenge like, "We've had three good years together; now it's up to you to carry on"; or, "God called me to speak the word, live the life, and die the death; now God is calling you to do the same."

Then he was transported away (verse 51). From now on, they would be without his physical presence. But this time their reaction was not one of fear, discouragement, and despair. Instead, they worshiped, returned joyfully, and began spending a lot of time in church ("the temple," verse 52). These three responses are significant. In worship, they turned their attention away from themselves and their grief and onto Jesus and his mission. In returning, they sought out familiar surroundings and a base of support for the awesome task that lay before them; and in doing this gladly, they became heartened by the awareness that their commission was divinely inspired. In going repeatedly to the Temple to praise God, they sought strength for the journey from both the community of faith and the Author of life.

Think About It: When Jesus withdrew and was transported, the disciples worshiped, returned joyfully, and began abiding in the Temple. How do you respond when faced with a great loss, shock, or challenge?

Reading From Acts: Acts 1:1-11

Like a continued story that appears in installments, Luke's "Book Two" summarizes the events before moving the narrative forward from the "acts of Jesus" to the "acts of the apostles." He is addressing Theophilus (meaning "lover of God"), referring either to an actual Gentile convert, or in general to any and all readers motivated by a desire to grow in the faith. He begins by briefly touching on Jesus' life, teachings, death, Resurrection appearances, and ascension (verses 1-3), then notes that he stayed (the verb could also mean "ate") with them for forty days, a number often used to denote an extended but indefinite period of time. This same number marked the days of rain leading up to Noah's flood (Genesis 7:4), the years the Hebrews spent in the desert (Numbers 14:33), the days of Moses on Mount Sinai (Exodus 24:18), and the days of Jesus' temptation in the wilderness (Mark 1:13).

This is different information from that presented in Luke 24:51, where Jesus appears to have ascended at the end of Easter Day, the timing also implied by his promise to the thief on the cross (Luke 23:43). This immediate departure is more likely, but in Acts Luke is making the theological point that the disciples' experience of the risen Christ—for which more time was needed—was the foundation on which their mission was to be based. They were to remain in Jerusalem, waiting for the infilling of the Spirit to empower them in a way that water baptism by itself could not (verses 4-5).

The instruction by Jesus, conducted in a Socratic, question-and-answer manner, dwelt on matters of the timing of the coming reign of God (Trust God; don't expect inside information—verse 7); mission strategy (Move out from Jerusalem in concentric circles—verse 8b); and the source of strength for the mission (God's Spirit, not their own—verse 8a).

Now all was ready for his final departure. When he had vanished into the air, the disciples were confronted by "two men in white robes" (not mentioned in Luke 24:44-53). This was the traditional clothing of divine emissaries (see Luke 24:4) and indicated that the words about to be spoken were to be a message from God. That message was an insistent invitation to turn their eyes from the skies (the uplifting experience with Jesus that had been) toward the future, in which their ministry in Jesus' name would lead to their meeting him again in ways demanding and costly, but equally uplifting and rewarding (verses 9-11).

Think About It: "Why do you stand looking up toward heaven?" When have you basked too long in the euphoria of a mountaintop experience and needed a reminder that the power of the Spirit is given to send us into mission?

Epistle: Ephesians 1:15-23

In the Epistle lection we come full circle. The Lord who was enthroned for a glorious reign in Psalm 47, who came to earth in Jesus to live, teach, die, be raised, commission disciples, and ascend, is now reigning in glory once again (Ephesians 1:20-21). This reign has the full power and authority of God almighty, exceeds the dominion of all other entities, both now and in all time to come, and rules over "all things."

To what end is this universal sovereignty devoted? "For the church!"—the body of Christ, the community in which God's Spirit now dwells in redemptive love and through which God works in reconciling power. Christ does not just sit on a heavenly throne basking in the glory he has earned through his earthly travail. Rather, in all his fullness, he has come again to dwell amongst his people, continuing his mission of healing, saving, reconciling love (verses 22-23).

The author of Ephesians, speaking in the name of Paul, commends his readers for their faith in Christ and love for their fellow believers, thanks God for their faithfulness, and prays that they will grow in discernment and insight to understand more deeply the mind of Christ (verses 15-17). He yearns for the illumination of "the eyes of their hearts." What a beautiful phrase this is! What a different vision of reality we get when we view from the depths of emotion and compassion rather than merely observe the surface appearance of things! When we do so we perceive hope when things seem hopeless, the potential richness of the faith community in the midst of petty bickering and mundane operations, and the great spiritual power available for standing firm and making a faithful witness when the odds seem stacked against us (verses 18-19).

> *Think About It:* "With the eyes of your heart enlightened." When have you caught a different vision of circumstances when you allowed God's Spirit to open your heart and overcome the one-dimensional view afforded by eyes fixed only on the ground before you? How did this afford fresh perspective? expand the options? change your life?

Study Suggestions

A. Set the Context

Begin by noting that this is Ascension Day, then asking: Why does the church observe this Sunday? What is its significance? What does it mean to you? What do you think really happened?

B. Summarize Themes

Explain that the usual sequence of lections is altered this week to show a chronological/theological sequence. Drawing on the commentary on pages 188–92, briefly summarize the themes of the four lections and show the progression—enthronement (Psalm 47), instruction after resurrection (Luke), preparation for mission (Acts), vision and power for the church's redemptive ministry (Ephesians).

C. Study the Lections

Assign one of the lections to each of four groups. Ask them to read their passage aloud in at least two translations, then develop a one-sentence statement of what they think is its main thrust. Write these four statements on chalkboard or posterboard, compare and contrast them with the summary themes mentioned in Activity B, and discuss similarities and differences. Encourage members to hear one another's statements with sensitivity and respect, but also to examine them carefully in terms of how well they think they reflect the text's meaning as they understand it.

D. Explore Questions

Take up the questions in the "Think About It" boxes one by one. Encourage members to share their own experiences of the issues raised, the choices they made, and the learnings gained. With reference to the Luke lection also ask: Which of the four types of blessing do you think Jesus might have given his disciples? Which did they need the most? Which would be most helpful or meaningful to you?

E. Move Toward Mission

Noting that, for the disciples, the outcome of the Ascension experience was to move them into mission, ask: How does our experience of Christ's presence, absence, direction, and empowerment lead us into mission? In what aspects of mission are we currently engaged? What are the needs around us that summon us to mission? What mission venture might we take on as a group?

F. Depart to Serve

Close by singing a hymn of mission and service like "The Church of Christ, in Every Age" or "Lord, Whose Love Through Humble Service." Then pray this prayer in unison:

"O Christ, you died that we might be reconciled; you arose that we might have life; in your Ascension you handed your mission to us. Empower us with your Spirit. Enlighten us with your vision in the eyes of our hearts, we pray, that we may view the needs of your people with compassion, engage the problems of the world with your divine energy, and be open to your coming into our midst with hope. In Christ we pray. Amen."

Lections for Seventh Sunday of Easter

First Reading: Acts 16:16-34

*W*HILE in Philippi, Paul and Silas met an unnamed slave girl who "had a spirit of divination." The Greek for this phrase means literally "a python spirit," comes from the Greek story of Apollo's killing a dragon at Delphi, and became a general term referring to all sorts of ventriloquism and soothsaying. Luke's Gentile readers would have recognized that this girl was seen to have received powers from the serpent associated with the Delphic oracle and practiced a pagan faith.

Think About It: Paul's healing of the girl hurt the business of those who were using her for profit. What are some similar situations in our day in which helping the oppressed offends and angers those who are exploiting them? (Consider: boycotts of products of Third World sweatshops; efforts to help sex workers find productive employment; the sale of fair trade coffee and cocoa to provide a living wage to Third World farmers; providing microcredit to small farmers and businesses so they can avoid paying exorbitant interest rates to large lending agencies.

Paul Silences a Slave Girl

Because she was able to divine the future, she brought her owners much wealth. She proclaimed that Paul and Silas were "slaves of the Most High God" (16:17)—a very different form of slavery than that into which she was bound. This may have been a prescient utterance. "Most High God" is a familiar Lukan title for God; see Luke 1:32, 35, 76; 6:35. It is also used in recognition of God by those possessed by a lesser spirit that required exorcism (see Luke 8:28-29). However, "Most High God" was a title given to Zeus, the highest deity in the Greek pantheon. Paul, upset by the exploitation of this slave girl for the material gain of her owners,

194

exorcised the spirit; and her powers of divination were silenced, thereby ruining their business.

Traditionally, interpreters point to this story as Luke's indication that Jesus' power had been continued in Paul just as it was in the twelve apostles (see Acts 3:1-26). Luke reports four main events in Paul's activity in Philippi that demonstrate the presence and power of the Holy Spirit: the conversion of Lydia, this healing of the possessed slave girl, the conversion of the jailer (16:24-34), and Paul's public vindication (16:35-40). In these episodes, it is clear that resistance is building against the thrust of Christian influence in Philippi, "a leading city of the district of Macedonia and a Roman colony" (16:12).

Roman Resistance

Paul's perceived attack on the livelihood of the girl's owners caused quite a stir. Paul cast out the spirit from the girl; and, thus, she lost her soothsaying capability. Irate over this loss of her ability and its potential for earning them money, the owners dragged Paul and Silas before the local authorities and accused them of "advocating customs that [were] not lawful for . . . Romans." It is unclear what customs they had violated—perhaps overtly proselytizing Roman citizens or somehow disturbing the Roman peace. This is Luke's first recorded account of Roman resistance to the Christian movement.

A Prison Conversion

Paul and Silas were thrown in prison where a late-night earthquake shook open prison doors and loosened chains. But, thanks to Paul's restraint, no one tried to escape. This incident implies God's power over those who attempt to suppress the gospel. Its main purpose, however, was to set the stage for another conversion story. The jailer, expecting to be punished for losing his prisoners, instead heard the gospel. Washing his prisoners' wounds as a sign of penitence, he was converted and baptized (16:26-34). He, like Lydia, demonstrated his faith by caring for Paul and Silas and confirmed the presence of the Spirit by rejoicing with his household at his new-found faith.

Psalter: Psalm 97

This is an "enthronement psalm" that celebrates the sovereign rule of YHWH. The first five verses portray God as a divine king who arrives in a storm. This image emphasizes God's reign as a cosmic reality. Yet, God's reign is also rooted in the human community and calls for our response. Besides rejoicing and giving thanks for God's sovereignty in the universe, we are also called to struggle against evil and to be righteous (personally) and just (socially) in human interactions. True worship is not just praising and rejoicing; it involves personal integrity action for social justice (see verses 2b, 6, 11-12). This theme is the heart of the Psalter and is also the core message of Jesus' ministry.

Psalm 97 is often used during the Christmas and Easter seasons because it reminds us of God's incarnational entry into the world through Jesus. Jesus announced and participated in God's new reality, faithfully pursuing justice and righteousness and opposing evil. This heralding of God's reign landed Jesus on a cross, a cross that his disciples are also called to take up.

Epistle: Revelation 22:12-14, 16-17, 20-21

John's vision ends at 22:7. The rest of Chapter 22 is a series of isolated sayings that have many parallels to the opening of Revelation. These closing verses function as an epilogue.

Reward or Rejection

One of the major conclusions of the vision of John is that when the new age arrives, some will be rewarded and others judged (22:12-15). People's actions and commitments have a price. Those who "wash their robes" will be blessed; that is, those who have remained faithful and kept witnessing to the gospel despite persecution from "the beast" (the power of evil) will be rewarded. They will have the right to the tree of life (salvation and eternal life) and will be welcomed into the New Jerusalem.

On the other hand, those who follow the ways of the beast will be rejected and denied entry into the heavenly city. For John, the beast was Rome (the Empire, with its "dogs, sorcerers, fornicators," and the like; see 22:15). For us, it might be the "ways of the world," such as individualism, materialism, greed, corporate crime, violence, racism, ageism, sexism, and destruction of the environment.

Authentic Witness

As he closes his Book of Revelation, John authenticates his vision. In verse 16, Jesus declares that he, the faithful witness, sent his angel to confirm the validity of all the things in John's vision. Jesus also identifies himself as "the root and descendant of David" (emphasizing messianic status) and as "the bright morning star" (emphasizing universal sovereignty).

Invitation and Prayer

Through images of the Spirit and the bride (the people of faith), John invites his readers to hear, heed, and receive the water of life (grace of God) and to share in the redemption of the faithful. He reminds his readers that those who do not hear and heed will discover that God comes not as a redeemer but as a judge.

Finally, John proclaims that all that he has seen and heard will transpire soon. The fitting response to this is "Amen. Come, Lord Jesus!" (22:20). This is probably a translation of an ancient Aramaic eucharistic formula (*maranatha*, or "our Lord, come") found in 1 Corinthians 16:22. The closing phrase, "the grace of the Lord Jesus be with all," offers universal blessing and affirmation at the end of a vision in which threat, division, and rejection have predominated. It promises the freely given water of life (liberating spiritual sustenance) to faithful believers.

> ***Think About It:*** John's revelation emphasized reward for the faithful and judgment of the unfaithful when God's plan for the world is finally implemented. Why was this an important message for a persecuted Christian minority to hear? How does John's vision speak to you? How do you think God's ultimate purpose for the world will be achieved?

Gospel: John 17:20-26

According to John's account, at the end of his farewell meal and discourse with his followers, Jesus stopped speaking to them and began to pray to God. Our Gospel passage is part of that final prayer.

An Ancient Farewell

Ancient farewell speeches of dying persons usually concluded with prayer. However, this is not a typical farewell prayer. Jesus' whole farewell discourse had been not only about his death but also about his resurrection and ascension (his "hour"). Thus this is a prayer of one who is about to give away his life willingly out of love for his followers, bringing his work for God to completion.

Overview of the Prayer

This passage is often identified as Jesus' "high priestly" prayer; but we see that it is about intercession, not sacrifice. Jesus first prayed for himself, his work, and his glorification (verses 1-5). For John, glorification meant revelation or disclosure. Jesus prayed that God would be revealed through him. Then he prayed for his "own"—those who believed and followed him (verses 6-19)—asking God to protect them as they remained "in the world" when he left it. When Jesus said he was not praying for the world (17:9), he did not mean earth or creation, but rather the enemies of God, those who did not accept, believe, and obey God (see, for example, John 1:10-11 and 7:7). He entrusted believers to the caring, protective hands of God.

Jesus then prayed for future believers, that they would all be one, just as he and the Father were one—unified in purpose, community, and love. He prayed for believers' mission in the world, asking that through the unity of all believers, the world would come to know that the Father had sent him and that God loved them (verses 20-23). Jesus was praying for the unity and mission of the church in every age.

Finally, Jesus prayed that through love for him, for God, and for each other, believers would join him some day in God's new age (verses 24-26). When he prayed for unity, Jesus was not really praying for the ecumenical, organizational unity of all branches of the church as we know it today, although we often read the prayer that way. Rather, he prayed a vision of the future in which God's unifying, reconciling love would reign. Living out God's love would bring that unity and—someday, in some way—God's new age. It is toward the realization of that vision that we yearn and strive.

Reflections on the Prayer

Several themes may be discerned in John's recording of this prayer: Jesus intercedes with God on behalf of the faith community; Jesus is on intimate, loving terms with God; and believers are promised a future, eternal life with God. In this intimate prayer Jesus boldly holds God to God's promises: You sent me, showing them that you love both me and them; now keep them safe, let them be one in their love for one another, and let them glimpse the glorious future offered in God's coming realm.

Think About It: Jesus prayed for believers then and now, entrusting the faith community to God's care and guidance. How might the reminder that Jesus is praying for the protection, unity, and mission of the faith community change the way we conduct ourselves in the church today?

Jesus' final words before his "hour" are thus cast as an intimate prayer entrusting to God the future of the faith community. One wonders how the church's understanding of itself and conduct of its affairs would be different if we would consistently remember that we are a community for whom Jesus prayed and that the future of that community is completely in God's hands, not our own.

Study Suggestions

A. Explore a Psalm

Read Psalm 97, and review the commentary on pages 195–96. Ask: What are the main points of this psalm? (God is sovereign over all yet is rooted in human relationship; the peoples' response must include acts of justice as well as praise and thanksgiving.) How does this psalm remind you of Jesus' life and message?

B. Listen to Jesus' Prayer

Read John 17 aloud as a prayer, starting with "Father, the hour has come" in verse 1. Pause for a few minutes of silent meditation.

Discuss: How did it feel to be "overhearing" Jesus' prayer to God? In John's view, what is Jesus' vision for the church? How does Jesus' prayer suggest that we might pray?

C. Examine Revelation

Read aloud Revelation 22:12-21, and review the commentary on pages 196–97. Discuss: What main conclusion can we draw from John's vision? (Reward for some; judgment for others.) For whom were these words originally intended? What was their situation? What encouragement would this message give them? What groups might find John's message most meaningful today? (The "reward" message could be for any Christians who, by witnessing to the gospel, are being discriminated against. Examples: Christians around the world who stand for justice in opposition to oppressive rulers; Christian churches who take bold, prophetic stances for the gospel; those who dare to lead and plan ecumenically and interculturally. The "rejection" message could be for any Christians or churches that conform to the ways of the world instead of boldly living out the gospel message of love, inclusion, and justice.)

D. Make Connections

Summarize: The Revelation lection bids the faithful to remain committed to the gospel message of love and justice. The psalm calls for acts of justice as well as praise. Acts tells of persons who assumed risk for the sake of the gospel. In John, Jesus, in the midst of grave injustice, calls believers to unity, love, mission, and hope. These passages all declare that believers are called to stand up for their faith, even though such faithful discipleship may have a high price.

Discuss: Who do you know who has paid a price for doing acts of justice or for struggling for justice to prevail? When have you had to make a decision to live out your commitment like Jesus did, regardless of the consequences? When have you felt caught between a call to unity (maintaining harmony and good feeling in the church) and a call to justice-love (taking a stand on a controversial issue)? What happened?

E. Sing a New Earth Vision

Sing or read together the hymn, "Come, All of You." (This Laotian hymn text weaves together biblical visions from Revelation, Matthew, John, and Isaiah, inviting all people to eat, drink, and rest peacefully in the promise of the reign of God.) Close with your own prayer for the unity of the faith community and for peace and justice in the world.

Lections for Day of Pentecost

First Lesson: Acts 2:1-21

*A*CTS 1 describes several appearances of the risen Christ that occurred between the first Easter and the Day of Pentecost. In one appearance, the disciples asked: "When will you restore the kingdom to Israel?" (They, of course, meant an earthly, political realm.) Jesus told them not to worry about the timing, but just to depend on God's Spirit to empower them to get out and spread the good news (Acts 1:6-8; see Ascension Day lection). In today's passage, Luke describes how that promise was fulfilled. The Pentecost event also fulfilled earlier promises made by John the Baptist and Jesus (Luke 3:16; 24:49).

Celebrating Pentecost

In Acts 2:1, Jesus' followers were gathered after his death for the Jewish Festival of Weeks. This festival was celebrated fifty days after Passover (see Exodus 23:16). The Greek word *pentecost* literally means "fiftieth." Our Christian celebration of Pentecost is rooted in this ancient Jewish festival, the second of three required observances, coming between Passover and Tabernacles. It was an agricultural celebration, like our Thanksgiving, in which the people gave thanks to God for the "first fruits," that is the early wheat harvest.

While Jesus' followers were gathered for this festival, a rush of wind filled the house where they were meeting. "What seemed to be tongues of fire" (Acts 2:3, NIV)—representing divine energy—appeared and rested on each of them. The Holy Spirit permeated their beings. They began to speak in foreign languages, so that devout Jews, who had come to Jerusalem for the festival from the various Near Eastern lands where they were living, overheard and understood them.

Some were impressed and curious, saying, "What is this amazing thing?"

The more skeptical merely scoffed, "They are filled with new wine." Although wine was sometimes thought to enhance prophetic speech, the scoffers were charging Jesus' followers with drunkenness.

Peter's Witness

Peter addressed the Jewish crowd, explaining that it was God's Spirit that had endowed them with these awesome new powers. He quoted the prophet Joel who, centuries earlier, had prophesied that God would "pour out my spirit upon all flesh" so that all—sons and daughters, young and old, slave and free, men and women—would prophesy, dream, and see signs, omens, and visions (see Joel 2:28-32).

Peter wanted the Jewish crowd to relate Joel's words to the rush of wind (Hebrew: *ruach,* which also means "spirit" and "breath") the followers had just experienced and to the vital energy that had now possessed them. By changing Joel's words slightly to refer to "the last days," Peter told the crowd that this interruption of normal events on Pentecost was a prelude to "the day of the Lord" (Acts 2:20) when Christ would return, history would end, and people would be judged. In Acts, Peter's speech was the first public Christian witness.

> **Think About It:** Throughout Acts, Luke emphasized that the work of the Holy Spirit was ongoing in the life of believers. Throughout history, the church has sometimes emphasized the sovereignty of God, sometimes the redemptive work of Christ, and sometimes the power and inspiration of the Spirit. Which do you think the church is primarily emphasizing today? Which part of God's nature is most important to you? How and when have you experienced being filled with the Spirit?

Other Spirit-Filled Moments

The Day of Pentecost in Acts was not the only time recorded in the New Testament when the Spirit appeared. In John 20:19-23, Jesus' followers received the Spirit on Easter night. Also, Luke describes other times when disciples and new believers received the Spirit (see Acts 8:17; 10:44-47; 19:1-6). Today we generally believe that the Spirit continues to touch and guide believers and communities of faith.

Psalter: Psalm 104:24-34, 35b

On Pentecost we celebrate God's gift of the Spirit that gave new energy and hope to Jesus' dispirited followers after his death. We often read Psalm 104 as part of that celebration. This psalm is a hymn of praise to God who has made all creatures on land and sea and provided them with their very breath (spirit). On Pentecost we affirm that God is the source of all life and that the Spirit works through us to renew and sustain life.

201

We affirm that we live by the power of God's renewing Spirit, rather than by our own abilities, merits, or ingenuity. We exist to praise God, our creator and sustainer.

In verse 26, Leviathan (elsewhere described as a monster of chaos) is seen as a playful whale. In verses 31-35, the psalmist hopes that God has joy from creating and that God's creation will endure. The psalmist also hopes his or her praise will please God and that no sin or evil will ever interrupt or interfere with God's good creation.

Epistle: Romans 8:14-17

Written after two decades of Paul's preaching, teaching, and writing, Romans expresses some of his most mature thoughts. Our verses offer God's solution to the human dilemma posed in Chapter 7: We know God's law holds out the promise of life to us; we want to follow the law; but because we are human—and thus sinful—we cannot do the good that it requires of us (Romans 7:14-25). Therefore, a gracious God sets us free to walk, not in the law, but in the Spirit (8:1-13). Through Christ and the Spirit, God has broken the power of the law to condemn us. If we are led by the Spirit, we become children of God, not slaves to the law. And, as children, we are the heirs God's good gifts (8:14-17).

The Law and Spirit

Spirit is the divine, life-giving power that is active within each of us. Spirit seeks to reshape our lives so that they are pleasing to God—something the law can never do. Paul's understanding of the law is that it was given by God to save. A quick scan of the books of the Torah reveals that God called a people to be a holy nation and gave them the law as guidance in achieving that intent. But, as Paul describes it, sin (a self-centered intent to violate the law), entered in to frustrate this godly intention; and it employs the law against the purpose of God. Something more is needed for salvation.

Choose Life in the Spirit

In Romans 8, Paul challenges us to choose life over death, to choose to be led by the Spirit rather than by the law. We have only to invite the Spirit to lead us—then commit ourselves to follow where it leads. To be "Spirit-led," however, we must first give up our dependence on the law, that is, on "being good" and obeying the rules, as the way to salvation. If we live by the law, we cannot avoid condemning ourselves and others, because none can totally fulfill the law. However, if we let ourselves be led by the Spirit, we focus on life, hope, freedom. We discover that God yearns for us to become Spirit-led children, exhibiting love and generosity, rather than law-bound slaves who are entrenched in rule and form over grace. We discover that God offers us unconditional love rather than judgment and condemnation. Even so, we often cling to the law.

Heirs of God

Even if we are Spirit-led, Paul believed that full freedom (the opposite of slavery) was to be gained only in the future (see Romans 8:19-21). In the meantime, Spirit-led children are heirs of God. Our entitlement is firmly established, but not yet fully delivered to us. Spirit-led children can be certain that our inheritance will ultimately bring "new life." We live in the hope of that inheritance.

> *Think About It:* Paul contrasts being "Spirit-led" (which brings life and vitality) with being "law-bound" (which brings death and rigidity). What corresponds to being "law-bound" in our experience? How does the church sometimes reinforce this preoccupation with being good and obeying the rules? What do we need to change—as individuals and congregations—to become more open to being more "Spirit-led"?

Gospel: John 14:8-17 (25-27)

The Gospel of John, written fifty to sixty years after Jesus' death, stresses that Jesus is the incarnate Word, the divine Son of God, who entered history to demonstrate God's love for humanity and to invite persons into a reconciled relationship with God (see John 3:16). John also claims that God sent the Spirit to the disciples to teach them truth they were not ready to hear from Jesus. Today, and in the next session, we explore John's understanding of the Spirit.

The Confused Disciples

According to John, the disciples believed that Jesus had "the words of eternal life" (John 6:68). Imagine their consternation as Jesus talked about leaving them. Would they no longer hear these words? In his farewell address, Jesus tried to explain what would happen in their future; but they could not comprehend it. He told them that where he was going they could not follow (13:36). Peter protested that he would follow Jesus anywhere, that he would lay down his life for Jesus. But Jesus pointed out that Peter would deny him three times (13:37-38).

Then, Jesus reassured the disciples: "Do not be troubled; . . . you will come later; . . . you know the way to the place I am going" (see 14:1-3). This time Thomas misunderstood, thinking in geographical terms, protesting that they knew neither the destina-

> *Think About It:* Jesus said, "I am the way, and the truth, and the life. No one comes to the Father except through me." What do you think this means?

tion nor how to get there (14:4-5). Jesus responded on an entirely different level: "I am the way, and the truth, and the life. . . . If you know me, you will know my Father also" (14:6-7). He was talking about himself as embodying a way to live (love) that would bring direction (the way), assurance (truth), and spiritual vitality (life). No one could understand the nature of God who did not see God in him. But still, they misunderstood.

> **Think About It:** Jesus said that believers would do greater works than he did. Has this happened? What do you think he meant?

When Philip asked for a concrete explanation of God (a contradiction in terms), Jesus could only repeat, "Any one who knows me, knows the Father. . . . *If you don't believe my words, believe my works!* Both my words and my works validate that God is in me, working through me" (see 14:9-11). The "works" were the things Jesus had done, signs that God had been in them and was revealed through them. With those words, Jesus invited the disciples—and us—to accept him as the incarnation of God.

Jesus also declared that believers would do his works, or even greater ones, and that to demonstrate their love for him they must live by his teachings. To help the confused disciples, Jesus promised that after he left God would send the *Paraclete*—the Holy Spirit (14:12-16).

The Promised Paraclete

The Greek word *paraclete* means literally "called to the side of." It refers to the Holy Spirit and is variously translated as "counselor," "comforter," and "advocate," highlighting that the Spirit has several functions. Unlike Paul, however, John does not connect the Spirit with baptism or spiritual gifts.

John asserts that, after Jesus was gone, the Spirit continued God's presence in the world so that succeeding generations could know God (14:12-15). The presence and work of the Spirit has at least two functions: to remind us about Jesus' teachings and to guide us toward deeper truth about God (14:25-26). Just as the disciples' ideas about Jesus changed after his death, so do we continue to grow in the faith—thanks to the work of God's Spirit.

> **Think About It:** The Spirit guides our growth in faith. How have your beliefs changed through the years? Have you sensed the Spirit's guidance in this? How do you discern it?

Study Suggestions

A. Experience God

Before class gather: a red cloth; a small table; chimes; candle and holder; red, orange, and yellow construction paper; red crepe paper; glue; scissors; matches. Invite persons to cover the table and hang chimes above the candle, create and hang a large paper flame, hand out three-foot lengths of red crepe paper stoles, and open their Bibles to Psalm 104:24-34, 35b.

Gather. Light the candle. Watch the flame. Listen to the chimes. Ask: What are you experiencing? What other natural phenomena give us this same sense? (Rainbows, sun through stained glass windows, rippling streams?) Read the psalm. Pause; then the extinguish candle.

B. Explain Pentecost

Comment that today is Pentecost Sunday, and give the background (see pages 200–201). Ask: How does our church observe it? What would you like us to make of it in the future?

C. Examine Confusion and Promise

Assign roles to Jesus, Peter, Thomas, Philip, and a narrator; then dramatically read John 13:33–14:15. Ask: Why were the disciples confused? (See "The Confused Disciples," pages 203–204.)

Read John 14:16-17, 25-27. Review "The Promised Paraclete" on page 204. Ask: Who is the "Paraclete"? How does the Spirit remind us of Jesus' teachings? (Helps us look back to Jesus' day and remember what he taught.) How does the Spirit "guide us into new truth"? (Opens our hearts and minds so we can gain fresh meanings.) Also discuss the "Think About It" questions.

D. Discuss the Spirit's Arrival

Read Acts 2:1-21 and the commentary on pages 200–201. Ask: Was Pentecost the only time Jesus' followers were filled with the Spirit? What do you think actually took place on that occasion? How have *you* experienced the Spirit?

Explore the "Think About It" questions related to the aspects of God the church has emphasized. Ask: What differences would these varied emphases make in the church's worship? program? outreach? our lives?

E. Explore Being Spirit-Led

Read aloud Romans 8:14-17, and review the commentary on pages 202–203. Ask: What does it mean to be "led by the Spirit of God"? What useful functions does law (rules and regulations) serve?

Invite members to share their understandings of the function and role of the Spirit. Remind them that God is Spirit and that we as human spirits encounter God who is Spirit.

F. Invite the Spirit

Relight the candle on the worship table. Form a prayer circle. Say: "O Holy Spirit, help us to be aware of your presence with our spirits. Any who wishes may offer sentence prayers aloud, then I will close."

Sing "Many and Great, O God" or another hymn about the Holy Spirit.

SUNDAYS AFTER
PENTECOST

Lections for Trinity Sunday

Old Testament: Proverbs 8:1-4, 22-31

*P*ROVERBS is a "wisdom book" similar to other wisdom literature in the ancient world. It says nothing about Israel's history, institutions, kings, or prophets. In wisdom literature, righteousness is not linked to observance of covenant, law, or rituals; so, in Proverbs, righteousness comes from following Wisdom. Wisdom literature has a strong didactic tone expressed in moral sayings and teachings.

Despite these common characteristics, biblical Wisdom Literature has a variety of narrative settings. For example, The Song of Solomon is a collection of love poems; Job is a dialogue on divine justice embodied within a tale of a man's suffering; and Proverbs offers parental instruction to young men (see Proverbs 1:2-7). Proverbs instructs by contrasting two ways of living: following folly or wisdom, both of which are personified as women. Today's verses are part of Proverbs' most fully developed poetic description of Woman Wisdom. (For a brief description of Woman Folly, see 9:13-18.)

Wisdom's Origins

Proverbs 8:22-31 is a striking claim about Woman Wisdom's antiquity and authority. She was present during the process of creation, participating as a master worker, pleasing the Creator and enjoying the human beings as they emerged. There is much scholarly debate about the personification of wisdom. Some scholars attest that Wisdom is a poetic way of describing the wisdom of God; others think the divine attribute of wisdom has become a separate entity, like an angelic power. Proverbs 8 shows wisdom with female attributes in service to the divine initiative of creation. Wisdom determines cosmic order and is the prior condition for the existence and functioning of all things.

Wisdom and Spirit

Christians usually identify Christ as God's Wisdom—the Word made flesh. The result is a male image of the Spirit. However, Woman Wisdom is also a cosmic image of the divine work of God in creation; together these images provide a potent understanding of God's relationship with all of humankind and balance the masculine and feminine aspects of God.

> **Think About It:** In Proverbs, Wisdom is personified as a woman. What images of God are most meaningful to you? Why is the creative dimension of God's nature expressed by a feminine image?

Wisdom's Nature

Proverbs was meant to teach young men who are ready for wife and wisdom, but prone to illicit love and folly. The city is held up as a microcosm of their human cultural world. Both Woman Folly and Woman Wisdom inhabit the openings or places of encounter and transition in human life. The young man's relationship to one "woman" or the other reflects his relationship to his goods and, ultimately, to his direction in life.

> **Think About It:** Woman Wisdom calls to humanity to understand the deepest ways of the universe and to exercise common sense in decisions and actions. How does Woman Wisdom guide you in your life?

Thus, in Proverbs 8:1-5, Wisdom is described as a female prophet or street teacher who appears at the crossroads and the city gates where men did business, settled disputes, arranged marriages, and obtained justice. She calls to young men to learn from her. Salvation does not come through grace or forgiveness, but through making wise choices. Those who succumb to the temptations of folly will find only ruin (verses 1-4).

Psalter: Psalm 8

This psalm first praises God as sovereign over all the earth and above the heavens (verse 1). Then it thanks God for exalting humans over all other creatures (verses 2-8). Sometimes we quote Psalm 8 to justify human decisions to change or control something or someone. However, when we forget the source of our sovereignty, we invite both ecological calamity (polluted streams, eroded hillsides, depleted ozone layer, extinction of species) and social disaster (mass hunger, poverty, disease, and war).

Forgetting the source of our autonomy also tempts us to act like God in judging one another, which leads to widespread discrimination and rejection of people. Psalm 8 reminds us that God has made us a "little lower" than divine beings and called us to be partners in caring for the earth and one another. After naming the creatures under the care of humankind, the psalmist concludes with a final reminder of the sovereignty of God, the ultimate source of being and authority.

Epistle: Romans 5:1-5

Romans, which may be Paul's last surviving letter, was written around A.D. 58 to a group of house churches in Rome that he intended to visit on his way to Spain after leaving Jerusalem (Romans 15:23-24). These house churches consisted of both Jewish and Gentile Christians. We do not know how much direct knowledge Paul had of these churches. It is possible that much of what he wrote was in the form of generic comment. It does appear he desired the support of Rome and that he may have feared he had to overcome some negative press that may have preceded him.

Early Christian Controversy

The Roman house churches mirrored a tension that existed in Christianity at the end of Paul's ministry. Paul spoke to that tension. To Gentile Christians in Rome, he explained how Jews understood the continuing validity of the Abrahamic tradition and of Jewish law in God's purpose. To Jewish Christians in Jerusalem (to whom he was delivering much-needed money donated by largely Gentile churches), Paul would defend the validity of the Gentile church by expounding on God's impartiality and on Jewish and Gentile equality as heirs of God's grace and salvation. In defending each side, Paul risked being misunderstood by both. Romans reflects his struggles with a weighty but practical matter: How might both sides learn a larger truth about the way(s) to reconciliation with God?

Justification

Romans 5:1 begins a summary of the groundwork laid in prior chapters: "Therefore, since we are justified by faith. . . ." The typical concept of justification was: to be found righteous when tested by God both in this life and in the Final Judgment. Paul argued that all persons sin and fall short, therefore no one can be justified (counted as righteous) through the law. In addition, a new age had opened with the coming of the Messiah. What the Jews had hoped for in God's intervention at the end time, Jesus had inaugurated in their present time. Justification was possible because of what God had done in Jesus Christ, and this was grounds for great hope.

From Suffering to Hope to Love

Paul wrote that since they had faith in Christ, they could have peace with God. Believers are justified (reckoned as righteous) by faith (trust in

Christ); their enmity with God is taken away; they are reconciled (brought into relationship) with God (5:18-21). The overcoming of separation from God provides them access to God's grace—undeserved acceptance and forgiveness.

Paul extended the benefits of this grace, in which one could exult, in a cascading pattern of effects and consequences that began with hope, moved through endurance and character, and ended with hope (5:2b-4). The faithful would not be disappointed, because they had received God's love through the gift of God's Spirit (5:5).

> **Think About It:** Paul said to boast (exult) in our suffering because suffering leads to hope. When have you found hope through pain or misfortune? Both success and failure can teach lessons. What can be learned from failure?

Gospel: John 16:12-15

In the last session, we explored Jesus' promise to the disciples that God would send the *Paraclete* (the Holy Spirit) who would serve as an advocate or counselor. In particular, Jesus noted that the Spirit would perform two kinds of roles, both reminding believers of what Jesus had taught and guiding them into all truth. Today's passage focuses on the Spirit's guiding role. The term "Spirit of truth" (along with *Paraclete*) is one of John's unique names for the Holy Spirit. "Spirit of truth" emphasizes the dependability of the Paraclete and links it to Jesus, who in John 14:6, refers to himself as the "truth."

Spirit as Guide

In John 16:12, Jesus notes that he has many things to tell the disciples. However, because they were in crisis over his imminent departure, they were not able to grasp some things he would teach them. Thus, he promised that the Spirit would guide them into other truth later. His comment that the Spirit would "declare to you the things that are to come" (16:13) is not a reference to prediction, but a further promise that the Spirit will make clear the meaning of future events for which he could not prepare them.

Sometimes we think that all religious truth was given to those who lived in biblical times and that we only have to remember and follow the old revealed truth. When we do this, we limit the Spirit's role to that of reminder of truth. We forget that Jesus promised that the Spirit would guide each new generation to new truth as it is needed.

Incarnation Extended

The verb *guide* in verse 13a appears only here in John. It is formed from compound verbs that together literally mean "lead in the way." This same verb is used in the Greek version (the Septuagint) of the Psalms to refer to the instructional role of God in leading the community into right and faithful behavior. It is also used to describe the teaching function of Wisdom. By choosing this verb, John claims that the guiding role of the Spirit is already present in some Jewish traditions. Since Jesus said that he spoke what he heard from God (John 12:49-50) and that he is "the way, and the truth, and the life" (John 14:6), John is underscoring that the Spirit is the abiding presence of God. John wrote the extended farewell dialogue between Jesus and the disciples to assure his readers that God remained with them and that the Spirit would continue to show them additional truth as they needed it.

New Occasions, New Truth

The great hymn "Once to Every Man and Nation" says, "New occasions teach new duties, / Time makes ancient good uncouth; / They must upward still and onward, / Who would keep abreast of truth." Jesus and John claim that new occasions bring new understandings of God's truth.

As our lives and our world change over the centuries, the circumstances we face are very different from those the disciples confronted. But we are promised that the Spirit will guide us beyond what Jesus could teach in the first century. God's gift of the Spirit in our lives ensures that Jesus' words are not locked in the past, restricted to a particular historical moment. The promise of 16:13 is that each new generation can receive fresh insight into God's truth appropriate to its situations. Through the Spirit, God remains with us and offers us new interpretations of God's life-giving revelation.

> **Think About It:** Jesus promised that the Spirit would guide us to new truth as we needed it. How has the Spirit helped your faith to grow with the acceptance of new truth? What difficulty do you have remaining open to new belief?

Study Suggestions

A. Sing About Spirit and Wisdom

Sing a song or hymn about the Holy Spirit, such as the African American spiritual, "I'm Goin'a Sing When the Spirit Says Sing." (Other stanzas: shout, pray, moan, praise.)

B. Relate the Lections for Trinity Sunday

Observe that today, on Trinity Sunday, the lections present different aspects of our belief in the Trinity. The Proverbs passage deals with Wisdom, God's creative Spirit. Psalm 8 speaks of God's sovereignty. Romans 5 expounds Christ the Redeemer. And John 14 explores the work of the Holy Spirit.

C. Identify Wisdom

Read aloud Proverbs 8:1-4, 22-31, and study the commentary on pages 208–209 carefully. Ask: Who is Wisdom and how is Wisdom portrayed? How are Woman Wisdom and Woman Folly portrayed and differentiated? How was Woman Wisdom meant to be instructive to young men in the ancient world? How do female- and male-specific images for God or God's character, such as Woman Wisdom, enhance or confuse our understanding of God?

D. Reflect on Hope and Spirit

Read aloud Romans 5:1-5, and review the commentary on pages 210–11. Discuss: What was the big debate in early Christianity? (Did Gentile Christians need to follow Jewish law and rituals in order to be people of God?) Paul felt called to defend Jewish and Gentile Christians to each other. What did Paul say to the two sides? How might Paul's approach be useful today as a means for settling differences among Christians?

E. Explore "Spirit of Truth"

Read aloud John 16:12-15, and review the commentary on pages 211–12. Discuss: How does John describe the work of the Spirit? (Reminder: guide, advocate, comforter, counselor.) What is talked about in today's lection? (Guide.) What kind of guide or teacher is the Spirit? (One who leads us to discover the truth we need to know, rather than one who tells us.) Whose truth is the Spirit leading us toward? (God's.)

Discuss further: Sometimes we tend to think that all religious truth was given to those who lived in Old and New Testament times and recorded in the Bible. But John says the Spirit leads each new generation to discover new truth as needed. What do you think about John's claim? How have you experienced the Spirit's guidance in the discovery of new truth? Also explore the "Think About It" questions.

F. Create Wisdom-Spirit Symbols

Provide modeling clay, large colorful pipe cleaners, colored markers, drawing paper, or other art supplies. Invite group members to create a figure, symbol, drawing, or other art form that conveys their understanding of wisdom and truth in relation to God. Show the results and discuss the images. Ask: How did it feel to create your image of this divine dimension of God? How has your understanding of wisdom and spirit changed? What difference will this make in your faith life?

G. Invite the Spirit

Sing again: "I'm Goin'a Sing When the Spirit Says Sing." Add two stanzas related to the lections: (1) "I'm goin'a learn when wisdom says learn, . . . and obey the wisdom of our God," and (2) "I'm goin'a hear when the Spirit says hear, . . . and follow the Spirit of our God."

Close with prayer asking the Spirit to guide us into new truth.

Lections for Sunday Between
May 29 and June 4

W Old Testament: 1 Kings 18:20-39

*W*HAT we call First Kings and Second Kings is, of course, a single writing. The division into two writings was made when the Hebrew text was translated into Greek in the third century B.C., called the Septuagint. The Kings document is part of the Deuteronomist tradition of political history, expressed in the books from Deuteronomy through Second Kings. These writings interpret history from the theological viewpoint that God's punishment of Israel and Judah was due to the sins of the kings and their people in violating the covenant with YHWH by practicing idolatry and injustice. The purpose of the writing was to persuade the people to repent, change their ways, and return to faithful obedience to YHWH's laws, both ceremonial and moral. Prophets like Elijah and Elisha were God's spokesmen in proclaiming this call to repentance and faithfulness.

Stories of Elijah

Chapters 17–19 tell several miracle stories about Elijah (whose name means "YHWH is God"). In 17:1-7, he confronted King Ahab with the prediction of a coming drought, fled the king's wrath, and was nurtured by ravens and the brook Cherith east of the Jordan, until the drought dried it up. Then, in next week's lection (17:8-24), Elijah went up to Zarephath, in present-day Lebanon, was cared for by a widow, and restored her dead son to life. In 18:1-19, Ahab and his chamberlain Obadiah went out searching for food for the animals, Obadiah (loyal to YHWH) hid a hundred prophets from Queen Jezebel's murderous rampage, and God sent Elijah to Ahab to announce the end of the drought. In this encounter, Ahab blamed Elijah for causing the drought; but Elijah retorted that it is Ahab's idolatry that brought God's punishment. Then he issued the challenge to assemble the prophets of Ba'al (a Canaanite weather god associated with thunderstorms) and Asherah (Ba'al's consort and a Canaanite goddess of the sea) for the decisive contest.

This week's lection (18:20-39) recounts the well-known encounter on Mount Carmel between Elijah and the prophets of Ba'al. Carmel is a precipice rising out of the sea overlooking present-day Haifa. It was viewed as a sacred site in ancient times. For the Canaanites (amongst whom the Israelites lived and whose ways they frequently adopted), Ba'al was worshiped as lord of Mount Carmel. Elijah challenged the Ba'al that was worshiped at Carmel.

"YHWH Indeed Is God!"

The people gathered to witness the event. Elijah demanded that they cease "hobbling on two crutches" (see 18:21). They must make a clear choice between YHWH and Ba'al—which is the central theme of the Deuteronomistic historian throughout these books. They remained silent, awaiting the outcome of the momentous contest. The god that would send down lightning to consume the oblation would be the one they would follow. The 450 prophets of Ba'al offered prayers and lacerated themselves, but nothing happened. Then Elijah repaired the altar, had it laid with wood and the bull, then doused it with water. When he prayed that YHWH would act so the people would know he was the prophet of YHWH, fire came from the sky. The bull, wood, water, altar, and dust were totally consumed. The people were convinced and bowed in worship. And Elijah summarily executed the prophets of Ba'al.

The power of God was invoked by a faithful prophet. The people's belief was induced by a miraculous demonstration. YHWH and his prophet were triumphant. The losers were annihilated. Ahab and Jezebel, the sponsors of syncretism, were discredited. The people shouted, "YHWH indeed is God!"

> **Think About It:** YHWH indeed is God! What would Jesus say about the way the Ba'al prophets were treated? What is your understanding of how God confronts opposing forces? What are the signs of God's activity in our world that might lead persons to faith? What has led you to faith?

Psalter: Psalm 96

The most complete of the enthronement psalms, Psalm 96 appears to be a fuller version of Psalm 29. It first ushers in a new reign and then describes its qualities. Verses 1-6 bid the congregation to worship God, calling them to sing (three times), bless, tell, and declare the greatness of God's majesty, goodness, and mighty acts among the nations. By comparison with the creator of the universe, other gods are mere empty idols. The glory of YHWH is revealed both in the world of nature and in the Temple where worship takes place.

Verses 7-9 closely parallel Psalm 29:1-2, the main difference being that it speaks to "families of the peoples" rather than "heavenly beings," who are called to participate in worship here on earth rather than to observe divine beings adoring God in heaven. The central affirmation of the psalm is that "YHWH reigns" (10a)! This is the announcement of the coronation. God's rule is now made evident and effective.

In verses 10b-13, the character of God's reign is proclaimed to the nations.

> **Think About It:** God can be trusted to make all things right. Have you found this to be so? What helps you keep on trusting when things keep going wrong?

God has been installed in the roles of maintaining creation and judging humanity. All nature (the heavens, earth, sea, field and its inhabitants, and trees in the forest) celebrate its divine ordering. People can also be content in the assurance that God's judgment will be fair and honest. The new king (YHWH) can be trusted to make all things right.

Epistle: Galatians 1:1-12

This letter of Paul was written around A.D. 50 to the churches he founded on his first missionary journey (see Acts 13, 14) in the Roman province of Galatia. It was written to address the controversy raging in those churches concerning the requirement that converted pagans needed to become observant Jews. Paul was a strong advocate for offering the gospel of Christ to pagans free from the restrictions of Jewish law and practice (epitomized by circumcision).

Returning to Antioch, Paul received word that the Judaizers (who taught that to become Christian Gentiles must first become Jewish proselytes) were upsetting the congregations he had just established in Pisidian Antioch, Iconium, Lystra, and Derbe with their teaching. Furthermore, they were demeaning Paul by declaring he was not a true apostle like the leaders of the Jerusalem church who had been Jesus' companions during his earthly ministry. So Paul wrote this letter to defend his theological position and his apostolic authority.

A Divine Commission

Today's lection begins with a salutation (verses 1-5), continues with a description of the situation in the Galatian churches (verses 6-10), and concludes with an affirmation of the divine source of Paul's message (verses 11-12). Paul claims that because he saw the risen Lord and had been sent to preach the Resurrection, he was a true apostle in every sense of the word. He was gravely concerned that they had so quickly departed from the truth he had taught them, led astray by persons coming after him who had been preaching a distorted gospel. His anger was expressed in the curse he pronounced on them (verses 6-10). He made clear right at the start that his message was revealed to him directly by Christ. Apparently his opponents were not among the witnesses of the Resurrection and thus had no superior claims over Paul (verses 11-12).

> **Think About It:** Paul asserts that his message was revealed by Christ. Imagine yourself as a new Galatian Christian reading these words and comparing them with the preaching of the Judaizers. Which would appeal to you more and why? How would you discern whom to believe?

Gospel: Luke 7:1-10

The Gospel of Luke was written between A.D. 70 and 90, well after the Galatian epistle. But the Gentile Christians in Galatia would have taken great encouragement from Jesus' affirmation of the Roman centurion's faith in this passage from Luke. The centurion was not circumcised and did not fully observe the Jewish law; yet he trusted in the power and love of Jesus. And Jesus sensed in him a deeper faith than he had found in his own people.

The scene was Capernaum, a fishing village on the shores of the Sea of Galilee, home of several of the disciples. As part of occupied territory, a Roman military contingent was stationed there, with an officer who had befriended the Jews and even built them a synagogue. He had a trusted slave who had become very sick. Hearing about Jesus and his powers of healing, he asked some leaders of the Jewish synagogue to ask Jesus to help. Apparently, the servant meant a lot to him, and the centurion was desperate to try to save him. So he was ready to try anything. The leaders trusted the centurion, who had been treating them kindly and fairly. So they went to get Jesus to bring him to the military barracks. Good relations seem to have prevailed here all around—the Romans with the Jews and the elders with Jesus.

A Humble Man

Then the centurion had second thoughts. A humble man he must have been, for he began to think it presumptuous of him, an outsider, to request help from this renowned Galilean healer. He realized that it might be offensive for a pious Jew to enter his house, so he did not want to create a problem. His faith in Jesus' curative powers led him to ask Jesus simply to say the healing words rather than enter his house and be made unclean. Whatever spirits or powers had inflicted the illness on his slave would heed the commands of Jesus, just as his foot soldiers obeyed his orders without question. Without Jesus ever entering the centurion's house or seeing or touching the slave, when the messengers returned home they found the slave restored to health.

An Unfavorable Comparison

The centurion's trust in the Son of God was comparable to a soldier's trust in his commanding officer. Jesus saw the parallel, was impressed by it, and commended the man's faith to the surrounding crowd. Perhaps the Jewish elders were taken aback, even offended, by the unfavorable comparison Jesus drew to the faith of their own people; and this may have been one of many incidents that began to disturb the good relations and build up opposition.

Think About It: The slave was healed by the word of Jesus. What do you think accomplishes healing—the faith of the recipient? the power of God? the skill of health-care professionals and caregivers? the compassion and support of the faith community? the power of prayer? Did God work in different ways in Jesus' time than now, or is the process of healing the same in all times and places?

Why does Luke include this story in his Gospel? First, because the event happened. Second, to indicate that many Roman soldiers were receptive to the gospel. Third, to indicate that Jesus was not an enemy of Rome and that anyone could be a disciple of Jesus without being an enemy of the Roman state. This story sets the stage for the story in Acts in which Cornelius was baptized and became the first Gentile convert.

Study Suggestions

A. Sing Praises to God

Open by singing a hymn of praise, such as "Let All the World in Every Corner Sing." Then read Psalm 96 responsively, with half the group reading the first line of each verse and the rest responding with the second line. Ask: What creates joy in Christian worship? Help the group appreciate the psalm's significance in Temple worship by summarizing the background information on pages 215–16. Discuss the "Think About It" questions regarding God making things right.

B. Pose the Issue

State that the other three lections this week address the relation between the faith community and outsiders in different ways. The Elijah story pits the power of YHWH against that of pagan priests and describes a mighty triumph. Paul in Galatians argues for the inclusion of Gentiles. Luke shows Jesus commending the faith of a Roman officer in contrast to that of his own people. The issue here is: How are we to relate to persons outside our faith community?

C. Examine Elijah's Way

Set the context for 1 Kings 18:20-39 by presenting the background about the theological commitment of the Deuteronomists and the Elijah stories leading up to the contest on Mount Carmel. Then read the lection aloud, and ask: Why were the people undecided as to which god to trust? Why did Ahab and Jezebel encourage worship of the Canaanite deities? Why was Elijah opposed to this practice? What led the people to believe in YHWH?

Continue with the "Think About It" questions related to contemporary parallels to this situation. Ask: What was Elijah's way of dealing with unfaithful Israelites and the foreign prophets of Ba'al? (He persuaded the unfaithful and executed the foreigners.)

D. Explore Paul's Way

Explain the aim of Paul's letter to the Galatians, then read aloud 1:1-12. Divide the class into three groups, assign one section of this passage to each (verses 1-5, 6-10, 11-12), and ask each group to develop a one-sentence statement of the main point of its passage. Write these summaries on chalk-board or posterboard. Ask: What problem was Paul addressing in Galatians? What was he advocating? How would the Christians in Galatia be likely to respond to his message? Also ask the "Think About It" questions. What was Paul's way of dealing with outsiders (persons of pagan background who believed the gospel)? (To emphasize that both Jews and Gentiles receive salvation through faith.)

E. Learn About Jesus' Way

Read aloud Luke 7:1-10. Supplement the story from the interpretation on pages 217-18. Discuss the question in the last paragraph of the commentary about why Luke included this story in his Gospel. Raise the questions in the "Think About It" box. Ask: What was Jesus' way of dealing with outsiders (persons of pagan background who trusted in him)? (To recognize faith wherever it was found.)

F. Compare the Ways

Ask: What are appropriate ways for Christians today to relate to persons of other faiths? to those who want to continue in their faiths? who want to accept Christ but do not accept many of our traditions? Who can we think of whom we might help to feel we want to include them?

G. In Closing

Read the poem, "Outwitted," by Edwin Markham:
"He drew a circle that shut me out—
Heretic, rebel, a thing to flout.
But Love and I had the wit to win:
We drew a circle that took him in!"

Offer an extemporaneous prayer expressing thanks for the learnings of this session.

Lections for Sunday Between
June 5 and 11

Old Testament: 1 Kings 17:8-24

*T*ODAY we go back a chapter from last week's passage to explore the encounter of Elijah with the widow of Zarephath, which was on the Phoenician coast, well beyond the area under Ahab's dominion. Still fleeing from Ahab's wrath because of the drought, he had left the Wadi Cherith east of the Jordan and traveled northwest to Sidon along the Mediterranean coast (present-day Lebanon). There, guided by YHWH, he found refuge in the home of a poor widow who gave him hospitality. As he entered town he saw her near the gate gathering firewood and asked her for something to eat and drink. She confessed that, due to the drought, she had next-to-nothing left in her larder. In fact, she was on her way home to bake a last loaf of bread for herself and her son and then settle down to starve to death (verses 8-12).

One Good Turn Deserves Another
Elijah tried to cheer her up by telling her not to fear, which, considering her dire circumstances, probably fell on deaf ears. Rather audaciously, he asked her to share this final meal with him. Then, in the name of YHWH—who was his God not hers—he made the astonishing promise that, until God brought the drought to an end, her supply of meal and oil would continue to supply her needs. According to the word of the prophet, she prepared the last meal. She found that the meal and oil never were depleted (verses 13-16).

Adding Insult to Injury
The woman's problems were not over. Her son fell ill and declined to the point of death. This development she blamed on Elijah. Next to his aura of holiness as a prophet of God, her sinfulness stood out in stark relief, and her

son's illness was her punishment. Here the Deuteronomist theology becomes apparent: misfortune, regardless of its natural causes, is inevitably a punishment for sin (verses 17-18).

Without trying to answer the woman's charge, Elijah, confident that the God who had kept the food supply going was adequate for this crisis as well, took the unconscious boy from his mother's arms, carried him upstairs, laid him on his own bed, and began to pray. God heard the prayer, the child was revived, and Elijah carried him down, laid him back in his mother's arms, alive and well. No doubt regretting her earlier intemperate accusations against Elijah, the grateful mother was quick to acknowledge Elijah as a true "man of God" (prophet, holy man) and to trust the truth of his words as coming from God (verses 19-24).

What Does It Mean?

That's the story; now what does it mean? Elijah, a prophet of YHWH, was in pagan territory. The Canaanite woman was suspicious of this alien refugee but took him in and treated him kindly. They were both victims of a severe drought, so perhaps misery loved company. Each met the other's need. Elijah returned a human favor with two saving acts of compassion that kept both her and her son alive. She was convinced of the authenticity of both him and his message. Being faithful to the law of hospitality did not lead to starvation, but provided for her survival.

> **Think About It:** Elijah and his message were authenticated by a compassionate, prayerful act. When have you been in doubt about a person or a truth claim? What convinced you of their validity? How, in your experience, is trust built? How can we convince others that we and our witness are real?

Psalter: Psalm 146

This is a psalm of personal thanksgiving. We are not told the specifics of how the psalmist has been blessed. But we know God has been good to him, for which he will be eternally grateful. Perhaps this psalm was sung during the peace offering (see Leviticus 7:11). The animal was offered, the psalm was sung, and then all who had gathered join in a feast. Human leaders fail, but God is faithful. Human beings are fallible; their plans and programs do not last (verses 3-4).

Far better is it to put one's trust and hope in the Creator God who administers justice fairly and provides for the needs of all who are oppressed, hungry, afflicted, downtrodden, marginalized, and faced with misfortune. These are all objects of God's compassion, but the way of those who practice evil and injustice will be undone (verses 5-9). God is good. God is just. God will rule forever. You can count on it, people! So praise God (verse 10)!

Epistle: Galatians 1:11-24

In this lection, Paul, still contending with those who had been undermining his ministry in the churches of Galatia, sets out a defense of his apostolic authority. First, supplementing Luke's account in Acts 9:1-30, he describes the circumstances of his conversion and call. Not one to do anything halfway, he had earlier gone all out in defending Pharisaism by rooting out members of the upstart Christian sect wherever he could find them. Because of his prodigious zeal he had moved up in the ranks of Pharisees quite rapidly (verses 13-14).

Called by God

But God, who had other plans for Paul from birth, tracked him down on the road to Damascus. There he met Jesus, his life was changed, and he was called to take the good news to the Gentiles. His commission and message came directly from God, he claimed, and not from any human source. After his call vision, he did not go to headquarters in Jerusalem to get instructions. Rather, he went out into the Arabian desert to commune directly with God. Only after this period of solitary preparation did he return to Damascus to take up his new task (verses 15-17). So Paul's ministry and message were valid—especially for Gentile Christians—because they had come directly from God and not from the leaders of the Jerusalem church.

Knowing that his reputation as a vigorous persecutor of Christians had spread far and wide, he needed to ascertain whether he would be accepted in his new role as a missionary for that same faith. It was altogether possible some might think he was a double-agent for the Pharisees. He was delighted to find that they welcomed him with open arms (verses 18-24). Paul understood that his welcome was an act of God's grace.

Think About It: Paul had both a divine sense of calling and human confirmation of the validity of his ministry. What constitutes a call to ministry today? Is an inner sense of God's blessing and vocation sufficient? What role does the church play in validating a call?

Paul's case with the Galatians was taking shape. A direct encounter with God in Christ and three years of preparation in the desert had established his credentials as one called and equipped for his missionary task. Bridges of trust had been built with the leading apostles, the Jewish church, and the growing Gentile constituency, all of whom could provide support and verification of his mission.

Gospel: Luke 7:11-17

Here we have another story of the raising of a widow's son, which Luke seems self-consciously to have patterned after Elijah's raising of the Canaanite widow's son in today's Old Testament lection. This happening is not reported in any of the other Gospels. It took place in the village of Nain, about twenty-five miles southwest of Capernaum and six miles southeast of Nazareth.

As Jesus was entering the town, a funeral procession was leaving the gate carrying a corpse on a stretcher to the burial ground. Burials were not permitted inside the walls of a town, for obvious reasons. The deceased was a grown man, not a little boy as was the widow's son in the Elijah story. The large crowd indicates that the man and his mother were either prominent citizens or much beloved in the community. The fact that he had been the only son of a widow meant that he was likely her only source of support, so the townsfolk were showing great sympathy for her.

"Do Not Fear"

Jesus took all this in at a glance, and immediately his heart of compassion went out to her. His words were, "Do not fear." These words constitute what is known as an oracle of salvation in the Hebrew Scriptures. The words mean that God has broken into a human situation in the presence of death and brings life and salvation. Jesus announced that salvation or deliverance had come to her, and she would live because her son was restored to life.

Jesus was addressing the right problem, but he did more than speak. He moved toward her and touched the corpse. This was surprising in itself, as it would have contaminated him with the ritual taint of death and demonstrated his willingness to identify with the depths of sorrow and suffering. Then he spoke again—this time not to the widow but to her son. With great authority he commanded, "Young man, I say to you, rise!" And lo and behold, to everyone's astonishment, the son sat up and began talking. The phrase, he "gave him to his mother," is identical to that used to describe Elijah's action (see 1 Kings 17:23).

A Different Kind of Fear

The only proper response to God's saving act is that of reverence and awe. Unlike the incident in last week's lection, in which opposition could have been stirred up by Jesus' affirmation of a Gentile's faith, here the crowd was enthusiastic and supportive. Another difference with last week's story of the healing of the centurion's slave is that here there is no mention of faith. The saving action came by God's act of salvation.

> **Think About It:** A revelatory event had taken place. Could it be any act through which God is seen and that leads persons to faith? How is the saving power of God revealed today?

In this event, who God is for us was revealed. The aura of God was present. The blessing was extended to his hearers. The word was getting around—not only in Galilee but also to Judea and beyond the borders of

Palestine. Jesus was one in whom God was truly present and made available to human need.

Study Suggestions

A. Count Your Blessings

Begin by singing the hymn, "Praise, My Soul, the King of Heaven," then ask the group what they are thankful for this day. As they name items, list them on chalkboard or a large sheet of paper. Now read Psalm 146. Ask: For what was the psalmist thankful? Write their answers alongside the first list. Summarize the information in the commentary on page 221. Turn these reasons for gratitude into a simple litany by reading them off one by one, with the group responding after each, "We give you thanks, O God."

B. Examine the Call to Ministry

Pose the questions in the "Think About It" box regarding what constitutes a call to ministry. Then read aloud Paul's argument for the authenticity of his call in Galatians 1:11-24. Drawing on the background information, point out that his claim had a twofold basis—his direct experience with Christ and validation by the church. Note how careful Paul was to stress God's call, his transformation from his previous life, his time of preparation in the desert, his building rapport with the Jerusalem leadership, and his testing the waters in a wider constituency.

Turning to our current situation, emphasize that today we too often limit the call to ministry to the ordained clergy and commissioned missionaries; all Christians are called to ministry in their baptism. Ask: Do you feel called? What is your ministry? How can you test your call? How can you carry out your ministry? How can the church be more intentional about validating the laity's call to ministry and using their gifts?

C. Compare Widow Stories

Explain that the Old Testament and Gospel lections both present stories about the raising of widow's sons from the dead. Give a brief synopsis of each. Then form two groups, assigning 1 Kings 17:8-24 to one and Luke 7:11-17 to the other. Write these instructions out for both groups to follow: "Read your passage and the commentary on it. Consider: What was the situation of the widow and her son? What were the circumstances facing Elijah/Jesus? What did Elijah/Jesus do? Why did he do it? What was the response? What teaching did the writer want to convey to readers through this story? Prepare a brief report."

Regroup and hear reports. Ask: What are the similarities and differences in these two stories? Why do you think Luke patterned his story after the

Elijah story? How does this week's Elijah story differ from that of last week? How does Luke's widow story differ from last week's centurion story?

D. God's Revelations

Pose and discuss the "Think About It" questions mentioned in the two boxes related to building trust and understanding miracles. Keep the focus on how these processes take place today, as compared with the events in Scripture. Encourage group members to share their experiences with how persons and their words are authenticated and how God's saving power is present in contemporary life.

E. Respond With Feeling

Summarize today's lections by noting that they have dealt with thanksgiving for God's blessings (Psalm 146), response to God's call (Galatians), validation of God's message and messenger (First Kings), and awareness of God's action in our lives (Luke). Form groups of three or four, and invite each group to stand and create with their bodies a "statue" that expresses how they can witness to God's saving power in their lives. When they have done so, ask the total group to look at each "statue" in turn and voice the feelings each evokes.

F. Close in Prayer

Merge the statue groups into one large circle. Sing "Spirit of the Living God, Fall Afresh on Me." Then invite sentence prayers expressing learnings gained and commitments made in this session.

Lections for Sunday Between
June 12 and 18

*A*FTER Old Testament: 1 Kings 21:1-21a

FTER Solomon died in 922 B.C., jealousy and infighting erupted
between the two kingdoms that had been ruled by the house of David
for nearly eighty years. As a result, Israel chose a king for itself; and
Solomon's son was left to rule Judah. Fifty-three years later Ahab
became the seventh king of Israel. His main palace was in Samaria; and
his winter palace was in the fertile plain of Jezreel, at the foot of Mount
Gilboa.

Ahab's Conflict

A Jezreelite man named Naboth owned a vineyard next to the winter
palace. Ahab wanted to turn the vineyard into a vegetable garden. Ahab
offered Naboth what he considered to be a fair trade for his land—either
money or a better vineyard. However, since Israel was often referred to as
God's vineyard, and vineyards were considered symbols of God's blessing,
it seemed like Ahab was demeaning God by proposing to trade something
lesser for God's blessings by wanting to turn a vineyard into a vegetable
garden.

Naboth refused Ahab's offer, saying, "The LORD forbid that I should give
you my ancestral inheritance" (21:3). Ancestral property was valued very
highly and was considered an inheritance from God, given when the
Israelites entered Canaan (see Numbers 36:1-12). So Naboth was not just
being difficult; he believed profoundly that God forbade the selling of his
inheritance. Israel placed limits on its kings. It was the excesses of Solomon
that caused the princes of Israel to reject the house of David. Now Ahab was
behaving in a similar, arrogant manner.

Jezebel's Plot

When Queen Jezebel, Ahab's foreign wife, discovered him pouting about his failed deal, she took over. She chided him for not exercising his royal power. As a Canaanite, she believed in the absolute right of the king. From the perspective of her royal upbringing, Naboth was just an insubordinate subject. So she arrogantly usurped Ahab's royal authority, writing letters in his name and using his royal seal. She ordered Jezreelite leaders (who may have been beholden to the king) to proclaim a religious fast where Naboth would be falsely charged with blasphemy and treason. After Naboth was executed on this trumped-up charge, Jezebel brazenly urged Ahab to go and claim the vineyard.

The Consequences

At the vineyard Ahab was confronted by the prophet Elijah. Even though Jezebel seems to be the main schemer in this story, Ahab knew himself to be guilty. He had married a foreigner who worshiped the Ba'als. Furthermore, he had allowed—and perhaps even subtly manipulated—Jezebel to do what she did on his behalf. The consequence of Ahab's crime was commensurate to the deed: He would die on the land he had stolen.

Because the Deuteronomists were sympathetic to Judah, Ahab, like all the kings of Israel, was judged negatively. Some scholars believe this story was rewritten after the Exile to place blame on Jezebel and set an example of the dangers of intermarriage with foreigners.

> **Think About It:** The narrator of Kings rendered a judgment that Ahab and all kings of Israel failed to put loyalty to YHWH above all else. What did they love more than God? What are we tempted to put above our love and loyalty to God and God's will? What are the consequences of failing to put God first in our lives?

Psalter: Psalm 5:1-8

In a morning prayer, the psalmist appeals to God to listen. He is assailed by boasting, lying, deceitful, and bloodthirsty enemies. The psalmist knows that God abhors this wickedness and that the evildoers will not stand before God or dwell with God. In verse 6, the verb *destroy* literally means "cause to perish." Those who practice evil (thus opposing God's sovereignty) will perish because they cut themselves off from the giver of life.

In contrast, the psalmist enters God's house and attributes his or her ability to do so to God's *hesed* (5:7), not to personal worthiness. The Hebrew word *hesed* describes God's character better than any other word, but it is hard to translate because it involves at least seven different English concepts: grace, mercy, compassion, patience, faithfulness, loyalty, and love. It is usually translated as "steadfast love," or, in the King James Version, "lovingkindness."

The psalm also describes God as sovereign or king. *Hesed* and sovereignty are both part of God's character. God exercises sovereignty, not as absolute power, but as *hesed*—committed love. The psalmist recognizes God's sovereignty, abandons self-reliance, and petitions God to lead him or her in this way of committed love.

Epistle: Galatians 2:15-21

Paul wrote to the churches in Galatia because he was astonished and disturbed that they were turning to a "false gospel." After first defending his apostolic *authority* (1:11–2:10; see last week's lection), Paul defended his apostolic *message*. He did so, first, by reporting on his confrontation with Cephas (Peter) at Antioch.

Peter's Inconsistency

When Peter visited the church in Antioch, he found Jewish and Gentile Christians participating together without regard for Jewish laws. They ate at an integrated table—and Peter willingly ate with them. However, when emissaries from James arrived, Peter withdrew from this integrated table fellowship and ate with the visitors. Others followed Peter's example.

Paul's Response

Paul publicly accused Peter of hypocrisy—of not acting consistently "with the truth of the gospel." He challenged Peter: "If you, . . . a Jew live like a Gentile, . . . how can you compel the Gentiles to live like Jews" (2:11-14)? Paul then directly expounded on the gospel message as he understood it. No one, not even Jews, would be justified (come into right relationship with God) by keeping the Jewish law. We are justified only by our faith in Christ. It is possible that Paul failed to understand Peter's motives. It may also explain why Paul and Barnabas ended their companionship and Paul was joined by Silas. Unfortunately, we are not provided with Peter's side of the argument.

> **Think About It:** Paul accused Peter of hypocritical actions because of fear of a certain faction's response. If you were Peter, how would you respond to such a charge? What happens when new leadership questions the character of old leaders in the church?

Still thinking about Peter and the Antioch situation, Paul acknowledged that some of his opponents were against an integrated table fellowship of Jews and Gentiles because the Christian doctrine of freedom might lead Jews to break the law. Paul's opponents claimed that Christ therefore was the minister of sin. But Paul responded, "Certainly not!"

Paul then pondered what would happen if *he* were to require Gentile Christians to follow Jewish law. He too would become a transgressor of the true gospel of freedom in Christ. But Paul quickly noted that his ego was dead to the law. Within his same old body, he had gained a new identity. While Paul talked about himself in this passage, he really was speaking more generally about Christian life and relationship to God. Christians do not earn God's favor by observing the Mosaic law. God's favor comes by grace received through faith.

Gospel: Luke 7:36–8:3

Our Gospel lection includes the story of the "woman in the city, who was a sinner" and a brief reference to women disciples of Jesus.

The Banquet Scene

Luke had previously noted that Pharisees rejected God's purpose for them (Luke 7:30). However, Jesus was still on relatively good terms with the Pharisees and accepted an invitation from one of them—a man named Simon—to a banquet, a much more public affair than we might assume. Townspeople gathered to see the Pharisee and his guests.

One person in the crowd was a "woman who had lived a sinful life in that town" (7:37, NIV). It is possible Luke meant to imply that the woman was a prostitute. This implication—and the story's placement after the accusations against the Son of Man (7:33-34) and just before Luke 8:2, which introduces several women—has led many to identify the unknown woman as Mary Magdalene and then to denigrate her as a prostitute. There is no evidence for this; Matthew (26:6-13) and Mark (14:3-9) simply identify her as a woman. John (12:1-7) attributes the action to Mary, the sister of Martha and Lazarus, who is characterized as upright and faithful. The woman and her sin remain unknown. In her anonymity she serves as a universal "repentant sinner" figure, one of the few mentioned in every Gospel.

Simon's Consternation

The woman created a scandalous scene at Simon's banquet. In his mind she violated social custom by washing Jesus' feet and letting down her hair. In Simon's Pharisee worldview, the woman had dishonored him and made Jesus unclean. Simon responded by making four pious and rather arrogant assumptions: the woman was a sinner; if Jesus had been a prophet, he would have known she was a sinner; if Jesus had known she was a sinner, he would not have allowed her to touch him; and, since Jesus did nothing to stop the woman, Jesus was not a prophet.

Jesus' Response

Jesus immediately confirmed that he *did* know what kind of woman had touched him and that he also knew Simon's character. Following a custom at banquets of posing riddles, Jesus told Simon a parable and asked a question. The answer was so obvious that the Pharisee responded cautiously. Jesus then made his point: The Pharisee, since he followed the law, believed he had little sin and thus neither needed nor received much forgiveness. Furthermore, he neglected to be hospitable to Jesus. The woman, on the other hand, knew her sin had been forgiven and demonstrated her gratitude with extravagant, loving actions.

> **Think About It:** Jesus contrasts the woman who recognized her sin with Simon who did not. She received much forgiveness; he received little. Where do you see the woman in yourself? Where do you find Simon in yourself? When have you pretended to be upright and self-sufficient? When have you acknowledged your need for help and grace?

We are left with a riddle in Luke 7:47: Did the woman love because she had been forgiven, or was she forgiven because she loved Jesus? Either way, Jesus forgave her sin, causing others at the banquet to wonder what manner of man this was who presumed to forgive sin (7:49). Many of Luke's stories posed this question, until finally he reported Peter confessing that Jesus was the Messiah, after which a voice from heaven declared, "This is my Son" (Luke 9:18-20, 28-36).

The Women Followers

After this story, Luke briefly mentions the unconventional practice of Jesus of permitting women to travel with him as disciples, thereby correcting an assumption that all Jesus' disciples were men. Unfortunately, we are told only a few of their names and very little about their roles. Biblical reports of women often refer to their roles of mother, widow, former prostitutes, passive followers, or nurturers of men. Most are unnamed. Here Luke identifies and names several prominent women who financed and nurtured the ministry of Jesus (8:1-3).

Study Suggestions

A. Create a Poster

On a large sheet of paper, print "Finding Our Way to God." Provide colored markers. Invite the group to add words, phrases, and sketches on how we find our way to a right relationship with God.

B. Identify Hindrances

Read Psalm 5 together. Review the commentary on pages 227–28. Ask: Who were the psalmist's enemies? What did the psalmist ask God for? What does the psalmist mean by "make straight your way"? What kind of sovereignty does God exercise? What hinders us from following God's way? What kinds of speech are hindrances? (Examples: boasting, gossiping, exaggerating, lying, giving false witness.) How does such speech do violence to people? How does destructive speech keep us from God's way of committed love? How can we stop destructive speech?

C. Examine Power

Act out 1 Kings 21:1-21a by assigning reading parts for Ahab, Naboth, Jezebel, Elijah, and a narrator. Review the commentary on pages 226–27. David also violated property rights by taking Bathsheba as a wife. How is it that this abuse of power is excused and Ahab's offense became fatal?

Discuss power. Ask: When power is abused, what elements exist in the situation? (Unequal positions, coveting something, being greedy, feeling superior to others?) Power is frequently abused. How is power limited so as to minimize its abuse?

D. Explore Forgiveness

Read aloud Luke 7:36–8:3, then summarize the commentary on pages 229–30. Ask: How did the woman experience God's *hesed* or grace? (Through recognizing her sin and having it forgiven.) Why did Simon not experience much forgiveness? How do we know *we* are forgiven? How do we respond to God's forgiveness? How does recognizing one's sin and being forgiven relate to finding our way to God?

Also discuss the "Think About It" questions.

Contrast Jezebel with the woman "sinner." How are the queen and the woman characterized? What would you expect of each if she fulfilled her stated role? What do the reversals in the characterizations and actual behavior tell us about sin? about being righteous before God? about repentance and the need for forgiveness?

E. Reflect on Faith and Law

Read Galatians 2:11-21, and review the commentary on pages 228–29. Ask: What point was Paul trying to make by telling the Galatians about his confrontation with Peter in Antioch? Does Paul's attack seem fair? (Review Acts 11:1-18 to learn what Peter believed.) What does Paul say is the true message of the gospel? (Faith in Christ.) How does faith help us find our way to God? How does depending on obedience to the law or moral behavior hinder us in finding our way to God?

F. Make Connections

List the major points of today's lections: God is sovereign; God exercises power through committed love; we gain right relationship with God by grace received through faith. Our proper response to God's loving forgiveness is to express love and gratitude. Look at the poster again (Activity A). Ask: Is there anything you would change? What else would you add? What do today's lections teach us about finding our way to God?

G. Sing and Pray

Sing "Help Us Accept Each Other." Pray: "Gracious sovereign God, help us recognize our sin. We trust that you forgive us. We give thanks for your steadfast love. Lead us in your way. Amen."

Lections for Sunday Between
June 19 and 25

Old Testament: 1 Kings 19:1-15a

*E*LIJAH was a prophet of YHWH who lived in the 800's B.C. during the reign of King Ahab of Israel. Centuries later, the narrator of Kings retold long-existing Elijah stories, including a report of Ahab's failures to obey YHWH. Our passage is the end of one such story.

The Drought and Contest

When Ahab married the Phoenician princess Jezebel, she gave support to the worship of ba'als and asherahs in Israel. The ba'als were believed to be the husband or lord of a particular place. The female consort of the ba'al was an asherah. The ba'al was represented by a pole, or phallic symbol, and the asherah by a tree. It was thought that for the land to be fertile, the ba'al of the place needed to be worshiped. Sexual fertility rites used sympathetic magic to assure productivity of the soil. This kind of religion was an abomination to any who worshiped YHWH.

A drought descended on the area; and Elijah, who insisted that to be faithful Israel must worship YHWH alone, proclaimed that this was YHWH's punishment on Israel for practicing this idolatry. Three years later, Elijah challenged the prophets of Ba'al and Asherah to a contest. They would prepare to sacrifice a bull and call on Ba'al to provide the fire; Elijah would do the same and call on YHWH; the god who answered would be the true God. Ba'al lost; God provided fire for Elijah's altar and was declared God. Elijah ordered the death of Ba'al's prophets. The rain returned—not through Ba'al—but by the word of God (1 Kings 17:1-7; 18:1, 17-40; see the lection and commentary of two weeks ago for a full discussion of this dramatic event).

Elijah's Flight

When Jezebel learned that her prophets were dead, she threatened to kill Elijah. He fled south into the desert wilderness, a journey of forty days and nights, reminiscent of the time Moses spent on the same mountain (Horeb or Sinai, verse 8). At the mountain, a voice asked why Elijah was there. Elijah was angry and depressed. Serving God was just too hard; his "zeal" for the people (the same term used to characterize God's "jealousy" for Israel's loyalty) had not stanched their idolatrous habits and behavior. In spite of his triumph on Mount Carmel, he still felt like a failure.

Elijah was directed to a cave to wait for God to "pass by"—another nod to the tradition of Moses having stood at the "cleft of the rock" for his own theophany (revelation of God's presence; Exodus 33:19-23). While he was hiding there, a rainstorm, an earthquake, and a fire all took place—but God was not in any of these signs. Finally, there was a "sound of sheer silence," which is a contradiction in terms suggesting the calm after a storm. Nevertheless, Elijah heard God in the hush that followed three violent, tumultuous acts of nature.

The Story's Point

Elijah was told to go about his prophetic business, including anointing Jehu as the new king of Israel. Later in Kings we discover that Jezebel was killed by Jehu (2 Kings 9:30–10:30). The narrator's point? God most often works quietly and naturally through ordinary historical events and people to accomplish the divine purpose. Ironically, it is usually in the mundane and commonplace that God is most active.

> **Think About It:** Elijah expected a dazzling act of God, but instead was told to return and go about his ordinary business. How do you experience God at work in your life? Does it take a spectacular intervention to make you aware of God's presence, or do you sense God's purpose and power moving in everyday events?

Psalter: Psalm 42

Psalms 42 and 43 are numbered separately, but scholars view them as one poem with a common theme and refrain. In the poem, the psalmist's soul "thirsts" (longs) for God, whose comforting presence is like the escape a deer finds in a stream when chased by dogs. The psalmist complains that he has been exiled from worshiping God at the Temple in Jerusalem and that his antagonists constantly taunt him by asking, "Where is your God?"

He tries to remember happier times of festivals and worship, but cannot forget his circumstances or his fear that God has forgotten him. Thus, in the refrain, he begins to despair: "Why are you cast down, O my soul?" Yet hope remains: "I shall again praise [God]" (42:5, 11; 43:5).

The poem ends in Psalm 43 with two petitions: for vindication (justification, support, approval) and for God's light and truth to lead him back to the Temple so he might praise God. Although expressed in personal language, this poem speaks for all who are cut off from God, calling them to continue trusting in God and to remain hopeful.

Epistle: Galatians 3:23-29

Jews believed that God gave them the law through Moses in order to teach them how to please God and find the path of life. Then Jesus came to the Jews with a new claim: Know me and you will know God; have faith in me and gain eternal life; respond to God's gift by loving your neighbor.

Paul's Struggle

When law-abiding Jews became disciples of Christ, they struggled to understand the place of the law in their new lives. Some of Paul's fellow Jewish Christians believed they should continue following the law. They also argued that Gentiles who became Christian needed to observe Jewish law in order to be fully Christian. Paul did not discourage Jews from their religious observance, but argued that Gentile Christians need not come to Christianity by way of Jewish law. All persons, Paul argued, are justified (brought into right relationship with God) by God's grace received through faith.

Paul's Argument

In our passage, Paul responds to Jewish Christians in Galatia who wanted Gentile Christians to follow Jewish dietary law. He tells the Jewish Christians that before Christ came, the law functioned as their *paidagogos* (a household slave who guarded children, supervised their discipline, and took them to and from school). The law was a disciplinarian for Jews, supervising them, guarding them, helping them to know and follow the way to God. However, when Christ came, believers no longer needed a disciplinarian. Through their baptism, they came to know God personally and received God's promise of eternal life. They became children of God—adult heirs, full members of God's household. Of course, Paul insisted that all Christians observe the moral laws revealed to Moses.

Gospel: Luke 8:26-39

In the first century, and in many parts of the world today, many people believe in a world inhabited by demons (as well as spirits, angels, centaurs, nymphs) who control natural processes and possess persons. Demon possession and mental illness are two different things; but this story may be seen to offer hope to those who suffer from the "demons" of depression, destructive compulsive behaviors, irrational fears, or anxiety. If today this man's possession were actually mental illness, our remedy would be counseling or medication. In any case, he was in desperate need of healing.

The Story

When Jesus stepped from his boat onto the shore of a non-Jewish area, he was met by a man tormented by demons. Although a "man of the city," he had been ostracized and was living unclothed in desolated tombs (considered unclean by Jewish standards). Jesus demanded to know the demons' name (thereby gaining power over them). The name "legion" implies power and strength in number. Jesus ordered the demons to leave the man alone, but they pled not to be returned to the abyss. Jesus obliged their request to be transferred in a herd of swine. (Swine were considered unclean by Jewish law.) The swine rushed down an embankment into the Sea of Galilee and were drowned. When the swineherds reported what happened, the people were afraid and asked Jesus to leave. The healed man begged to go with Jesus, but Jesus told him to return home and witness to what God had done for him.

From a first-century, Jewish Christian point of view, justice had prevailed: The man had been delivered from the torment of demons and the unclean tombs; the demons got what they wanted; the unclean herd of swine was destroyed. No Jewish Christian reader would have questioned the ethics of Jesus destroying the livelihood of Gentile swineherds. The story showed that Jesus outwitted evil, which, when it gets its way, is always destructive, even self-destructive.

The Unvoiced Question

Luke's stories of Jesus in Chapters 7, 8, and 9 continually raise one question: "Who is this person Jesus?" In our last session the question was "Who is this who forgives sins?" When Jesus stilled a raging storm at sea the disciples asked: "Who then is this, that he commands even the winds and the water?" (8:22-25). Today's lection implies a similar question: "Who is this person who casts out demons?" The question is not voiced, but is buried beneath the people's fear. Just as they had ostracized the man who was filled with demons, so they sent away the one who had healed him. They did not recognize God's power at work in Jesus.

The Story's Significance

On a historical level, Luke's only story of Jesus' ministry beyond Jewish territory foreshadows the Christian mission to the Gentile world that would begin after Jesus' death. This story showed Luke's first readers that Jesus approved of such a mission. The healed man is a prototype of the Gentile convert who, freed from evil, became a strong and vocal witness to all that God had done. He did not need to become a part of the Jewish community, but could remain in his Gentile world.

Think About It: The Gerasene man responded to Jesus' healing action with faith; the people responded with fear and rejection. How do you respond to an unusual or awesome event—with doubt and suspicion, or with openness to see signs of God at work in new ways? How do you respond to persons who do and say good things in ways that are new and different?

On a personal level, Jesus' healing of the Gerasene man is a story of hope. Although we experience the oppression of evil, the torment of illness and disorders, and the damaging effects of sinful behaviors (committed both by and against us), we are assured by this story of Jesus' compassion that a loving God seeks to heal and save us.

Study Suggestions

A. Illustrate Despair and Hope

Read Psalms 42 and 43 as one poem. Review the notes on pages 233–34. Invite members to use paper and colored markers to illustrate the psalmist's movement between despair and hope. Show and talk about these drawings. Discuss: What is the sanctuary the deer finds in the water? What is the cause of the psalmist's despair? What gives him hope? How do we find respite from the pressures of life that seek to overcome us?

B. Examine Elijah's "Burnout"

Read aloud 1 Kings 19:1-15a, and review the commentary on pages 232–33. Ask: Why did Elijah flee? What is his complaint? What is the narrator of Kings saying by retelling this story? (God can act in nature, God works through ordinary historical events and people.) Why do you think Elijah was so despondent? How might we describe Elijah's state today? (Frustrated, burned-out, depressed, suicidal.) What kinds of burnout situations have led you to seek sanctuary?

C. Reflect on Fear and Faith

Read Luke 8:26-39 and the interpretation on pages 234–36. Ask: How are the mentally ill treated in modern society? Why did Luke tell this story? (It demonstrated Jesus' power and how persons touched by the gospel could live as Gentiles in a Gentile world as faithful disciples.)

Compare Elijah's situation with that of the Gerasene man. (Both felt desperate in their particular circumstances.) Discuss: What did faith in God and God's intervention accomplish in each situation? What changes were wrought in the beneficiary of God's action? How have we experienced God's presence at times when we felt discouraged or possessed by circumstances or powers beyond our control?

D. Explore Law and Faith

Read aloud Galatians 3:23-29. Summarize the commentary on page 234. Discuss: What did first-century Jewish Christians struggle over? What is Paul's answer in this struggle? Where do we encounter this same struggle between salvation by human accomplishment and our salvation by grace through faith today?

The language about belonging and unity refers not just to a change in membership or status, but to a change in one's being, an actual shift in identity. Ask: What is it that Paul suggests is "no longer," and what has taken its place? How would you formulate these thoughts in your own words? What have you relinquished because of your faithful relationship to Christ? Also discuss the "Think About It" questions.

E. Make Connections

On chalkboard or a large sheet of paper, make three columns: "Human Emotions," "Human Responses," and "Common Message." Ask: What are the common emotions, responses, and message in the lections today? (Possibilities: *Emotions*: loneliness, despair, hopelessness, anger, fear. *Responses*: fleeing from enemies, rejecting others, seeking sanctuary, seeking divine direction, remaining hopeful. *Message*: release yourselves from the seeming safety of laws; live by faith in a steadfastly loving God who promises eternal life; accept all believers into one community.)

F. Sing a Petition

Sing "Let My People Seek Their Freedom," and close with prayer for faith and for healing for all God's children.

Lections for Sunday Between
June 26 and July 2

*T*HIS passage narrates the ascent of Elijah and the commissioning of

Old Testament: 2 Kings 2:1-2, 6-14

Elisha, two great prophets. Elijah, who raised a child from the dead (1 Kings 17:17-24) and triumphed over the priests of Ba'al (1 Kings 18:20-40), makes way for his disciple, Elisha, who would prophesy through the reigns of four kings of Israel (850–800 B.C.). His name means "El [God] is salvation."

The stories of Elisha in Second Kings portray him as a wise man who performed wonders, both to help his nation during trying times and to meet the needs of individuals. Unlike his predecessor Elijah, who moved about alone and dwelt in caves, Elisha lived in cities (2 Kings 6:13, 19, 32) and traveled with groups of prophets (the "sons of the prophets," 2 Kings 2:3-15; 4:1; 5:22; 9:1). His prophetic activity took him to religious centers like Bethel (2 Kings 2:23), Gilgal (2:1; 4:38), and Mount Carmel (2:25; 4:25). He used his staff (2 Kings 4:29) and music (2 Kings 3:15) to manifest his prophetic power.

"I Will Not Leave You"

Elisha had been warned by other prophets that Elijah, his mentor, would be taken by God that very day (2 Kings 2:3-5). As they traveled from Gilgal to other cultic sites, Elijah tried to get Elisha to stay behind. But Elisha insisted on accompanying him (2:4, 6), much like Ruth insisted she would not leave Naomi (Ruth 1:16-17).

When the two prophets reached the Jordan River, Elijah rolled up his mantle and struck the water with it. The water divided so they could cross on dry ground, a miracle echoing the Exodus (Exodus 14:21-22) and Joshua's leading of the people of Israel across the Jordan (Joshua 3:14-17). The mantle, a loose-fitting, knee-length cloak made of rough hair, was commonly worn by prophets and in this case symbolized the prophet's power.

Power in the Spirit

Elisha asked Elijah for "a double share of your spirit" (2 Kings 2:9). Ancient peoples believed that God-given charismatic gifts could be apportioned out and transferred to others, as when God gave some of Moses' spirit to the seventy elders in the wilderness (Numbers 11:16-17). The "double share" of spirit alludes to the firstborn son's share of a father's estate, which gave equal portions to each son except for the eldest, who received an added portion (Deuteronomy 21:15-17). A careful counting of the wonders performed by Elisha compared to Elijah will reveal that Elisha received an exact double portion.

> *Think About It:* A chariot of fire within a whirlwind whisked Elijah away. Chariot, fire, and whirlwind are all symbols of power. What do these symbols represent to you?

The Chariots of Israel

Elisha cried out "Father, father! The chariots of Israel and its horsemen!" (2:12). This enigmatic cry could mean that Elisha was having a vision of the heavenly armies led by "YHWH of Hosts," who was believed to fight alongside the armies of Israel. Or, the phrase could refer to Elisha's later role as advisor during Israel's battles (see 2 Kings 3:9-27; 6:8-23). When Elijah disappeared, Elisha tore his clothes as a sign of mourning.

Picking Up the Mantle

Picking up Elijah's discarded mantle, Elisha struck the water with it, saying "Where is the LORD, the God of Elijah?" (2:14). This act represented evidence that he was Elijah's successor.

> *Think About It:* "Where is the LORD?" Elisha asked. What evidence of God's presence in your life do you seek?

Psalter: Psalm 77:1-2, 11-20

This psalm affirms God's care in the face of circumstances that seem to belie it. Exhibiting the sleeplessness and inner turmoil characteristic of depression (verses 2-4), the psalmist does not specify the nature of the trouble; but unceasing prayer brings no relief (verse 2). The severity and urgency of the psalmist's distress are underscored by the repetition in the opening verse, "I pray aloud to God, aloud to God." The psalmist fears that God has stopped loving his people (verses 7-9).

How does the psalmist find relief? By remembering the mighty acts of God during the Exodus and the wilderness wanderings (verses 14-20; see Exodus 15:1-18). Verse 16 also suggests the power of God manifested over the waters of chaos during Creation (see Genesis 1:2). This poem would have been sung in Temple worship. Recalling God's power while being surrounded by other worshipers, the psalmist experiences reassurance that God still cares.

In fact, the psalmist concludes, just as God left no footprints during the Exodus (verse 19), human beings do not always recognize what God is doing in the world. The same mighty God who led the people "like a flock" can, however, be trusted to act again (verse 20). This shepherd imagery is also used by the prophet Ezekiel (34:11-16) and Jesus (John 10:11-16).

Epistle: Galatians 5:1, 13-25

As we have seen, Paul, in his letter to the Galatians, argued against the teaching of Jewish Christian missionaries who said that Gentile Christians must become observant Jews. The pressure of these missionaries had heightened divisions within the Galatian church. For Paul, Jesus' death paid the ransom and set believers free from slavery to sin. Because a slave's labor belongs to his master, no work the slave can do can purchase freedom. One can be set free only when a freeman purchases his freedom. The words "for freedom" are a direct quotation from the legal document given to slaves when they were set free by being redeemed by another. Paul writes, because Christ has purchased your freedom, do not behave as if you are slaves any longer. Learn to live as the free persons you have become (5:1).

Desires of the Flesh?

Conditioned by a sex-saturated media, Americans often assume Paul meant sexual desire when he used the word *flesh*. In fact, Paul understood *flesh* in a much larger sense—any self-seeking human desire was opposed to God's will. Paul's list of vices in 5:19-21 includes eight sins against community unity: enmities, strife, jealousy, anger, quarrels, dissensions, factions, and envy. Paul compared the Galatians to dogs who snap and bite at each other (5:15).

> **Think About It:** Paul lists sins against community unity. How are these "sins of the flesh"? What damage do these sins do in our churches? What is the remedy?

Life in the Spirit

The way of life guided by the Spirit, on the other hand, is characterized by love, joy, peace, patience, and other community-enhancing virtues (5:22-23). Lists of vices and virtues were common in the Hellenistic literature of Paul's day (see 1 Corinthians 6:9-11 and 2 Peter 1:5-7). With such lists Paul showed what life in the Spirit does and does not look like. Paradoxically, after saying the Galatians were free, Paul told them to "become slaves to one another" (mutually commit to serving each other's best interests) through love (Galatians 5:13). Mutual love was their only obligation, just as Christ had said (Mark 12:28-34).

Gospel: Luke 9:51-62

This passage opens a major section in the Gospel of Luke (9:51–19:27), when Jesus set his face to go to Jerusalem. For ten chapters Jesus is described as traveling with and teaching his disciples, with the shadow of the cross looming over him (9:22, 44). "Taken up" (9:51) is the same phrase used to describe the ascension of Elijah, which suggests that Jesus, like Elijah, would fulfill God's purposes in a mighty way.

While they traveled together, Jesus tried to prepare his disciples for the hardships and hostility they would encounter. Traveling the road to Jerusalem became a symbol of discipleship for the early church, the Christian movement becoming known as "the Way" (Acts 9:2). The phrase, "set his face," suggests Jesus' fierce determination to go where God was leading him regardless of the consequences.

Rejection

The response of the Samaritan village showed what lay ahead. Having sent messengers ahead to request accommodations, Jesus was rejected, much like he had been in his hometown of Nazareth (4:16-30). Samaritans were accustomed to Jews traveling through their territory on the way to Jerusalem, but relations were hostile. Jews regarded Samaritans as half-pagan descendants of Assyrian colonists. Samaritans saw themselves as true Israelites, and their mountain (Mount Gerizim and not Zion) as God's true holy place.

Though Jews and Samaritans hated one another, Luke shows Jesus as having an unusually positive attitude toward Samaritans. He commended the one leper, a Samaritan, who returned to give thanks (17:11-19) and told a parable in which a Samaritan was the hero (10:30-37). Here, though, the Samaritans refused Jesus. Perhaps they were angry that, despite his openness to them, he did not recognize their holy site, heading instead to Jerusalem. Jesus did not allow himself to be owned by anyone, either his townspeople or those who might see him as a potential ally.

Refusing Revenge

Jesus' disciples were incensed at this rejection, particularly James and John, two of the disciples closest to Jesus (5:10; 9:28). They wanted to call down lightning from God to destroy the whole village, as Elijah had invoked fire from above on the soldiers of Ahaziah (9:54; see 2 Kings 1:10). Jesus, however, rebuked their eagerness to employ destructive power on his behalf (see 9:49; Mark 10:35-40).

When Jesus had first sent out the disciples to teach and heal, he had told them how to respond to rejection—to wipe the dust from their feet and go on (Luke 9:5; see also 10:10-11). Jesus' refusal to seek vengeance on those who rejected him foreshadows the Passion, when Jesus told his disciples to

Think About It: Jesus rebuked the disciples' eagerness to employ power on his behalf, refusing to seek vengeance on those who rejected him. It is natural to want to lash out when we are hurt or to show our loyalty to Jesus by turning our backs on those who reject him. What does Jesus want us to do in such situations? How can we stay in relationship with persons who hurt us or repudiate Christ?

put their swords away and then asked forgiveness for his enemies from the cross. This is the Christian way.

Costs of Discipleship

When three would-be disciples came to Jesus, he warned them of the cost of following him. They would be homeless; and they would have to put loyalty to Jesus above everything, even their families. Jesus demanded more of them than Elijah had asked of Elisha, who was at least given permission to say goodbye to his family (1 Kings 19:19-21). Jesus' words, "Let the dead bury their own dead," seem harsh, especially since care of deceased loved ones was considered an important religious duty (Genesis 50:5).

Any disciple who wants to travel with Jesus must "count the cost" (Luke 14:25-33) before signing on. What are the barriers to your complete commitment?

Study Suggestions

A. Open With Singing

Read Psalm 77:11-15 aloud, and sing "O God, Our Help in Ages Past." Drawing on the commentary on pages 239–40, explain the flow and the significance of this psalm. Ask: What message does this psalm convey to us today? How are the psalm and this hymn similar?

B. Create a Drama

Present 2 Kings 2:1-15 as a dramatic reading, by asking three group members to read the parts of Elijah, Elisha, and a narrator, and others to speak in unison the words of the company of the prophets. After the reading, ask the whole group: What struck you during the drama? How would you describe the relationship between Elijah and Elisha? Where did you witness God's presence and power?

C. God's Presence

Review the commentary on the Elisha story (pages 238–39) and discuss the "Think About It" questions. How do you seek to be assured that God is with you? Do you often become aware that God was with you *after* you thought you were alone?

D. Remember God's Acts

A common theme for 2 Kings 2:1-2, 6-14 and Psalm 77 is how remembering God's actions can help us through difficult times. Form two groups. Ask the Second Kings group also to read Exodus 14:21-25 and the Psalm group also to read Exodus 15:1-18. Have each group discuss: How does your passage echo the events of the Exodus story? When has the memory of God's actions comforted you?

E. Define *Flesh*

Read Galatians 5:1, 13-25, and review the commentary on page 240. Ask: What does Paul mean by "flesh"? How does he describe life in the flesh? Give contemporary examples of "fleshly" behavior. (Be sure your definition and examples go beyond sexual sins.) How do they affect the unity of your church, family, or workplace? How do they affect you? Also discuss the "Think About It" questions.

F. Describe Life in the Spirit

How does Paul describe life in the Spirit? Make a list of the behaviors that characterize a Spirit-filled life, then pair off. Ask participants to relate how they have seen one or more of these qualities or behaviors in their partner or another person in the church. Invite members to copy the list and circle those fruits they desire to live out more fully.

G. Consider the Costs

Read aloud Luke 9:51-62, and summarize the commentary on pages 241–42. Discuss first the "Think About It" questions regarding our response to those who hurt us or spurn Christ. Then ask: How do you react to Jesus' words in 9:57-61? What does Jesus want from his followers? What does he offer? What stands in the way of our full and whole-hearted commitment to Christian discipleship?

H. Close With Exhortation

Stand in a circle. Assign each person one or two words from Galatians 5:22. Say, "The fruit of the Spirit is . . . ," and have each person say his or her word in sequence around the circle. After each word is spoken, have the group respond with, "Fill us with your Spirit, O God." Offer a closing prayer, asking God's Spirit to strengthen them in that resolve. Then sing, "Spirit of the Living God, Fall Afresh on Me."

Lections for Sunday Between July 3 and 9

T ## Old Testament: 2 Kings 5:1-14

HE Old Testament, Psalter, and Gospel lections today are healing stories. A foreign military official seeks it, the psalmist celebrates it, and the disciples of Jesus are sent out to perform it. The story of the cleansing of Naaman the Syrian demonstrates the miraculous healing power of God through the mighty prophet Elisha. Despite Naaman's skepticism and resistance, Elisha healed him, an act that would be cited by a later prophet with healing powers, Jesus of Nazareth (Luke 4:27). Though accomplished in diverse ways through a variety of agents, the source of healing power is always the same: God.

A Proud Seeker

Naaman, the commander of the Syrian army that had made successful raids on Israel earlier (1 Kings 22:19-23), inspired respect and fear in enemies and allies alike (2 Kings 5:1, 7). Told by an Israelite slave girl that he could be cured of his leprosy by a prophet in Samaria (5:3), Naaman set out for the neighboring nation with an entourage on horseback and in chariots, carrying lavish gifts (5:5, 9). He was directed from the royal court to Elisha by the distraught king of Israel (5:6-8). No doubt expecting instant obeisance and dutiful homage, Naaman's procession halted at the prophet Elisha's house.

Thwarted Expectations

Elisha, however, did not even come outside. Instead, he apparently snubbed him, merely sending a messenger to tell Naaman to dismount and go down to bathe in the Jordan River seven times. Naaman, who had hoped

244

for a dramatic display of prophetic power on his behalf, complete with shouting, hand-waving, and immediate cure (5:11), was furious at this lack of proper respect. He proclaimed the superiority of Syrian rivers (5:12), and left in a huff, uncured.

The picture that Naaman had in mind of how he should be treated threatened to keep him from receiving the gift that was offered. But the proud commander's servants calmed him down and prevailed on him to follow the prophet's simple instructions. When he did, his flesh was "restored like the flesh of a young boy" (5:14). Elisha did not even have to be present for the healing.

> **Think About It:** Naaman's arrogant expectation of how he should be treated threatened to keep him from receiving the gift that was offered. How do our expectations of special treatment or proper procedure distance us from others or prevent us from receiving God's gifts? How can we stay open to the presence and activity of God coming to us in expected places and ways?

Biblical Bias

The story of Naaman reveals the biblical bias against the proud (see 1 Samuel 2:3; Psalm 101:5; Luke 1:51); Naaman received healing when he humbled himself to accept the counsel of his inferiors and follow the prophet's instructions. Naaman accepted the God of Israel as his own, loading two mules with dirt from Samaria to take back to Syria so he could offer sacrifices from the land of the God he now worshiped. He thought that YHWH was a local deity who could only be worshiped on his own soil. Nevertheless, he further glorified the God of Israel and the mighty prophet Elisha.

> **Think About It:** Naaman thought YHWH was a local deity who could only be worshiped on his own soil. In what ways do we limit God and our own experience by assuming that God can only be approached in certain set forms or places? What can we learn about God and faith from persons who live in other places and worship in other ways?

Psalter: Psalm 30

This psalm expresses thanks and praise to God for healing in a near-death experience (verse 3), "sheol" and "pit" being synonyms for the place of the dead. The psalmist had thought his or her security was guaranteed by a prosperous life (verse 6), which afforded a false confidence that was shaken by mortal illness. The psalmist felt cut off from God during the illness (verse 7b), ancient peoples believing that illness and defeat resulted from the withdrawal of God's presence. The psalmist's enemies may have been gloating that the illness was a punishment from God (verse 1). Some commentators have suggested that verse 9 seems like an appeal to God's self-interest: If the psalmist were to die, it would mean one less person to sing God's praise. The candor of this verse suggests the trustful intimacy of the psalmist's relationship with God.

God grants healing after the psalmist's supplications (verse 8-10), having "drawn up" the psalmist like one draws water from a well. The psalmist exults in God's faithfulness, who turns mourning into dancing (verse 11) and ends the night of weeping with joy (verse 5). The experience of deliverance reminds the psalmist that God is the source of all human blessings (verse 7). Buoyant with gratitude, the psalmist urges the congregation to join in life-long praise (verses 4, 12).

Epistle: Galatians 6:(1-6) 7-16

In this chapter Paul describes community life in the Spirit. His directives emphasize the twin themes of personal accountability and mutual dependence. All persons will stand before God's judgment in the last days. Will their lives demonstrate reliance on the Spirit or upon human desires and works?

Mutual Correction

Paul begins by counseling the Galatians on how to deal with a person who has gone astray. They should "restore" the guilty person to the community "in a spirit of gentleness" (6:1a), humbly remembering their own propensity to sin (6:1b, 3). The verb meaning "to restore" is also used in Mark 1:19 to describe the mending of fishing nets, in both instances suggesting a return to wholeness and usefulness.

Paul's assumption that believers will reprove one another may sound strange to individualistic American Christians raised in a climate of "live and let live" and "do your own thing." Yet several biblical passages deal with the issue of restoring transgressors to the community (see Leviticus 19:17; Matthew 18:15-22; Luke 17:3-4; James 5:19-20). "Love your neighbor as yourself" (Galatians 5:14, 6:2) means that one must care enough to confront.

Think About It: "Bear one another's burdens" seems to contradict "all must carry their own loads." Which is more important to you: helping others or taking individual responsibility? How do you put these together in your own life? Which is more important in the church?

Personal Accountability

Verse 5 seems directly to contradict verse 2. First the Galatians are told to "bear one another's burdens" (6:2), then that "all must carry their own loads" (6:5). Paul's reasoning progresses from the need for mutual support within the body of Christ (6:1-2), to calling for appropriate humility in one's own conduct (6:3-4), to recognizing that in the end each is called to personal account, not just by other believers but by God. Thus, the two ideas complement rather than contradict each other. The only way we can stand before God is by rigorous self-examination reinforced by loving confrontation from others.

Rely on Christ

The remaining verses summarize Paul's earlier arguments against the circumcision party in the Galatian churches. He warns that even religious rites and rules like being circumcised or obeying the law can be "works of the flesh," unless they are seen as means of grace rather than ends in themselves (6:7-8, 12-15). Finally, echoing a synagogue prayer, the blessing in verse 16 pronounced upon "the Israel of God" redefines Israel to include uncircumcised Gentile converts and all who put their trust in Jesus Christ alone.

Gospel: Luke 10:1-11, 16-20

This passage, in which seventy persons are sent out by Jesus—in addition to the Twelve (9:1-6)—to cure the sick and proclaim the reign of God has no parallel in the other Gospels. This special material from Luke reinforces Jesus' earlier instructions, prefigures the wider mission in Acts, and emphasizes that the work of preparing the world for Christ belongs to all believers.

Seventy Sent

After stressing the rigors of discipleship to several would-be followers (9:57-62), Jesus commissioned a willing group to go before him on his planned itinerary. The number *seventy* is significant, possibly representing the seventy nations descended from Noah after the Flood (Genesis 10) or the seventy elders chosen to assist Moses in his work (Numbers 11:16-17). Either symbolism reinforces Luke's concern with worldwide mission and shared proclamation.

The disciples went out in pairs because, in Jewish custom, two witnesses were required for a testimony to be considered credible (Deuteronomy 19:15). Pairing off also provided support and protection, a missionary strategy adopted in the Book of Acts by Peter and John (Acts 8:14), Judas and Silas (15:32), and Paul and Barnabas (15:35).

A Template for Witness

Jesus' instructions provided a template for early Christian witnessing, anticipating the difficulties and forestalling the temptations his followers would face. By telling them to carry no money or extra possessions, for example, Jesus protected them from robbery and forced them to depend wholly on the hospitality of others, a dependence that strengthened their trust in God.

Remaining in one place deepened their relationship with their hosts and set up the possibility of a church in the future. (The early Christian movement was staged from private homes, as in Acts 10:1-2; 12:12; 18:7.) If they did not move from house to house, they also avoided the impression that they were profiting from preaching the gospel, as Paul stressed in Acts 20:33: "I coveted no one's silver or gold or clothing." And, by graciously eating whatever was set before them, their meals could become an occasion for sharing and teaching, just as Jesus used table fellowship.

Expect Rejection

Since the mission was urgent, they did not speak to anyone on the road to avoid the customary formality of long greetings (Luke 10:4). As "lambs in the midst of wolves" (10:3b), they could expect hostility. When a town did not welcome them, it was as if they had rejected Jesus himself (10:16); but they were not to retaliate, as James and John wanted (9:51-55). Rather, they were to wipe the dust off their feet in a symbolic gesture, declaring that, despite rejection, the realm of God had come near (10:11).

Returning With Joy

> **Think About It:** Joy is a hallmark of the inbreaking reign of God. Where do you see signs of God's presence and power in our world? Where is joy erupting? Where are people happy and content?

When the seventy returned to Jesus, they were jubilant. "Even the demons submit to us!" they said (10:17). Joy is a hallmark of the inbreaking reign of God. Like Zechariah and Elizabeth (1:14), like Mary (1:47), like the angels and shepherds (2:10), the returning disciples rejoiced at God's mighty power displayed in their midst.

Study Suggestions

A. Open With Song

Sing a hymn about healing such as "When Jesus the Healer Passed Through Galilee" or "There Is a Balm in Gilead." Comment that healing is a central theme in today's lections.

B. Study the Situation

Read aloud 2 Kings 5:1-14, and summarize the commentary on pages 244–45. Ask participants to describe the political situation between Israel and Syria (Aram). Ask: What are the surprising turns in the plot? How does God work through each character?

C. Expect the Unexpected

Focus more closely on verses 9-14. Discuss: What picture did Naaman have in his mind about how he should be treated and how Elisha would act? How were his expectations thwarted? What enabled him to be healed?

Invite participants to reflect on these personal questions: What do you want from God? What happens if God wants to give you something other than what you expect? Also pose the questions in the "Think About It" box.

D. Challenge the Complacent

Read Psalm 30 responsively, with half the group reading the first part of each verse and the others the second line. Then review the commentary on pages 245–46. Focus on verses 6-7. Ask the group to describe ways prosperity and comfort can make us complacent. When has an illness or other difficulty shaken you out of complacency? Where was God in that process?

E. Compare Healing Stories

Second Kings 5:1-14, Psalm 30, and Luke 10:1-11, 16-20 all describe occasions of healing by the power of God. Form three groups and assign each group one passage. Ask each group to discuss: What events preceded the healing? What kind of healing took place? How was the healing accomplished? What reactions to the healing were reported? Compare findings in the whole group. Discuss: What healing ministries does your church support? What kind of healing takes place? How does your church celebrate occasions of healing?

F. Compassion Fatigue

Post this advice by John Wesley in the room: "Do all the good you can, by all means you can, in all the ways you can, in all the places you can, at all the times you can, to all people you can, as long as ever you can." Read Galatians 6:9-10 aloud. Ask: What are the similarities and differences between these verses and the Wesley quote? How does the Holy Spirit undergird us?

G. Roleplay

Read Luke 10:1-11, 16-20; and review the commentary on pages 247–48. Form pairs, and send them to different parts of the room. Ask them to imagine themselves being sent out by Jesus to preach and heal. What are they thinking? What are they feeling? Give each pair a scenario, such as a robber confronts them; an acquaintance accosts them; a village rejects them; a host welcomes them; a servant feeds them; a sick person beseeches them; a demon challenges them. What will they do? What will Jesus say when they return? Either act these out before the whole group or report the experience to another pair.

H. Close With Praise

Close with prayer thanking God for learnings gained in this session and asking for wisdom and strength to live them out this week.

Lections for Sunday Between
July 10 and 16

Amos 7:7-17

*A*MOS was the earliest of the great eighth-century prophets to pronounce judgment on the nation of Israel. He prophesied during the reign of Jeroboam II (786–746 B.C.), who had brought peace and prosperity, restoring earlier boundaries and supporting national shrines. Things were looking good.

Prophecy of Judgment

Yet Amos warned that YHWH would "rise against the house of Jeroboam with a sword," because the nation had failed to keep its covenant with YHWH. Wealthy persons lived indolent lives, exploiting the poor (6:4-6; 8:4-6), believing that their religious rituals assured their special standing with God (4:4-5). They did not remember God's deep and abiding concern for the weak and powerless (Exodus 22:21-27). Since they did not listen to Amos's call to repent and change their ways, his prophecy was fulfilled in 722 B.C. The Assyrian king, Sargon, conquered Israel and scattered the people throughout his empire. The Assyrians brought foreign settlers into Israel to create an Assyrian colony.

> **Think About It:** Jeroboam had brought peace and prosperity, but the nation had failed to keep its covenant with YHWH. What are some modern parallels in personal and national lives where the outer signs all look good, but inner, spiritual decay has set in?

Plumb Line or Tin?

Amos reported a vision he had seen of YHWH standing before him holding a "plumb line," a cord and weight used in construction to make sure

250

walls were true. God was measuring the people of Israel, and they were not proving to be plumb and true to God's standards.

However, the meaning of the Hebrew word *anak,* translated "plumb line," is unclear, as the word occurs no other place in the Old Testament. The "plumb line" translation originated with medieval Jewish scholars. Scholars now recognize the word to mean "tin" in Akkadian, but that metaphor makes no sense in the oracle.

No More Time

Whatever translation we may choose, it is clear that Amos understood the symbol to convey God's judgment for Israel's failure. In two previous visions, Amos had seen God preparing a plague of locusts and a destructive inferno (7:1-6). On those occasions, when the prophet interceded for the people, YHWH relented and delayed the judgment. This time, however, Amos was given no opportunity to plead for the people; for YHWH declared in no uncertain terms: "I will never again pass them by" (7:8). Their opportunity to repent has passed (4:6-11).

Amos's prophecy was challenged by the priest at Bethel, Amaziah, who was supported by the royal house. Amaziah told the king that Amos was "conspiring" against him (a charge often leveled against social critics); and he told Amos that the sanctuary belonged to the king. God's house had been co-opted by a political ruler.

> ***Think About It:*** God's house had been co-opted by the king. What are some present-day examples of how modern politicians use religion to further their political agendas? What might Amos say to them?

No Prophet

Amos retorted that he was not a professional prophet (7:14). Raised as a humble herdsman and a dresser of sycamore trees, God had taken him "from following the flock" (like young David in 2 Samuel 7:8). Thus, it was not Amos whom Amaziah was opposing, but YHWH. Therefore, Amaziah would suffer the fate in store for all Israel—his wife violated, his children slain, his land taken, himself in exile.

Psalter: Psalm 82

The psalmist portrays a remarkable scene: The God of Israel indicts other gods on behalf of the poor. People of the ancient Near East believed that the universe was governed by a divine council, an assembly of the gods of the various nations. Here, YHWH, God of Israel, the supreme God (1 Kings 22:19; Psalm 89:6-8), calls the other gods to account for allowing oppression of the weak. The other gods are so ignorant of the demands of justice that the very order of the cosmos is at risk (verse 5).

"How long?" is a lament usually addressed to God by suffering individuals or communities (see Psalm 6:3). But here God turns the lament against other divine beings, in the same way as the prophets cried "How long" against powerful and corrupt mortals (see Jeremiah 4:14). In a kind of mock trial, God speaks on behalf of the underclass of Israelite society—the weak, the orphan, the lowly, the destitute, the needy.

Because the other gods have failed to observe justice, they are stripped of their immortality (verses 6-7). The psalmist then asks God to rise up in the same manner and judge the rulers of the nations (verse 8). Attributed to Asaph, one of David's chief musicians, the psalm is a stunning and imaginative literary creation, demonstrating the extent to which God would go in acting on behalf of the poor. If God would depose other gods for their injustice, how much more would the wicked rulers of the world be called to account!

Epistle: Colossians 1:1-14

Who wrote Colossians? In New Testament times, disciples of a great leader sometimes composed a letter to sound as if he had written it, which was an accepted literary practice called "pseudonymous writing." In this way, the teaching of the leader was passed on and re-applied for later times. Because the grammar, syntax, and terminology of Colossians differ so greatly from undisputed Pauline letters, some scholars believe this letter was pseudonymous.

Other scholars argue, however, that the letter's close links to Philemon, its specific personal references (1:1-2; 1:24–2:5; 4:7-18), and its direct address to a particular local problem support Pauline authorship. These scholars suggest that the differences between Colossians and other undisputed letters can be explained by a natural development of Paul's thought over time, or by the shaping of phrases by a co-editor or secretary. Whether penned by Paul or not, the early church accepted the letter as canonical; that is, standing in the apostolic tradition and expressing basic truths of the Christian faith.

False Teachers

> **Think About It:** Mistaken teachers advocated a syncretism that detracted from focus on Christ. What spiritual beliefs and practices undergird faith in Christ? Which detract? How can we tell the difference?

Colossae was a small town near Laodicea in the Lycus Valley on the ancient road running east from Ephesus. Colossians was written to combat gnostic (belief in salvation through special knowledge) teachers who advocated asceticism, special days and rituals, and worship of angels (2:16-23). They were advocating a syncretism (mixture of Christian and pagan ideas) that detracted from focus on Christ. These teachers claimed to have superior wisdom that gave them access to God.

The author of Colossians counters that Christ alone makes possible a saving relationship with God (1:15-20). True spiritual wisdom consists of knowing God's will (1:9) and leading lives worthy of Christ (1:10).

Bearing Fruit

Having heard about the faith of the congregation at Colossae, a church founded not by him but by Epaphras (1:7-8), the author gives thanks to God for them (1:3-8), particularly for how the gospel is "bearing fruit" (finding expression) in their lives (1:6). The writer prays that the recipients of the letter will live faithful, effective Christian lives, will endure trials and controversies with consistency and dedication, giving thanks to God throughout (1:10-12).

Gospel: Luke 10:25-37

The parable of the good Samaritan is so well-known that it has a class of laws named after it, laws that protect persons who aid strangers. Nonetheless, this beloved and familiar story has an edge, a sharp or touchy dimension. Part of the edge comes from the setting given by Luke. The other aspect of its edge is seen in how Jesus twice undercut the expectations of his hearers.

Public Debate

Jesus' telling of this parable concludes a confrontation with a lawyer, that is, a teacher of the law of Moses. In his time, rabbis commonly debated in public, exchanging questions and retorts. Though this lawyer asked Jesus a legitimate question about how to inherit eternal life, Luke disparaged the lawyer's motives, saying he wanted to "test" Jesus (10:25) and to "justify" himself (10:29). (The only other persons who "tempt" Jesus in Luke are the devil in 4:2 and the "evil" crowd in 11:16, 29.) For Luke, the lawyer was more concerned with appearing religious and advancing himself than with loving God.

What Must I Do?

"What must I do to inherit eternal life?" (10:25) is the same question the rich ruler asks in 18:18-23. In both cases, Jesus turned the question back on the questioner, asking what the law required. Here the lawyer answered with two of the basic teachings of Jewish faith, the *Shema* (Deuteronomy 6:5), which pious Jews recited daily, and a portion of the Holiness Code (Leviticus 19:18), which detailed the ritual and ethical requirements of holy living. Jesus approved the lawyer's answer (10:28) but told him to put it into practice.

Who Is My Neighbor?

The lawyer, employing a time-tested method of avoiding action, challenged Jesus to define *neighbor*. Jesus then told a story about a man travel-

Think About It: The lawyer, employing a time-tested method of avoiding action, challenged Jesus to define *neighbor.* When have you preferred to discuss a problem rather than act on it? What needed ministries in your church still await action? What is behind the delay?

ing the wild and dangerous stretch of road from Jerusalem to Jericho who was assaulted by thieves and left for dead. This road descends nearly 3,300 feet over 17 miles through rough, isolated terrain, a perfect setting for an ambush. Purely by chance, a priest came by but did not stop. Likewise, a Levite (another high Temple official) saw the injured man and also avoided him.

The Good Samaritan

At this point in the parable, since the first two passersby were clergy, Jesus' hearers would have expected the third to be an ordinary person, thus giving the story an anti-clerical thrust popular with the people. Jesus, however, confounded his hearers by saying that the third person, the one who stopped to give the victim aid, was a Samaritan. Jews despised Samaritans, stereotyping them as half-pagan descendants of mixed marriages. This Samaritan, unlike the Jewish religious leaders, gave what the suffering man needed, binding his wounds, carrying him to safety, providing for further care, and footing the whole bill.

Go and Do Likewise

Jesus moved the discussion back to its starting point: "What must I do?" His imperative has the force of "You, go, now." To love one's neighbor as one's self means showing mercy to anyone in need, regardless of social status. This teaching echoes Luke 6:31-36, where Jesus exhorted his hearers to "do to others as you would have them do to you" and to "be merciful, just as your Father is merciful." God's own compassion is the source and model for neighbor-love. Jesus pushed his hearers to expand the limits of their concern to the sinner, the poor, the outcast, and the enemy.

Study Suggestions

A. Open With Prayer

Invite group members to share joys and concerns. Respond to each in unison with, "God, in your mercy, hear our prayer."

B. Hear the Prophet

Read Amos 7:7-17 and the commentary on pages 250–51. Form three groups, assigning each one a text: Amos 6:4-6; 8:4-6; or 4:4-5. Have each group determine Amos's complaint against the people in its passage. Report findings to the whole group, and compile a master list. Read Amos 7:11 aloud to indicate Israel's fate.

C. Discuss Repentance

Amos predicted harsh punishment with no possibility of repentance. Discuss: Does God always give people a second chance? When have you experienced a time when it was too late to avert the consequences of wrong-doing? Where was God in that experience?

D. Write a Letter

Read Colossians 1:1-14 and the interpretation on pages 252–53. Give members pencil, paper, and these instructions: "Pretend you are a friend of the author of Colossians. Choose several verses from the passage and put them in your own words, applying them specifically to your personal or church situation. Read your paraphrase to a partner, comparing each version to the original." Ask: What did you highlight? What did you omit? What new insights emerged from the paraphrase?

E. Update the Parable

Read Luke 10:25-37, and review the commentary on pages 253–54. Make a chart with three columns headed "Road to Jericho," "Respectable People," and "Samaritans." Fill this in with modern equivalents—such as "inner city" or "tavern" under "Road to Jericho," "bishop" or "televangelist" under "Respectable People," an "immigrant" or "Islamic terrorist" under "Samaritans."

Form small groups and recreate the story, choosing one entry from each column. Discuss: What new understandings does the retelling offer? What is Jesus saying to us through this story?

F. Tie It Together

Note in closing that all four lections emphasize concern for the needy: Amos stresses justice for the oppressed; in Psalm 92, God judges other gods on behalf of the poor; Colossians urges bearing fruit through good works; and the good Samaritan aids a suffering man.

G. Close With Prayer

Offer a prayer of confession, following with the group response, "O God, judge the earth; all nations belong to you." Close with the hymn, "The Voice of God Is Calling."

Lections for Sunday Between July 17 and 23

Old Testament: Amos 8:1-12

*I*N this lection, the fourth of five oracles recorded in the Book of Amos, the prophet sees a basket of summer fruit, after which God pronounces the judgment that "the end has come upon my people Israel" (8:2). All the vision reports follow a similar pattern: First God shows Amos something; then Amos describes what he sees; next there is a dialogue between God and Amos; and finally God explains what the vision means.

Play on Words

In the Hebrew, a pun makes the point: The Hebrew *qayits* or "summer fruit" is played against *qes*, a homonym meaning "the time is ripe" (translated here as "the end"). Prophets often drove home a point with word play. Prophetic oracles have the distilled imagery and luminous brevity of Japanese *haiku* poetry and, in addition, infuse ordinary objects with divine meaning.

A Terrible Judgment

Though puns are often associated with humor, in this instance the word of God spoken by Amos is frighteningly final. Summer fruit symbolizes judgment; God will destroy the people of Israel; the fruit is ripe, indicating that the end is near. The day of the Lord will come with earthquake (8:8), eclipse (8:9), mourning (8:3, 10), and famine (8:11-14). The mourning will be agonizing; when an only child is lost (8:10) the grief is overwhelming. Corpses will be piled high (8:3b) on that dreadful day. Hymns of praise will turn to sorrowful dirges (8:3a).

The worst part of the famine will be a dearth of God's word (8:11). The

256

people will traverse the whole nation seeking a word of hope, but God will have abandoned them (8:12). The vision is so terrible that verse 3 sounds like a series of hysterical outcries. The New International Version translates the verse: "The songs in the temple will turn to wailing. Many, many bodies—flung everywhere! Silence!" (8:3, NIV).

Greed—Not Good

Why would this terrible fate befall Israel? Greedy merchants had broken God's law, treating the poor as sources of profit rather than as neighbors and kin under the covenant. The merchants' own words accuse them: They cannot wait for the religious festivals to be over so they can resume their cheating of the poor (8:4-6).

They use different weights for buying and selling, and they tamper with standard units of measurement, the *ephah* and *shekel* (Amos 8:5c). They even sell grain mixed with chaff and dirt (8:6b). Their corrupt practices have driven some people so far into debt that they have to sell themselves as slaves (8:6). What the merchants see as shrewd business dealings Amos views as an irreversible rupture in their relationship with God. These oppressors of the poor have moved far away from God because they have broken God's law, denied God's justice, and trampled on God's people.

Amos is clear about what he expects to befall the nation. The fifth vision in Chapter 9 is the most devastating: "All the sinners of my people shall die by the sword" (9:10). The note of hope found in 9:11-15 is generally regarded as a later addition to the text.

> **Think About It:** What the merchants see as shrewd business dealings Amos sees as an irreversible rupture in their relationship with God. Where do you see greed and corruption in the American marketplace? What groups today would correspond to the merchants in Amos's time? What would Amos say to them? How might God's justice fall on them? What is the church's responsibility in relation to situations of injustice in our time?

Psalter: Psalm 52

Very little of Psalm 52 consists of prayer or praise offered to God; rather, it seems to be a psalm of accusation. The speaker invokes disaster on his enemy, sarcastically called "O mighty one" (verse 1). This "mighty one" deserves a downfall because of his deceitful speech and evil plots against the godly (verses 1-4), actions that may include fraud or extortion against the poor.

The psalmist predicts that God will "uproot" this evildoer from "the land of the living" (verse 5), while the righteous look on in approval (verse 6). His fate is in sharp contrast to the speaker of the psalm, who flourishes "like a green olive tree" planted by the Temple (verse 8). The worst sin of this enemy is that he has trusted in riches rather than in God (verse 7).

The superscription refers to 1 Samuel 21:1-7 and 22:6-19, passages that describe the treachery of Doeg, an Edomite mercenary. Thus, these introductory words, which were added later, interpret "mischief done against the godly" as plots against David and his supporters.

This psalm sets forth two opposing ways of life: one embodied in the "mighty one," who trusts only in himself, and the other found in the righteous who trust in God. Like the rich fool in Jesus' parable, the life of the wayward one is demanded of him, for he has stored up treasures for himself but is not rich toward God (see Luke 12:20-21).

Epistle: Colossians 1:15-28

After giving thanks for the faith and love of the congregation at Colossae (1:3-14), the author of the letter breaks into song, an early hymn exalting the person and work of Jesus Christ. The hymn, probably familiar to the Colossians, helps establish a bond between the author and this congregation founded by someone else (1:7-8). The hymn's elevated language, repetitive phrasing, and declarative style create a powerful effect. No wonder the author later urges the Colossians to sing psalms, hymns, and spiritual songs to God with gratitude (3:16).

> **Think About It:** The hymn, probably familiar to the Colossians, helps establish a bond between the author and tis congregation. What role has hymn-singing played in your faith? How does hymn-singing draw a congregation together? Which hymns do this best for you?

Christ in Creation and Redemption

The sweeping affirmations of the hymn (1:15-23) declare Christ's role in creation and redemption: the image of God, created by God and co-creator with God; and the first to rise from the dead, in whom the whole universe is held together (1:15-17). This cosmic, preeminent Christ is also the head of the church, reconciling all creation to God through his reconciling death (1:18-20). The affirmations of the hymn echo the description of Wisdom's role in Creation (Proverbs 8:22-31), as well as the preexistent Logos of John 1:1-4.

Humble Jesus to Cosmic Christ

The high regard and universal scope of the hymn is startling when juxtaposed with the career of the earthly Jesus, born as the son of a Galilean artisan. How did early Christians make the leap from the humble historical Jesus to the cosmic, eternal Christ? Colossians 1:27 provides a clue: "Christ in you." The powerful

> **Think About It:** From "Humble Jesus to Cosmic Christ." How do you put these two aspects of Jesus Christ together in your thinking?

experience of the resurrected Christ within the church prompted several hymns: Philippians 2:6-11; 1 Timothy 3:16; Hebrews 1:3-4; 1 Peter 2:22-25.

Hold to Christ

Remain steadfast in faith, the writer says, not shifting to some other teaching that diminishes the preeminence of Christ (Colossians 1:23). The mystery of Christian faith is attested to not only by exalted hymnody but also by the hardships willingly endured by Paul ("completing . . . Christ's afflictions") that helped extend the gospel to the Gentiles (1:24). Only by holding to Christ can the Colossians mature in faith (1:28) and feel accepted in God's presence (1:22).

Gospel: Luke 10:38-42

This brief passage reporting Jesus' visit with Martha and Mary contains several surprises. Though Martha welcomed Jesus into her home, reversing the rejection he had experienced from a Samaritan village (9:51-56), Jesus did not express gratitude for her hospitality. And, though he usually commended those who serve the needs of others (10:30-37; 22:25-27), Jesus did not tell Mary to help Martha with the mealtime chores. Instead, he defended the non-working sister, affirming her choice of a learning over a serving role and assuring her that she would be encouraged to continue in this mode (10:42).

Jesus' defense of Mary defied the cultural expectations for women in that time. Women were expected to serve the meals and were not usually given religious instruction. The phrase, "sat at the Lord's feet," was a technical term for a disciple learning from a rabbi, as Paul did with his teacher Gamaliel (Acts 22:3). Thus, Jesus surprised the sisters (and others observing this scene) on several counts.

Distracted and Anxious

The Gospel writer Luke depicts Martha as "distracted by her many tasks" (Luke 10:40) and has Jesus chiding his hostess for her harried demeanor (10:41). This was a diagnosis of her soul's condition. The repetition of her name ("Martha, Martha") was a mild rebuke or impatient lament over her distraction from the things that really mattered. But at the same time Jesus was expressing a deep love and concern for her, a closeness further revealed in John 11:1-44; 12:1-8. It requires a good friend to care enough to challenge our self-destructive behavior. In early Christian literature, "distracted" or "drawn away" referred to the

> **Think About It:** Good friends challenge our self-destructive behavior. When has a good friend helped you see something in your life that needed changing? How might you do this for a friend of yours? What might Jesus say to you?

cares of the world that pull someone from God, like the thorns that choked the growth of seed in the parable of the sower (Luke 8:14).

A Different Posture

Jesus desires something more for his disciples than tense shoulders and furrowed brows. "Do not worry about your life, what you will eat, or about your body, what you will wear," he says in Luke 12:22-31. Trust God to provide. Jesus wants his disciples to sit and be nourished by his word.

Only One Thing

Martha's real task is given in the phrase variously translated, "there is need of only one thing," or "few things are necessary" (Luke 10:42). The literal meaning of the phrase may refer to the variety of dishes on the table. Jesus did not need a seven-course meal. Simple food would suffice. Besides, Mary had already chosen the "good portion" (10:42, RSV). Jesus also may have been suggesting that Martha needed to determine what was most important in her life at that time, the "one thing needful" (10:42, RSV) for her.

Discernment

Thus, Jesus presented Martha with a task of discernment. Sometimes the disciple sits and receives from Jesus. At other times the disciple rises to serve. The early church faced a similar moment of discernment when leaders were needed to oversee the ministry of hospitality (Acts 6:1-6). Stephen, who helped manage the daily distribution of food to widows, at other times preached the gospel with power (6:8-15). Preaching the word is not better than serving food; each has its essential place.

Luke underscores the disciples' need for trust and discernment by preceding the Martha and Mary story with the good Samaritan parable (both stories have unlikely heroes). He then followed it with Jesus' teaching on prayer: "Give us each day our daily bread" (Luke 11:1-4). Active service to the needy across barriers of prejudice and prayerful trust in God for the provision of life's essentials are both basic aspects of faithful discipleship.

Study Suggestions

A. Open With Singing

Sing or read a hymn glorifying Christ such as "Fairest Lord Jesus" or "At the Name of Jesus." Ask that the hymn be remembered in the discussion of the Colossians lection coming later in the session.

B. Read and Respond

Read aloud Amos 8:1-12, and review the commentary on pages 256–57. Form two groups, assigning them Amos 8:5-6 (merchants group) and Amos

8:1-4, 7-12 (God group). Ask the merchants group to list the items from their verses that detail what they hope to do once the sabbath is over. Have the God group list the things God plans to do as punishment. When the lists are complete, ask members of each group to read the items aloud, alternating between groups until all items have been read. Discuss: Why was what the merchants were doing displeasing to God? What does this exercise suggest about God's response to injustice?

C. Compare Christ Hymns

Read Colossians 1:15-28 and the interpretive comments on pages 258–59. Ask participants to recall one of their own favorite hymns about Christ (or review one of the hymns mentioned in Activity A). Write down key phrases. Compare them to Colossians 1:15-20. What does each hymn affirm about Christ and our relationship to him?

D. Paraphrase a Psalm

Read aloud Psalm 52, and review the commentary on pages 257–58. Invite group members to rewrite the psalm, using contemporary descriptions, sarcasm, and insults. Ask: Should a Christian wish God's vengeance upon another person? How does God treat evildoers? How do you feel about psalms that express strong negative emotions? Should they be read in worship or for personal devotions?

E. Roleplay Sibling Rivalry

Read aloud Luke 10:38-42, and review the commentary on pages 259–60. Ask three persons to roleplay the story of Martha, Mary, and Jesus. (Roles do not have to be gender-specific.) After the roleplay, ask the three participants to share how they felt in their roles. Then invite observers to comment: What important contributions do persons like Martha and Mary each make to the Christian community? With whom do you most identify? How does Jesus help them transcend competitiveness? Also discuss the "Think About It" questions.

Invite two men to imagine and roleplay an analogous scenario with two brothers, asking observers the same questions as above. Or, compare the relationship of the brothers in the parable of the prodigal and his brother (Luke 15:11-32) with the relationship of the sisters here in Luke 10:38-42. Discuss: What are the similarities and differences? What are comparable situations in family relationships today? What approaches would you suggest for working these things through? What is the good news in each case?

F. Close With Prayer

Invite group members to reflect silently on the question, What is the "one thing needful" for me today? Invite any who wish to offer sentence prayers. Close this time of reflection with the benediction, "Thy will be done, O God."

Lections for Sunday Between July 24 and 30

Old Testament: Hosea 1:2-10

*H*OSEA prophesied in Israel in the eighth century B.C. His book presents a provocative and troublesome image for God's love. His marriage and family become metaphors for YHWH's relationship with his people.

Promiscuous People

The prophet Hosea felt YHWH leading him to marry a promiscuous woman because the people of Israel had sought out other gods (1:2). As Hosea saw it, the Israelites were religiously "promiscuous" because they worshiped the Canaanite ba'als (2:13), the Assyro-Babylonian goddess Ishtar (3:1), and local deities, as well as YHWH. They had forgotten their exclusive covenant relationship with YHWH forged at Sinai: "You shall have no other gods before me" (Exodus 20:2).

Promiscuous is a judgmental term. The descriptive word for combining elements of various religions in one's belief and worship is "syncretistic." The Israelites lived among neighbors whose customs and agricultural practices were long-standing, inseparable from their culture and lifestyle, and believed effective in controlling the weather and protecting them from harm. The Israelites naturally and pragmatically adopted the cultural mores of these indigenous inhabitants. It took a prophet like Hosea to call them back to exclusive loyalty to YHWH, their deliverer.

> **Think About It:** Hosea judged the syncretistic religious practices of his people to be "promiscuous." They saw them as natural and pragmatic. What aspects of our religious practice are more cultural than Christian? Which might be considered as unChristian or unfaithful by a prophet like Hosea? How do we determine the appropriate mix of what is cultural and what is Christian in our religious life and faith?

The Children

God provided names for Hosea's children to indicate how the people would be punished for their religious infidelity. The name of the first child, *Jezreel*, referred to the site of political intrigue and bloodshed that brought King Jehu to power (2 Kings 9:17-26, 10:1-11). YHWH would likewise depose the kings of Israel, a prophecy fulfilled in 722 B.C. with Assyria's invasion.

The second child was named *Lo-ruhama* (Hosea 1:6), the verb *ruhamah* conveying compassion for a child or kindred (related to the noun, *rehem*, for "womb"). The prefix *Lo* negates the verb, giving the meaning "not pitied," "not accepted," "not loved." The same YHWH who had heard the groaning of the Israelites in slavery and remembered the covenant with them (Exodus 2:24) would have no pity now. Hosea 1:7 suggests that for now the neighboring nation of Judah would escape Israel's fate. The name of the third child, *Lo-ammi*, also contains a negation, "not my people" (1:9)—reversing Exodus 6:7, "I will take you as my people, and I will be your God."

Difficult Metaphor

We may question a metaphor that seems to equate God with abusive behavior (Hosea 2:1-13). Would the well-being of Hosea's own family be sacrificed to make the point that YHWH was going to allow both nations to be destroyed? Was what the people were doing so terrible? Yes, said Hosea. When people put their trust in false gods, it is they who break the relationship with God, not the other way around.

> **Think About It:** We may question a metaphor that seems to equate God with abusive behavior. How do you react to the image of God presented in Hosea?

Repentance and Return

The broken relationship conveyed by the names of Hosea's children would eventually be mended, says the prophet. After a time of punishment (2:3-13), husband and wife would be reconciled (2:14-20). *Shalom* would replace bloodshed; the people would prosper and multiply once again (1:10a). "Lo-ammi" would be renamed "Children of the living God" (1:10b). God would have pity on "Lo-ruhamah," and say to "Lo-ammi," "You *are* my people" after all (2:23, italics added). YHWH would reclaim and restore his family when they repented and returned.

Psalter: Psalm 85

Psalm 85, a community prayer for deliverance, is a "perennial psalm," because God's people are always in need of forgiveness and restoration. The psalm has three parts. The first section recalls what God has done for Israel, restoring the fortunes of the people and forgiving their sin (verses 1-3). The psalmist may recall the return from exile in 538 B.C. The second portion pleads for restoration and forgiveness in present circumstances that are not specified (verses 4-7). The returning exiles had a more difficult time than expected, facing hostile inhabitants, poor crop yield, and ruined cities.

The third part of the psalm promises that God would speak a word of *shalom* to the people (verses 8-13). This future of peace and well-being would be characterized by social harmony and agricultural bounty (verse 12). The psalmist imagines various attributes of God—steadfast love, faithfulness, righteousness, and peace—as heralds who would announce God's renewed favor and would greet one another with the kiss of hospitality (verses 10-11, 13).

Epistle: Colossians 2:6-15 (16-19)

"Fully claim the gift you have already been given," is the message to the Colossians. The gift is Jesus Christ himself—incarnate (2:9), crucified (2:11), resurrected (2:12), and ruler over all the powers of the universe (2:10, 15).

The Gift of Christ

In this lection, all aspects of Jesus' life, death, and resurrection serve a salvific purpose. The Crucifixion relates to functioning as a whole body "circumcision" (redemptive sacrifice) of Christ (2:11b), provides a "spiritual circumcision" (purification, transformation) for Gentile believers (2:11a), initiating them into the new community of faith. The Christian, "buried" with Christ in baptism (dying to sin), receives forgiveness and new life because of the resurrected Christ (2:12-13). The "record" of the believer's sin, like a legal writ of indebtedness, has been dismissed, nailed to the cross (2:14). Christ's victory over worldly authorities and elemental spirits gives Christians freedom from fear, equipping them for faithful in witness in the face of persecution and tribulation.

Placating the Powers

The Greco-Roman world believed that the universe was ruled by hostile, capricious celestial powers that had to be placated by elaborate rituals (2:8). Apparently, some teachers in the Colossian church were advocating such practices as abstaining from certain food or drink, observing special festivals, abusing the body, and seeking assistance from heavenly beings (2:16-18) to appease these powers. These syncretistic practices did not strengthen Christian faith, but actually weakened it by diminishing the sense of full trust in Christ's redemptive work in the cross.

> **Think About It:** What ideologies or systems compete with Christ for authority in our lives? What sources of security and well-being do we rely on out of our lack of faith in God's guidance and protection?

True Substance

The author uses the categories of Greek metaphysics to describe Christ's role in the church. Such ideas are only a "shadow," he says, but Christ has true "substance" (2:17). Christ is the head of the body (2:10, 1:18), the church; and believers grow in him when they claim the gifts he has given and use them for the well-being of all.

Gospel: Luke 11:1-13

Of the four Gospels, Luke gives the greatest emphasis to Jesus as a man of prayer. Jesus prayed at every juncture: the baptism (3:21-22), the call of the disciples (6:12-16), the Transfiguration (9:28), Gethsemane (22:40-42), and the cross (23:34, 46)—as well as at regular times of withdrawal (5:16). Having set an example, Jesus here provides a model prayer (11:2-4), a parable (11:5-8), and sayings about prayer (11:9-13).

A Community Prayer

First-century Jews knew the psalms, traditional prayers for morning and evening, and the "eighteen benedictions" spoken during synagogue worship. The Lord's Prayer in Luke follows traditional form. The plural pronoun *us* shows that this was the community prayer of Jesus' disciples.

Father . . .

Though God is referred to as *father* elsewhere in Jewish writings (see Deuteronomy 32:6; Psalm 68:5; Isaiah 64:8; Jeremiah 3:4; Malachi 1:6), God is never directly addressed by this title. Not only does the prayer say "Father" in the vocative (the case for direct address), Jesus also used the affectionate Aramaic form, which is translated "Daddy." *Abba* occurs also in Romans 8:15 and Galatians 4:6, showing how the early church preserved Jesus' distinctive way of addressing God. Jesus wanted his disciples to claim an intimate relationship with God.

The Petitions

For biblical people, one's name and character were closely related. To hallow God's name meant to recognize God as holy. "Your kingdom come" expressed the disciples' desire that the transforming reign of God they were proclaiming (4:43; 9:2; 10:9) would be fully realized. These first two petitions speak to God's nature and power.

The next three petitions ask God for basic human needs: food, forgiveness, and freedom. Praying for daily bread as the Israelites did in the wilderness (Exodus 16:4) puts a cap on human greed. Rather than stockpiling goods like the rich fool (Luke 12:16-21), we are to ask only what we need for each day, in trust that God will provide (12:29-31). Forgiveness is a basic need for life in community, since we all sin against one another. Receiving forgiveness from God requires us to offer it to everyone.

Freedom From Evil

Think About It: With what powers and adversaries do you struggle? Do you believe God is testing you in some way? What helps you surmount these tests?

The final petition, "do not bring us to the time of trial," takes seriously the power of evil in the world. We face conflicts with both spiritual powers and human adversaries, circumstances that test our faith in God—as did Abraham (Genesis 22:1-9), Job (Job 1:1–2:10), and Jesus (Luke 22:39-46). Jesus reminded the disciples of this petition twice in Gethsemane (22:40, 46).

Prayer Works

The passage continues with two teachings that urge persistence in prayer. The parable of the friend at midnight presumes the ancient Near Eastern etiquette of hospitality. Hosts were expected to provide for their own guests and to share with neighbors so they could care for their guests. If the needy host could not rouse his friend through the bonds of their relationship, his persistent shouts would shame the friend into providing service. In the same way, prayer can be honest and direct with God about what we need. Prayers do not have to become oblique references to what we want.

Think About It: The imperatives to ask, search, and knock urge persistence in prayer and promise a response. If God already knows what we need, what is the point of this persistence? How do you deal with times when you ask, seek, and knock, but the response does not come as expected?

The three imperatives—ask, search, and knock—even further give us permission to persist in prayer and promise a response. If only we will ask, God will bestow the greatest gift: the Holy Spirit.

Study Suggestions

A. Open With Singing

Open with a hymn about repentance and forgiveness, such as "Amazing Grace" or "Forgive Our Sins as We Forgive."

B. What's in a Name?

Bring a baby name book to class. Look up the names of group members, and read the meanings given. Ask: What impact do our names have on how we feel about ourselves? What do our names say about us? Should names be used to make a statement about parents' beliefs? Why or why not?

C. Change Names

Distribute stick-on nametags, each tag inscribed either with "Jezreel," "Lo-ruhamah," or "Lo-ammi." After putting on nametags, form small groups according to name, and ask each group to imagine the situation implied by its name. For example, what would it be like for "Jezreel" to live under the threat of bloodshed or for "Lo-ammi" to be disowned? Then distribute new nametags inscribed either with "Shalom," "Children of the Living God," or "Has Pity." Have participants describe their changed situation. Ask: How do you feel now?

D. Voice Repentance

Read Psalm 85 and the commentary on pages 263–64. Notice where the themes of remembrance, repentance, and forgiveness occur. Imagine the people of Hosea's time reciting this psalm. Ask: To what other occasions in the life of Israel might this psalm have spoken? To what occasions in our national or personal lives might it be relevant?

E. Claim Christ's Gifts

In relation to the commentary discussion of Christ's lordship (Colossians 2:6-15, 16-19) and competing ideologies and systems (pages 264–65), invite the group to brainstorm a list of the institutions, ideologies, or competing activities that undermine our allegiance to Christ. Ask: Do we really trust Christ to conquer evil in our world? How can we manifest our trust in relation to forces that compete for our loyalty? What does Christ expect of us in the struggle against evil?

F. Discuss Prayer

Discuss these questions in groups of three: How did you learn how to pray? What are your prayer practices now? What are your struggles in relation to prayer? How would you like to grow in your prayer life?

Compare the versions of the Lord's Prayer in Luke 11:2-4 and Matthew 6:9-13 from various Bible translations and liturgical resources. Ask: What do the differences teach us? Which version do you prefer? Why? Then develop a paraphrase of the Lord's Prayer following these three criteria: as few of the original words as possible; faithful to the original intent; meaningful to "our people."

G. Close With Prayer

Pray your paraphrase of the Lord's Prayer in unison.

Lections for Sunday Between
July 31 and August 6

H Old Testament: Hosea 11:1-11

OSEA prophesied during the last decades of the life of the kingdom of Israel, about 750–721 B.C. Jeroboam II, who died in 726 B.C., was the last strong king of Israel. After him, four kings rose and fell in quick succession. It was a period of decline and decay, all played out against the background of the westward and southward expansion of the Assyrian Empire, which eventually conquered Israel in 721 B.C.

Devastation

In last week's lection, the prophet enacted YHWH's message in his own personal life, marrying an unfaithful wife who symbolized the people's covenant unfaithfulness and giving names to his children that expressed God's displeasure with Israel. The prophet used this dysfunctional family situation as a living parable that revealed God's steadfast love (*hesed*) toward a wayward covenant partner, God's redemptive purposes for his bride and her children, and upon whom God would again have compassion.

I once met a single mother of a rebellious teenage son who was running with a wild crowd, had started taking drugs, and had been arrested for shoplifting. Her pressure, scolding, and punishments, though motivated by concern, came across as rejection and only made matters worse. Then, in a church Bible study she read this passage from Hosea, saw the contrast between her own rejection of her son's behavior and God's compassionate acceptance of Israel, and began to lighten up and be more understanding. This began a long, slow process of behavior change, reconciliation, and improved relationship.

Today's lection falls hard on the heels of a series of oracles foretelling the imminent devastation to befall Israel (often called "Ephraim" or "Samaria" [its capital], the most prominent tribe). The devastation came as Assyria invaded and subjugated Israel, making it a vassal territory of a Gentile empire and reversing, in effect, the Exodus experience of liberation and resulting political independence. This realization drew Hosea's attention back to the Exodus from Egypt (verse 1), as YHWH recalls, using the tender images of a parent nurturing and teaching a child, the manner in which YHWH had been rejected while trying to guide Israel toward maturity and responsibility.

> *Think About It:* Hosea compares God's feelings toward a sinful people to those of a husband for his wife and a parent for a child. What changes do Hosea's images of "took them up in my arms," "led with cords of human kindness and bands of love," "taught to walk," "lift to their cheeks," and "bent down and fed them" (verses 3-4) suggest for your attitudes and relationships with loved ones?

Between Justice and Compassion

The prophet paints a picture of a heartbroken God. The "child" God protected and tended so carefully failed to acknowledge that loving care, rejected its true Parent, YHWH, and instead adopted the polytheistic ways of worship and sacrifice of their Canaanite neighbors. God laments this painful rejection like a mother who grieves as her child neither returns her affections nor allows her care to awaken loyalty and love, but instead adopts a lifestyle that can only bring the child harm.

Here we see the tension between justice and compassion, the latter being passionately expressed in verses 8-9. So, rather than punish in anger and retribution (as human parents sometimes do), God decides to act with compassion and forbearance. Though Assyria will swallow up Israel for a time, the place carved in God's heart for Israel would in the end ensure redemption and restoration.

Psalter: Psalm 107:1-9, 43

This excerpt comes from one of the most carefully structured thanksgiving psalms. The psalmist invites all who have experienced God's saving power in one trial or another to give testimony to what God has done to save those who called upon God (verse 2). Verses 4-9 announce a pattern that will be repeated successively in verses 10-16, 17-22, and 23-32.

In each, some circumstance of dire trouble is described, followed by a first refrain narrating the turning point in distress ("Then they cried to the LORD in their trouble, / and he delivered them from their distress," 6, 13, 19, 28).

Next comes a description of the deliverance God has provided, then a second refrain calling for the appropriate response ("Let them thank the LORD for his steadfast love, / for his wonderful works to humankind," 8, 15, 21, 31), and finally a conclusion. Verses 33-43 provide a summary of the mighty acts of God, calling upon the "wise" (those who honor God) to pay attention to the ways in which God's faithfulness manifests itself in the world.

Epistle: Colossians 3:1-11

This reading begins an artfully structured instruction in the kind of behavior that reflects the new life into which Jesus has called us.

A New Reality

In verses 1-4, Paul sets out the necessary consequences of the new realities of Christian life in the world. We have been given to share in Christ's death and resurrection, and our life and hope are set fully in Christ, "seated at the right hand of God" (a metaphor for Christ's sovereignty in relationship to the Creator). In response to this gift, our ambitions, desires, and thoughts are to be focused there as well. This does not mean that we should be of "no earthly good." On the contrary, we are enabled by Christ to choose how we act toward others, what we pour ourselves into and out for, and what we set as the goals of our lives, in light of eternity.

Conflicting Desires

In verses 5-11, the author develops the negative side of this ethical exhortation. Having died with Christ, we must put to death that which reflects the world and its cravings to make way for the love of Christ to find full expression in our hearts and lives.

In the passage that follows (verses 12-17), the author develops the positive side, namely the new life that the believer takes on in Christ. The whole is governed by the metaphor of clothing (3:9-10, 12, 14), which represents both the "old self" (former life) and the characteristics and driving passions that used to dominate us, and the "new self" (transformed being) that we long to become through the power of the Spirit. This image expresses a conviction that people can change and grow and thus stands opposed to the deterministic views of behavior and personality that are often used as excuses for remaining mired in self-centered, self-serving lifestyles.

A Renewed Vision of Humanity

A person is characterized by many traits that neither reflect God's character nor embody God's desires for human beings in their relationships with one another. Verses 5 and 8 list some of these attitudes and behaviors. Few of us can hear the list without feeling some pang of guilt. Whether we put money ahead of people, give vent to road rage, bear ill will against another, or seek personal sexual gratification at the expense of the well-being of our partner, we have failed to embody God's vision for human community.

This contest does not instantly disappear when we are initiated into the body of Christ. Nevertheless, having entered into God's new creation in Christ, it becomes our proper response to purge ourselves of all that stands in the way of that vision, in which "Christ is all and in all" (verse 11).

> **Think About It:** Colossians calls us to strip off the "old self" and clothe ourselves with a "new self." How is this struggle between the old and the new manifested in your life? How much free rein do you give your "old self"? How do you reflect the "image of your creator"? What help do you need to persevere in this struggle?

Gospel: Luke 12:13-21

An all-too-familiar family dispute—the fair division of an inheritance—becomes the occasion for a series of teachings by Jesus about possessions.

A Proper Legacy

Classical authors recognized the dangers to the unity and harmony of siblings in dividing an inheritance. Plutarch, for example, cautioned that the most important legacy a parent could leave behind was the gift of brothers and sisters one to another. To sacrifice the enjoyment of that gift for the sake of ownership over some part of the material inheritance was to lose the best part of the inheritance. Rather, he advised, the whole estate ought to be considered the common property of all the siblings (*On Fraternal Affection,* 483D-E). Therefore siblings ought to allow one another to choose over what part of the estate they would be stewards (rather than owners). Plutarch would probably have counseled the disputant to allow his brother to keep the money rather than break the bond of love over the claim (as Paul urged brothers and sisters in Christ; see 1 Corinthians 6:7-8).

Handling Our Assets

If we were to extend the definition of "sibling" to "fellow human being," we would come close to the underlying logic of Jesus' response to this person from the crowd. First declining to act as arbitrator in such a divisive dispute over ownership, Jesus used the occasion to warn the crowd against "all kinds of greed," the disputes over inheritances being only one form among many (Luke 12:15).

Jesus then offered a difficult parable on how a person dealt with surplus (verses 16-21). At this point, Jesus shifted the focus to the testator and away from the heir. While wealth may be a sign of God's blessing, the Hebrew

271

Scriptures were clear that one's ultimate reliance was to be upon God and not on material possessions. We may find this teaching uncomfortable because, in America at least, we are considered wise if we hold onto our surplus and lay it up for the future. This is called "financial planning." The other tendency is to use surplus to acquire more extravagant consumer items. This could be called "upgrading."

The "rich man" in the parable, who could count up his amassed fortune and sit back and relax, living well off the interest, is the model for American retirement. Jesus shows us this "rich man" in a very different way that convicts us all. God confronted this man, mocking his efforts to lay up enough to feel secure, with the announcement of his impending death. What treasure had he laid up for that future?

A Word From the Wise

The parable shows Jesus' connection with the wisdom tradition of Israel. The author of Ecclesiastes, for example, comments on those who gain wealth but who, at death, are prevented by God from enjoying it (6:2). Ben Sira speaks of the one who labors hard to become rich: "When he says, 'I have found rest, / and now I shall feast on my goods!' / he does not know how long it will be / until he leaves them to others and dies" (Sirach 11:18-19, the Apocrypha).

> **Think About It:** Jesus' timely warning allows those who hear to start paying attention to becoming "rich toward God." Consider the quality of your life and the nature of your relationship with God. How can you invest more fully in that relationship and the things of eternal value? What assets will you have to reallocate to do so?

The earlier wisdom authors wrote of the futility of laying up riches rather than enjoying them as one goes along and the folly of postponing pleasure for the sake of amassing wealth. Jesus, however, pointed to a greater danger, namely standing before God at the judgment with nothing of lasting value to show for one's life. Having played the world's game and come out, in the bank accounts, a "winner," the person finds out at the end that he or she has nothing but empty hands, an empty heart, and an empty life.

Study Suggestions

A. Thank the Lord

Begin by inviting the group to read Psalm 107:1-9 in unison and then tell of times when they have known God's timely intervention in response to prayer. Close this time of sharing by reading verse 43.

B. Consider God's Heart

Set Hosea 11:1-11 in context by drawing on the commentary on pages 268–69; then read the lection aloud. Ask: Why is God so compassionate toward these people? What does this say about God? How does history square with the prophet's reading of God's heart?

Mention the above instance of the woman and her teenage son. Ask: When have you had a similar experience? What did you do? What was the result?

C. Take Stock of Your Wealth

Read Luke 12:13-21, and review the commentary on pages 271–72. Ask: Why did Jesus refuse to sort out the man's family problem? What did he expect the man to do? Share and discuss instances of family conflict provoked by inheritance disputes. Ask: What guidance does this passage offer to families on these matters? What help might the church provide?

Ask: In what ways have you approached wealth like the rich man in the parable? What exactly does Jesus take issue with concerning that rich man? Have the group paraphrase verse 15 ("Be on your guard against all kinds of greed; for one's life does not consist in the abundance of possessions"), using words different from these but faithful to Jesus' intent. Ask: What "kinds of greed" are seen in present-day America?

D. Update Your Wardrobe

Read Colossians 3:1-17, and ask: How does the image of clothing work in this passage? What do vices, virtues, and clothing all have in common? What pieces of the "old wardrobe" do you still wear occasionally? In what ways do these conflict with your being in Christ? How full is your "spring wardrobe" of Christlikeness? How can you better accessorize so your actions are color-coordinated with the complexion of Christ?

E. Tie It Together

The three principal lections are linked by the theme of divestment. Israel was challenged by Hosea to cast off its waywardness, to respond to their divine Parent in love and obedience, and thus to experience the richness of God's love. Paul challenged the Colossians to divest themselves of the vices that marred their relationships so God's vision for community might be realized. Jesus' hearers were challenged to divest themselves of wealth and possessions and the illusion that hoarding could result in security.

Ask: How have you been challenged to divest yourself today, so you can clothe yourself more fully with Christ? How can we as a group support and hold one another accountable as we seek to make these changes? Close by first singing "Are Ye Able?" then humming it again as persons offer sentence prayers seeking to heed God's challenge and find God's help to grow in these ways.

Lections for Sunday Between August 7 and 13

I## Old Testament: Isaiah 1:1, 10-20

SAIAH of Jerusalem was active during the last half of the eighth century B.C., proclaiming the word of God to the kingdom of Judah. (Isaiah was a contemporary of Hosea, who prophesied in the kingdom of Israel.) This was a tumultuous period for Judah. The Assyrian king Tiglath-pileser had exacted tribute from King Ahaz (2 Kings 16:7-8). His successor Sennacherib would soon attempt to force Hezekiah of Judah to do likewise (2 Kings 18:14-16).

Defeat and Humiliation

In the midst of this turmoil—and in keeping with the prophetic message of contemporaries Amos, Hosea, and Micah, with whose emphases he seems to be familiar—Isaiah called upon the people of Judah to return to YHWH with both their hearts and their actions. He condemned social injustice as unfaithfulness to God and urged his people to put their trust in God alone and to exhibit their faith in both private lives of integrity and in a just and equitable social order.

In this lection, Isaiah refers to the defeat and humiliation Judah has suffered at the hands of the Assyrians as "bleeding wounds" inflicted by God to discipline Judah and correct its wayward heart (Isaiah 1:6-9). Isaiah is amazed that the people of Judah were still prone to rebel against God's commands after such discipline. Though "sick" and "faint," they seek "further beatings" (verse 5).

A Painful Oracle

In today's lection, Isaiah pours forth God's heart for just dealings among God's people. He addresses the principal players in Judah as rulers of Sodom and Gomorrah, implying that the lot of Judah would be no different from the devastating fate of those cities if the Judahites were to continue living in the same idolatrous, unrighteous ways (1:9-10; see Genesis 18:16–19:28; Jeremiah 23:14; Ezekiel 16:46-48). This is but a whiff of a dominant prophetic scent, namely that election by God without ethical responsibility is meaningless and affords no guarantee of protection or prosperity.

Shockingly, the oracle proceeds to denounce the whole sacrificial cult in the Temple as worthless, even offensive, in God's sight (verses 11-15). Without justice for the poor and downtrodden, the ceremonial acts are an affront to God, who would turn a deaf ear to prayers offered by persons with greed in their hearts and blood on their hands.

The Limits of Worship

What would make YHWH pronounce this verdict on the impeccable performance of the very sacrificial system that had been ordained in the Torah? It was the fact that the Judahites acted as if sacrifices and rituals could serve as a substitute for a just and righteous society. No animal sacrifices or cultic acts could secure God's favor for the worshipers if those same people did not share God's heart for justice and refused to demonstrate compassion for the weak and defenseless.

The prophet's intent was not to discredit the sacrificial system, but to align the worshipers' daily life and behavior with God's standards and expectations. This theme (found also, for example, in Isaiah 58:1-12; Hosea 6:6) became an important formative influence on the preaching of Jesus. Jesus frequently drew on such prophetic texts as a means to elevate love, mercy, and mutual care above the performance of cultic rites and observance of purity regulations (see, for example Matthew 15:1-9).

> **Think About It:** As always with God, chastisement and rebuke come together with an invitation to turn from what displeases God and to enter again into God's favor (verses 18-20) by seeking to do God's will. How has piety been a cloak or compensation for injustice or apathy toward others in our lives? How will we respond to God's rebuke and invitation? What changes might God want us to make in our lives and society in order to avoid the judgment Isaiah was pronouncing on the people of Judah?

Psalter: Psalm 50:1-8, 22-23

The decision to omit verses 9-21 from this lection was unfortunate, since these verses contain the prophetic heart of Psalm 50. The first seven verses are a summons to judgment before God. To understand how God's justice has been provoked we must read the indictment contained in verses 9-21. The psalmist explains that God has no need of sacrifices, as if the Almighty depended on them for nourishment. The whole earth already belongs to God. The Holy One seeks not animal sacrifices, but gratitude for divine mercies, the honoring of vows, righteous behavior, truthful, edifying speech, and respect for the commandments. God prefers obedience rather than sacrifice.

Epistle: Hebrews 11:1-3, 8-16

The Letter to the Hebrews was written, either in the 60's or the 80's, to a mixed community of Gentile and Jewish Christians by a Christian leader.

Challenged and Abused
Because their neighbors regarded the Christian group as subversive, this community had suffered their hostility, insults, and abuse. All had lost respect, many experienced financial loss, and some were even imprisoned as part of society's attempts to "reform" these deviants; but they had endured (10:32-34). After some time, a few believers had withdrawn from the fellowship, seeking to distance themselves from the group associations that had cost them so much (10:25). Others pondered whether God's friendship was worth the world's enmity (2:1-2; 3:12-14; 4:1). Still others, perhaps the majority, remained steadfast and committed (6:9-10).

Have Faith
To such a situation the author addresses this famous chapter on *faith*, which we might better think of as *trust*. The word does not simply denote *belief*, as in intellectual convictions about theoretical matters of religion. It denotes trust in a person who has made promises, so that one acts in the present on the basis of what one believes will happen in the future. At the same time, it denotes firmness and loyalty to that person, the opposite of the "shrinking back" that characterizes those who will be lost (10:37-39). The author wants to impress upon the hearers that, as long as they continue to trust God, they will have a firm grasp on what God has promised.

A Legacy of Trust
The author argues that belief is seeing what is promised to be more certain than what can be seen in the present; but the visible creation offers proof that the unseen is more permanent and reliable than the seen. Abraham, Isaac, Jacob, and Sarah are held up as shining examples of this kind of trust (11:8-12). Having been promised an inheritance by God, they voluntarily left behind all the respect, rootedness, security they enjoyed in Chaldea and accepted the lower status of "strangers and foreigners" (see also Moses' example in 11:24-28).

Their circumstances became a witness to the homeland God had prepared, as they were neither willing to return to their old comforts nor to settle down to a permanent existence in Canaan. Wandering like Bedouins (whose forerunners they were), they nevertheless enjoyed the honor of being personally related to God on account of their trust in and commitment to the unseen but real promised things of God. The example of their faith was offered as a challenge to those to whom the Epistle was written, to embrace their new, lower status not as a loss, but as part of faith's rite of passage, leading on to an abiding home.

> **Think About It:** The essential tension expressed in Hebrews is between rootedness here, in this world's comfort and respect, and seeking to be grounded in the abiding realm of God. Where are your roots? How does this affect your witness and walk? How can we both live meaningfully and effectively in this world and at the same time maintain an eternal perspective? How do you handle this tension?

Gospel: Luke 12:32-40

Our appreciation of this week's Gospel lection is greatly enhanced as we compare the sayings Luke has brought together here with the parallel sayings in Matthew and Mark (compare Luke 12:33-34 with Matthew 6:19-21; Luke 12:35-40 with Matthew 24:42-44 and Mark 13:32-37). This process is called "Synoptic comparison," a process in which one gives careful attention to the specific wording an Evangelist has given to a Jesus saying as well as to the place he chose to weave that saying into his Gospel. By doing this, we can see more clearly how Luke, acting as a preacher and evangelist, interpreted and applied the sayings of Jesus.

Lay Up Treasure in Heaven

In the first part of the lection, we find that only Luke gives specific instructions concerning how one is to lay up treasure in heaven—"sell your possessions, and give alms" (Luke 12:33; absent from Matthew 6:19-21). This nuance resonates with similar advice preserved by Luke throughout Jesus' teachings on what it means to be a disciple (see 14:33; 16:9-13, 19-31; 18:22; 19:8-9; Acts 2:44-45; 4:32, 34-37), so that commitment to poverty and service can rightly be said to be a major emphasis in Luke-Acts.

The Shepherd of Hermas

Luke's word to the churches was effectively captured by the second-century author of *The Shepherd of Hermas,* whose expansive application of the passage merits attention: "Why are you preparing fields and extravagant furnishings and buildings and empty rooms here? As one who lives on foreign soil, prepare for yourself nothing more than what is sufficient to supply your needs. Be ready—whenever the master of this city should desire to banish you as one who lives contrary to his law—to leave his city and go to your own city, and to live by your law rejoicing and free from injury. So instead of fields, purchase souls in trouble—each as he or she is able—and watch over widows and orphans and do not neglect them. Spend your wealth and possessions, which you received from God, freely on fields and houses of this kind, which you will find in your city when you come home to it. Therefore, do not practice the extravagance of the nations, but practice your distinctive extravagance, in which you can rejoice" (*The Third Book of Hermas* or *Similitude* 1:1-11). Investing in people in need—this, according to Luke, is the financial planning advice of Jesus and the early church.

> *Think About It:* The money we lay up for tomorrow can save a life, relieve a persecuted sister or brother, or bring healing to the sick today. How does this reality, and the mandate of the gospel, shape your financial planning objectives?

Be Ready

As we compare the second part of the passage in Luke (12:35-40) with the parallels in Mark and Matthew, we notice that Luke has chosen to place sayings about being prepared for the return of the Son of Man in the context of Jesus' teachings about possessions. Matthew and Mark postpone them to a final discourse about the signs of the end, which might be considered the more natural setting.

In light of the parable of the rich fool (12:13-21), however, Luke's logic becomes quite clear. Whether through our own death or Christ's return, we must be prepared to meet God and give an account of our lives. Using the imagery of both the wedding party in which the slave must have all ready for his returning master and of a homeowner protecting his property from theft, Luke underscores the importance of being ready for an unexpected coming. Thus Luke links the exhortations to live so as to be ready for the returning Christ with Jesus' emphasis on stewardship rather than ownership of possessions, thereby freeing us to allocate funds according to God's heart for all people (see James 5:1-5).

Study Suggestions

A. God's Call to Worship

Read Psalm 50:1-23 antiphonally. Review the commentary on pages 275–76. Say that some ancient religions regarded animal sacrifices as their duty to "feed" the gods, but the true God has no need of such things. Ask: According to this psalm, what does God really want from worshipers? How can we offer this today?

B. Offer Acceptable Sacrifices

Set the context for the Isaiah lection by reviewing the first three paragraphs of the commentary (page 274). Then read aloud Isaiah 1:1, 10-20. Ask: Why did YHWH find fault with the abundant sacrifices and bustling cultic activity in Jerusalem? What contrast existed between that ostentatious worship life and social justice concerns in the Judahite society? How had the worshipers been using sacrifices? What were the consequences? What reform did God require?

C. Seek Investment Advice

Invite comparison of Luke 12:32-34 with Matthew 6:19-21. Ask: What differences do you notice? What might this say about Luke's emphasis? How well can one's values and commitments be discerned by reviewing one's checkbook register?

Read the quotation from *The Shepherd of Hermas*. Ask: How does this text compare with Jesus' teaching in today's Luke passage? How does being a stranger on earth and a native of heaven affect our view of wealth as Christians? What would constitute a sound financial investment strategy from this point of view? How do we justify "laying up treasures on earth"? What does faithful discipleship require?

D. Sharpen the Eyes of Faith

Introduce the Epistle lection with a review of the commentary (pages 276–77); then read Hebrews 11:1-3, 8-16. Discuss: What does the definition of faith in verse 1 suggest about faith? What is the relationship between being "at home" in society and being a person of faith? How might this crafting of Abraham's story have encouraged the readers of Hebrews in the midst of their challenges? Ask: How does this understanding of faith relate to Luke and *Hermas*?

At the close of this discussion distribute paper and markers, and invite members to draw a symbolic representation of *faith* as reflected in this passage. Collect the drawings without names, and display them for review at the end of the session.

E. Tie It Together

The Psalm, Old Testament, and Gospel lections all share in common a witness to God's passion for people and for God's followers to act with justice, generosity, and care toward all. The Epistle lection brings an added dimension: being on a pilgrimage of faith, detachment from the values of this world, and commitment to the eternal justice and righteousness of the realm of God. Ask: How do these passages call us to something new?

Close by silently viewing the symbolic drawings of faith. Then sing "Hymn of Promise," and pray for firmness of purpose in pursuing our pilgrimages of faith.

Lections for Sunday Between August 14 and 20

I Old Testament: Isaiah 5:1-7

*I*N order to illustrate God's care for, expectations of, and frustration with the house of Judah, Isaiah told a parable about a vineyard. YHWH had cultivated the people of Israel and Judah (verse 7) with great foresight and labor, just as a person would plant a vineyard and keep it. The cultivator must make extensive preparations if the vineyard is to be protected against animals and thieves and become productive. All this tending and cultivating, however, was done with the expectation of a harvest. The people were expected to be faithful to the covenant, worship YHWH alone, and treat one another with justice and compassion. But YHWH was disappointed in the return. The vineyard had produced only "wild grapes"—small, hard, and bitter. Because the harvest was wild grapes, YHWH concluded he would return the vineyard to its wild state, so it could continue to produce wild grapes.

Patron and Client

Isaiah's parable preserves one of the earlier examples of the use of agricultural imagery as a vehicle for describing the expectations of reciprocal relationships: relationships of patrons and clients, benefactors and beneficiaries. A patron would cultivate a client, providing assistance, protection, access to promotion, and the like, with the expectation that the client would prove himself or herself a loyal and grateful friend. To do what brought grief and frustration to the patron who had taken the client into his favor and trust would have been regarded as dishonorable in the extreme and would result in exchanging favor for wrath. (A similar logic appears in Hebrews 6:4-8, where ground is judged in terms of whether it produces a useful crop or thorns and thistles, and this is used as a metaphor for believers who have fallen away.)

God as Patron

This, Isaiah claimed, was precisely what Judah had done to God. God had lavished benefits on Judah, protected it from enemies, done everything possible to promote its growth (verses 1-2), and held the just expectation of seeing the Judahites do what pleased God (verses 3-5). They were expected to show gratitude for their prosperity by honoring God and treating one another fairly and equitably. Instead, the soil of the Judahites had brought forth injustice, oppression, and violence (verse 7).

Enriched and kept safe from enemies outside, the people of Judah had preyed upon one another instead of loving and showing fraternal care for one another, from the strongest to the weakest. The punishment would be appropriate to Judah's sin. Wild grapes need no protection. So YHWH would remove his protection and permit Judah to become wild.

Bear Fruits (or the Consequences)

Jesus would later appropriate this parable in his own "parable of the wicked tenants" (Matthew 21:33-44). Despite a key change, in which God's own vineyard becomes a vineyard let out to tenant farmers (the new focus falling on the people renting the vineyard and on the slaves and son sent to collect the rent), the message is essentially the same. Failure to bring forth the "fruits of the kingdom" in terms of righteous living, caring relationships, and trust in God, for which purpose God has offered us providence and grace, will result in the forfeiture of God's favor and the resulting encounter with calamity.

> **Think About It:** God's nurture, grace, and favor are meant to stimulate a response in the form of grateful worship, just living, and caring relationships. When we say, "God bless America," how does God intend for us to use divine blessing? How do we establish justice and show mercy?

Psalter: Psalm 80:1-2, 8-19

This psalm aptly complements the reading from Isaiah, continuing the use of the metaphor of the vine to represent Israel. The psalmist recounts how YHWH had carried the vine out of Egypt, prepared a place for it to grow, and carefully planted and tended it as it took root and spread (verses 8-11). But now it has been forsaken and laid waste, its fruit ravaged by strangers and wild animals (verses 12-13).

The psalm then turns into a national lament for the people of Israel, written when that territory was under attack from some outside power, or in the lingering aftermath of such an attack, quite possibly the Assyrian invasion that ended their political independence (14-16). At its close it becomes a prayer asking God to restore and save the nation, in response to which the people will return to faithfulness (verses 17-19).

Epistle: Hebrews 11:29–12:2

This week's lesson from Hebrews concludes the so-called "faith chapter." The examples of Abel, Enoch, Noah, Abraham, Sarah, Isaac, Jacob, and Moses had all contributed something important to the author's portrait of faith in action in the world (11:4-28), and several of these emphases reappear in this concluding collage.

Secure in God's Power
Hebrews 11:29 recalls the Exodus, a crisis where faith made the difference between deliverance and destruction, just as in Noah's situation (11:7) and in the experience of readers (10:37-39). Hebrews 11:30-31 reinforces the fact that the most secure structures of this world (city walls and mighty armies) shake and fall when confronted by people of faith acting in the name and power of God. So, alignment with the people of God rather than with the worldly camp is the faithful choice, as demonstrated by Joshua at Jericho and Rahab, the Canaanite woman who aided the Hebrew spies.

Winning by Faith
In the paragraph that follows the author first looks at those who, by faith, accomplished what even the world would admire (11:32-35a), and then at those who, by faith, made themselves "losers" from a worldly point of view (11:35b-38). The figures in the former group are readily identified from the Old Testament. The latter group include some unfamiliar traditions—the Maccabean martyrs in 11:35b; see 2 Maccabees 7 in the Apocrypha; and traditions about the deaths of the prophets Isaiah, Jeremiah, and Zechariah in 11:37a.

The author's point is quite clear: we best please and serve God by being faithful, regardless of the consequences for status and comfort in this world. Indeed, as society pushes the witnesses of faith out into the margins—to rejection, ignominy, persecution, and even death—the verdict it passes is really on itself—"of [them] the world was not worthy" (11:38).

> **Think About It:** Look toward the "great cloud of witnesses" (persons of faith) and the "pioneer and perfecter of our faith" (Jesus), rather than to those who reject what God values in a person. What witnesses in this cloud have set a faithful example for you? How have they influenced your life? Who might be looking to you to model faithful living? How is your witness setting such an example for them?

The Perfect Example
The climactic example of faith is Jesus himself—"the pioneer and perfecter of our faith"

(12:2)—and the faithful are called to "look to" that example. "Look to" literally means "to look away to," which suggests turning away from everything except Jesus, who endured the greatest assaults in his trial and execution. His perseverance in embodying sacrificial, redemptive love, even to the point of death, gained him a place of highest honor in the eternal realm.

In Jesus, then, one sees that faith entails ignoring human opinion and enduring temporal loss in order to stand firm for God and God's purposes. The fact that Jesus did this on our behalf, by going to the cross out of his great love for humanity, should arouse similar faith in us, in the sense of keeping faith with Jesus by living lives of faithful discipleship and service.

Gospel: Luke 12:49-56

In the opening sayings of this lection, we catch a glimpse of Jesus' frame of mind in the midst of his earthly ministry. He knew that, contrary to popular hopes about a messiah ushering in an era of peace and political independence for Judea, the aftermath of his own work would be division, strife, and fiery crisis. This point would be important for Luke, who wrote during a time of struggle in the wake of the Roman destruction of the Temple in A.D. 70, which led also to a schism between the infant church and the Jewish synagogue.

Division and Strife

This division of which Jesus spoke was not antithetical to his realm, which is characterized by peace. Rather, the coming of the Kingdom requires decision and commitment, which can always be divisive. "From now on" (12:52) might be taken as a period of purging and refining, or simply (and more plausibly) as divine judgment.

Nevertheless, this was the beginning of the fulfillment of God's final redemptive purpose for the world, and Jesus was eager—even "stressed"—to see his work, the inception of the end, completed. He refers to his passion as a "baptism" that he must undergo (12:50, as in Mark 10:38-39), an appropriate image for one who is about to be immersed in death and to rise to a new kind of life (indeed, for all baptized Christians).

Family Breakdown

Most disturbing, perhaps, is Jesus' statement about what his work will mean for human families. One might think that families ought to hold together in harmony, cooperation, and love, and that God's work should only foster that. Indeed, the text from Micah 7:6 that Jesus quoted in Luke 12:53 is an indictment of the breakdown of trust and cooperation in the family as a result of ungodliness, causing the prophet to be on guard against his nearest and dearest, trusting in God alone. Nevertheless, this Jesus saying reflects the reality that natural kinship networks will fail as some members respond positively to this Messiah, while others reject him and disown those who follow him. It is likely that the loss of kinship support networks played a large role in the poverty that befell the Judean Christians during the decades after Jesus' death and resurrection.

> **Think About It:** It is often said that if we would just follow Jesus, we could live in harmony; yet, Jesus causes division. When has it been necessary for you to "make waves" in your family in order to be faithful to your understanding of God's will for you?

In light of this reality, Jesus' redefinition of kinship—his creation of a new family support network among his followers—became essential for the perseverance, support, and survival of individual disciples and the faith community (see Matthew 12:46-50; Mark 10:29-30). As their kinfolk applied emotional and financial pressure through shunning, threat, and rejection, in an effort to dissuade the disciples from associating with the name of Jesus, they needed one another all the more in order to remain faithful. Nearly every New Testament author shows an awareness of this dynamic, urging believers to support one another with the same love, and to the same level, that one might expect from family.

Interpret the Times

The passage closes with Jesus challenging the crowds to discern the significance of the times in which they were living. They could tell that clouds from the west (the Mediterranean) meant coming rain and that wind from the south would drive up hot air from the desert. When it came to spiritual discernment of the "present time" and what it would bring, however, they were without insight.

In its Lukan context, this seems to refer to the troubles that were looming on the horizon for the Judean people, particularly the rise of anti-Roman nationalism that would eventually result in the Jewish War and the destruction of Jerusalem and the Temple by the Romans in A.D. 70. Pursuing peace with such an adversary (see Luke 12:57-59) would certainly have been the more astute policy.

Study Suggestions

A. Cry Out to the Lord

Read Psalm 80:1-2, 8-19 responsively. After sharing insights from the commentary on pages 281–82, ask: How does remembering God's earlier nurture of the "vine" build up the psalmist's confidence that God will help in the present crisis? Ask if any are facing troubles today, and pray for those who share concerns. Recite verse 19 together.

B. Inspect God's Vineyard

Read aloud Isaiah 5:1-7, and review the commentary on pages 280–81. Note that the vineyard represents Judah. Ask: How does the vinedresser's care of the vineyard correspond to God's acts on behalf of Judah in history? Why would the vinedresser feel entitled to have certain expectations about the produce of that which was so carefully tended? What fruit was God expecting Judah to produce? What were the "wild [sour] grapes" that the prophet specifically names? Why would God/the vinedresser react so destructively to the vineyard?

C. Gear Up for the Race

Read aloud Hebrews 11:29–12:2. Ask: What do the examples in 11:29-31 add to our understanding of how faith acts in the world and the consequences faithful action brings? With regard to these verses and those that follow, help the group recall the biblical stories of faith behind these brief references.

Next review the notes on pages 282–83 interpreting the Hebrews passage. What does Jesus' example contribute to our understanding of how faith acts in the world? When has standing up for Jesus meant ridicule or rejection by your neighbors, co-workers, or friends? In the church, how do we support one another in facing and evaluating these tensions?

D. Consider the Consequences

Read aloud Luke 12:49-56. Ask: What is the "baptism" to which Jesus refers? What do verses 49-50 and 54-56 tell us about Jesus' understanding of his mission?

Read the "Family Breakdown" paragraphs. Ask: Why would such divisions happen in ancient Jewish and Gentile families as a result of Jesus' ministry? When have you felt torn between faithfulness to God and pleasing your family?

Roleplay a situation involving conflict between faithful discipleship and expectations of family and friends, with another member playing the role of the person presenting the problem, so he or she can see how another handles it. Then debrief with questions about how persons felt, interpersonal dynamics, and what might have been said or done differently. Pray for strength and wisdom for the presenter as he or she goes back into the situation with these new insights and resolves.

E. Tie It Together

Ask: What important or challenging thoughts came out of our study of this week's lections? What do you hear God telling you to keep in mind, do, or change in the week ahead? Remind the group of the support and example of the "cloud of witnesses" who precede and surround us; then sing "For All the Saints."

Close with prayer for each person's focus and resolve that the seeds planted today will bear pleasant fruit for God.

Lections for Sunday Between
August 21 and 27

J Old Testament: Jeremiah 1:4-10

JEREMIAH exercised a prophetic ministry from 627 B.C. through 586 B.C. and the aftermath of the destruction of Jerusalem by Babylon, which marked the end of the kingdom of Judah. Most of the material in Jeremiah, including the extensive narrative accounts of the prophet's activities and trials, comes from the second half of this period.

"Only a Boy"

Today's lection may well represent the prophet's reminiscence of the earliest of his experiences as a prophet—his call by God. Jeremiah was called when he was "only a boy," a word designating an adolescent male too young to bear arms. Though young, Jeremiah's lack of experience would not hinder God's plans for him, nor excuse him from God's service (verses 6-7). In this brief exchange, Jeremiah's story recalls Moses' similar reluctance to accept God's commission (see Exodus 3:1-14).

A key element of this call narrative was God's assurance that Jeremiah did not need to be intimidated by the power and prestige of those to whom he would be asked to proclaim the word of God, since God had promised to stand by him and guide and protect him (verse 8). This aspect of Jeremiah's commission is embellished in verses 17-19. (Verse 8, in fact, is repeated in verse 19.) If Jeremiah were to fail to deliver God's message boldly—that is, if he were to allow fear of the people to derail his obedience to God—God would shatter him in full view of everyone, thereby humiliating and disgracing him (verse 17).

Such timidity would indicate a lack of trust in God's promises (richly described with vivid imagery in verses 18-19) and would show a poor grasp of the imperative to obey God rather than seek to please people. With the promise of God's presence and guidance comes the responsibility to represent this God well and fearlessly to the world Jeremiah would encounter. This is a task and an opportunity that the apostles would share with Jeremiah in times to come (see Acts 4:19; 5:29).

Standing Firm

Jeremiah would stand courageously, delivering his unpopular predictions of doom for Judah, often opposing other prophets, such as Hananiah, who predicted prosperity and peace for Judah and mistakenly promised a miraculous divine deliverance from the invading Babylonians (see Jeremiah 28). Hananiah's Pollyannaish message was much more in keeping with the spirit of the day. The Assyrian Empire was in rapid decay. This offered great hope for Judah; as a result, there was a rising sense of nationalistic fervor. Jeremiah recognized the threat presented by Babylon. The great tragedy is not that Judah was conquered by Babylon, but that the horrors of that war could have been averted had the king and his people been willing to heed the word of the Lord that was spoken by Jeremiah. Hananiah was no friend of Judah. His popular nostrums were deadly.

> **Think About It:** All servants of God are called to speak the truth of the antiicpated or actual response. When you have felt led to speak or sand up for God's standards and priorities? To what extent did you allow fear or intimidation to color, shape, or limit your words?

Psalter: Psalm 71:1-6

This psalm is the prayer of an aged worshiper of YHWH (see verses 9, 17-19), now in trouble, beset by enemies, but without the vigor of youth for dealing with them. The worshiper, robbed by time of natural resources, looks to God as the only source of help to cope with external threats to his well-being, dignity, and life itself. The psalm speaks of the worshiper's lifelong experience of God's faithfulness and deliverance, the memory of which fills him with hope for deliverance from present trials and tribulations (verses 20-21).

Epistle: Hebrews 12:18-29

The author's major strategies expressed throughout his letter-sermon are brought together in this lection.

Access to God

First, he has laid special emphasis on the quality of access to God that Jesus opened up for his followers. Prior to Jesus, the only access to the God of Israel was mediated through the Levitical (priestly) cult, in which stringent boundaries and limitations on access or contact with God were applied and observed. When Jesus died, the curtain of the Temple was torn in two. The Holy Presence upon the altar, or the "Shekinah," departed the Holy of Holies, tearing the veil as it left. So the Temple of Jerusalem, devoid of the presence of YHWH, was no longer the center for the authentic worship of God. The earthly Jerusalem was replaced with the heavenly Jerusalem where Jesus is present and where his blood ratifies, or guarantees, a new covenant (12:22-24).

The first point made by the author is to contrast the fear-filled, taboo-laden, boundary-marked encounter with God experienced by the Exodus generation at Sinai (see Exodus 19:12-22; 20:18-21) with the festive, joyous, unrestricted access to God that Christian believers are now allowed to enjoy as they keep moving forward in faith toward their eternal home, the "heavenly Jerusalem." How could they ever be tempted to give up such an unparalleled benefit won for them by Jesus?

Do Not Refuse

The second point stresses the great dignity of the One who has called them into favor. He warns of the incomparable danger of insulting that One through disobedience, distrust of the promises, or faithlessly seeking the world's friendship or fearing the world's hostility (see Hebrews 2:1-3; 10:26-31). So here in 12:25, the author drops a parting reminder that to reject a greater benefit from God than those enjoyed by Moses' generation would also mean incurring a worse punishment than that experienced by those who defied God in the wilderness.

An Unshakable Kingdom

A third point contrasts the temporary nature of all the goods that this world has to offer—the "fleeting pleasures of sin" (11:25)—with the "lasting" or permanent goods that God has prepared for those who trust God and remain steadfastly loyal. These blessings are described as "better and more lasting" possessions (10:34), "a better country, that is, a heavenly one" (11:16), a "lasting" city (13:14)—all metaphors for the spiritual benefits resulting from faithful, unswerving devotion to God above all else.

> **Think About It:** God's assurance of the unshakable kingdom should arouse gratitude and commiment. When have you felt the tension between Christ's gift of grace and desire for temporal advantage, physical comfort, or status and recognition? What makes us want to reject what is given us by grace through faith and seek to make ourselves acceptable to God by our own efforts of moral reform?

In the author's expectation, the visible existence of earth and heaven is not permanent, but will be removed on the day of the Lord. This will open up admission for believers into an eternal realm, which Christ entered as a forerunner (2:10; 6:19-20). This is the sense of

12:26-27 (see also 1:10-12). God's assurance of the gift of a place in the "unshakable kingdom" should arouse a full measure of gratitude (12:28), leading to a commitment to honor God through loyalty, witness, and service. The author gives specific shape to these assurances in 13:1-19.

Gospel: Luke 13:10-17

The four Evangelists sometimes show Jesus in conflict with other Jewish teachers concerning the propriety of healing on the sabbath. (In Luke, see 6:6-11; 14:1-6; see also John 5:1-19.)

Keeping Sabbath

That healing should ever provoke opposition from the religious leaders might strike us as strange, or even petty, until we consider the paramount importance of keeping the sabbath among Jews. This was one of the most distinctive marks that set Jews apart from their neighbors. The sabbath commandment was given following the Exodus (20:8-11), was affirmed in their holiness laws, and was particularly observed from the time under Ezra (mid-sixth century B.C.) when the exiles were allowed to return from Babylon and rebuild the Temple.

Even if Gentiles knew very little about the Jews, they at least knew that they rested one day in seven, circumcised their sons, and avoided pork. Sabbath observance was thus a pillar of Jewish identity, and, more to the point, of fulfillment of their mandate to be a people distinctly devoted to YHWH among the nations (see Leviticus 20:26; Deuteronomy 14:2). The seriousness with which YHWH was held to view the sabbath is seen in the fact that the "work" of carrying wood on sabbath was punishable by the death penalty (see Exodus 31:12-17).

In Rhythm With God

Resting on the sabbath was, for the observant Jew, a means of living in tune with the rhythm of God's activity, who worked six days creating the world and rested on the seventh (Genesis 2:1-3; Exodus 20:8-11; 31:15, 17). Setting apart the seventh day, keeping it uncontaminated from the work of the six ordinary days, was also a living witness to the one God who created the universe, as well as to the redemptive acts of God who gave rest and freedom to a people once enslaved (Deuteronomy 5:12-15).

The Pharisees, one Jewish sect, developed a very strict sabbath tradition and felt that those who disagreed with their tradition also violated the law. As a Jew, Jesus kept the sabbath; but he did not observe the sabbath in keeping with Pharisaic tradition. In John 5:1-19, for example, Jesus declared that, where acts of love, redemption, and compassion are concerned, "My Father is still working, and I also am working" (5:17). If the sabbath is meant to allow God's people to reflect the divine character and move in harmony with

289

God's movement, then acts of compassion and redemption are never untimely. Rather, withholding kindness on the sabbath is the true violation of the day, since that violates the character of God.

Jesus' Argument

To support his actions, Jesus employed a common rabbinic method for interpreting the Torah: namely the "lesser to greater" argument. He cited the practice of untying one's animals to lead them to water on the sabbath, which was acceptable to most Jews (all save the Qumran community). Establishing that a "daughter of Abraham" is of greater value than any animal, he argued that "untying" her from the affliction that had kept her bound was perfectly acceptable, even commendable.

Jesus' expression actually emphasized not just the possibility, but the necessity of liberating this woman on the sabbath—softened by the English "ought" (Luke 13:16), but better rendered as "is it not necessary?" which clearly implies an affirmative response. The sabbath was the weekly remembrance of God's liberation of Israel from slavery and God's gift of "rest" to the former captives. Now that the reign of God was breaking in on the world, it was all the more appropriate for Satan's captives to be "set free from this bondage on the sabbath day."

> **Think About It:** Our main calling is to reflect God's character and heart to the world, as Jesus did in this healing on the sabbath. To what extent do your religious practices and daily life reveal the nature of the God you worship?

Study Suggestions

A. Lean on the Lord

Invite the group to read all of Psalm 71 antiphonally. Comment that this is a very personal psalm, giving us a clear glimpse into the psalmist's own frame of mind and feelings in his circumstances. Ask: When have you been wrongly accused and were unable to prove your innocence? How can God bring vindication to the righteous? How does truth eventually emerge?

Look closely at verses 6, 17, 20-21. Discuss: How does the psalmist's long-standing experience of God influence him in his current distress? Invite group members briefly to share with one another the heritage of their past experience of God, for mutual encouragement.

B. Prophets Wanted

Set the Old Testament passage in historical context by reviewing the background in the commentary on pages 286–87. Then read Jeremiah 1:4-10. Ask: Why did Jeremiah feel unequal to the task? How did God encourage and empower him for his vocation?

Read the paragraph titled "Only a Boy" and then Exodus 3:1-14. Compare the Exodus reading with the passage from Jeremiah. Invite three persons to take the roles of Moses, Jeremiah, and God and to recreate their call and dialogue with God. Expand this in your own words to allow Moses and Jeremiah to express the full range of their fears, reservations, and expectations. Then ask observers to share their own call experiences and to describe how receiving a clear call from God can be greeted. Then discuss the "Think About It" questions. Comment that in Jeremiah's time religious perspectives were used to legitimate and/or critique political policy. Ask: What is the responsibility of Christian prophets to witness to God's standards in our country today?

C. Respond With Gratitude

Invite members to read Exodus 19:12-22 and 20:18-21 as background material, and then concentrate on Hebrews 12:18-29. Ask: What feelings and attitudes characterize the two different approaches to God (fear and confidence) described in 12:18-24? Which of these feelings and attitudes have characterized the ways you have approached God at different stages in your life? Read the commentary sections, "Access to God" and "Do Not Refuse." Ask: How can you best show appreciation for the access to God Jesus has opened up for you?

Read the section, "An Unshakable Kingdom." Ask: What events is the author looking forward to in Hebrews 12:26-28? How does the author think this should affect believers' attitudes and attachments in this world? Discuss the questions in the "Think About It" box.

D. Be Attuned to God's Rhythms

Luke 13:10-17 lends itself to a dramatic reading. Invite four participants to take the parts of narrator, Jesus, the healed woman, and the leader of the synagogue. Use the ideas in "Keeping Sabbath" and "In Rhythm With God" to provide background material on the significance of the sabbath. Ask: Why would the Pharisees criticize Jesus for challenging tradition? Why did Jesus feel compelled to heal this woman on the sabbath? What religious rules and practices might correspond to sabbath observance in Jesus' time? How do these sometimes get in the way of showing respect and compassion for others? What might Jesus say about these?

After the group has discussed the passage from Luke, share the ideas in the "Jesus' Argument" paragraph. Then discuss the "Think About It" questions. What happens when some Christians demand that all other Christians observe their traditions or adhere to their beliefs and practices?

E. Tie It Together

Note that the themes of divine calling, faithful witness, and challenge to prevailing thought and custom are common to several of this week's passages. Ask: When is tradition best preserved by changing the tradition? Sing the hymn, "Take My Life, and Let It Be Consecrated"; then offer an extemporaneous prayer asking God to help us respond faithfully and confidently to God's leading in our lives.

Lections for Sunday Between August 28 and September 3

Old Testament: Jeremiah 2:4-13

*T*HIS passage is set in a section of Jeremiah devoted to accusations and denunciations of the people of Judah for forsaking YHWH, their God. They no doubt had not abandoned YHWH completely, but were mixing loyalty to YHWH with worship of other Canaanite gods. Jeremiah represented the point of view that nothing short of exclusive allegiance to YHWH was acceptable.

Chapter 2 begins with Jeremiah receiving a directive from YHWH to make a public pronouncement to the people of Jerusalem in the name of God (verse 1). The prophet's statement begins by recalling the golden days in the desert when Israel was wholly devoted to YHWH, like a new bride to her husband. (Notice that the desert wanderings had a different meaning to other prophets. The desert was a place of doubt and death.) Even after they entered Canaan, in the early years they were careful to offer the best of their harvest to God and to punish the selfish ones who tried to keep for themselves what should belong to YHWH (verses 2-3). These were signs of their initial faithfulness.

Think About It: In seeking worthless things the people of made themselves worthless. To what do we devote our time, money, and energy that in the end leave us feeling empty and unfulfilled? What do these pursuits do to our own sense of worth, dignity, and self-respect?

Worthless Pursuits Demean Self-Worth

But these days were long gone, says Jeremiah. For now they were neglecting their original commitments, having forgotten how YHWH had delivered them from bondage in Egypt, guided them safely through the dangers of the desert, and brought them to a place of bounty and security. "What went wrong," the prophet has YHWH asking, "that this people have departed so far from devotion to me?" From worship of the only One of supreme worth they had fallen into the pursuit of worthless things. And in so doing, they had demeaned their own value (verses 3-7a).

Specific Accusations

The prophet then got more specific in his complaints against the people. They had befouled the land and turned God's gift from a blessing into a curse. They had corrupted YHWH worship with the obscene rites of pagan gods. Wealthy landowners had hoarded the fruits of their abundant harvests for themselves and denied fair benefits to their tenants and laborers. Priests and prophets had served the ba'als rather than YHWH, and lawyers and rulers had conducted their affairs as though God did not exist (verses 7b-8).

YHWH, through Jeremiah, brought an indictment. Not only the present hearers would suffer for these sins, but future generations as well (verse 9; this may be an oblique reference to the suffering of the coming fall of Jerusalem and exile in Babylon). Even in pagan nations like Cyprus (an island in the eastern Mediterranean near the coast of western Syria and southern Turkey) and Kedar (a collection of Arab tribes in the north Arabian desert) people do not forsake their gods, false and powerless though they be (verse 10). Yet, YHWH complains that the people of Judah have been blessed by their God but have turned their backs on him. They have given up their distinctive greatness for values that were fleeting and unreliable (verse 11).

Cracked Cisterns

The powers on high must be appalled at such faulty judgment and misplaced commitment. For the people whom YHWH had so favored had now made two fatal mistakes. They had forsaken YHWH, the sure source of wisdom and blessing ("living water") and instead put their trust in unreliable allies, leaders, and religious practices ("cracked cisterns") that are doomed to failure and disappointment (verses 12-13). By wrong choices and misplaced values, they had sealed their own fate.

Psalter: Psalm 81:1, 10-16

This psalm originated not in Judah but in the kingdom of Israel before its fall to Assyria in 721 B.C., as is indicated by the linking of Joseph with Israel in verse 5. The psalm expresses the same theme as this week's Jeremiah passage—the call to exclusive allegiance to YHWH. Verses 1-5a are a summons to worship the mighty God of Jacob with both vocal and instrumental music—probably at the time of the festival of booths (Succoth; see

Deuteronomy 16:13-15). In verses 5b-9, the psalmist, like Jeremiah, voices God's complaint that the people whom YHWH had so blessed had now abandoned him and turned to the worship of Canaanite deities.

Then, in the verses selected for today's lection (10-16), a priest or Temple prophet delivers an oracle reminding the people that it was YHWH, not these gods, who liberated them from slavery in Egypt and who would fill them with blessing, protect them from their enemies, and bestow on them the fruit of the land—both wheat from the plains and honey from the rocky mountains. But these promises hinge on an all-important condition—the people must heed God's words and follow God's ways (13).

Epistle: Hebrews 13:1-8, 15-16

The concluding chapter of Hebrews contains practical advice for Christian living in the community of faith. Verses 1-6 consist of exhortations on conduct, and verses 7-17 admonish respect for leaders. The key to vital Christian community is mutual love. The foundation of Christian ethics is unreserved, self-giving care, respect, service, regard, and acceptance of one another (verse 1).

Practice Hospitality

From this base flows hospitality to fellow believers visiting from other places ("strangers," verse 2), and empathy, concern, and support for those who have been imprisoned and tortured for their faith (verse 3). The reference to "angels" recalls the mysterious, anonymous visitors entertained by Abraham and Sarah (Genesis 18:1-8) and by Lot (Genesis 19:1-3) and also reflects the long-standing Middle Eastern custom of gracious, generous hospitality.

The author encouraged fidelity in marriage, avoidance of greed, and simplicity of lifestyle. There is no need to hanker after sexual liaisons, accumulation of wealth, or conspicuous consumption. Trust in God's presence, protection, aid, and guidance are sufficient (Hebrews 13:4-6).

> **Think About It:** "Jesus Christ is the same yesterday and today and forever." What do you think this means? Is it a theological affirmation of an unchanging God who can be depended on to remain constant in the midst of a sea of change? Or is it an affirmation of dependable succor and aid? How do we relate the permanence of God to changing circumstances and demands in ways that affirm essentials while remaining open to new challenges and opportunities?

Follow Leaders' Example

Readers are urged to hold in their hearts the teaching and example of the leaders who had brought them to Christ. Their faith and pattern of living had sustained them and kept them faithful, so were worth emulating. Solid faith in Jesus Christ had provided earlier

Christians with a sure foundation for committed discipleship and would serve present and future generations equally well (verses 7-8).

Finally, Christians are urged to continue offering sacrifices pleasing to God in both word and deed. The Christian life involves both regular participation in worship that forms and undergirds our identity by confessing who we are as a people of God and serving and sharing with one another the good gifts with which God has blessed us (verses 15-16).

Gospel: Luke 14:1, 7-14

The events in this lection provide a lesson in humility, a rebuke to the Pharisees, and the promise of a great eschatological reversal. Jesus had been invited to a sabbath meal in the home of a prominent Pharisee in Jerusalem. Other scribes and Pharisees were present, apparently hoping to gather evidence against this upstart rabbi from provincial Galilee (verse 1).

In their presence, as an act of mercy that presented a deliberate challenge to their interpretation of the law, Jesus broke the sabbath rules by healing a man of dropsy (edema, an abnormal accumulation of fluid in the tissues). Anticipating the Pharisees' criticism, he reminded them that to save a child or an animal from a pit on the sabbath was permissible, even though this involved exertion. Jesus' implication was that certainly one also could cure a person of a painful affliction on the sabbath. Impressed by his power and compassion and confounded by his logic, the Pharisees were speechless (verses 2-6). Luke presents his belief that power rather than words would silence the critics.

Take the Lowest Place

No doubt knowing he was taking a risk, Jesus still did not let up. In Palestinian feasts of the time, reclining couches were arranged in groups of three, with the center grouping reserved for persons of wealth and prestige. If persons came early, as some apparently did on this occasion, they were best advised not to take these seats, as they could later be displaced by late arrivals who outranked them. This would be embarrassing for all concerned. Instead, one should take a lower place and then possibly be honored by being invited to move higher.

In offering this prudent conventional advice, Jesus was merely making practical common sense, which also reflected ancient Jewish wisdom (see Proverbs 25:6-7). But he was at the same time chiding the Pharisees, who habitually claimed "the seat of honor in the synagogues" and demanded "respect in the marketplaces" (Luke 11:43). They would get their comeuppance, though, in the time to come when the places of the high and mighty and the meek and lowly would be reversed (verses 7-11).

Invite the Lowest Guests

Continuing in the same vein, Jesus turned to his host and advised him that for future parties he should not just invite friends and acquaintances who could reciprocate at the same level, but rather include the poor, sick, and outcast, who were needy but could not repay in kind. His reward for this generosity and compassion would come not in material benefits or social recognition in this life, nor even in direct personal benefit in eternity, but rather in the assurance that ultimately other-regarding love and service (*agape*) would be vindicated ("the resurrection of the righteous"; verses 12-14). Again, the eschatological reversal would surprise everyone by honoring the lowly and those who had cared for them in this life. And again, the Pharisees were given something to think about that challenged their present modus operandi.

> *Think About It:* Jesus took the risk of confronting a social and religious power structure based on rank and hierarchy. How does his teaching and example in this instance challenge customary practice and hierarchy in church and society today? What practices, corresponding to taking the higher seats and inviting the prominent guests, would have to be changed if we took his teaching seriously? How does belief in a great eschatological reversal influence your day-to-day life and decisions?

Study Suggestions

A. State the Central Theme

Begin by writing on chalkboard or a large sheet of paper, "Worthful and Worthless Ways." Comment that the thread that ties this week's four lections together is the call to and rewards of faithful living, in contrast to the consequences of forsaking God and God's ways.

B. Divide for Group Study

Divide into four groups, giving each group one of the four lections and the related commentary to study. Distribute a prepared guide sheet, giving the following steps for each group to follow:

(1) Read your passage and commentary silently.

(2) Have one person read the passage aloud, slowly.

(3) Collaborate on stating the central message of your passage in one compact sentence.

(4) What conditions or practices at the time of its writing was the author addressing?

(5) What conditions or practices in our lives and society today are challenged by this passage? (Select just one of these to report to the total group.)

(6) Discuss the "Think About It" questions. (Have the psalm group make a list of the gods we worship, that is, the values we pursue, today—as individuals, churches, and a culture.)

(7) Prepare a skit or roleplay illustrating the central message of your lection in a contemporary setting.

C. Assemble to Share

Bring the groups back together, and ask each to report the results of its discussion. In turn, have each group

(1) Write its one-sentence summary on chalkboard or large sheet of paper for all to see.

(2) Give the background and summary of the passage.

(3) Share the issues arising out of the discussion of the "Think About It" questions (and list of gods we worship), and engage the total group in further discussion of the most significant or troubling of these. For each of these ask: What about this issue provoked interest or controversy in your group? What further information or understanding do we need to probe this more fully? What other passages in the Bible throw light on this matter?

(4) Present the one present-day condition or practice most challenged by the passage. Tell why the group selected it, what is troubling about it, and what changes group members think are needed to bring present practice into conformity with the teaching of their passage. Invite the total group to discuss the matter further.

(5) Present a roleplay of a contemporary application of the message of the passage.

D. Debrief the Roleplay

After each group has presented a skit, explore the following questions as a total group:

(1) How did each participant feel in his or her role?

(2) Why did the players bring the situation to the conclusion they did?

(3) What alternative outcomes or endings might be considered?

(4) What are the obstacles in our contemporary world to living the way this passage proposes?

(5) What is the word of grace in this situation?

(6) What have we learned from this experience that will influence our lives this week?

(7) What are the "Worthful and Worthless Ways" we have discovered through these lections? Write these on chalkboard or large sheet of paper as they are mentioned by group members.

E. Close With Worship

Read Psalm 81:1 as a call to worship. Form the four summary statements into a litany by having each group read its aloud, followed by the common refrain, "Help us to be faithful to this mandate, O God." Recite Hebrews 13:8 as an affirmation of faith. Sing "Where Charity and Love Prevail" as a closing hymn. Read Hebrews 13:1 as a sending forth statement.

Lections for Sunday Between September 4 and 10

Old Testament: Jeremiah 18:1-11

*A*S noted last week, Jeremiah lived and preached in the dark days prior to, during, and after the fall of Judah to Babylon. During his public ministry, usually dated 627 to 587 B.C., he saw the great religious reform of Josiah, the death of Josiah and the collapse of his nation, the conquest of Judah and the deportation to Babylon in 597, and finally, the destruction of Jerusalem and the Temple in 587. He was a constant irritation because he kept advising Judah to surrender to Babylon rather than be destroyed, saying that this was God's judgment on the king and his people for their unfaithfulness.

The Potter's Wheel

In this text, Jeremiah was urged by God to go down to the potter's shop and watch him at work. As he watched, he began to think about Judah as the clay and God as the potter. There are parallels to other biblical images here. Some scholars see in this potter/clay image a reminder of creation, when God shaped a human from the dust of the ground (Genesis 2:7). Some of the rabbinical writings saw a parallel between a potter creating on a wheel set between his legs and the act of giving birth, implying that God has a motherly affection for humanity.

The Insight

What Jeremiah seems to be saying, though, is different from creation or birth images. The insight that comes to Jeremiah is that God is the potter and can do with Judah as the potter does with the clay—make a useful, beautiful vessel. This could mean that God would be patient with Judah and ultimately shape this rebellious people into a vessel for divine use.

It is not a given, however, that the potter would keep trying to come up with a beautiful or useful vessel. It could be that the clay would prove so impossible to work that the potter would squash a defective pot and start over. Just so, people might prove to be so unwilling to seek and obey God, that God would just give up on them and begin all over again (as is depicted in the account of Noah). The quality and receptivity of the people determines what God can do with them.

So Jeremiah's message is this: presently God would judge the nation. That's the point of the clay being discarded. But, if the people repent, if they become the kind of clay the potter can actually use—pliable and responsive—then they still have a chance.

So, What About Us?

We know that Judah did not listen to God's word through Jeremiah. The Babylonians overran them in 597 B.C. and carried the cream of society into exile. Then in 587, following a ruinous rebellion led by Zedekiah, the Babylonians laid siege to Jerusalem, breached its walls, and completely destroyed the city and the Temple. All the ruling class and aristocracy were exiled. Jeremiah, appointed by the Babylonians, remained in Jerusalem as an adviser to the governor. The peasants, who posed no threat, remained in the country.

What happens when we do not listen to the word of God? (A deeper question is, how can we discern what God's word for us is?) The account of the potter and the clay suggests that God will not be patient with us forever, that there comes a time when the clay is thrown aside because it cannot be worked. So maybe the question is, how can we be faithful to what we understand God is calling us to be and do? What does it mean to be responsive to God's will for our lives?

> **Think About It:** It is important not to push the metaphor too far and wonder about the inability of the clay to determine its shape. The point of the parable is that God can reshape misshapen lives. How has God re-formed you? Are there converts in your congregation whose lives are a testimony to God's saving power because they have been changed?

Psalter: Psalm 139:1-6, 13-18

Two important ideas leap out at us from this psalm. First, in verses 1-6, the key is that God knows me. This is an intimate, penetrating knowing, not a casual acquaintance. To be fully known means to be vulnerable to the knower; the psalmist rejoices that his life is so open to God all the time and in all ways.

Second, in verses 13-18, life is not just a biological accident, but the result of God's will and work. God is with us; we are with God. This gives us the confidence to trust all of life to God.

The psalmist's image for God is different from Jeremiah's potter. Here God is seen as a weaver, as one who "knits together" our lives and causes us to be "fearfully and wonderfully made."

Epistle: Philemon 1-21

This brief epistle follows the outline typical of Paul's letters. It begins with an address to the church and a greeting ("Grace to you and peace"). Then there is a short section of thanksgiving for the faith of the recipients, which also sets out the themes of the letter. Finally comes the body, in which Paul deals at some length with his main point.

The Point Is . . .

Onesimus was a runaway slave who had become a Christian. Under law, he needed to return to his owner, Philemon. Paul insisted that Onesimus make things right with Philemon. Paul also hoped that Philemon would release Onesimus and permit him to return to Paul. We need to remember that perhaps as many as three-fourths of the people in the Roman Empire were slaves. Many of them were given great responsibility.

The name *Onesimus* means "useful," so Paul was punning on the name when he said that Onesimus had become useful to him. In fact, Onesimus had apparently become a Christian while he was with Paul and therefore was *truly* useful.

The Strategy Is . . .

Paul could demand that Onesimus be allowed to stay with him. As an apostle he had the authority to do that. Philemon apparently was somehow in Paul's debt (perhaps because Paul had led him to faith) and owed Paul a favor. But Paul preferred that Onesimus stay with him as an expression of Philemon's free will. (Nowhere in the letter is there any indication of what Onesimus might have wanted.)

Paul reminded Philemon that Onesimus was now more than just a slave—he was a brother in Christ, dear to Paul. So dear, in fact, that Paul was willing to assume any debts or penalties that Onesimus might have had outstanding. That is the point of verses 18-19, which are a kind of legal bond.

> **Think About It:** Onesimus was a slave. Paul does not challenge the institution of slavery but works within it, leading Onesimus to faith and seeking to keep him by his side. Should Paul be faulted for this? How can we discern when to challenge an evil system and when to work within it to make it as humane as possible?

The Result Is . . .

At the beginning of the second century, the bishop of Ephesus (from which Paul probably wrote this letter) was Onesimus. We cannot, of course, be sure that this was the same man, although tradition suggests it. Ignatius of Antioch wrote about Onesimus as if he had been a companion of Paul. Apparently Paul got what he wanted.

Gospel: Luke 14:25-33

Jesus was moving about the Galilean countryside, and large crowds followed. So these sayings were addressed to the crowds. "If," he said, "you think you want to be a disciple, first be sure you can pay the price." (This is not a good recruitment technique!) Being a disciple is not easy. Jesus made clear that discipleship was a difficult choice; a disciple had to "hate" (lower the priority of) one's family, carry the cross, and give up all one's possessions! In this context, Jesus told two brief parables about counting the cost.

"Hating" Father and Mother

One of the values Christian groups stress in our day is family. Yet here was Jesus saying that no one could be his disciple without "hating" one's family. Jesus sometimes seemed to be at odds with his family—at one point he seemed to reject them in favor of "whoever does the will of God." (See Mark 3:31-35.) And yet, it was members of his family who became leaders of the church in Jerusalem together for nearly one hundred years after his death.

Most scholars agree that Jesus did not mean we literally have to hate our family members, but that the demands of discipleship must take precedence, even over family relationships. This in turn could lead to the family disputes that Matthew mentions (Matthew 10:34-39), in which "one's foes will be members of one's own household." For members of the early church, this was often true. Even today, converts to Christianity in many parts of the world risk being cast out by their families because of their new faith.

Carrying the Cross

Cross is a word that has been greatly cheapened in our day. We talk about relatively minor aches and pains as our "cross to bear," as if putting up with a whiny child or a demanding boss were equal to being crucified. Faithfulness means more than that, and discipleship sometimes comes at a greater cost than we expect.

Elsewhere Luke mentions the necessity of carrying one's cross daily (Luke 9:23). Discipleship is not a faddish, sporadic, or voluntary activity. It is an ongoing, demanding vocation that requires diligence, courage, and sacrifice.

Giving Up Possessions

Cruciform discipleship requires that we "give up all your possessions" (verse 33). Many in the early church had all their possessions confiscated. To be Christian meant to be like Jesus—a wanderer, celibate, and to give up all one had. Most American Christians are quite well off materially. Does Jesus ask us to give all this up to become his disciple? Or is it more the attachment to or preoccupation with possessions with which he was concerned?

Later, in the fourth century, Saint Antony of Egypt gave away all he owned and went out into the desert to live close to God—and began the great movement we know as monasticism. In our time, Mother Teresa gave away all she had to care for the poor in Calcutta.

Warnings About Counting the Cost

The two short parables in verses 28-32, on one level, refer to planning ahead. We must be sure we can get the job done before we bid on it. On another level, they warn that discipleship is for the long term and that one cannot remain a faithful disciple based on an impetuous decision. Jesus did not want followers who were mindlessly enthusiastic and impulsive. He wanted followers who had looked ahead, who saw what discipleship would cost, and who then decided they were willing to pay that price.

> **Think About It:** Discipleship sometimes comes at unexpected costs. What mght these costs be for you? Can you "carry your cross daily"?

Study Suggestions

A. Sing a Hymn

Open by singing "Have Thine Own Way." Ask: For what are we praying in this hymn? Invite members to remember the words of the hymn as they move through the session.

B. Explore Jeremiah's Message

Read Jeremiah 18:1-11, and review the commentary on pages 298–99. Recap the historical setting and Jeremiah's prophetic role. Note that he often used images and object lessons to convey God's message. Invite a potter to bring a wheel and clay and "throw" a pot. If this is not possible, have someone with experience in ceramics talk about what is involved— how they know when the clay is working the way it should, what one does when it is not working well, and how they feel when a pot is not turning out as anticipated.

Now talk about Jeremiah's interpretation of the potter and clay. Ask: Do you see how Jeremiah got his insight into God's plan while watching the potter? How do you now see this passage differently from before? How have lives been changed through the ministry of our church?

C. Consider Slavery and Being "Useful"

Read Philemon 1-21 and the interpretation on pages 300–301. Pay attention to the play on words with *useful* and *useless*. Ask: How, as a slave, was Onesimus useful and to whom? When he became a Christian, should his slave status have changed? In the negotiations over where Onesimus would end up, what risks would have to be taken by Onesimus, Philemon, and Paul? Discuss the "Think About It" questions relative to slavery and other evils, and our responsibility to challenge them.

D. Examine "Counting the Cost"

Ask: Who has a household budget? a retirement plan? What do you do when there are unexpected expenses or when you want to do something costly? How do you decide if you can afford it? How do you assess risk before beginning a venture?

Read Luke 14:25-33, with particular attention to the two parables about counting the cost. Review the commentary (pages 301–302).

Review what Jesus had to say here about the demands of discipleship versus attachment to family and possessions. Ask: What do you think he meant by "to hate father and mother"? to carry a cross? to give up possessions? What does he expect of us in these and other areas where the demands of discipleship conflict with other values and commitments? How do we resolve these issues? How can we support one another in these struggles?

E. Consider Your Discipleship

Summarize the main ideas in the four lections. Identify their common themes (obedience, taking risks, faithfulness, counting the cost, making commitments). Ask: What have we learned about our relationship with God? about our discipleship? Write the comments on chalkboard or a large sheet of paper as they come from the group.

G. Celebrate God's Grace

Build these ideas into a closing litany by reading them off one by one, with the group responding after each, "Make us faithful in this, O God." Read responsively Psalm 139, a hymn of grace about God as intimate presence and source of strength, with the group responding, "Thank you, God, for knowing and loving us this much. Amen."

Lections for Sunday Between September 11 and 17

*T*Old Testament: Jeremiah 4:11-12, 22-28

HE background against which this oracle was written was "the foe from the north," a common theme in the early prophets. Because of Judah's geographical location between the desert and the sea, enemies from the north or east, all had to approach from the north. Jeremiah was particularly aware of the potential danger from the north (which became real when Nebuchadnezzar invaded the territory in 605 B.C.).

The Wind Is Too Strong . . .

The "foe from the north" is also a metaphor for the calamity soon to descend on "my poor people." YHWH's judgment will come like the sirocco, the hot wind blowing off the desert that sucks the moisture (and the life) out of plants and animals alike. This is not a gentle breeze, the kind the farmers use for winnowing grain. (The grain was beaten out of the husks, then husks and grain were tossed into the air. The breeze blew away the lighter husks, while the heavier grain fell back into the winnowing pan.) This is a destroying wind that scorched the earth and caused all vegetation to wither (verses 11-12).

Creation Is Undone

The description in verses 23-26 is like the undoing of Creation. The earth would once again become "waste and void," the same words that were used to describe the situation at the time of Creation; Genesis 1:2). There would be no light in the heavens (a reversal of the first day of Creation; Genesis 1:3). The mountains and hills would quake, the birds would all flee. These two elements describe an earthquake, which would compound the terror of

304

the invasion. The fruitful land would become a desert, either because the invading armies would strip it bare, or because the peasants who farmed the land would all be killed or taken captive. The cities would all be laid in ruins.

All the creativity, order, and harmony about the land would be destroyed; all that would be left would be primal chaos. This is what the world was like before the beginning of God's creative work. (There is a similar description of "uncreation" in Job 3:1-10, where Job cries out that he is so filled with pain that he wishes the world would return to a state of chaos.)

> **Think About It:** The Creation would be undone and all would return to chaos and devastation. Do you ever wonder about present-day prospects for such a catastrophe? Does this sound like a nuclear winter? Has the prospect of such a calamity come closer since September 11, 2001? How does your faith guide your understanding and action in such a time as this?

When Jeremiah looked on all this destruction in his vision, his heart was torn apart by the thought of this suffering and devastation to be visited upon his people. But he stood firm in his conviction that YHWH would bring judgment on the people because of their unfaithfulness.

God's Purpose

Jeremiah says that things have gone too far: all God can do is bring judgment and make an end to the people of Judah. He insists that YHWH has spoken and will not go back on this declaration (verse 28). But there is one tiny ray of hope in all the despair. In verse 27, God says, "Yet I will not make a full end." Even in all the devastation and chaos, the destruction will not be complete. God will be present, still working for the salvation of the people.

> **Think About It:** In the midst of such sin and chaos, God "will not make a full end." In the face of sin, crisis, and chaos, what is your source of hope? What do you believe God is doing in the midst of today's world situation? How is God calling you to respond?

Psalter: Psalm 14

This is a prophetic psalm that begins with a comment on sinfulness and then reminds us that sin does not have the final word. A "fool" is one who does not recognize or serve God. This also speaks of a "practical atheism," in which we act as if we are not accountable to God. What this psalm calls foolish is exactly what our culture values—autonomy, self-direction, self-sufficiency. These are important, but not when they lead us to believe we do not need other people, or God.

Verses 4-6 may reflect a society in which there is a strong well-to-do class that oppresses the poor and marginalized. But the psalmist says, God will act on behalf of the poor; and the oppressors will be terrified. Selfishness and oppression do not have the final word; that word belongs to the God who does justice.

Epistle: 1 Timothy 1:12-17

This passage is about gratitude for God's mercy. Surely Paul needed that mercy, given his previous attempts to destroy the infant church. Remember that he received his vision while on his way to Damascus to arrest Christians and return them to Jerusalem in chains. In the words of verse 13, Paul had been "a blasphemer, a persecutor, and a man of violence." Yet, in spite of this, Jesus changed Paul and called him for service in the church.

Grace and Faith

Paul did not become an apostle and a missionary because he deserved it, but because of the mercy of God in Christ. Grace "overflowed" for him. This word reminds us of Jesus saying, "I came that they may have life, and have it abundantly" (John 10:10). The word *abundantly* can also mean "overflowing" or "effervescently" or "running over." Grace is like that. God gives it in a measure far greater than the need of our lives.

The response to grace is faith. In First Timothy (probably written by a later disciple of Paul in the late first or early second century) faith had come to mean belief or conviction, holding to the received teaching, rather than the radical trust and commitment to God that faith communicates in the Pauline letters.

Verse 15 sounds like a quotation. Was it a proverb that circulated in the church? Or a fragment from an early creed? The language ("came into the world," "save sinners") is more like John than Paul. Certainly the saying is sure and one on which we can depend. Christ did come into the world to save sinners. We may not be the "foremost" (verse 15) sinner, but we surely do need the grace of God for our lives. Just so, God's mercy came to Paul as a sign of Christ's patience with sinners.

Paul concedes too that he has been "ignorant" and unbelieving. Wisdom literature characterizes humankind in three ways: wise, foolish, and simple. The simple are those who are thus far ignorant of the law. Perhaps Paul here alludes to his own previous myopic focus on law to the exclusion of the truth of Jesus Christ. God in Christ is patient with us, waiting in hope that we will come to our senses and turn to God. Christ's patience also allowed Paul, once convicted, to become an example, a prototype, for believers.

> **Think About It:** Jesus Christ offers "overflowing" grace. How does your life overflow with grace from Christ and for others? What are the signs of this grace? How can we remain aware of and responsive to it?

306

The Doxology

Verse 17 is a doxology (an expression of praise to God), similar to what we sing in worship on Sunday morning. This one may have been borrowed from the synagogue. The hymn "Immortal, Invisible, God Only Wise" is based on this verse.

Gospel: Luke 15:1-10

The context of these verses is the complaint about Jesus "eating with sinners." *Sinners*, here, means people who were in violation of Pharisaic traditions related to the law. The scandal of the situation—and the parables that follow—is that God shows mercy to sinners and rejoices over their salvation (inclusion). The scandal is heightened by the implied question: Will we join the celebration? The problem is, if we want to celebrate with God, we must also share in God's mercy and acceptance of outcasts.

The Lost Sheep

Even though Israel's history is full of references to God as the "good shepherd" (Psalm 23; Isaiah 40; Ezekiel 34), in the first century shepherds were generally not held in high esteem. Most were poor and their occupation was dirty, backbreaking work. So an unspoken meaning of this parable is that God is seen in the outcasts, just as in the parable of the good Samaritan.

The parable itself is familiar: the shepherd leaves the flock (presumably with his fellow shepherds) and goes to find the one sheep that is lost. We have celebrated the parable in art and music. The gospel song "The Ninety and Nine" depicts the shepherd searching through the wilderness for the lost sheep. Then comes the glad cry, "Rejoice! I have found my sheep!" When the shepherd returns home, he calls the community together to celebrate.

The key to the parable is in verse 7, where Jesus says there is more joy in heaven over one sinner who repents than over the ninety-nine righteous. God is gracious to those who are held in contempt by the religious leaders. Today opposing groups in the church condemn one another and view only themselves as righteous. This parable calls us all to rejoice that God calls people whom we hold in contempt, rather than trying to shut them out of the church.

The Lost Coin

Put this story in perspective: this is not your house. This is a one-room stone and adobe house, with a dirt floor, a tiny door, and no windows. It would be very easy to lose even a shiny silver coin in a setting like this.

To focus further, consider that the money lost is a drachma, quite a small amount, but still a day's wage for a laborer. Would a business executive drop everything to search for a check for one day's pay at minimum wage? Perhaps not, but what does the woman do? She proceeded very carefully in her search. First she lit a lamp—a tiny clay lamp with a bit of oil that was not used often because the oil was expensive. Then she swept the floor, slowly and cautiously, looking everywhere for the lost coin. When she found it, she rejoiced and called her neighbors to celebrate with her as well.

This parable is one of proportion. The well-to-do Pharisees may consider that coin to be "peanuts," not worth their time. But even the smallest of the small is important to God. It is not only worth the search; its discovery is worthy of celebration.

> **Think About It:** Don't ask God for what you deserve. You might get it! Always ask for mercy. And this: If we find God's mercy to others offensive, we are cutting ourselves off from God's grace for ourselves. When have you received just "what you deserve"?

The parable does not call sinners to repent. Rather, it calls the righteous to join the celebration. If we rejoice upon finding what was lost, we proclaim that relationships are based on mercy. If, on the other hand, we refuse to join the party, we proclaim that relationships are based merely on what we deserve.

Study Suggestions

A. Take a Poll

Open the session by polling group members on this question: "Do you think God judges and punishes people because of their sins? Why or why not?" Allow some time for silence and reflection. Then repeat the question. If necessary, encourage one or two persons to begin. List responses on chalkboard or a piece of paper. (Do not let the members' conversation slide into argument or into rehashing the same idea.)

B. Investigate the History

Using the background information and commentaries on the passages (pages 304–308), spend a few minutes establishing the historical context of each of the three main lections. (The psalms are most important for their contribution to the worship life of the community.) About each lection ask: What is the context of this passage? What is going on in the life of the faith community? What historical issues in the community of faith help you understand the passage? What are the theological issues that arise in each passage?

C. See What the Bible Says

Explain that, today, we have four texts that approach the question of judgment in different ways. Not only do they interpret judgment quite differently, but they also describe it in varied ways.

Form four groups, and assign a separate passage and the commentary on it to each group. Ask each to try to summarize in one or two sentences what the text says about judgment and what form the judgment will take. List responses on chalkboard or a sheet of paper, and then discuss them briefly to ensure that group members understand the import of the passage. Invite members to mention any phrases from their text they find memorable and to indicate to the larger group why they are meaningful.

D. Check Out the Reason for Judgment

Ask: As you thought about the meaning of judgment in your texts, what did you see as the reason for judgment? What sins were being judged?

Focus particularly on the passage from Luke, where the real sin is identified as not joining the party when persons find God's grace. Ask: Why is this a problem? Does God really want us to rejoice over somebody who is a major sinner finding acceptance and coming into the church? Aren't there standards? (Note: the temptation in answering this question will be to parade prejudices. Keep asking, over and over, "What does the text say?" Help persons to be honest to what they read.)

E. Identify Signs of Grace

Remind participants that grace is God's love in action. Ask: As you read your text, what signs or hints of grace did you see? (For example, "God's patience" in the First Timothy text.) What do these indicators of grace mean to you as a disciple? How might our group or church reach out to include persons on the margins?

F. Think About Where to Go Now

Discuss the "Think About It" questions for each passage. Ask: How do these Scriptures touch you personally? How do they help you claim faith and strength to exercise your own gifts for service to God? What do they call you to do now?

G. Close With Worship

To close the session, sing or read aloud together either "Immortal, Invisible, God Only Wise" or "The Ninety and Nine." Invite those who wish to affirm or reaffirm their commitment to Jesus Christ, to offer an extemporaneous prayer thanking God for redeeming grace and asking for help in offering this grace in concrete, caring ways to those on the margins of our community.

Lections for Sunday Between September 18 and 24

Old Testament: Jeremiah 8:18–9:1

*I*N this text, Jeremiah is "pushed" by God to confront the people of Judah, his countrymen and women. Jeremiah pours out his heart and soul to us, sharing his pain and grief and longing for something better. This text is a glimpse of the inner Jeremiah, who grieves for his people in their suffering even as he pronounces God's judgment on them.

In verses 14-15, the people are in a panic over the consequences of their sin. There is no safety in fortified cities, there is no peace or well-being; there is only "poisoned water" (bitter misfortune) and "terror instead" (verse 15). In the midst of this there seems also to be a natural disaster in the making, probably a severe drought (verse 20; see 14:3-6).

"The Cry of My Poor People . . ."

We know how Jeremiah felt. We stand by the side of the grave, or in the middle of a pile of rubble that used to be home before the tornado struck, or on the edge of the bluff watching the river tear away the work of a lifetime, or by a hospital bed seeing disease suck away the life from one we love. And we wish for words as powerful as Jeremiah's to express our grief. Our joy is gone, our hearts are sick.

Jeremiah felt this way when he looked at his people. "The cry of my poor people" comes from all over the land. Isn't YHWH our God? Why doesn't God help? In verse 20, *harvest* refers to the grain harvest in the spring, and *summer* to the gathering of summer fruits. Normally, if the grain harvest was short, the people could still look forward to harvesting fruits (dates, figs, olives, grapes) in the summer. But, this year the drought was so bad that there was no harvest. Everything on which they could count for food had failed them. People and animals alike were beginning to look like the news clips from Somalia or other crisis points where whole populations starve.

The Scripture gives no sign that the crop failure is a punishment for sin. The last part of verse 19, which suggests sin, is in parentheses in the NRSV because most scholars agree it is not original with Jeremiah but was added later. For Jeremiah, the crop failure was a disaster, pure and simple. He was torn apart by the suffering of his "poor people." No matter what he might have said about sin and judgment at other times, here he was expressing pain and grief.

Is There No Balm in Gilead?

Balm is a type of resin used for medicinal purposes. It was not grown in Gilead (modern Jordan) but apparently was processed and shipped from there. In the ancient world the balm had proverbial healing powers. The rhetorical questions in verse 22 are cries for help: If there are remedies available, why have my poor people not been helped? The Christian folk song answers Jeremiah's questions in the affirmative: "There is a balm in Gilead to make the wounded whole; there is a balm in Gilead to heal the sinsick soul."

Jeremiah's grief was so extreme that he wished his head were a spring, so that he might cry day and night. And this was not a selfish grief—"woe is me." It was a grief over his beloved "poor people" who were dying of starvation.

> **Think About It:** As Christians we affirm that there is a "balm in Gilead" (healing and help in time of need). When have you received a much-needed "balm" (comfort, succor, support, help) for pain or misfortune? What was its source? When have you provided such "balm" for others? How is your church organized to offer "balm" to persons in need?

Psalter: Psalm 79:1-9

This psalm reminds us so much of Jeremiah's laments of pain and grief. It comes from about the same time in history, and mourns the destruction of Jerusalem in 587 B.C. and the Exile that followed. Verses 1-5 are a complaint to God about the disaster that has happened. The complaint moves from what the nations have done in destroying Jerusalem (verses 1-3), to how the people feel about that catastrophe (verse 4), to a protest against YHWH (verse 5).

Verses 6-9 voice prayers for help, with reasons why the people need it. For example, verse 8 asks God for compassion, because "we are brought very low." The petitions also move from prayers against the nations (verses 6-7), to prayers for the people (verse 8), to a prayer for God's direct intervention (verse 9).

In the report of the taunts of the nations and the doubts and fears of the people, there is the question: Where is God in all this calamity and suffering? The psalm reminds us that God's people were frank and open about their feelings, even to the point of complaining to, or being angry with, God—which gives us encouragement us to open our hearts to God in this same honest way.

Epistle: 1 Timothy 2:1-7

This lection is about prayer and about the universal mission of Christian faith. Something has turned the writer's church inward and made it exclusivistic. So readers are urged to pray for all people.

Pray for Kings and Rulers

These are people who may, in fact, be persecuting the church. Romans 13, Revelation 13, and 1 Peter 2:13-17 tell us that the church's relationship to the rulers was a serious problem. By the time First Timothy was written, there had been persecutions of the church in Rome and Asia Minor; and Christians could be prosecuted simply for being Christians. The writer is saying: (1) if we pray for the rulers, maybe they won't accuse us of disloyalty, and we can lead a peaceful life; and (2) God really wants all people, including the rulers, to be saved.

The Knowledge of the Truth

Verses 3 and 4 emphasize God's intention for all to be saved. There is a big difference between this statement and what is called predestination. God wants all persons to be saved, but does not force us if we choose not to be. The "knowledge of the truth" is a technical term, meaning "accepting the truth of the faith received from the apostles."

God Is One

> **Think About It:** There is only one God and no exclusivism. How do you understand these two affirmations? On what conditions does God invite all persons into relationship? If there is no exclusivism in God, what is the basis for our setting limits on who is welcome in the church?

"God is One" (verse 5a) was a rallying cry of the early church against the multiplicity of pagan gods. Verses 5 and 6 sound like part of a creed, possibly used in baptism. It explains why we are to pray for everyone and shows that preparation for baptism in the second century taught the universal claims of the gospel. There is one God for all people and one mediator, Christ Jesus. Note also the emphasis on the humanity of Christ (an important issue in early doctrinal disputes) and the suffering and death of Christ as a ransom (release) from evil powers for all.

312

This creed has two important messages. First, there is only one God. There are not many paths to the same goal; there is only one goal, one God. Second, there is no exclusivism. God calls all persons to salvation and into the church. Salvation and the church are open to all people, because God has made it so.

Jesus gave up himself for all, and this writer is prepared to give his all, having been "appointed a herald and an apostle" and passionately claiming the legitimacy of that appointment: "I am telling the truth, I am not lying." He is very much in earnest.

Gospel: Luke 16:1-13

This has always been a troubling parable. Why would Jesus praise such blatant dishonesty? What is going on here that we seem to miss?

Here's the Plot
It's pretty simple. The steward had squandered the rich man's property, like embezzling to cover gambling debts or something. The rich man discovered the theft and fired him. The steward did not have a lot of options. He was not strong enough for physical labor, and he was too proud to beg for alms. So he developed a plan to ensure his future.

Here's the Plan—and the Problem
The rich man rented out his land to tenants, who agreed to pay him a fixed sum in either grain or olive oil for the use of the land. (There is a potential for oppression here; the rich man was owed the rent whether the crop is good or not.) For example, the first tenant owed over 900 gallons of olive oil; the second somewhere between 650 and 1200 bushels of grain. This was serious commercial farming. What the steward did was change the amount of rent owed in the various contracts, with the apparent help of the tenants.

How did this help? It was a clever solution: If the rich man reversed the steward's actions, he would lose face. The steward gained the gratitude of all the tenants, along with a debt of honor that they owe him. (But who would want to hire someone known to cheat or steal from his employer?)

We can look at the steward's actions three ways: (1) He is still cheating his master by reducing the size of the debts. (2) He is acting righteously by not charging the interest written into the contract. Deuteronomy 23:19-20 forbids usury and charging interest to another Israelite. (3) He is reducing the debt by the amount of his own commission. It would be nice to jump on one of the last two, because then no one would really be a "bad guy."

Unfortunately, the parable seems to demand the first explanation—the only one that provides the "punch" the story needs.

Think About It: The man is still a crook. Why praise him for covering one set of crooked acts with another set?

The man was a crook. Why did the master praise him? Even though the master lost a lot of money, the steward made him look good and earned him good will in the community. At the same time, the steward acted shrewdly to take care of his own future. The debtors needed to reciprocate his generosity.

Here's the Point

Jesus was talking about faithfulness and honesty. And he made several points in verses 10-13. First, faithfulness is not tied to wealth and power. If you are faithful in little things, you can be counted on to be faithful in big things. If you fail the little ones, you will fail the big ones, too. So, no big dreams of all the things you would do for Jesus when the chips are down, if you are not doing the little things for Jesus on a daily basis.

Second, faithfulness in earthly matters has a direct relationship to our treasure in heaven where our true wealth is to be found. Third, the most familiar part of this passage: You cannot serve two masters, in this case, God and wealth. This does not mean that wealthy people cannot serve God. We all know they can and do. The issue is not over having wealth; it is a matter of who owns what. That is, do we own our wealth, so that we make decisions about its use for God? Or does our wealth own us, so that all our decisions and actions are based on holding on to it?

Think About It: Do you own your possessions or do they own you?

Study Suggestions

A. Sing Together

Sing the spiritual, "There Is a Balm in Gilead," which is based on today's passage from Jeremiah. Comment that this week's lections look at the theme of faithfulness in three different ways.

B. Deal With Faith and Suffering

Invite group members to mention persons who have suffered greatly but were still faithful to God. Ask: What were these persons like? How could you tell that they were faithful? Ask a reader with good oral interpretation skills to read Jeremiah 8:18–9:1 aloud, with as much passion as possible. Then ask: What are signs of suffering in these verses? What are signs of faithfulness? Summarize the background material to show the depth of the suffering among Jeremiah's people.

C. Explore Biblical Prayer

Look at Psalm 79:1-9 together, and review the commentary on pages 311–12. Mention that in verses 6-9, we have specific prayers of petition, with reasons for them. Ask participants to identify the prayers and the reasons for them. Point out that the writer is complaining about his sense of God's absence from his suffering and that God welcomes all our feelings, including negative ones, because God wants to be in relationship with us as we really are.

Ask: How honest can we be in prayer? If we cannot be honest in prayer, why pray at all?

D. Look at a Strange Faithfulness

Read Luke 16:1-13. Drawing on the interpretation on pages 313–14, ask about this passage (as for all Scripture): What is the context? the audience? After establishing this, analyze the message. Discuss: Why would Jesus praise such blatant dishonesty? What is this steward doing? How does being a crook (twice) deserve praise for faithfulness? Is there any circumstance now in which being dishonest or unethical could be praiseworthy? (Consider situations in which lying could save life, protect from abuse, defend against oppression, or serve a greater good.)

Then review the background material to be sure participants understand the depth of the situation. (The commentary in *The New Interpreter's Bible* [Abingdon, 1995] is comprehensive and very helpful.)

E. Be Open in Faithfulness

Say: "First Timothy 2:1-7 says that faithfulness is related to being open to all people in the church. Let's see what this means for us." Read the passage, and review the commentary (pages 312-13). Then ask: What does this passage say about "all paths lead to the same goal"? about being exclusive? Who can be excluded from the church, according to this passage? Review the "Think About It" questions. Discuss: How do these questions make the lesson from Scripture personal and compelling? What do you feel called to do with these insights?

F. Draw Things Together

Review the three forms of faithfulness represented in today's lections: In Jeremiah and Psalm 79 it is caring for people's suffering. In First Timothy it is welcoming all persons into saving relationship with the one God in and through the church. In Luke it is serving God in all things, both small and big, and putting loyalty to God before the desire for wealth and possessions. Ask: What guidance for living do these three takes on faithfulness offer us? Invite members to offer sentence prayers asking for God's help in being faithful in these and other ways. Close with the Lord's Prayer.

Lections for Sunday Between September 25 and October 1

I Old Testament: Jeremiah 32:1-3a, 6-15

IN the midst of God's judgment that Jeremiah pronounced on Judah, and all the pain that he felt over the sin and suffering of his people, there were also signs of hope. This lection describes how Jeremiah showed his people one of those signs.

First, the Bad News

Jerusalem was under siege by the Babylonian army. The enemy was camped around the city so that no one could get in or out. The siege had begun in January of 588 and had been lifted briefly, only once, when an Egyptian army appeared in southern Judah. The citizens of Jerusalem had hoped the Egyptians would drive off the Babylonians, but that hope had quickly died. Nebuchadnezzar was more than a match for the Egyptians, who retreated back to Egypt after only a token attempt at battle.

Jeremiah himself was imprisoned—actually in open arrest in the palace court. He had been arrested when he tried to leave the city during the short interval when the Babylonians were off dealing with the Egyptians. Trying to leave the city was interpreted as treason, since he angered the king by advising him and his people to surrender to the Babylonians because Jerusalem was doomed.

Second, the Strange News

Now, Jeremiah decided to make a long-term investment in land, an act that seemed stupid on the face of it, since the land around the city was already occupied by the Babylonians and Jeremiah had no chance of even seeing it, let alone cultivating it. His cousin Hanamel came to him offering to sell a field in Anathoth (Jeremiah's home town). What he offered Jeremiah was the right of redemption (see Leviticus 25:25-34). The purpose of the law of redemption was to keep property within the family. Ostensibly, Jeremiah bought the field to keep it from being taken over by a creditor or being sold outside the family. But his real reason was to symbolize to his people that YHWH was faithful and would one day bring them back to this place.

It is interesting that so much detail about the sale is recorded in this Scripture. Jeremiah weighed out the silver, approximately seven ounces. Coins were not yet in use at that point in time, so the purchase price was paid by weight. Two copies of the deed were made. The official copy was rolled up, folded over, and sealed. The second was also rolled up, then tied to the sealed copy. This was the "open copy," which could be consulted any time. The deeds were given to Baruch, Jeremiah's scribe, with instructions to put them in a pottery jar, so they would be safe during the Babylonian occupation and last a long time.

Lastly, the Good News

For Jeremiah, this transaction was a response to God's leading and a sign that there was a future for his people. Normal life would one day return. Land would be bought and sold, and the Judahites would again live in this place. His redemption of the field, in accordance with the law, was a vivid symbol of YHWH's coming redemption of his people.

> **Think About It:** While his city and people were facing imminent catastrophe, Jeremiah went out of his way to make this prophetic gesture of affirmation in the future and faith in YHWH's redemptive purpose and power. When you and your people are facing difficulty and disappointment, what gives you hope? What signs point you to God's redemptive activity in the midst of turmoil?

Psalter: Psalm 91:1-6, 14-16

The message of this psalm is that God alone provides ultimate security. We can trust God in every circumstance, day and night—even the most fearsome calamity.

In verses 14-16, the psalmist gives voice to YHWH's promise of deliverance, protection, respect, comforting presence, and grace-filled salvation, to those who love and serve God faithfully. A profound intimacy in the divine-human relationship is seen here.

Epistle: 1 Timothy 6:6-19

This lection begins with teachings about greed and possessions (verses 6-10), moves to an exhortation about keeping the faith (verses 11-16), then ends with an appeal to the wealthy to replace the arrogance of affluence with generosity, sharing, and good works (verses 17-19). Let's look at the details.

The Love of Money

This little homily (verses 6-10) is a hard saying for people who are caught up in getting ahead in the world. It suggests that the desire for money and material goods is a source of peril; we risk our souls when we set our hearts on accumulating wealth. The writer enjoins us to be satisfied with the minimum necessities of life—food, clothing, and shelter. When we start focusing on acquiring more and more and living better and better, we lose our single-minded devotion to Christ.

> **Think About It:** "The love of money [greed] is the root of all evil." What is it about money (or the human heart) that seems always to lead us to want more? What evils (personal, relational, societal, global) can you name that are produced by greed? How can greed be contained? How can these evils be overcome?

Some Christian leaders today teach that if we follow God faithfully we will be blessed with material prosperity. The writer of First Timothy tells us, however, that the real gain in being a Christian is not in wealth, but in a sense of spiritual fulfillment that helps us rise above material desires. Truly godly disciples are content with what they have and are ready to live a simple life.

The Call for Faith and Righteousness

The godly disciple shuns the quest for wealth and instead "fights the good fight" of faith, holding on to the faith (teaching) received from the apostles. Adherence to right doctrine was an important theme for second-century Christians, who by then were contending with a variety of interpretations and philosophies. Holding to one's beliefs in the midst of these controversies is tantamount to taking hold of eternal life by preparing for the Last Judgment.

The writer urges his readers to bear faithful witness, by living an exemplary life and by contending for the true faith. By confessing Christ publicly in the face of opposition or persecution, we follow the example of Christ before Pilate, give him honor and praise, and prepare to meet him in all his glory at the judgment seat. The "good confession" (verse 13) refers to baptism, during which the new believer affirms that "Jesus is Lord." Verses 13-16 were likely part of an early baptismal liturgy, and the confession of Jesus before Pilate may be a reflection of the creedal affirmation that he "suffered under Pontius Pilate."

Faithful Use of Wealth

Returning to the subject of riches in verses 17-19, the writer of First Timothy issues a caution against haughtiness and inappropriate self-confidence. The wealthy are urged to do good with their wealth, to be generous and share it, and thereby lay a foundation for future happiness in both this life and the next. A life devoted to service, using our material resources to glorify God and benefit the needy, provides a sense of fulfillment far superior to conspicuous consumption and a big bank account.

This does not suggest salvation by works or the idea of buying one's way into heaven—or even that charitable giving is enough in itself. It does, however, suggest that Christians can appreciate money as a gift from God to be used in the service of God. Those who have the ability must help those in need (see 1 Timothy 5:3-8).

Gospel: Luke 16:19-31

This parable of Jesus speaks of a rich man who served wealth rather than God, and a poor man who had nothing except God. It is also the story of all of us, as we choose what we serve.

The Characters in the Story

First, there is the rich man, who is not named. (He is sometimes called *Dives*, which is Latin for "rich man.") He practiced conspicuous consumption in both dress and diet. He wore purple (an expensive cloth dyed with a secretion from a rare species of shellfish), which suggests that he was either a high-ranking official or a member of the nobility. He lived in a "gated community," with firm barriers between him and the poor and marginalized "riffraff." He enjoyed frequent lavish banquets.

Lazarus (not to be confused with the brother of Mary and Martha) is the only character in Jesus' parables who is named. He was a crippled, starving beggar, covered with running sores. His name derives from Eleazar, meaning "God helps," which is ironic since it seems that no one helped him. He was separated from the rich man by a gate, which he could not get past to secure the help he needed. He was hungry enough to fight the dogs for the bread the rich man discarded. The "bread" refers to the flat bread used to wipe the grease from one's hands—much as we would use a napkin—and then discarded.

The First Step in the Plot

Both men died. Lazarus was transported to be with Abraham in the place of highest bliss. Lazarus and Abraham were in sight of the rich man, who was suffering torment. We often think of heaven and hell as being discrete places distant from each other. But in this story, Hades and the "bosom of Abraham," as the King James Bible describes it, were within view of each other, yet separated by an untraversable chasm. More important, this story challenged the conventional wisdom that wealth was a mark of God's blessing and poverty a sign of divine displeasure.

The Plot Thickens

The rich man begged Abraham for water. In an ironic twist, he still saw Lazarus as available to serve his personal needs. After all, we amass wealth at the expense of others in this life; why shouldn't the pattern continue? But just as there was a barrier between the two men in life, so now there was a great chasm that could not be crossed. On earth the chasm was indifference and contempt, and the rich man could have come to Lazarus at any time. Now there was no crossing of the divide.

The Final Act

At last the rich man thought of someone else—his brothers. But he still wanted Lazarus to take care of things for him. He implored "Father" Abraham (suggesting his own privilege as a "child of Abraham") to send Lazarus to warn them. But Abraham, speaking on Lazarus's behalf, advised the rich man that his brothers had Moses and the prophets (representing the five books of Moses and the prophetic writings); that should be enough. (See Deuteronomy 15:7 and Isaiah 58:6-7 for examples of what Moses and the prophets taught.)

Since his own status as Abraham's "kin" was not enough, surely, "if someone came from the dead" to warn them, that should be enough to save his blood kin. "Not so," said Abraham. "If they don't heed the Scriptures and show mercy on the poor, they have placed themselves so far beyond the reach of God's mercy that not even someone coming to them from beyond the grave can help." In the final reversal on the presumed benefits of wealth, we see no satisfaction for this tormented man of riches.

> **Think About It:** How does this parable suggest that the church understood the Hebrew Scriptures differently than the synagogue and that the proclamation of Jesus' resurrection was not believed by persons outside the church?

Study Suggestions

A. Setting the Stage

Explain that this week's lections all deal with the theme of trust in God. Jeremiah trusted God to make a future for his people and demonstrated it by buying a field. The psalmist trusted God to provide security and protection. The writer of First Timothy urged his readers to demonstrate their trust in God rather than riches by their exemplary witness and defense of the faith. Jesus' parable of the rich man and Lazarus teaches that not the quest for wealth, but only trust in God shown in care for the needy leads to abundant life.

B. Buying a Field

Read Jeremiah 32:1-3a, 6-15. Recall the historical situation of the siege of Jerusalem. To highlight the apparent absurdity of Jeremiah's action and the significance of his symbolic act, ask: Where was Anathoth? (Three miles from Jerusalem.) Why did Jeremiah buy property there? (It was his hometown.) Who occupied it now? (The Babylonian army.) What was the field worth to Jeremiah? (Nothing; he couldn't get to it.) Why did he pay good money for an apparently worthless plot? (On one level, to secure the right of redemption for his family; on a deeper level, as a sign of hope that, though things looked bleak now, God would one day restore the people.) What led him to take this absurd step? (Trust in God.)

C. Examining Greed

Repeat these statements from the NIV: "Godliness with contentment is great gain. For we brought nothing into the world, and we can take nothing out of it" (1 Timothy 6:6-7). People who want to get rich fall into temptation: "For the love of money is a root of all kinds of evil" (verses 9-10). "Command them to do good, to be rich in good deeds, and to be generous and willing to share. In this way they will lay up treasure for themselves as a firm foundation" (verses 18-19a).

Then ask: What is the difference between money itself and the love of money (greed)? What is the faithful attitude toward the use of money? What is the relationship between our use of money and our eternal reward? How is trust in God related to all of this?

D. Bridging a Chasm

Ask three members to take the roles of narrator, rich man, and Abraham, and read Luke 16:19-31. Explore its meaning with these questions: What did the rich man want from Lazarus and Abraham? Why was his request denied?

Then focus on the contemporary relevance of the parable by discussing: What "Lazaruses" do we often pass by? How do we decide how much of our resources to spend on ourselves and how much to use to meet human need? How would a fuller trust in God free us up to give and share more? Which is the stronger motivation to generosity—fear of judgment or love of God and neighbor?

E. Affirming Trust

Read Psalm 91:1-6, 14-16 responsively. Sing the refrain, "All things come of thee, O Lord, and of thine own have we given thee." Close with prayer thanking God for all gifts, material and spiritual, and asking for help in being faithful stewards.

Lections for Sunday Between October 2 and 8

T　Old Testament: Lamentations 1:1-6

*T*HE Book of Lamentations is exactly that: a collection of poetic laments mourning the fall of Jerusalem to the Babylonians in 587 B.C. The five poems that make up the book give insight into the hearts and minds of the people of Judah as they struggled to understand and cope with their exile from the land their forebears had wrested from the Canaanites. The raw emotions and severe imagery underscore their feelings of desolation and humiliation. There is no misunderstanding that the people's own faithlessness had brought about these consequences, nor that YHWH had allowed the Babylonians to triumph as judgment for their waywardness. "The LORD has made her suffer / for the multitude of her transgressions" (1:5b).

In the first poem (Chapter 1) Jerusalem is personified as a woman, a destitute widow (later a prostitute in 1:8-9). The bitterness of Jerusalem's defeat is heightened by the remembrance of her former glory. Nothing remains of her prosperous past. The complaint "no one to comfort her" (1:2), repeated in various forms in verses 9, 16, 17, and 21, highlights both the people's utter devastation and their need to reach out to God.

Form and Function

The authorship of Lamentations is uncertain, although at one time the work was credited to the prophet Jeremiah. (Second Chronicles 35:25 mentions Jeremiah's lament over Josiah "recorded in the Laments.") Still read by Jews at the Wailing Wall in Jerusalem each Friday and during the Hebrew month of *Ab* (July/August) in observance of the fall of Jerusalem, the poems may have originally been developed for use in worship. The first four poems are alphabetic acrostics, each having twenty-two stanzas beginning with successive letters of the Hebrew alphabet. (In Chapter 3 all three lines of each stanza begin with the same Hebrew letter, and each line is numbered—hence 66 verses.) This form may have aided in memorization.

Psalter: Psalm 137

Like the preceding lection, today's psalm focuses on the Babylonian Exile. While Lamentations offers a view of the Exile from those who stayed behind in Jerusalem, Psalm 137 expresses the anguish of the Jews who had been taken away from Judah and forced to sing Zion's songs for the amusement of their captors. It also gives expression to their fierce determination to remember who and whose they were and from whence they had come (verse 5-6). Its setting makes it one of the easiest psalms to date with accuracy—587 to 539 B.C.

> **Think About It:** The songs of Zion spoke of YHWH's triumph over Judah's foes. As exiles in Babylon, it was clear YHWH had lost the battle. The request to sing was utter torment. When have you been in deep sorrow and then had to endure the ridicule of others?

Psalm 137, like two-fifths of the entire Psalter, can be characterized as a "lament," following, with some variation, a standard five-part form: the cry to God, the description of the affliction, the profession of God's faithfulness, the petition for God's intervention, and the vow to proclaim before the community God's action in response to the supplications. This psalm (along with Psalms 35, 59, 69, 70, 109, and 140) is known as an "imprecatory psalm" because it includes an impassioned plea for vengeance against Judah's enemies. In this case the enemies are the Babylonians who conquered Jerusalem and the Edomites who aided Babylon in its destruction.

The violent—even bloodthirsty—imagery of verses 7-9 often results in their omission from public reading. They stand, however, as a testimony to the Judahites' belief in a God to whom they could turn when all other defenses failed. They were confident that the justice of YHWH would prevail.

Epistle: 2 Timothy 1:1-14

Today begins a four-week exploration of Paul's Second Letter to Timothy. While verses from each of the four chapters will be covered in order, it is important to read the entire Epistle before studying the individual lections. To read it as a whole is to see it more clearly as a letter, an intimate letter from the imprisoned apostle to the young pastor. Also, a reading of First Timothy will provide a background understanding of the development of their relationship and ministry.

Letters in the Greek Tradition

The style of Paul's writing itself is evidence of his fluency in literary Greek and his familiarity with Greek culture. With few exceptions, his letters follow closely the five-part format of Greek correspondence: (1) the salutation, containing the identity of sender/s and recipient/s, and greeting; (2) the thanksgiving, modified to include a brief exhortation and reference to the coming reign of Christ; (3) the body, containing at least three components: the reason for writing, an autobiographical reference, and travel plans; (4) moral and ethical instruction: a theological discourse or response to previously posed questions; and (5) the closing, which is expanded to include a doxology or benediction in addition to a farewell and wishes for good health.

Addressed primarily to churches, Paul's letters were intended to be experienced as they are today—read aloud in the midst of the worshiping congregation. The "Pastoral Epistles" (First Timothy, Second Timothy, and Titus) offer instruction for the ordering of church life in the late first and early second century and outline the gifts and responsibilities of pastoral leadership.

Timothy's Relationship With Paul

Perhaps there was no other coworker in the gospel as dear to Paul as Timothy, the son of a devout Jewish mother and a Greek Gentile father. Paul engaged Timothy on his first missionary journey to Lystra (A.D. 45–48), had him circumcised (Acts 16:1-5), and became his teacher, mentor, and spiritual father. Timothy became for Paul "a beloved and faithful child in the Lord" (1 Corinthians 4:17) and as "a son with a father" (Philippians 2:22). Timothy appears in Acts, Romans, First Corinthians, and First Thessalonians, and is included in the salutations of Second Corinthians, Philippians, Colossians, First and Second Thessalonians, and Philemon.

Second Timothy

If Paul wrote the letter from prison as he neared the time of his own death (A.D. 67–68), he and Timothy would have been companions in mission for twenty years. Paul was seeking to encourage the younger pastor to hold fast to his faith in the face of challenge. In sharing the inevitability of his own suffering and death, Paul comforts Timothy while exhorting him not to be ashamed of testifying to Christ or to Paul's own imprisonment.

Paul begins his letter by claiming his authority as an apostle and by giving thanks for Timothy's faith, a faith nurtured by his grandmother Lois and by his mother Eunice, strong Jewish Christian women well-known and respected by Paul. By recalling the inheritance of faith given Timothy, Paul looks to the ongoing transmission of the gospel through its sharing from generation to generation.

The future of the ministry was now in Timothy's hands—hands empowered by the Holy Spirit "living in us" (1:14). For the church to continue its mission, Paul reminds Timothy of the need to stoke the fires of the gift of God imparted through the laying on of hands—his "ordination" (1 Timothy 4:14)—and through the spiritual gifts received at his baptism: power (energy), love (compassion), and self-control (discipline).

> ***Think About It:*** The future was now in Timothy's hands. What tasks have been given over to you by those who have gone before? What help do you need to remain faithful to them?

Gospel: Luke 17:5-10

Luke places the disciples' plea for faith in the midst of a series of parables and teachings that offer a warning: the rich man and Lazarus, the admonition against becoming a "stumbling block," and the call to forgive the one who repents. The parables that follow exemplify the power of faith and the duty of servanthood.

Much of the impact of Jesus' parables on his hearers lay in the specificity of detail he used to illustrate his point. The characters, objects, and situations described in the parables were well-known in his day. Jesus knew his audience (and human nature) well; more than eliciting the "Aha!" of recognition, his stories evoked an emotional response. While the imagery may be less familiar today, their message remains fresh because of this emotional connection and the note of urgency. When we get the point, we cannot ignore their call to change or act.

The Seed and the Tree

Each of the Synoptic Gospels contains a similar account of the power of faith. In Matthew 17:20, Jesus uses the example of the mustard seed, but replaces the tree with a moving mountain. In Mark 11:23, he also refers to a mountain, "taken up and thrown into the sea," as an example of what will be done for believers who "do not doubt." These sayings of Jesus appear to have been familiar to Paul who, in 1 Corinthians 13:2, speaks of having the faith "so as to remove mountains."

The mustard seed and the mulberry (sycamine) tree were extreme opposites. More than saying, "just a little faith can do big things," Jesus juxtaposes one of the tiniest of seeds against a tree known for its size and the depth and strength of its root system. So extensive were its roots that the *Mishnah,* the second-century collection of authoritative rabbinical teachings, prohibited its planting within 50 cubits (approximately 75 feet) of a cistern.

When the disciples asked Jesus to "increase our faith," his answer implied that the measure of one's faith was not at issue, but whether faith was present at all. It was not a question of a little versus a lot. The question was simply, "Do you have faith?" If a mustard seed's worth of faith is enough to tear

> **Think About It:** Whether you have faith like the tree or the seed, it is still enough to live by Jesus' teachings. What is the state of your faith? Do you live up to this potential?

loose the mulberry tree and plant it in the sea, how much more would it take for the disciples to trust and follow?

The Nature of Faith

Faith in the account of the mustard seed is both absolute and concrete. Just as in the healing stories where Jesus credits the restoration of health to "your faith," it is experienced in a specific context that calls for a response of both trust and obedience. Faith enables us to recognize and respond to the power of God that is present and active in Jesus.

The Master and His Slave

The image of slavery is uncomfortable for us because it is a painful reminder of a not-too-distant past. For Jesus' hearers, however, the image illustrated a well-defined relationship. To substitute *servant* for *slave* does not change the basic understanding—the servant was not free to choose whether to obey the master. The servant was expected to serve. Tasks were not performed in response to the master's goodness or kindness or out of the servant's desire to please. *Servanthood* meant the faithful carrying out of one's required duty—no reward, not even a "thank you," was promised or expected. Disciples cannot do *more* than is expected because our *all* is required.

Study Suggestions

A. Singing a Hymn

Sing a hymn of faith, such as "Through It All" or "Trust and Obey." Then ask members to share feelings elicited by the hymn.

B. "Lamenting" Together

Drawing on the commentary on pages 322–23, set the two Old Testament passages in their historical context. Note that Lamentations views the Exile from the perspective of those who remained behind; Psalm 137 voices the feelings of those forcibly separated from their roots.

Form two groups; assign the Lamentations passage to one and the Psalm to the other. After reading the passage aloud, have each group list the emotions expressed in its passage. Compare the lists; then ask: What do these writings tell us about the intensity of the Exile experience? How does this kind of emotional outpouring help? How do we understand the brutality of the imagery?

C. Exploring Exile

Ask participants to list examples of modern-day exile. (The Dalai Lama, political or economic refugees from Cuba, Haiti, Mexico, Africa, Bosnia.)

Comment that the biblical community brought their complaints and feelings into worship and made no secret of their despair. Ask: Do we feel free to offer laments in worship (or at church)? Why or why not? What purpose could it serve? Does pouring out our hurt, despair, and anger to God or to others mean that we have abandoned our faith?

Distribute paper and pens and invite members to write a personal reflection on their own experience of "exile"—times when they have felt alienated, disoriented, lonely, discouraged, because of a change of circumstances (loss of job, pain, illness, separation). Write these questions on chalkboard or large sheet of paper to guide this reflection: What is my strange land? How do I feel there? What is "the Lord's song" I am called to sing there? What does it mean to remain faithful in this circumstance? What help do I need to be faithful?

Divide into groups of three to share these reflections, with the guideline being: Share only what you feel comfortable talking about in this group. After reconvening as a total group, invite members to report significant learnings from this experience.

D. Finding Strength Through Faith

Have someone read aloud 2 Timothy 1:1-14 while others jot down the passage's images of hope, faith, and power. Ask: In light of the discussion of exile and lamentation, how do we rekindle the "spirit of power and love and self-control"? How do we "guard the good treasure entrusted to [us], with the help of the Holy Spirit"? How do we hold onto faith in times of crisis? What sustains us? How can we support one another at such times?

E. Examining Faith and Obedience

Read aloud Luke 17:5-6. Ask participants for one-word reactions to Jesus' response to the disciples. Discuss: What did Jesus mean by the metaphors of the seed and the tree? (Consult the commentary on pages 325–26.) Do we really believe that faith is this powerful? If so, what does this imply about our own faith?

Read verses 7-10 together. Ask: How do you characterize the master? the slave? Is this a comfortable image of the relationship between God and God's people? Do we expect reward (or at least thanks) for doing what we are called to do? What is the relationship between faith and obedience? Using this lection, work together to develop a definition of *servanthood*. Then invite members to apply this definition to their respective occupations— teacher, laborer, homemaker, business, health care, student, farmer. What would it look like to be a "servant" in each of these settings?

F. Commissioning to Service

Invite each member in turn to stand or kneel in the center of the circle, with others laying hands on his or her shoulders and sending him or her forth with prayer to a life of servanthood during the coming week.

Lections for Sunday Between
October 9 and 15

T Jeremiah 29:1, 4-7

ODAY'S Old Testament passage is part of a letter written by the
prophet Jeremiah to the exiled Jews in Babylon. This message, like all he
delivered, came from God. The people, however, were not always ready (and
rarely willing) to hear what God had to say to them through Jeremiah.

The Reluctant Prophet

Born in Anathoth (a half hour's walk northeast of Jerusalem in the territory of Benjamin), Jeremiah received the "word of the Lord" (Jeremiah
1:1-3) around 627 B.C. during the thirteenth year of King Josiah's reign. Born
into a priestly family, he was told by God that he was known and consecrated to be a "prophet to the nations" while still in his mother's womb. His
first response was to decline God's call, claiming youth and inexperience.
God prevailed, however, telling Jeremiah that he would go where he was sent
and speak the word given to him. God sealed the call by touching his mouth,
promising to be with him and deliver him (1:4-8).

Jeremiah's initial reluctance may have reflected a premonition of the sad
events to come, the hard words he would have to speak, and the painful
rejection he would later encounter. Much of the poetry in the Book of
Jeremiah consists of laments. One of the most familiar of these is found in
Chapter 20: "For whenever I speak, I must cry out, / I must shout "Violence
and destruction!" / For the word of the LORD has become for me / a reproach
and derision all day long" (20:8). The word God had placed in his mouth,
however, could not be silenced; if Jeremiah were to try to refrain from delivering God's message, he would be overcome by the "fire shut up in [his]
bones" (20:9).

Being a prophet was never more difficult than during the time leading up to the Babylonian Exile. Josiah's reign had produced a new prosperity for Judah. Hopes were high. Josiah's reforms had even produced a renewed (if short-lived) zeal for God's law. The people scoffed at Jeremiah's warnings; they had no use for his prophecies of gloom and doom, especially when the popular prophets of the day told them what they wanted to hear.

After the Fall

If Jeremiah's message before the Exile astounded the people of Judah, his later message to the captives certainly confounded them. Unlike the sanguine words of the popular prophets who had mistakenly predicted that God would act swiftly against the Babylonians, Jeremiah delivered another unexpected (and equally unwelcome) message: "Bloom where you're planted." In his letter, Jeremiah told the exiles to carry on with their lives—build houses, plant gardens, marry, and raise families ("multiply there, and do not decrease"). Beyond that, they were to seek the welfare (*shalom*) of their new home and pray to YHWH on its behalf, because it was YHWH who had sent them there (29:4-7). *Shalom* carries a depth of meaning well beyond the mere absence of conflict. It implies the sublime peace, both personal and social (wholeness, well-being, justice, completeness, fulfillment) that is only possible through God.

To struggle against the Exile was to defy God's will. The exiles must learn to sing the old songs in a new land. They might no longer have Jerusalem or the Temple or their lands or the comforts of their former home. They had God's word, and God's word would be sufficient.

> **Think About It:** To struggle against the Exile was to defy God's will. What unhappy circumstance do you struggle against? What purpose might God have for you in that situation? How might God's word replace the things or relationships that formerly made life meaningful? What specific word from God do you need to hear?

Psalter: Psalm 66:1-12

The Vulgate (the earliest Latin translation of Scripture) and the Septuagint (the Greek translation of Hebrew Scripture) label Psalm 66 a "psalm of resurrection." Its sheer exuberance in praise—loud, joyful celebration—explains this title. All creation is invited to join in the recognition of God's "awesome" deeds, and "all the earth" responds: "they sing praises to you / sing praises to your name" (66:4). The same adjective appears in Exodus 15:11 to describe God's deliverance, a true passage from death to life, which expresses God's will for all people.

The first twelve verses of this psalm, included in today's lection, give evidence of God's great deeds in the life of the community: "You have brought us out to a spacious place" (66:12). The verses that follow testify to God's work in the life of the individual: "I will tell what he has done for me" (66:15). The community has been tested by God (66:10-12), but the emphasis is on God's deliverance. The people have been "tried as silver" (66:10), but ultimately delivered to new life.

The Ancient Hymnal

The 150 psalms collected in the Psalter most probably received their form and order from those in charge of Temple worship in the years following the Exile (most likely in stages between the fifth and second centuries B.C.). The many notations concerning music and liturgy suggest that the psalms were sung in worship. The Hebrew word *Selah*, which occurs in today's selection, may have noted the place where a refrain, or other musical interlude, would be included. Other rubrics "for the leader" (or choirmaster) are found at the beginning of many of the psalms.

Epistle: 2 Timothy 2:8-15

"Remember Jesus Christ. . . ." Today's lection begins with an early Christian creed affirming the dual nature of Christ: the divine, "raised from the dead," and the human, "a descendant of David" (2:8). In this proclamation, Paul embraces both the suffering of the crucified Jesus and the glory of his resurrection. Jesus was the fulfillment of the promise made to David; his resurrection secured Paul's hope.

Paul counts it a privilege to share in any small part of that suffering, knowing that he will benefit in full measure from Christ's resurrection from the dead (2:11-12). The proclamation is at the heart of his exhortation to Timothy, the pastor. "Remember Jesus Christ. . . ."

The Apostle in Chains

It was the remembrance that empowered Paul not only to endure his imprisonment but to proclaim victory over it: "I suffer hardship, even to the point of being chained like a criminal. But the word of God is not chained" (2:9). With an exuberance reminiscent of his imprisonment with Silas in Philippi (Acts 16:25), Paul continued to praise God in spite of his chains. Implicit in this is the understanding that suffering—even to the point of death—may become the lot of any who follow Christ. Paul's imprisonment served to illuminate more fully his freedom in Christ. He did not celebrate suffering for suffering's sake; he celebrated the reign of Christ.

> **Think About It:** Paul's imprisonment served to illuminate his freedom in Christ. From what confining "prison" might you gain release by claiming your freedom in Christ?

The Nature of God

Just as Paul's imprisonment underscores his freedom in Christ, so our faithlessness only serves to accent the faithfulness of God. "If we deny him, he will also deny us" (2:12b). Jesus himself offered such a warning (Matthew 10:32-33), but "if we are faithless, he remains faithful—for he cannot deny himself" (2 Timothy 2:13). God's very nature is love. God's faithfulness does not depend on our loyalty; it is part of who God is.

Gospel: Luke 17:11-19

Jesus' encounter with the ten lepers confronted those around him with their worst fears and deepest prejudices. Luke places this story "on the way to Jerusalem" (17:11). Traveling along the border implies that they were skirting Samaria (Gentile territory) on purpose. In addition, Luke reminds his readers that even as he moved toward the cross, Jesus was concerned with bringing the suffering and marginalized members of society into the embrace of the realm of God. The healing Jesus offers in this setting goes beyond the removal of a bodily ill; it touches the very core of brokenness that separates people from one another and, ultimately, from God.

"Leprosy" in the Bible

In our day, "Hansen's Disease" is the preferred designation for the illness formerly known as "leprosy," although in biblical times a variety of skin diseases was included under this term. (Leviticus 13 and 14 provide extensive lists and descriptions of these skin conditions.) While the diagnosis and treatment of Hansen's Disease is probably unfamiliar to those outside the medical community, the connotation—and stigma—of "leper" is still widely understood. The only form of disease prevention available in those days was quarantine.

Lepers were unclean, set apart, isolated, marked by their clothing and hair, as well as by the requirement to cover their upper lip and cry "Unclean! Unclean!" (Leviticus 13:45). Persons with leprosy suffered doubly, their physical condition often less severe than their social ostracism. The leper was an outcast who, along with tax collectors and beggars, had no place in the religious community. In Luke's Gospel, however, such outcasts were precisely the focus of Jesus' ministry.

Jesus' command to "show yourselves to the priests" recognizes that the physical healing of the ten men was necessary to restore them into the Jewish community. Only upon examination by the priests with ritual cleansing and sacrifice (Leviticus 14:1-32) could the one healed be pronounced "clean" and reunited with the community. The ten were healed on their way to see the priests (in contrast to the healing in Luke 5:12-16 of another similarly afflicted man who was cleansed before being sent to the priest), but the story did not end there. Jesus shifted the focus from the miraculous curing of leprosy to the response of those whose lives had been restored.

The One Who Returned

The change in situation for all ten healed was astounding. More profound than the easing of their physical suffering was the end of their estrangement from the community. Nine continued toward the priests to complete the restoration; only one recognized that the God who had brought about the miracle must be glorified. In falling down before Jesus in thanksgiving, the one who returned acknowledged the power of God present in Jesus. To thank Jesus is to praise the One who has sent him.

Then, as if to add insult to injury, Jesus pointed out that the only one who stopped to thank God for his healing was a Samaritan—a double outcast.

> **Think About It:** Jesus praised the faith of a "double outcast." What can we learn from the faith and lives of those whom society (and sometimes the church) rejects?

Not only was this man unclean, he was a foreigner. The only one to praise God was the one most loathed. Just as in the story of the good Samaritan (Luke 10:29-37), Jesus knew that a Jew would find it difficult even to speak the word *Samaritan*. The outcast possessed a faith deep enough to recognize and to respond to God's saving power.

Study Suggestions

A. Sing a Hymn

Begin by singing a song of healing, such as "Jesus' Hands Were Kind Hands," or a hymn of thanksgiving such as "Now Thank We All Our God."

B. Consider Jeremiah

Invite participants to share what they know about Jeremiah. Using the group's knowledge, the commentary on pages 328–29, and previous sessions, describe Jeremiah's origin and call, historical circumstances, prophetic ministry, and message. Read Jeremiah 29:1, 4-7 in unison. Look up *welfare* (verse 7) and *shalom* in a Bible dictionary. Compare the two. Ask: What was Jeremiah's advice to the exiles? How did they respond to this message? How might you respond? Does faithfulness sometimes require living with the consequences of our actions? What helps us come to terms with an unpleasant turn of events?

C. Take Part in the Gospel Story

As a group, review the background information (pages 331–32), taking note of the place of "lepers" and "Samaritans" in the society of Jesus' day. Read

Luke 17:11-19 as a drama, assigning the roles of narrator, Jesus, the men who cried out for mercy (you don't have to have ten), and the one who returned. Discuss: When did the healing occur—the moment the ten men left? or only following the priestly ritual? Why did Jesus tell the one who returned that "his faith" had made him well? Does healing take place without acknowledgment of God's action? What is the efficacious element in a healing?

D. Apply the Story

Work as a group to rewrite the story in a modern setting. Ask: Who are regarded as today's "lepers" (persons with HIV/AIDS, persons with schizophrenia or other mental illness, the homeless), and who are considered as contemporary "Samaritans" (substance abusers, homosexuals, child molesters)?

Ask: Why would Jesus pick a societal outcast to make his point? What is the message of the story for those inside the faith community? Briefly review Leviticus 14:1-32. Ask: What are your reactions to these cleansing rituals? How can those identified as outcasts in your adaptation of the story be restored to the community?

E. Examine Faithfulness

Read 2 Timothy 2:8-15 together. Review the prison conditions that may have affected Paul's attitude and hope. Ask: Why was remembering Jesus' humanity and divinity critical to Paul as he awaited his own death? How do you understand his attitude toward suffering? Would this passage encourage you if you thought you might be called upon to suffer or die for Christ?

Examine faithfulness in light of this lection (as well as the Gospel passage). Does our faithlessness or weakness in faith have an impact on God's faithfulness? What does this passage show us about God's nature? What response to God's faithfulness is called for from God's people? How ready and able are you to live fully in faith? Also discuss the "Think About It" question.

F. Draw the Themes Together

These Scriptures lead us through the gamut from suffering or estrangement to healing or acceptance to rejoicing and praise. Review these themes and their relationship. Encourage group members to envision what these passages call them to do and be, as both individuals and a faith community. Invite persons to share briefly some of their experiences of God's deliverance from suffering or rejection to a point of shalom and thanksgiving. Handle these stories with sensitivity and care.

G. Close With Praise

Read Psalm 66:1-3 aloud, then sing the doxology. Pray for the strength to praise God "with a joyful noise" in times of adversity as well as in times of fulfillment.

Lections for Sunday Between October 16 and 22

Old Testament: Jeremiah 31:27-34

*T*HE best thing about hitting bottom is that there is no place to go but up. For the exiles in Babylon, who had spent more than seventy years away from Canaan, the promise of restoration given by God through Jeremiah must have seemed an incredible dream. When their years of discipline came to an end; God's forgiveness would create for them a fresh start: "I will remember their sin no more" (Jeremiah 31:34). A new community forged from the reunited peoples of Judah and Israel would become reality, and a new covenant—initiated (like the first) by God—would be written on hearts of faithful people.

Verses 27-28 of today's passage hearken back to Jeremiah's own call so many years before. Called to "pluck up and to pull down, / to destroy and to overthrow, / to build and to plant" (1:10), the prophet was now given a vision of a time of restoration, rebuilding, and reunification. Future generations would no longer be held accountable for the sins of their parents. Each person would be judged according to his or her own actions. "The days are surely coming, says the LORD" (31:27, 31).

A New Covenant

The old covenant, given to the people through Moses at Sinai, could not be restored through religious ritual and observance or even through attempts at reformation. The new covenant would be imparted inwardly, "written on the heart," imprinted upon the minds and will of the people. No longer would the Torah need to be taught, for all people would know God as intimately as a wife knows her husband. The image of God as the husband of the Hebrew people (31:32) illustrates the depth of the covenant as well as the

334

depth of the pain of their unfaithfulness. The new covenant, made possible through God's forgiveness, would give birth to a new community.

Christians interpret the new covenant in light of the coming of Jesus Christ: New Testament means "New Covenant." More than an expression of Christian history, however, the "coming days" speak of the future of Christ's reign and the fulfillment of human destiny in light of his redeeming purpose.

> *Think About It:* God's covenant is written on the heart. What does this mean in your experience? What binds you to God and to the community of faith? How do you know God loves, guides, and judges you?

At Home Away From Home

When the Jews were free to return to Canaan, some did. Many others, however, decided to stay in the only home they had ever known. Known as the Jews of the "dispersion" or "Diaspora," they continued to practice their faith (as they had done throughout the Exile) away from Jerusalem and the Temple. The prophets, Jeremiah in particular, had shown the people that God was not bound to the Temple and could be worshiped and served anywhere. God had indeed been with them through all their years in exile. God heard their prayers. God was their sanctuary. God was universal and omnipresent.

The synagogue developed during the postexilic period as a gathering place for prayer and study. The Babylonians had driven the Jews' faith into the world. Jerusalem would always be their spiritual home, but they did not need to be there to experience the covenant or to claim their heritage.

> *Think About It:* God was their sanctuary. If the Jews in exile learned that God is with them there, why is Jerusalem so important to the Jews today? to Muslims? to Christians? How might God be guiding all three "peoples of the Book" to find and share a spirital home?

Psalter: Psalm 119:97-104

These selected verses can be considered as the core of the entire work that praises God's law. The length (Psalm 119 is the longest in the Psalter) and repetitions exist due to its very structured form. Psalm 119 is an alphabetical acrostic: each section is composed of eight lines (which may correspond to the eight synonyms for "law" repeated throughout), each of which begins with the same letter of the Hebrew alphabet. There is a section for each letter in alphabetical order. The psalm is a celebration of structure; structure itself is a feature of the law.

Torah, the most important of the synonyms, is used more in verses 97-104 than in any of the other sections. Many scholars suggest that "instruction" is a better translation of Torah than "law." Torah may also be understood as "scripture" or "revelation." The psalmist loves God's "instruction," which is sweeter than honey to [the] mouth" (119:103). This love of God's instruction is accompanied by the "[hatred of] every false way" (119:104), showing the depth of the psalmist's devotion to God. Other synonyms for law used by the psalmist are associated with written instruction given by God—*statute, precept, commandment,* and *decree.* Another, *ordinances,* is a plural form of the Hebrew word for "justice." To love God's law, then, is to love justice.

Epistle: 2 Timothy 3:14–4:5

Timothy's heritage of faith again becomes the focus for Paul in his letter. In order to prepare him for the challenges that lay ahead, Paul reminded Timothy of the training he had received from his family, from Paul himself, and from the word of God in Scripture. These are the resources upon which the younger pastor could depend.

Paul highlights the importance of Timothy's childhood instruction. Often accused of minimizing the role of women in the church, Paul's high regard for Timothy's mother and grandmother is here very apparent. He urges Timothy to "continue in what you have learned and have become convinced of, because you know those from whom you learned it" (3:14, NIV).

Sacred Writings

Timothy's "childhood in the faith" had also included thorough training in the "sacred writings," the Scriptures that are not to be abandoned by the Christian pastor. To study these is to see the salvation of God fulfilled in the coming of Jesus Christ.

The assertion "All scripture is inspired by God" (3:16) is a basic tenet of Christian faith, although scholars tend to disagree on its interpretation. The Greek *pasa* interpreted as "all" can also mean "every"; the Greek *theopneustos* for "inspired" rarely appears in Scripture. Just how the process of inspiration takes place is not at issue here; the employment of Scripture is. "Inspiration" refers essentially to the work of the Spirit. For discerning truth or reproving false teaching, the disciple of Jesus Christ is incomplete and ill-equipped without it.

For the Pastor

There is an urgency in Paul's exhortation to Timothy as a pastoral leader. He evokes images of Christ's reign and second coming as he charges him to "proclaim, . . . convince, rebuke, and encourage" (4:2). Timothy is not to wait for the right moment, but to "carry out [his] ministry fully" (4:5) right now. He must deliver the message urgently . . . with patience. People's ears will itch for a word that is comfortable. False teachers will emerge to provide quick, easy answers and promote unreliable doctrine.

Gnosticism, a dualistic system contrasting the good (spiritual, nonphysical) with the evil (earthly, physical), threatened the early church with its denial of the humanity of Jesus. Only the steadfast pastor, grounded in Scripture and ready to endure suffering for the sake of the gospel, would prevail against it.

Gospel: Luke 18:1-8

In the midst of a series of stories about the faith of those deemed outcasts, comes this remarkable parable of the unrighteous judge and the persistent widow. Knowing there was no better example of powerlessness in Jewish society than a widow, Jesus chose one such woman's feisty determination to exemplify his call to "always pray and not give up" (18:1, NIV). The story of the seemingly powerless little woman mercilessly pestering the ruthless judge into submission was undoubtedly as amusing to those who heard it firsthand as it remains for us today.

The Widow's Place

No one in Jesus' day was more vulnerable to poverty and exploitation than a woman whose husband—and means of support—had died. Justice for the widow was required by the law, but adherence to the law (particularly justice for the downtrodden) was not a high priority. The old covenant requirements for the care of widows (Deuteronomy 24:19-21), as well as the stern warnings against their mistreatment (Isaiah 1:17, 23; Exodus 22:22-24), were features of the early church as well (Acts 6:1; 1 Timothy 5:3; James 1:27). Jesus' example of the "widow's mite" not only exemplified her faithfulness in giving all she had (Luke 21:2-4), but also exposed the community's failure to secure her basic needs.

A widow under the care of the early Christian community would also be understood by Luke's readers as a model of devotion. A woman without a husband to care for could devote herself fully to a life of prayer. The widow Anna (Luke 2:36-38), who recognized and proclaimed God's presence in the infant Jesus, was praised for her persistence in prayer and fasting. Luke also notes the devotion of the widows attending to Tabitha, first in death and later when she was raised by Peter (Acts 9:36-41).

The Unjust Judge

With the law on her side, a widow's only hope for justice was to appeal to the one charged with upholding that law. Unfortunately, this judge had no concern for his lawful duty. He "neither feared God nor had respect for people" (Luke 18:2); the law mattered little to him. As a judge, he had power over the rich and influential; the needs of a mere widow were not enough to merit his attention. He had no idea what he was in for.

Just as water can wear away stone, the widow's constant pleas for justice penetrated the judge's indifference. Often translated as "wear me out," the Greek verb *hypopiazo,* a boxing term, literally means to "give a black eye" (18:5). The beleaguered judge "threw in the towel," feeling both badgered and battered by her incessant petitions. Jesus' audience overheard his reasoning: "Though I have no fear, . . . I will grant her justice" (18:4-5). The crowd must have cheered at the widow's triumph.

Think About It: God's faithfulness is the key. Because God is just, we can persist in faith. Does God have to be persuaded to answer our prayers? How does prayer influence God and the outcome of events?

The Just Judge
The emphasis is not on the widow's persistence, but on God the righteous. Jesus employed the rabbinical practice of arguing from the less to the greater. If even a corrupt judge must do justice, how much more will a righteous God do justice. Like the widow, we must never lose heart.

Study Suggestions

A. Sing a Hymn
Open with a hymn celebrating the sacred word, such as "Thy Word Is a Lamp Unto My Feet," or "Wonderful Words of Life."

B. Compose a Psalm
Read Psalm 119:97-104, taking turns, line by line. Using the word *instruction*, write an acrostic psalm of praise for God's word (the first line beginning with "I," the second with "N," and so on). Divide into pairs and assign one letter (or more) to each. When finished, ask each pair to read its line aloud in order.

C. Look at the "Coming Days"
Ask one person to read Jeremiah 31:27-34 aloud. Ask: What makes this passage especially meaningful to Christians? Jeremiah's prophecies were often filled with images of downfall and destruction; what images of hope do you see in this message to the people of the Exile? How would such a message be understood by people who have "hit bottom"? How do we hear it today? Christians associate the "new covenant" with the promised coming of Jesus Christ; how can this message from God through the prophet bolster our hope in Christ's return?

D. Examine Faith Resources

Read 2 Timothy 3:14–4:5 together. Ask: From what sources did Timothy learn about God? Why does Paul highlight (for the second time in this letter) the importance of Timothy's faith inheritance? How does this inheritance prepare him for his work as a pastor? From what sources have you learned of God? How have these influences shaped your life?

When Paul spoke of "scripture" he was referring to our Old Testament. Discuss: What value do we place on studying the Hebrew Scriptures? How are they related to the New Testament? How does this passage inform the way we view Christian education and nurture?

Examine what your group understands by the inspiration of Scripture in 2 Timothy 3:16-17. Does it refer to God's dynamic working and continuing revelation through the biblical word? God's guiding presence with those who wrote and those who read? something else?

E. Discuss Perseverance in Faith

Read Luke 18:1-8, and review the commentary on pages 337–38. Ask: What adjectives would you use to describe the widow? the judge? Note that the parable was effective in Jesus' day because the characters so clearly exemplified the powerless versus the mighty. Ask: In updating the story, whom would you pick for each part? To what do you credit the widow's success? Does the story inspire you to "pray without ceasing"? Does it encourage you to "not give up"? How does God's faithfulness to us inspire our remaining faithful to God?

F. Summarize Themes

Justice, hope in God's law, Christian nurture, scriptural inspiration, and persistence in faith mark these passages. Ask: How do you see these themes working in your life? What questions remain about them? How do Scripture, prayer, and nurture sustain your hope and commitment to justice? How can we in this group and congregation better foster these elements in the Christian life?

G. Close in Prayer

Join hands in a circle, and invite participants to offer sentence prayers asking God's Spirit to guide and strengthen our understanding of Scripture, practice of prayer and nurture, vision of hope, and devotion to justice.

Lections for Sunday Between
October 23 and 29

Old Testament: Joel 2:23-32

*L*ITTLE is known about the prophet Joel other than what appears in the first verse of the book, "son of Pethu'el." His prophecy is thought to date from the time preceding Ezra and Nehemiah, during the period of 500 to 350 B.C. The meaning of his name, "YHWH is God," is shared with many other Old Testament characters. The liturgical style of his prophecy suggests that he was familiar with and knowledgeable of the Temple in Jerusalem as well as its services and priesthood. As such, Joel can be termed a "cultic prophet" (along with Haggai, Zechariah, and anonymous others) whose message would be shared in the context of Temple worship.

Warning and Promise
Joel's preaching focuses on an infestation of locusts that threatened to destroy the land. To Joel the locusts represented a "nation" (Joel 1:6)—an "army" (2:25)—visiting God's judgment upon the people's faithlessness (as a plague of locusts had been used to "soften" Pharaoh's heart in Exodus 10:1-20) and to announce the coming day of YHWH (Joel 1:15). The relentless swarm is "powerful and innumerable; its teeth are lions' teeth" (1:6) and "like war-horses they charge" (2:4). The devastation was felt throughout the nation, causing the prophet to issue an urgent call to repentance, sackcloth, and fasting.

The urgency of Joel's exhortation is, however, balanced by the promise of restoration that will "sanctify" (make holy) the repentant people of God (2:16). They are called to "rend [their] hearts and not [their] clothing," to "return to the LORD" who is "gracious and merciful, / slow to anger, and abounding in steadfast love" (2:13). "Return to me with all your heart," says the Lord, "and I will no more make you a mockery among the nations"

(2:12, 19). The autumn rains, which come at the time for planting the spring crops, follow the locusts as a sign of God's mercy (2:23-25). Joel's prophecy connects these events to God's final judgment and ultimate redemption at the "great and terrible day" of YHWH (2:31), a cataclysmic intervention in history that will right all wrongs and rescue the faithful.

Apocalyptic Literature

Joel's description of the day of YHWH (2:30-32) is an example of apocalyptic (from the Greek *apokaluptein,* meaning to uncover or reveal) literature. Often produced during times of persecution or tribulation, apocalyptic literature contains highly symbolic, supernatural imagery to depict the end times when God's righteousness would prevail. The books of Daniel and Revelation are prime examples of this type of literature.

The Coming Day

The apocalyptic images of blood, smoke, and fire will usher in the day of judgment; but when the Spirit is poured upon "all flesh" (meaning "the Jews" for Joel, but "all nations" for Peter on the Day of Pentecost), redemption shall be known by those—regardless of human distinction—who call upon YHWH. Scholars suggest that verse 32 more accurately reads, "and in Jerusalem shall be survivors on whom the Lord calls," rather than "among the survivors," which implies that not all are called by God. Unmistakable, however, is the message that redemption succeeds judgment as God's final word.

> **Think About It:** Apocalyptic images usher in the day of judgment. What images inform your understanding of God's activity in history? Do you look forward to a cataclysmic Last Judgment? In light of God's revelation in Jesus, how do you relate judgment and redemption within the divine nature and purpose?

Psalter: Psalm 65

The images of the restorative powers of rain and the joining of "all flesh" before God in today's psalm echo the prophecy of Joel. Again, those who cry out to God experience satisfaction and salvation, having witnessed YHWH's "awesome deeds" and signs. Such a psalm of thanksgiving would be sweeter still to those who had experienced the ravages of a plague of locusts (or other natural disaster) and interpreted it in light of God's ultimate plan. The hope in God's redemption points once more to the inevitability of a final triumph of righteousness.

Verses 9-13 focus exclusively on God's activity in providing life-sustaining rain for the land, causing some scholars to treat this section as a separate psalm. These verses also offer a view of YHWH as provider and caretaker, thereby rejecting the Canaanite belief in a fertility god, as well as humanity's reliance solely on its own efforts in bringing forth the harvest.

Unity is maintained throughout the psalm by its direct address to God: "to you" praise is due, "to you all flesh shall come," "your wagon tracks overflow with richness." The effect of God's goodness is experienced in the congregation (verses 1-4), through forgiveness of sins; in the world (verses 5-8), as God's "awesome" acts in creation are recalled; and in the earth (verses 9-13), through the images of water and new life.

Epistle: 2 Timothy 4:6-8, 16-18

Throughout this letter, Paul has encouraged young Timothy to take hold of his ministry that waits to be fulfilled, anticipating this moment when Paul's ministry—even his life—is coming to an end. As a priest pours the drink offering on the altar to end the sacrifice (Numbers 28:7), so Paul's "sacrifice" is at the point of completion.

Departure

Paul's choice of the word *departure* as opposed to *death* is not an attempt to soften the blow for Timothy or to deny his situation; the subtlety of meaning connotes Paul's understanding of his transition from one life to the next.

The Greek word for "departure" carries shades of meaning similar to those of dismantling a tent or untying a boat. The tent provides shelter, but is not a permanent home. The "freeing" of a boat from the dock signals the beginning of the voyage. Paul's understanding of his death is that of release—"from the bonds of prison and, more significant, from the confines of this life in anticipation of the endless life that is to come.

> **Think About It:** Paul sees his death as a release and as the beginning of a new life. How do you view the prospect of death—as a terminus, a trauma, or a transition? What gives you hope as you contemplate your own (and others') mortality?

The fight has been fought; the race has been run. Crowns of leaves or flowers were worn by Jews as symbols of honor or celebration (during feasts or weddings). Greeks awarded crowns to triumphant athletes who had stayed the course and crossed the finish line. In contrast to such rewards for personal achievement, however, Paul awaited the "victor's crown," not trusting in his own merits or righteousness, but in God's promise to all those "who have longed for his appearing" (2 Timothy 4:8).

"Come Soon . . ."

Verses 9-15 and 19-22, omitted from today's lection, urge Timothy to come quickly to Rome. The urgency of his appeal suggests that death is very near. These verses also attend to personal effects and exhortations about individuals who had deserted Paul along the way. God, however, had never abandoned Paul, delivering him (figuratively, as in Psalm 22) from the "lion's mouth" and assuring his rescue "from every evil attack." He would be saved for God's heavenly realm, to God "be the glory forever and ever" (4:17-18).

Gospel: Luke 18:9-14

In last week's parable of the widow and the unjust judge, Jesus accentuated the need to be persistent in prayer. Today's passage follows directly, with examples of two men going to God in prayer. Like the characters in the previous story, the Pharisee and the tax collector would bring an immediate picture to mind of "insider versus outsider" in Jewish understanding, as well as "righteous-in-self versus righteous-in-God" for those familiar with Luke's emphasis on Jesus' ministry with the outcast and excluded. A similar distinction had already been drawn between Pharisee and tax collector specifically (Luke 5:29-32; 7:29-30; 15:1-2), and the parable's conclusion—the moral—repeats verbatim Jesus' teaching on humility found in the parable of the wedding feast (14:11).

> **Think About It:** The Pharisee was burdened by his self-righteousness; the tax collector by his life choices. With which do you most identify? What type of burden most limits your relationship with God?

Those "who trusted in themselves that they were righteous and regarded others with contempt" (18:9) apparently had not learned the lesson. It is interesting to note that the disciples themselves struggled to take Jesus' admonition to heart. Immediately following this encounter they rebuked those bringing infants (another striking example of the powerless in Jewish society) to Jesus for blessing (18:15-17).

Pharisees and Tax Collectors

To be sure, Jesus was not designating all Pharisees as villains or all tax collectors as pillars of morality—or humility. Pharisees, as a sect, advocated strict adherence to the practices of faith that maintained their separateness from the Gentile world (prayer, fasting, circumcision, diet) in anticipation of the time when God's reign would be established and the people liberated from alien domination. Unlike the Sadducees, they opposed any collaboration with foreign rulers. Tax collectors, while Jews, acted as agents of Rome. Perceived as traitors to their own people, they often collected more than they would "render unto Caesar." Few persons were more reviled within the community.

"O, Lord, It's Hard to Be Humble . . ."

Compare the Pharisee's prayer of thanksgiving with that of the writer of Psalm 65. The source of goodness and bounty for the psalmist is clearly God.

The Pharisee, however, is thankful for what he himself has done. He has tithed and fasted above and beyond the law's "call of duty." His devotion is above reproach. The trouble is that he knows it and celebrates it as his own accomplishment. Even his stance, "by himself," illustrates the object of his prayer. (Note the number of times he uses "I" while offering thanks.) His contempt for others is his true downfall, however, as he weighs his own righteousness against the tax collector who has also turned to God in penitence.

"Be Merciful to Me . . ."

The tax collector has no accomplishments to present. Absent too is a list of faults and failures. His simple request, "have mercy on me," with the beating of his breast (a sign of deep anguish) and down-turned eyes, stand in sharp contrast to the confidence of the Pharisee. The tax collector recognizes God as the source of mercy and the focus of prayer. The Greek *hilaskomai*, translated "be merciful," rarely appears in the New Testament and refers to the expiation of sin through sacrificial offering.

It is the second man whom Jesus declares as "justified" before God. From the Greek *dikaioo*, "justified" is related to "righteous." The tax collector was "accepted as righteous" or "made righteous" through the earnestness of his prayer. Societal preconceptions were turned upside down. Knowing one's place before God, and in relation to one another, takes precedence over adherence to—or boasting in—"righteous" behavior.

Study Suggestions

A. Sing a Hymn

Sing a hymn of humility, such as "Take Time to Be Holy" or "Dear Jesus, in Whose Life I See." Read Psalm 65 in unison or responsively. Share expressions of thanksgiving to God; pray together for humility and guidance as you embark on today's study.

B. Experience the Prophecy

Assign the five senses to five individuals or teams. Read Joel 2:23-32 aloud, instructing teams to take notice of the sights, sounds, smells, touches, and tastes they experience in response to the passage. As they call them out at the end, write these on chalkboard or a large sheet of paper in scattered fashion.

Use these questions to reflect on the reading: How do these images strike you? What feelings do they evoke? What does Joel's interpretation tell us of the nature of judgment and the nature of redemption? What does it tell us of the nature of God? Why do you think Peter quoted Joel at Pentecost? What picture of the "end times" do we see in Joel? Are these pictures frightening or hopeful for you? Explain the context and significance of apocalyptic thinking. Discuss the "Think About It" questions related to God's activity in history and contrasting images of judgment and redemption.

C. Explore Pride and Humility

Read Luke 18:9-14 together, asking two volunteers to read the prayers of the Pharisee and tax collector aloud. Ask group members to write brief descriptions of each "pray-er." Share the responses together.

Think of examples of persons who have publicly admitted their sin. (Jimmy Swaggart; Karla Faye Tucker, the born-again woman executed in Texas; Charles Colson; President Clinton; others.) Ask: Do we view these confessions with trust or skepticism? Why? What justified the tax collector in Jesus' eyes? What did Jesus mean by justification? When is pride a stumbling block?

D. Evaluate Good Advice

Read aloud 2 Timothy 4:6-8, 16-18. Discuss Paul's summation of his life and ministry. Ask: What words of advice does Paul want to secure for Timothy? How timely is this counsel? What is it calling us to do or be? Also explore the "Think About It" questions regarding views of our death and mortality.

E. Write an Epitaph

Using the above information about Paul's "departure," as well as the previous discussion of justification, ask members to compose their own epitaphs. What would they like to able to say when their own faith journeys come to an end? What legacy do they want to leave? What help might they need between now and then?

F. Summarize Themes

God's judgment and redemption, our death and immortality, and pride and humility are found in today's Scriptures. Summarize your learning about these concepts. Ask: How are these ideas inter-related? How are they illuminated in the various passages? What guidance do you draw from them for your own sense of meaning and discipleship?

G. Write Individual Prayers

Ask members to write two prayers (one of thanksgiving, one of confession) side by side on the same sheet of paper. Use the words of the Pharisee, "God, I thank you that I am . . . ," and the words of the tax collector, "God, be merciful to me, a sinner!" to begin the prayers. Instruct them to make their prayers as personal and specific to their own situations as possible. In closing, invite willing participants to read their prayers to the group. Then end by saying the Lord's Prayer in unison.

Lections for Sunday Between October 30 and November 5

H Old Testament: Habakkuk 1:1-4; 2:1-4

ABAKKUK is often called "the skeptical prophet" because he questions the traditional Deuteronomic view that God automatically rewards the faithful and punishes the sinner in tangible ways. His name comes from an Akkadian word meaning "a garden plant," suggesting that he may have been a foreigner transplanted in Judah, perhaps for the very purpose of delivering God's message. His book opens by posing the problem of why righteous Judah was suffering under the heel of pagan foreigners and closes with an affirmation of trust in God's goodness and righteousness.

Habakkuk was a contemporary of Jeremiah, who prophesied before the Exile. His message was delivered either between the rise of the Chaldeans in 626 and the reforms of Josiah in 622 B.C., or else around 605 when Nebuchadrezzar conquered Judah. Habakkuk's agonizing question amidst all this was: Where is God? Why does God permit Judah to suffer under unjust oppression? Was YHWH too weak to prevent this, too indifferent to care, or pursuing an unknown purpose through these calamitous events?

> **Think About It:** Habakkuk's question was: Why does God permit people to suffer unjustly? How do you answer this question?

Habakkuk's Message

While agonizing over this dilemma, Habakkuk had a vision that provided an answer (1:2-4, 13; 2:1). In this vision YHWH made clear that he was neither powerless nor apathetic, but was using the Babylonians to carry out God's judgment on those who were abusing God's people. They were being used as God's agents without their knowledge or consent, following their own god and acting under their own power (1:7-11). When they had finished punishing Judah, those they were oppressing would rebel and destroy them (2:7-8). The Chaldeans' punishment would bring glory to YHWH in the eyes of all the nations (2:14).

The righteous must wait patiently for God's vindication and strive to remain faithful through it all (2:3-4). When vindication did come, however, the righteous would rejoice and all would recognize that God reigns over the earth (2:20). Although all present signs were discouraging (3:17), this confidence in God's power enables the righteous to proclaim, "I will rejoice in the LORD; I will exult in the God of my salvation" (3:18).

Habakkuk's Influence

Habakkuk's struggle with the problem of righteous suffering and his eventual affirmation of hope became an important source of encouragement for the Essene community of Qumran in Jesus' time. One of the Dead Sea Scrolls is a commentary on Habakkuk that applied his message to their own time. The apostle Paul also relied on Habakkuk in developing his theme of salvation by faith. In short, Habakkuk's trust in a God who overcomes evil and upholds the righteous, provides assurance and hope to all who undergo injustice and oppression for no good reason.

The book is entitled "the oracle which Habakkuk the prophet saw" (1:1). The Hebrew word for "oracle" means "burden," and refers to the burden of a message that God laid on a prophet to deliver. The verb "saw" suggests that the message came to him in a vision which he was commanded to pass on (2:2). The oracle consists primarily of a dialogue between Habakkuk and God. The two brief passages included in today's lection come from the book's first section containing questions to God about pagan tyrants (1:2-2:4). The first (1:1-4) is Habakkuk's first charge: injustice abounds; and the second (2:1-4) is God's response: remain faithful and wait patiently for God's deliverance.

Psalter: Psalm 119:137-144

The structure of Psalm 119 as an alphabetical acrostic and its emphasis on God's law through repetitive use of eight synonyms were explained two weeks ago. Today's selection affirms God's righteousness and faithfulness (verses 137a, 138b, 142a) and attests to the dependability and veracity of God's law (judgments, 137b; decrees, 138a, 144a; promise, 140a; precepts, 141b; law, 142b; commandments, 143b). Though a mere inconsequential mortal (141a), and beset by enemies (139b) and woes (143a), the psalmist is passionate in his devotion to God (139a).

With only a passing reference to the kind of doubts with which Habakkuk was openly struggling, the psalmist comes out with a very similar confession of trust in God's faithfulness and justice. Such a ringing affirmation of faith and unswerving devotion to God's purpose sets a standard to which all can aspire.

347

Epistle: 2 Thessalonians 1:1-4, 11-12

In contrast to First Thessalonians, which is tender and caring, this letter is more reserved, austere, and doctrinal. Paul's mission in Thessalonica had met with a mixed response (Acts 17:1-13). Now, a few years later and from a distance, he was writing to nurture the faith of his converts and counter the influence of those who had rejected his message and were persecuting the faithful. In the first letter Paul had sought to strengthen the resolve of the Thessalonians as new Christians to persevere and grow in the faith. Now he was adding to this encouragement a note of sterner demand that they hold fast to the standards of belief and conduct which he had taught them.

Many scholars believe that the early Paul was convinced that Christ would soon return. As the years passed, the gospel spread, the church became more firmly established, and history showed no sign of coming to an abrupt end, the urgency of guiding a growing movement to more mature standards of faith and practice led him to turn his attention to other issues.

Words of Encouragement

The expectation of Christ's coming was uppermost in the minds of these Thessalonians, so Paul dealt with it. They were facing severe persecution, so—after a formal greeting (1:1-2)—Paul immediately launches into words of praise for their unwavering devotion and ongoing improvement in their relationships with God (faith) and one another (love) (1:3). He admiringly commends their courage and loyalty to Christ in the face of opposition—not only to them but to other churches as well (1:4). He promises to continue to pray for them, asking for God's affirmation, blessing, strength, and grace, so they may remain firm in their determined witness, and thereby bring honor to both Christ and themselves as his faithful servants (1:11-12).

Think About It: When Jesus returns wrongs will be righted and rewards and punishments meted out. What is your view of the second coming of Christ and the Last Judgment? How do we prepare for the end of history? What would your message be to Christians struggling with opposition or persecution today?

In the verses omitted from this lection (5-10), Paul asserts that the Thessalonians' faithfulness through suffering is proof that God is both good and just and that they are deserving of acceptance into the realm of God. When Jesus returns in glory, wrongs will be righted, rewards and punishments meted out, Paul's teaching vindicated, and scoffers confounded by the wonders of that day. The long-suffering faithful will be given permanent relief from their tribulations, and their persecutors will suffer lasting separation from the loving, uplifting presence of God.

Gospel: Luke 19:1-10

Habakkuk experienced God's grace through a vision of divine deliverance and faithful endurance. The psalmist found it through trust in the reliability and truth of God's word (law). The Thessalonians were promised grace to sustain them in current suffering and reward them through Christ's coming. Now Zacchaeus finds it through Jesus' forgiving look and his own resolve to share.

A Familiar Story

It is a well-known story. Zacchaeus, a rich tax collector in Jericho, who had gained his wealth by cheating the poor, heard that Jesus was coming to town and went down to the main street to get a look at him—whether for purposes of curiosity, criticism, or gnawing need we do not know. From the text it is not clear whether Jesus or Zacchaeus was the one who was short. Zacchaeus climbed a tree to get a better look. As Jesus passed he looked up at him in all his finery, sensed a lost soul, and signaled his intention to visit his home for dinner and serious conversation. The self-righteous townspeople, possibly stirred up by their religious leaders, voiced resentment against Jesus for spending time with one they had written off as a turncoat and a cheat.

Jesus, however, knowing spiritual hunger when he saw it, accepted Zacchaeus and honored his demonstration of penitence by declaring the restoration of genuine Jewish identity to this one who had so wantonly betrayed it. In response, Zacchaeus generously offered to give half his wealth to the poor and to restore his ill-gotten gain to those he had defrauded. What happened between Jesus and Zacchaeus was a fulfillment of Jesus' mission to the lost sheep.

A Host of Learnings

Several aspects of this event deserve closer scrutiny. First, as was his practice in Luke's portrayal, Jesus sought the company of a person whom the majority rejected. Zacchaeus was ostracized because he had become a crony of the Romans, violating the law and the canons of justice by making a tidy living for himself through gouging his countrymen. But Jesus chose to accept, forgive, and help turn his life around. Grace bridges the boundaries of human prejudice and resentment.

Second, salvation for Zacchaeus, while precipitated by Jesus' understanding look and ready acceptance, was not complete until he responded with penitence and a commitment to justice and generosity. He was *saved by* the grace of Jesus, *saved from* a continuing life of self-centered greed, loneliness, and despair, and *saved into* the joy of giving, sharing, and restoration to community. In contrast to the grasping servant in the parable that follows (Luke 19:11-27), Zacchaeus was willing, even eager, to be

349

liberated from a strangling attachment to possessions that was stifling his soul.

Third, the "salvation" Jesus proclaimed was not just to Zacchaeus the individual but to his whole "house"—family, relatives, servants, establishment. All had benefited from his greed and treachery, all had been tainted by affluence and indulgence, all needed redemption and a fresh start. The corrupt network of relationships fostered by their master's exploitative lifestyle was in dire need of revitalization. The transformation Jesus proclaimed was to be thoroughgoing and revolutionary for the whole household. They would never be the same again.

Think About It: As Zacchaeus experienced it, salvation crosses boundaries, requires our participation, involves communities, and fulfills God's eternal purpose. In what ways are you like Zacchaeus? How do you experience salvation? How can you participate in God's redemptive purpose?

Finally, Luke makes this encounter a paradigm for God's redemptive purpose—"to seek out and to save what was lost" (19:10, NIV). God, as manifested in Jesus, is the "hound of heaven" working in the world to seek, find, nudge, invite, corral, welcome, redeem all who have turned their backs on the purpose for which they were intended. In so doing, we are restored to the image of God in which we were created, thereby bringing spiritual renewal and holistic fulfillment to us and to our communities.

Study Suggestions

A. Celebrate God's Grace

Open by singing stanzas 1–3 of "Amazing Grace." Ask: In common parlance, how do we usually think of grace? (Gracious, generous, graceful, elegant, Grace Kelly, Gracie Allen.) What is grace in the religious sense? (God's unmerited favor.) How do you experience this kind of grace? (Invite members to tell of experiences of acceptance, forgiveness, compassion, redemption.) Comment that today's lections speak of grace from four different, yet consistent, angles.

B. Examine the Lections

Form four groups, and assign one lection and its accompanying commentary to each. Ask each group to read its passage and its interpretation, then discuss and be ready to report on the following: (1) Who is the speaker and who is the audience? (2) What were the circumstances being addressed? (3) What is the central message of this passage? Summarize it in one sentence. (4) How is grace being understood and experienced in this passage?

350

C. Share Findings

Reconvene as a total class, and have each group report in turn. Write the one-sentence summaries on chalkboard or posterboard. Then discuss: What does each lection contribute to our understanding of grace? How can our group and congregation better respond to and represent God's grace in our world?

D. Explore Theological Issues

Discuss the questions raised in the "Think About It" boxes. In relation to Habakkuk's question about the suffering of the righteous, explain the historical context of the Babylonian conquest and the impending exile. Note Jeremiah's explanation that the suffering was due to Judah's idolatry and disobedience, and compare it with Habakkuk's promise of God's ultimate vindication and deliverance. Ask: How do we understand why bad things happen to good people? How can we be supportive of one another in times of undeserved and unexplainable suffering?

With regard to the matter of the second coming of Christ and the Last Judgment raised in Second Thessalonians, review the several interpretations mentioned in the "Think About It" box. Invite members to move to different corners of the room according to the explanation they prefer, and discuss there why this view is meaningful to them. Then come back together and have each group share its thinking. Ask: Why was an imminent coming and a decisive judgment important to the Thessalonians in the mid-first century? Ask: How can we accept and affirm one another as brothers and sisters in Christ even though we disagree on matters like the second coming?

The Zacchaeus story poses the question of salvation. Review the four dimensions mentioned in the commentary on pages 349–50, and discuss the issues of crossing boundaries, divine vs. human initiative, and individual vs. communal salvation. Ask: How are we like and unlike Zacchaeus? How do we understand and experience salvation?

E. Celebrate Grace

Refer back to the four small-group statements summarizing the key ideas in today's lections. Note how each is a manifestation of God's grace. Form these into a brief litany, with a leader reading the statements one by one and the group responding after each, "We thank you for your grace, O God." Add to these this final statement, "For the sense of acceptance and support we find in this group, . . . We thank you for your grace, O God." Close by singing the last three stanzas of "Amazing Grace."

Lections for All Saints (November 1, or may be used on first Sunday in November)

Old Testament: Daniel 7:1-3, 15-18

CHAPTERS 1–6 of Daniel are stories set in the Babylonian and Persian courts, told in the third person, and seem like romantic fiction, while Chapters 7–12 are apocalyptic oracles narrated in the first person.

Stories and Vision

Daniel is composed of six stories and four visions and represents the only apocalyptic (end-time) book in the Old Testament, though other apocryphal apocalyptic writings appeared in the same time period (second and first centuries B.C.) of social turmoil and distress. They seek to interpret current events through signs and symbols that predict an end to tribulation and a coming time of vindication and tranquility. The authors are anonymous, but present their thought in the name of ancient well-known figures like Enoch, Noah, or Abraham. The name of Daniel, or Danel, is mentioned both in Ezekiel 14:14; 28:3, and in North Canaanite clay tablets found by archaeologists at Ras Shamra.

The author was a pious Jew living under the oppression of the Hellenistic king, Antiochus Epiphanes IV in 167–164 B.C. The stories in Chapters 1–6, purportedly set in Babylon in earlier times just before and after the Persian triumph. Antiochus Epiphanes intensified the Seleucid persecution of the Jews and defiled the Temple at Jerusalem by conducting worship of Zeus and other Greek gods. The writer of Daniel sought to encourage his people to stand firm against such evils and remain loyal to YHWH at all costs.

These stories, however, present a number of historical problems. The transformation of Nebuchadnezzar into a beast described in Chapter 4 can be traced to an event in the life of Nabonidus, the last Babylonian king. Chapter 5 has Belshazzar as king of Babylon at the time of its fall, even though he was never king. Chapter 6 mentions an unhistorical Darius the Mede as the conqueror of Babylon, although it was only the later Persian kings who were named Darius. These inaccuracies suggest that these stories must have been written long after the Babylonian Exile by persons who had no clear memory of the actual events—even though they present inspiring examples of courage and devotion.

In contrast to the narrative style and past-orientation of the first half of the book, Chapters 7–12 draw on symbolic, apocalyptic imagery, focus on the future, and describe the actions of God that are soon to take place. Thus, just as God has been faithful in the past, so the persecuted faithful can count on coming divine action to conquer evil and save believers from destruction.

The first vision, the dream of the four beasts (7:1-28), is the source of much of the imagery in subsequent apocalyptic works, including the thought of Jesus recorded in the Synoptic Gospels and in the Book of Revelation. It speaks of the four empires (verses 1-8), the judgment of God (verses 9-12), the Son of Man (verses 13-14), and the coming rule of the saints (verses 15-28). The four beasts represent past temporal kingdoms that have all fallen to make way for the triumph of the coming reign of God.

The Reign of the Saints

In the first of the two brief excerpts chosen for All Saints Day (7:1-3), Daniel is depicted in bed dreaming, then arising to record his vision of the four beasts blown up out of the sea (traditional symbol of chaos; see Isaiah 51:9-10; 27:1; Job 26:12; Revelation 13:1) by the four winds (representing the power of God's Spirit coming from all four directions). In the second (7:15-18), Daniel gets a headache from all he has seen, which is only cured by the explanation that the four beasts are kings who have reigned on earth and then fallen, while the "holy ones of the Most High" (the saints, the faithful) are to be honored and eternally blessed in the coming reign of God.

> **Think About It:** Daniel's apocalyptic visions gave hope to the faithful. What is our source of hope when things look bleak?

Psalter: Psalm 149

The saints are here called to "sing a new song" of joy and praise, complete with dancing, the melody of stringed instruments, and the beat of percussion instruments. Just as God delights in the faithful (verse 4), so they are invited to rejoice in their Maker (verse 2). The "assembly of the faithful" (verse 1) probably refers to the gathering for Temple worship.

The rejoicing is not only in the glory of God, but also in the defeat of enemies and oppressors (verses 6-9), a vengeful attitude that is humanly understandable but morally inferior to the universalistic tone of much of the
prophetic literature, and the forgiving, compassionate utterances of Jesus on
the cross.

Epistle: Ephesians 1:11-23

Whether Ephesians was written by Paul or later by one of his disciples, it
clearly conveys a Pauline message, has Pauline roots, and is similar in emphasis to Colossians. There are no specific references or addresses to persons in
the church at Ephesus, which suggests that it may be a general letter to all
recently converted Gentiles. The letter lifts up the grace of God as the source
of strength for all the faithful, that is, the saints.

Unity

The overall theme of the Epistle is unity—the unity of all creation in Christ
(Chapter 1), the unity of Jew and Gentile in the church (Chapter 2), the unity
of believers in the body of Christ (Chapter 3), the unity of leadership gifts to
"equip the saints" and of all believers in mutuality and good will as "members of one another" in the body of Christ (Chapter 4), and the unity of
upright living, family harmony, and social responsibility (Chapters 5 and 6).

Identity

In today's passage the writer tells the Ephesians that they, who have
inherited the gift of salvation as part of God's eternal plan, and thereby
have found hope in Christ, are called in response to serve God's purpose
and praise God's glory (verses 11-12). Because they have heard and
responded to the gospel, they have, thankfully, been imprinted with a spiritual identity as people of God (verses 13-14). This is evidenced by both
their exemplary faith and their devoted care for one another, news of
which has reached the writer, and for which he is deeply grateful to God
(verses 14-15a).

The writer prays for them regularly, asking that God will give them spiritual insight, knowledge, hope, and awareness of how blessed they are as the
saints of God to have the power of the Spirit available to them (verses 15b-
19). This is the same power that God used to raise Christ from the dead and
give him authority over all humanity and history, both now and in all time
to come (verses 20-21). This awesome power is shared with the church,
Christ's body, which brings both great opportunity and awesome responsibility (verses 22-23).

Intentionality

As members of the body of which Christ is the head, the community of saints is re-created by its communion with him. Christ is found wherever people suffer—in the gutter, on the battlefield, in a demolished or broken home, in the ghetto, in both abused and the abuser, both oppressed and oppressor, both pauper and president. And it is here that the saints, members of the body of Christ, must go with intentionality, in company with the One who died that all might live.

> **Think About It:** The church, Christ's body, is given both power and responsibility. Does your church have a sense of its power? What does the way Christ used his body (offered it in death) imply about the vocation of the church as body of Christ?

Gospel: Luke 6:20-31

Sainthood is discipleship. Members of the body of Christ are called to live the cruciform life. Luke's "sermon on the plain" (so-called, in contrast to Matthew's "Sermon on the Mount" [Matthew 5–7] because of the reference in Luke 6:17 to Jesus standing on a level place) makes this very "plain"! But location is not the only difference between Matthew's and Luke's versions of the Beatitudes. Luke has fewer (four instead of nine); he parallels blessings with woes; his are briefer and offer less interpretation; he stresses material rather than spiritual need (blessing the poor and hungry not the spiritually deprived). Luke has Jesus speaking directly to his hearers ("blessed are you;" "woe to you"—in contrast to Matthew's more impersonal use of the third person).

Blessings and Woes

The blessings and woes are concrete and to the point. Specifically, the materially poor are promised admission to the realm of God (verse 20), while the rich have already gotten all that is coming to them (verse 24). The justice of God will provide means for the hungry to be fed (verse 21a); but the affluent and content face a time of want and deprivation (verse 25a). Those made distraught by sadness and grief will have cause for rejoicing (verse 21b), while those enjoying life now will be brought low and made to weep (verse 25b).

Those now scorned and rejected by polite society because of their love and loyalty to him who is fully human (Jesus' self-identification as the Messiah)—even as the prophets of old were repudiated and mocked—will surely be elevated and honored in the reign of God (verses 22-23). But those who are high and mighty now—recipients of awards and adulation—are likened to the fawning courtiers and unreliable advisors of the weak kings in Israel's history who led their people to doom and oblivion (verse 26). In the coming Great Reversal, the present celebrities will lose out and be forgotten, while today's rejects will become tomorrow's saints.

The Standards of Sainthood

Jesus sets the standards of sainthood high. Not only family and friends but enemies are to be loved (respected as persons of dignity and worth; verse 27). Curses must evoke blessings; mistreatment calls for prayers of concern (verse 28). A nonviolent but self-respecting response to the backhanded slap of contempt can be made by offering the other cheek. An unjust demand for one's outer garment as surety for an unpayable debt can be met by quietly but defiantly removing one's inner garment as well, thereby shaming the greedy creditor by standing naked before him (verse 29). The beggar's request calls for generosity; unjust theft and extortion must not be difnified or reinforced by self-demeaning groveling (verse 30). The saintly life is summarized in the golden rule—treat others as you would like to be treated, with dignity, respect, justice, and generosity (verse 31).

> **Think About It:** Whom do you know who embodies some of these qualities? What is the source of their dignity and compassion?

Study Suggestions

A. Affirm the Saints

Open by noting that we today celebrate All Saints Day. Sing "I Sing a Song of the Saints of God." Ask members to name aloud or in their hearts the saints (ordinary believers, special people, giants of faith) who have touched their lives and have gone to their reward. After each is named, voice the corporate response, "Praise God for . . . (person's name)." State that today's lections are chosen to commemorate this special occasion in the church year.

B. Struggle With Daniel

Read Daniel 7:1-3, 15-18 aloud. Explain the background (pages 352–53): the historical background, the meaning and significance of apocalyptic literature, the two contrasting yet complementary parts of the book, the historical inaccuracies, the need for this message of hope, and the interpretation of the vision of the four beasts. Stress the promise to the saints, the "holy ones of the Most High." Discuss the questions in the "Think About It" box having to do with the need for and relevance of an apocalyptic message for today.

C. Explore the Unity in Ephesians

After drawing on the commentary on pages 354–55 to explain the authorship and overall message of Ephesians, have members open their Bibles and look for the dimensions of the unity theme in each of the six chapters. Read aloud 1:11-23; and highlight the message to the saints, in terms of unity, identity, and intentionality. Then focus on the "Think About It" questions relative to being the body of Christ by giving oneself as Jesus did to the vocation of sainthood as service.

D. Hear the Blessings and Woes

Ask two persons to read aloud the blessings and woes in Luke's version of the Beatitudes by alternating the contrasting blessing and woe on each of the four subjects (verses 20-26). Do this three times, pausing several minutes after each reading to allow persons to jot down whatever thoughts or feelings come to mind. Invite participants to share and discuss their responses. Now read the Beatitudes in Matthew (5:3-12); note and discuss the differences. Read the paragraph describing the contrasts between Luke's sermon on the plain and Matthew's Sermon on the Mount (page 355). Ask: Which version is most meaningful to you? Which is most needed by church and society today?

E. Encounter the Standards of Sainthood

Next read Luke 6:27-31 one by one, following each with the interpretation given on page 356. Ask: How does this interpretation compare with the one you have usually heard? Form five groups, and assign each group to paraphrase one of these five verses, following three guidelines: (1) Use as few of the original words as possible. (2) Be faithful to the original intent. (3) Make it relevant to the needs of our people. Reassemble, share the paraphrases, evaluate them in terms of the three criteria, and compare them with the interpretation given on page 355. Discuss: What is Jesus really asking of us here? How can we live up to these demands? Where is grace? Also explore the "Think About It" questions.

F. Draw Things Together

Review the perspectives on sainthood offered by each of the three main lections: the promise of future reward for present suffering in Daniel; the divine plan for unity, the imprinting of spiritual identity, and the call for intentional servanthood among members of the body of Christ in Ephesians; and the expectation of treating others as we would like to be treated in Luke. Ask: What are the different understandings of sainthood in these lections? What is your definition of *sainthood*? What synonym would you use to describe a faithful believer?

G. Raise Saintly Voices

Read Psalm 149:6-9, and discuss the moral shortcomings of the vengeful attitude it expresses. Then stand and read verses 1-5a in unison as an expression of praise and celebration of the assembly of saints. Close by singing "For All the Saints Who from Their Labors Rest," then offering a prayer of gratitude for the witness of those who have gone before, the blessings God bestows on saints like us, and the challenge to live like saints in response to Jesus' call to faithful discipleship.

Lections for Sunday Between
November 6 and 12

H Old Testament: Haggai 1:5b–2:9

*H*AGGAI and Zechariah commenced the third period of Hebrew prophecy. The prophets of the first period, prior to the Exile, proclaimed that YHWH would judge Israel and Judah for their unfaithfulness. When this came to pass in the Exile, the next generation of prophets offered encouragement and hope of a return. Once this took place, the third wave of prophets sought to motivate their people to adhere closely to God's law. On the material level, Haggai and Zechariah were successful in persuading the leaders, Zerubbabel and Joshua, to resume building the Temple. But their greater challenge was a spiritual one—to imbue a sense of hope and confidence in the remnant that lived in a desolate Jerusalem and struggled to restore the glories of old.

After functioning as a prophet among the exiles, Haggai returned with Zerubbabel (Ezra 2:2). When the Persian king Cyrus first gave permission in 538 A.D., Sheshbazzar, a Judahite prince, led a small group back to Palestine to begin the rebuilding task (Ezra 1:5-11). But not much progress had been made, for when Haggai arrived he upbraided the people for devoting their energies to rebuilding their own homes rather than the house of YHWH (Haggai 1:4, 9). What they did was understandable since everything had been demolished; rubble was everywhere, the land had not been cultivated, they were plagued by drought and hostile neighbors, and mere survival was the foremost need.

Haggai's Four Prophecies

The priority of Haggai and Zechariah was to motivate their people to begin work on the Temple and then to see it through to completion. Four of Haggai's dated prophecies are recorded in his book: (1) YHWH's demand that the governor, high priest, and people commence the Temple reconstruction, and their response (1:1-15, today's lection; August–September, 520 B.C.); (2) YHWH's assurances that the future Temple would be a thing of beauty and grandeur (2:1-9, today's lection; October, 520); (3) YHWH's concern about ritual impurities that would be held against the people and sully their future (2:10-19; December, 520); and (4) a prophecy of the emergence of Zerubbabel as messianic ruler (2:20-23; December, 520). These were all based on Haggai's abiding concern for the centrality of Temple worship in the life of the faith community. He preached that, if they would put God first, their fortunes would change and the messianic age would soon be upon them. YHWH would channel the wealth of neighboring nations into their coffers, providing resources to erect a temple more elegant than even that of Solomon (2:6-9).

When the people complained that the emerging temple was looking shabby compared to their memory of the glory of that of Solomon (a memory that had likely grown in grandeur through frequent retelling), Haggai assured them that YHWH would embellish its features in years to come.

Haggai's Central Message

Haggai's central message was: Give God priority and a grand future awaits you, regardless of past wrongdoing and misfortune. His stress on putting God first and his condemnation of selfish materialism are of timeless value. But his assurance that God-centeredness would bring material good fortune was belied by righteous people's actual experience of undeserved suffering, an issue raised previously by Habakkuk (see lection for two weeks ago).

> **Think About It:** In what ways can we put God first in our lives? What is today's equivalent of building God's house?

Epistle: 2 Thessalonians 2:1-5, 13-17

The first of these passages reveals the purpose of the entire letter. It is hard to understand because it seems unconnected to previous and subsequent verses and because the terms of the argument are unclear to persons unfamiliar with the first-century dispute about the time of the end. The problem is posed in verses 1-2:.

The "coming" refers to Christ's return (see 1 Thessalonians 4:13-18); "our assembling to meet him" applies to the Christian community a common apocalyptic belief that the Jews of the Diaspora would all be gathered together in the end time (see 2 Maccabees 2:7). But Paul's adversaries had been teaching, not that "the day of the Lord is near" as he believed, but rather that it "is already here." This is what we today might call "realized eschatology"—

that Christian hope has been fulfilled and we are already living under the reign of God. It is true Paul taught that salvation had already been made available through Christ's death and resurrection. He also asserted that the complete redemption of history and creation and the full establishment of God's reign were still to come. This is the tension we still feel between the "already" of Christ's first advent and the "not yet" of his second.

A Crucial Issue

The idea that this tension had been resolved was the product of first-century gnosticism, which claimed that full salvation was available through a mystical knowledge of a small in-group of believers gained through participation in the "mysteries." The stakes in this debate were huge. Was Jesus the Lord of the cosmos and history, or merely of a select group of saved souls? Was the gospel about the future redemption of the entire universe or only the rescue of individual believers? Was God moving history toward a momentous final consummation, or simply plucking the elect out of a maelstrom of worldly evil?

> **Think About It:** Is Jesus the Lord of the cosmos and history or merely of a few saved souls? How do you see God working in individual hearts and lives? in the events of history?

Two Prerequisite Events

Paul makes his rebuttal to the gnostic argument in verses 3-5. Paul contends that the end has not yet arrived because the two events that must first occur have not yet happened—the "rebellion" and the exposure of the "lawless one . . . destined for destruction." In apocalyptic teaching, the "rebellion" referred to a repeat of the revolt of the angels prior to Creation and was interpreted to mean an overall uprising against religion by the forces opposed to God that would take place prior to the final cataclysm (see 2 Timothy 3:5; Revelation 13:3-4).

The "lawless one" is another name for the antichrist. (See 1 John 2:18, 22; 4:3; and Revelation 13, which calls him "the beast.") As the ultimate in idolatry, he would set himself up in God's place and seek to draw people to follow and serve him. This extreme act of rebellion would look like the eclipse of God's sovereignty, and only after this occurred would God reassert the divine authority and carry out a complete and terrible triumph over the forces of evil.

Cordial Encouragement

The second passage (verses 13-17) marks an abrupt change from the foregoing apocalyptic discourse. In verse 13, in the congenial spirit of 1:3, Paul thanks God for his readers, "brothers and sisters, beloved in the Lord." They are some of his first converts, called by God through his preaching to find salvation in Christ and receive the heavenly reward (verses 14-15). To that end Paul urges them to remain faithful to the doctrinal and moral standards he had taught them and to support one another in the faith with both words of encouragement and acts of love (verses 16-17).

Gospel: Luke 20:27-38

This passage records one of the times when Jesus' understanding of the law astonished the religious leaders, multitudes, and disciples. Questions about resurrection were prevalent before Jesus' death. Mosaic law did not overtly mention resurrection, and many of the laws with their detailed interpretations had become quite complex. Raising questions about interpretation of the law was not unusual. Jesus' opponents often sought to trap him into an erroneous interpretation. The Sadducees, in their only appearance in Luke, posed a question here and were skillfully outmaneuvered by Jesus' mastery of the law.

The Sadducees
The Sadducees' most pressing issue was the question of resurrection, on which they disagreed with the Pharisees. The Sadducees did not believe in resurrection; yet they raised a question about it, combining it with the concept of levirate marriage. Their aim was not only to push Jesus on a question of the law but also to make the concept of resurrection seem ridiculous. In typical fashion, Jesus turned their question upside down.

Levirate Marriage
The law on levirate marriage assumed that one would live on through one's descendants and that a man's lineage could be preserved through his brothers. If a married man died childless, his brother was compelled to take the widow as his wife and to produce children, with the first-born son regarded as the legal heir of the first husband. There were strong social sanctions against a brother-in-law who refused to take the widow as his wife (Deuteronomy 25:5-10).

The Contest
Aligned with the priestly and aristocratic classes, the Sadducees had social authority and prestige. In contrast to the Pharisees, they did not believe in angels, rejected the oral traditions of the law, and debated the prophetic writings. Their argument here may have been as much with the Pharisees as with Jesus. This contest hinged not only on beliefs about the law but also on authority. Who was to be believed? Jesus' response to the Sadducees made use of their disbelief in angels.

The Response

Jesus addressed the first two issues (angels and resurrection) by correcting the notion of what life after death is. Life after death, he said, is not the same as in the present age. The resurrected are like angels, and the idea of marriage is irrelevant; indeed the very idea of death is irrelevant. Those who do not die have no need of marriage nor of continuing their family line.

Then, Jesus used a typical form of rabbinic argument to refute the rest of the Sadducees' argument. He based the idea of resurrection on the Torah by recalling the revelation of God in the burning bush. God was the Lord of Abraham, Isaac, and Jacob, the God of the living, not the dead. By asserting that these famous forebears were alive, Jesus invoked the names of some of the most authoritative and revered persons in Jewish tradition to support his comments on resurrection and to confound his critics.

Think About It: Jesus confounded his critics through his interpretation of Scripture. How can you deepen your knowledge of Scripture as a foundation for your faith and witness?

Psalter: Psalm 145:1-5, 17-21

This is a personal hymn to be sung as a solo in the congregation. That it is one of the later psalms is indicated by its use of Aramaic and its emphasis on the reign of God. The psalm opens with a lengthy introduction (verses 1-7) extolling the profound greatness of YHWH and urging successive generations to praise God's awesome grandeur, mighty deeds, and superb justice and holiness. The magnificent qualities of YHWH are expanded in verses 8-9 to include graciousness, compassion, forbearance, mercy, and steadfast love.

Verses 10-12 add to praise of God's nature and deeds the element of God's everlasting reign. This theme, which developed in late Jewish tradition and was pivotal in the teachings of Jesus, is then expounded in verses 13-19 as the psalm's central message. In God's realm all creatures are sustained and provided for (verses 14-16), God is responsive to the needs of all who seek him (verses 17-19). God protects the faithful but crushes those who reject his ways (verse 20). In the summation (verse 21), the psalmist returns to the first person with which he began, expressing the hope that his individual song of praise will evoke an equally adoring and long-lasting response from the entire creation.

Study Suggestions

A. Posing the Issues

Introduce the session by stating that the three main lections, while not dealing with common themes, all involve controversy. Haggai urged his people to put building God's house ahead of their personal comfort and security. Paul in Second Thessalonians contended against gnostic teaching in advocating for an apocalyptic view of the end times. Jesus refuted the Sadducees' arguments against the resurrection with his superior knowledge of Jewish law and tradition. Only in the psalm is controversy overcome in a lofty song of praise for God's grandeur, goodness, and everlasting reign.

B. Putting God First

Note Haggai's postexilic historical setting, four prophecies, central message, and dubious promise of material reward for faithfulness. For discussing the first issue regarding religious versus personal priorities, explain the extenuating circumstances that led the returnees to give priority to securing their own homes. Ask: How do we decide how much of our time, energy, and resources to devote to God and how much to spend on ourselves, our families, personal comfort, and future security?

Regarding the second issue on rewards, explore the questions in the "Think About It" box, plus the following: What is our motivation for choosing to serve God? What place do anticipated rewards play in this decision? Why might loyalty to God sometimes bring unfortunate results?

C. Is It Already or Not Yet?

Read aloud 2 Thessalonians 2:1-5. Explain apocalyptic teaching, drawing on the commentary on pages 359–61. What effect has the two-thousand–year delay in Christ's return had on the importance with which this issue is viewed today? What do you believe about the second coming of Christ and the Last Judgment? How does this belief influence your day-to-day life and behavior?

D. Discussing Marriage and the Resurrection

Read Luke 2:27-38, review the commentary on pages 361–62, and explain the issues on which Jesus disagreed with the Sadducees and how he handled them. Ask: How can we make discussions about biblical interpretation constructive rather than divisive? How can our congregation better equip us with biblical understanding as a foundation for our faith?

E. Affirming Christian Unity

Open Bibles to Psalm 145. Explain that this is a song of praise composed as a solo for congregational worship to highlight the glorious reign of the sovereign God. Read verses 1-3 and 21 in unison. Sing the hymn "Glorious Things of Thee Are Spoken." Close with sentence prayers giving thanks for the unity in Christ that enables us to accept and affirm one another as brothers and sisters in the midst of controversy and disagreement.

Lections for Sunday Between November 13 and 19

Old Testament: Isaiah 65:17-25

CHAPTERS 56–66 are usually referred to as Third Isaiah and come out of the period of exile in Babylon, roughly 586–520 B.C. Isaiah 65 is a composite unit and must be seen as a whole. In verses 1-7, the prophet pronounces YHWH's judgment upon a people that continue to be unfaithful, even in exile. But in verses 8-10, redeeming virtue is found among God's servants; and for this reason the hand of judgment will be stayed and future blessing is promised. However, says the prophet in verses 11-12, the people should not become complacent, for fearsome destruction will fall on those who have forsaken YHWH and gone over to the worship of Fortune and Destiny (in Hebrew, *Gad* and *Meni,* the Syrian gods of fate).

The contrast between the fate of the faithful and the destiny of those who turn their backs on YHWH will be sharp and awful to behold (verses 13-15)—plentiful food versus the pangs of hunger, water to drink versus the agony of thirst, smiles of joy versus the shadow of shame, happy versus tormented hearts, names of curse versus identities of blessing. This time of division and antagonism is sure to end; the messianic age will dawn, in which these calamities will be put in the past, and both those who bless (offer benefit) and those who swear (attest to truth) will do so only in the name and by the power of YHWH the faithful (verse 16). This verse sets the stage for the messianic vision to follow (verses 25, today's lection), which is the climax of the chapter and the culmination of the whole book.

New Heavens and a New Earth

This passage, depicting God's coming creation of the new heavens and new earth, is a repetition and expansion of Chapters 60–62. Its grandeur will cause all that has gone before, both comfort and misery, both conquest and defeat, to pale into insignificance and be forgotten (verse 17). God will bring into being a new Jerusalem (Holy City, paradise, ideal realm), which will bring gladness and joy to all its inhabitants (verse 18). The people's contentment and the banishment of tribulation and grief will bring pleasure to God as well (verse 19). Infant mortality will be a thing of the past, and good health will extend long into the golden years as well (verse 20).

Violence Replaced by Shalom

A sense of permanence and contentment will prevail, as those who build and plant will be free from the fear of exploitation and invasion and will be assured of being able to live to enjoy the fruits of their labors (verses 21-22a). Life will be as stable as a deeply rooted tree, and work will be both profitable and fulfilling (verse 22b). Laborers will be confident that their efforts are appreciated and rewarded, and women will be able to bear children in the assurance that they can grow to maturity in a climate of peace and justice (verse 23a). God's blessing will be felt and God's purpose assured for all time (verse 23b). A sense of the divine presence will prevail and all will be in direct communion with God (verse 24). Harmony will replace aggression in the natural world, although for some reason snakes are singled out for continued abhorrence (verse 25a). In sum, YHWH says, the reign of violence and destruction will come to an end, as the realm of shalom and justice for all is established.

> **Think About It:** God through Isaiah promises "new heavens and a new earth." How do you think this will come about? How can we create "small spaces" of shalom in the interim while we pray and wait for the ultimate culmination of God's purpose?

This depiction of an ideal realm, similar to those found in Genesis 2, Isaiah 2:1-4, and Isaiah 11:6-9, portrays the prophet's idea of the kind of world God intends. The creative power of God is devoted not only to forming a physical universe, but to shaping a just and harmonious human society as well.

Psalter: Psalm 118

This psalm is bracketed front and back by a stirring affirmation: "O give thanks to the LORD, for [God] is good; / [God's] steadfast love [Hebrew: *hesed*] endures forever!" The testimony of the individual in verses 5-18 and the witness of the congregation in verses 22-25 make the psalm a thanksgiving hymn for any who have lost much and feel they have nowhere to turn. God can been depended on (verse 14); life and hope are still possible (verses 17-18); the open gates of goodness still beckon (verses 19-20); prayers are being answered (verse 21); rejection is reversed (verse 22); salvation and success are still possible (verses 21, 25). The bountiful goodness of God is dramatized in the Temple procession right up to the Holy of Holies, in which the representative of YHWH pronounces a benediction upon all who worship (verses 26-27). The psalmist feels God's presence in a very personal way ("you are my God") and offers praise for this close communion (verse 28).

Verses 19-20, referring to the righteous entering the open gates, are sometimes related to Jesus' triumphal entry into Jerusalem on Palm Sunday. The phrase "save us" (Hebrew: *Hoshianna*, Hosanna) in verse 25 is taken up as a refrain by the Palm Sunday crowds, as reported in Matthew 21:9. The mention of the rejected stone becoming the chief cornerstone is interpreted by several New Testament writers (Matthew 21:42; Acts 4:11; 1 Peter 2:7) as an allusion to the rejected Jesus being acclaimed as messiah and sovereign of all.

Epistle: 2 Thessalonians 3:6-13

Having first dealt with the crucial doctrinal issue of apocalypticism versus gnosticism, Paul now turns to a practical problem. It appears that in anticipation of Christ's early return, some Thessalonians had stopped working just to wait and were depending on others to support them. While ministering among them, Paul had set a diligent example of working hard to pay his own way and not be a burden (verses 7-8). Though he might have pulled rank or presumed on their hospitality, he had been very careful to model responsible behavior (verse 9). Because we cannot know the time or season of Christ's second coming, he is saying, we must continue living honorably day by day right up to the last moment. Every member of the body of Christ must pull his or her own weight.

Work or Starve

These indolent believers had missed the point. Like some later-day enthusiasts who have mistakenly set the date of Christ's return, quit their jobs, sold their possessions, and retired to some mountaintop to wait, these misguided Thessalonians had become a hindrance to mutuality and community. So Paul recommends ostracism (verse 6). Avoid them, shut them out, force them to work or starve. If they will not work they do not deserve to be fed (verse 10).

Never Tire of Well-Doing

Following this advice to the leaders of the congregation, Paul then turns to address the idlers themselves: You are no longer constructively busy, but have become mere busybodies, he tells them (verse 11). You are constantly flapping your wings but never taking off. You pretend to make a contribution, but have actually become a drag. I both order and urge you, by the authority of Jesus Christ, to stop talking and start producing. Then to the whole congregation he concludes, "never tire of doing what is right" (verse 13). Once we start slacking off, we send the wrong signal both to our fellow believers and to the watching world. The faithful Christian must exhibit ongoing, unflagging devotion to loving service, regardless of opposition, temptation, or the notion of some that because the goal has already been achieved we are free to let up and coast.

> **Think About It:** "Never tire of doing what is right." What are some present-day parallels to the lazy Thessalonians? When do you feel tempted to tire of doing what is right? How can we support one another in the effort to "keep on keeping on"?

Gospel: Luke 21:5-19

Luke's version of Jesus' apocalyptic discourse (which actually extends through 21:36) is based primarily on Mark 13:1-37 (see also Matthew 24:1-44). There are some differences, however. Jesus' remarks are evoked by the comments of "some" (verse 5), not the disciples. The location for this discourse—and for all Jesus' teachings in Jerusalem—is the public setting of the Temple (verses 5-7, 37-38), not the Mount of Olives to which he retired at night and where private conversations with the disciples could take place (verse 37). In Luke, the teaching about the Parousia (second coming) had already been dealt with in 17:20-37; so this passage is restricted to the fall of Jerusalem and destruction of the Temple.

Reading the Signs

Hearing bystanders admiring the Temple's splendor and the generosity of people's offerings, Jesus seized the opportunity to predict its coming downfall. Shocked, his hearers asked two questions: when? and what signs? (verses 5-7). Four kinds of signs are mentioned: impostors claiming to be the Messiah and to know the precise time, wars and rebellions, natural disasters, and fearsome supernatural warnings (verses 8-11). But these are not sure indicators and can easily be misread.

A Time of Testing

More important for Jesus' followers is the time of testing they will face, in which faithful, courageous witness will be necessary (verses 12-19). Here Luke goes beyond Jesus' conversation on the Temple steps and speaks directly to the church decades later. Christians are being detained and harassed. They are being arraigned in synagogue hearings (see Acts 4-5), put in prison (Acts 16), and hauled before rulers (Acts 24-26).

Such situations gave them an opportunity to bear witness to their faith. They need not worry about what they will say, for the Spirit will direct their

Think About It: More important is the time of testing they will face. As the Scripture references in parentheses indicate, all these things did happen to the early Christians. How do you think you would have measured up to these tests? What kinds of tests has your faith faced? How can we support one another in times of testing?

minds and mouths (see Luke 21:15; 12:11-12) in persuasive ways (Acts 4:8-13; 6:10). They will be called upon to face enmity, treachery by family, friends, and relatives, and even death. Verses 16 and 18 are apparently contradictory. Taken together, perhaps they mean that some will perish, but God will preserve the saints. Or, the reference to not a hair being harmed in verse 18 may be taken as a metaphor for a spiritual triumph over physical suffering and death. This interpretation is supported by verse 19, which promises that courage and stamina will preserve one's spiritual integrity. Faithfulness insures everlasting life.

In the remainder of the discourse, Jesus speaks of the destruction of Jerusalem (verses 20-24), global turmoil followed by the coming of the Son of Man in the clouds (verses 25-28), the parable of a sprouting fig tree as a parallel to the certainty of the signs leading to an imminent end (verses 29-31), the assurance that these things will occur while the hearers are still living (verses 32-33), and the warning to keep vigilant and pray for strength to endure (verses 34-36). Such watchfulness and reliance on God will help guard against indifference, self-centeredness, and spiritual neglect on the one hand, and anxiety and overzealousness on the other hand, thereby equipping the faithful both for effective witness and to face God in the coming Parousia.

The chapter concludes by describing Jesus' habit of spending his days teaching in the Temple and his nights at rest on the Mount of Olives, thereby bringing to an end his public ministry and pointing toward his passion and death in the days to come (verses 37-38).

Study Suggestions

A. Celebrate God's Steadfast Love

Ask the group to memorize the first verse from Psalm 118. Then divide the group in half and read this entire hymn of thanksgiving antiphonally. Sing the chorus, "This Is the Day," which is based on Psalm 118:24. Summarize the interpretation of the psalm (pages 365–66), with particular reference to the messianic allusions.

B. Response to Isaiah's Vision

Ask three members to read aloud Isaiah 65:17-25 from three different translations of the Bible. Allow a lengthy pause after each reading for persons to reflect and record thoughts and feelings evoked by the readings. Form groups of three to share these responses. Then ask each group to together create a "statue" with their bodies, depicting nonverbally their conception of Isaiah's vision of the new heaven and earth. Invite each triad to portray their vision, then call for brief responses from the group. Next, discuss the significance of this experience, review the commentary on the passage (pages 364–65), and examine the "Think About It" questions, with particular reference to our responsibility while praying and waiting for the vision to be realized.

C. Motivation for Keeping On

Set the context for discussing 2 Thessalonians 3:6-13 by describing how tempting it must have been for persons convinced that the end was nigh to relax and coast in. Ask members to mention some things that compete with faihful discipleship and list them on chalkboard or a large sheet of paper. Ask: What do you think of Paul's advice for dealing with the "idlers"? What help do we need to "keep on keeping on"?

D. Exploring Jesus' Apocalyptic Discourse

Read Luke 21:5-19 and the commentary on pages 367–68. Refer to explanations of *apocalypticism* in previous sessions. Ask: Why do you think apocalypticism was so strong in the time of Jesus? Look up the Scripture references in parentheses to show how the types of testing Luke mentions actually took place in the early church. Ask: How are we tested today? What opportunities does this give for witness? How can we help one another to become more faithful witnesses?

Invite members to roleplay one or more of the testing situations to experience how these may be turned into opportunities for witness.

After each roleplay, debrief with these questions: How did you feel in your role? How did you feel toward one another? How did you respond to the attempt at witness? What might be said or done differently? How will this discussion and experience influence your response to future times of testing and opportunities for witness?

E. Summarize and Pray

Review the themes emphasized in today's lections: celebration of God's faithfulness, vision and hope in God's future, approaching times of testing with courage and hard work, rejoicing in the strength of God in the midst of trouble, attitudes, and responses to the end times. Ask: What light has our study of these Scriptures shed on understanding and committing to the life of discipleship?

Close by joining hands in a circle, offering brief prayers for strength to keep on, pursue the vision, and make a faithful witness in times of testing. Then recite the verse from the psalm that was memorized at the beginning of the session.

Lections for Reign of Christ, Sunday Between November 20 and 26

T Old Testament: Jeremiah 23:1-6

*T*HIS lection is the concluding portion of a longer literary unit in Jeremiah (21:1–23:8) dealing with the kings of Judah around the unifying theme of justice and righteousness as the standard for royal behavior (21:12; 22:3, 13-17; 23:56; see Psalm 72). As such it is an appropriate choice for Reign of Christ (Christ the King) Sunday. It begins with Jeremiah's prose sermon in response to Zedekiah (21:1-10; see the similar narrative in Jeremiah 37 and 38). Zedekiah had sent messengers to ask Jeremiah to plead with YHWH to spare Jerusalem. Jeremiah replied that it was too late—because of their disobedience the city would be destroyed (21:10; 37:10). They had only two choices left: stay in the city and die or go out and surrender.

A Series of Oracles
The remainder of this section is a series of oracles. These start out with an overall pronouncement of judgment against the Judahite monarchy (house of David; 21:11–22:9), containing two parallel condemnations. The first, in poetry, is critical of persons who gain a false sense of security from the belief that YHWH will not let the nation fall (21:13). The second, in prose, draws on the Deuteronomistic interpretation that the punishment is a direct result of the people's betrayal of their covenant with YHWH (22:8-9).

The oracles then move from general condemnation of the monarchy to treatment of the sins of specific kings in Judah's recent history—Jehoahaz (22:10-12), Jehoiakim (22:13-19), and Jehoiachin (22:24-30). This sequence is interrupted in 22:20-23 by a general lament—issued from the vantage point of the high mountain peaks of Lebanon—over the impending destruction and suffering of Jerusalem, the betrayal and defeat of supposed allies ("lovers"), and the scattering of its leaders ("shepherds") to the winds.

370

The Kings as Shepherds

Finally, following all this talk of punishment and disaster, the unit concludes on a hopeful note—the prophecy in today's lection (23:1-8)—of the eventual end of desolation, return from exile, and reprieve and restoration of the Davidic line ("Branch," see Isaiah 11:1; Zechariah 6:12). That the kings are referred to as shepherds is an indication that their primary responsibility was to protect, nurture, and care for their people (sheep), a duty that they had grievously betrayed and for which YHWH would punish them (verses 1-2).

> *Think About It:* The kings are called shepherds, whose duty is to care for their people. How are the "sheep" faring under present-day "shepherds"? How might the church assume the prophetic role of calling them to account?

Then YHWH (the great, good shepherd), would take over, restore and protect them, provide new, conscientious rulers, and guarantee their safety and productivity (verses 3-4). The new ruler in the Davidic line would be a true king (see Isaiah 9:2-7) and not a mere puppet of a foreign power like Zedekiah (whose names means "YHWH is my righteousness"). He would be given the name "The Lord is our Righteousness" (a pointed and unmistakable reference to the hypocrisy of Zedekiah). This restoration from exile by YHWH would be just as memorable as the liberation from Egypt and would give the people a new cause for gratitude and celebration (verses 7-8).

This passage is an early messianic prophecy. The messiah is not a supernatural being, only a good king like Josiah; his reign is not seen as a future ideal paradise but just a coming time of peace, security, and prosperity. Thus, Jeremiah may be referred to as one of the earliest prophets of the messianic hope. His words can be seen in hindsight to be fulfilled by Jesus in the reign of God he embodied and proclaimed as the Good Shepherd (John 10).

Epistle: Colossians 1:11-20

Colossae in Paul's time was a large city and a center of the industries of wool-working and cloth-making. As a major metropolitan area, it would have had a cosmopolitan mixture of ethnic groups and religions, including Gentile Christians. This Gentile Christian community was probably founded by Epaphras (4:12)—a missionary in the Lycus valley, which included Colossae, Hierapolis, and Laodicea. The author of this letter wrote to remind them of the grandeur and all-sufficiency of Christ, "the image of the invisible God, the firstborn of all creation" (1:15).

Faith in the Midst of Controversy

Epaphras very probably would have supplied the author with details of the community's joys and challenges. The words of encouragement implied that the congregation was contending with the "power of darkness" (verse 13), a designation given to the prestige, cogency, and influence of the (what Christians viewed as false) systems of thought arrayed against them. The most popular of these was gnosticism, a dualistic philosophy that, among other beliefs, conceived of the cosmos in terms of opposing arenas of evil and good. One attained the good by way of secret wisdom, which lifted the believer out of the condemned physical world and into the redeemed cosmic realm. Gnosticism also asserted that Jesus could not have been human, since all physical beings were tainted and evil.

The argument in this lection seized on these dualistic images and used them to refute the gnostic contentions. Jesus Christ is the prime physical product of the cosmos; he has a wisdom from God that is not secret or selective, but available to all by God's grace, through Christ's death and resurrection (verse 20).

The Christ Hymn

The underlying theme, in what has been called the "Christ hymn" (verses 15-20)—in reference to the possibility that it was part of an early Christian liturgy (verses 15-20)—is directly related to God's revelation in Jesus as the *Logos* (God's creative energy; verses 16b, 17b, 19). Of equal importance with Christ's creating and sustaining of the cosmos (verses 16-17) was his establishment of and rule over the church (verse 18). Any worship of cosmic or angelic beings, such as advocated and practiced by the gnostics, was therefore unnecessary and an affront to God in Christ.

The Colossians shared "in the inheritance of the saints in the light" (verse 12). Light and darkness were among the dualistic images of gnosticism and corresponded to good and evil. Through Christ's death on the cross, "all things" (not only human beings but the entire creation) had been reconciled (brought back into relationship) with God (verse 20). Persons so redeemed were rescued from darkness, restored to the light, and made members of the church over which Christ reigned and who were called to witness in his name.

Think About It: The reign of Christ had begun and was firmly in place. Gnostics take note! Against what "powers of darkness" (alien systems of thought and centers of influence) are the church and the gospel contending today? What beliefs and values do they threaten? How can the church deal with them?

Christ Is Lord of All

Redemption through Christ was a universal act. Even those who may have had connection with pagan gods were welcome to seek this forgiveness (verses 13-14). Christ was Lord of all, and his redemptive power was manifest in the transforming light of resurrection (verse 12). God has initiated the opportunity for all to be pardoned from sin and to acknowledge Christ's reign over the powers of the universe. The church at Colossae had a friend in Jesus

Christ, ruler of heaven and earth and savior of the whole world. The reign of Christ had begun and was firmly in place. There were no powers, spirits, or beings that could contend with him. Gnostics take note!

A New Testament Psalm: Luke 1:68-79

Zechariah, aging father of John the Baptist, had been struck dumb. But when he concurred with Elizabeth's choice to name the boy John, his tongue was loosed and the Spirit filled him with this psalm of praise, which we call the "Benedictus" (from the Latin for the first word, "Blessed"). Containing many Old Testament references, the first part (verses 68-75) resembles a Jewish messianic hymn, similar to the psalms of gratitude in the Dead Sea Scrolls. It celebrates the fulfillment of Jewish hopes in God's redemption through sending a deliverer in the Davidic line (verses 68-69). This is a fulfillment of the prophetic promises that God would provide protection and forgiveness, in keeping with the covenant with Abraham (verses 70-73a). People would be freed from anxiety to serve God faithfully throughout their lives (verses 73b-75).

In the second part of the hymn (verses 76-79), Zechariah proclaims that John would be the prophetic harbinger of the Messiah, preparing his way, announcing that God's liberation and grace were on the way (verses 76-77). This is a reference to Malachi 4:2, 5, which predicts that Elijah would return as the prophet of the end time to pave the way for the "sun of righteousness." The darkness was ending, dawn was at hand, the light of God's compassion would illuminate the way to God's shalom (verses 78-79). Thus, the third of our lections also anticipates the coming reign of Christ.

Gospel: Luke 23:33-43

This portion of Luke's Crucifixion account includes the name of the place—"The Skull"; the scorn of the leaders; the taunts of the soldiers; the offering of sour wine; the inscription, "King of the Jews"; the derision of one thief, the penitent plea of the other, and Jesus' promise of salvation to the latter.

Jesus' decision to complete his journey in faithful response to God's call to face his accusers in Jerusalem led him reluctantly but inevitably on the path to the cross. He explored every avenue to win over his critics and lead them into God's way of love and justice, but all to no avail; they wanted him dead. Little did they know that their opposition would open the door of salvation for all the world to enter. Jesus' life, death, and resurrection brought blessing to all of God's creation, and inaugurated the messianic realm.

Agony on a Cross

Crucifixion seems to have begun among the Persians. From there it spread to the Greeks and then to the Romans, who regarded it as a supreme form of execution usually reserved for rebellious slaves and insurrectionists. Intended as a deterrent, crucifixion usually was carried out in a public place. Death often came slowly, sometimes only after several days—brought about by the cumulative effect of the scourging, loss of blood, exposure, pain, thirst, and suffocation from the weight on the victim's diaphragm.

A Penitent Thief

Unique to Luke is the conversation between Jesus and the two thieves. One thief exhibited an attitude of outright contempt; in the midst of his own torment, he used his ebbing energy to deride Jesus. The other was more vulnerable and honest, begging for mercy. Both pleaded for their lives—the first sarcastically and desperately, the second humbly and trustingly. This sincere repentance, even at the point of death, touched Jesus' heart; and he went beyond the request for salvation and extended to him security and companionship in the next life.

The Prince of Peace

The Crucifixion presents a paradox: through the violent suffering of Jesus, the world is offered a peaceful existence. Jesus' life was the epitome of sensitivity, service, and sacrifice. His every encounter was affirming, nonviolent, and compassionate. All who came to him penitent and searching, left with a newfound peace and a challenge to share that shalom with others. God intends for our lives to mirror this way of peace—peace in our world, our institutions, our neighborhoods, our families, and in our souls. This is the realm of God over which Christ—the Prince of Peace—reigns as sovereign.

> **Think About It:** The Crucifixion presents a paradox: peaceful existence coming through violent suffering. What brings real peace? Is it ever easily achieved or maintained? How do we participate in it and help bring it into being?

Study Suggestions

A. Proclaiming the Reign of Christ

State that this day in the church year celebrates the reign of Christ and that the lections are chosen in relation to this theme. The Jeremiah passage is an early messianic prophecy promising a reign of peace with justice under a restored Davidic monarchy. The "Christ Hymn" in Colossians 1 is a portion of an early church liturgy countering gnostic dualism and its downgrading of Jesus' divinity. The Benedictus of Zechariah proclaims the coming messianic age, inaugurated by John the Baptist. And Luke's Crucifixion story promises paradise to the penitent thief—and to all who seek forgiveness and peace—in the dawning reign of the Prince of Peace. Commemorate this significant tradition by singing, "God Hath Spoken by the Prophets."

B. Reflecting on Shepherds and Sheep

Read aloud Jeremiah 23:1-6. Assign class members as individuals or teams to look up, read, and be prepared to summarize Psalm 72, Jeremiah 37 and 38, and the several sections of Jeremiah 21:1-23:8 mentioned in the commentary (pages 370–71), as these come up in the discussion.

Use the "Think About It" questions to relate this to the assessment of present-day leaders in church and government in terms of this standard. Also ask: What new insights do we gain from Jeremiah's use of the shepherd metaphor to refer to God's expectations of kings and leaders? What other analogy would you draw to emphasize political accountability under God?

C. Singing the Christ Hymn

Read aloud Colossians 1:11-20. Drawing on the commentary on pages 371–73, review the background relative to gnostic teaching, the *Logos*, light and darkness, and the reign of Christ. Explore the "Think About It" questions relative to contending with today's "powers of darkness." Consider such forces as materialism, militarism, consumerism, racism, large institutions, corporate media, lobbies. Also ask: What is the place of these powers within the reign of Christ?

D. Preparing the Way

Read aloud Luke 1:68-79, review the commentary on page 373, tell the story of Zechariah's announcement, and point out the two parts of his Benedictus and their different points of focus. Note that this perspective on the reign of Christ stresses the fulfillment of Old Testament prophecy in the coming of John the Baptist. Ask: What is the significance of Zechariah's losing his voice, then getting it back to make this announcement?

E. Welcoming to Paradise

Read Luke 23:33-43. Review the key elements in the story as summarized in the commentary on pages 373–74. Concentrate on Jesus' conversation and his assurance to the penitent one that he would soon be with him in paradise. Ask: What do you think Jesus meant by "paradise"? Is the primary manifestation of the reign of Christ on earth or in heaven? Explore the "Think About It" questions about the relationship of crucifixion to peace in the realm of the Prince of Peace.

F. Pointing Toward Advent

Summarize the four dimensions of Christ's reign found in today's lections, and note that they all point in different ways toward the season of Advent that begins next Sunday. Sing or read in unison one or more stanzas of the hymn, "Rejoice the Lord is King," then end with the Lord's Prayer.

List of Scriptures

Revised Common Lectionary, Year C

SEASON OF ADVENT
First Sunday of Advent
Jeremiah 33:14-16
Psalm 25:1-10
1 Thessalonians 3:9-13
Luke 21:25-36
Second Sunday of Advent
Malachi 3:1-4
Luke 1:68-79
Philippians 1:3-11
Luke 3:1-6
Third Sunday of Advent
Zephaniah 3:14-20
Isaiah 12:2-6
Philippians 4:4-7
Luke 3:7-18
Fourth Sunday of Advent
Micah 5:2-5a
Luke 1:47-55
Hebrews 10:5-10
Luke 1:39-45 (46-55)

SEASON OF CHRISTMAS
Christmas Day
Isaiah 52:7-10
Psalm 98
Hebrews 1:1-4 (5-12)

John 1:1-14
First Sunday After Christmas Day
1 Samuel 2:18-20, 26
Psalm 148
Colossians 3:12-17
Luke 2:41-52

SEASON OF EPIPHANY
Epiphany of the Lord
Isaiah 60:1-6
Psalm 72:1-7, 10-14
Ephesians 3:1-12
Matthew 2:1-12
Baptism of the Lord, First Sunday After the Epiphany
Isaiah 43:1-7
Psalm 29
Acts 8:14-17
Luke 3:15-17, 21-22
Second Sunday After the Epiphany
Isaiah 62:1-5
Psalm 36:5-10
1 Corinthians 12:1-11
John 2:1-11
Third Sunday After the Epiphany
Nehemiah 8:1-3, 5-6, 8-10
Psalm 19

377

1 Corinthians 12:12-31a
Luke 4:14-21
Fourth Sunday After the Epiphany
Jeremiah 1:4-10
Psalm 71:1-6
1 Corinthians 13:1-13
Luke 4:21-30
Fifth Sunday After the Epiphany
Isaiah 6:1-8 (9-13)
Psalm 138
1 Corinthians 15:1-11
Luke 5:1-11
Sixth Sunday After the Epiphany
Jeremiah 17:5-10
Psalm 1
1 Corinthians 15:12-20
Luke 6:17-26
Seventh Sunday After the Epiphany
Genesis 45:3-11, 15
Psalm 37:1-11, 39-40
1 Corinthians 15:35-38, 42-50
Luke 6:27-38
Eighth Sunday After the Epiphany
Isaiah 55:10-13
Psalm 92:1-4, 12-15
1 Corinthians 15:15-58
Luke 6:39-49
Transfiguration Sunday
Exodus 34:29-35
Psalm 99
2 Corinthians 3:12-4:2
Luke 9:28-36 (37-43)

SEASON OF LENT
First Sunday in Lent
Deuteronomy 26:1-11
Psalm 91:1-2, 9-16
Romans 10:8b-13
Luke 4:1-13
Second Sunday in Lent
Genesis 15:1-12, 17-18
Psalm 27
Philippians 3:17–4:1
Luke 13:31-35

Third Sunday in Lent
Isaiah 55:1-9
Psalm 63:1-8
1 Corinthians 10:1-13
Luke 13:1-9
Fourth Sunday in Lent
Joshua 5:9-12
Psalm 32
2 Corinthians 5:16-21
Luke 15:1-3, 11b-32
Fifth Sunday in Lent
Isaiah 43:16-21
Psalm 126
Philippians 3:4b-14
John 12:1-8
Passion/Palm Sunday
Isaiah 50:4-9a
Psalm 31:9-16
Philippians 2:5-11
Luke 22:14–23:56

SEASON OF EASTER
Easter Day
Acts 10:34-43
Psalm 118:1-2, 14-24
1 Corinthians 15:19-26
John 20:1-18
Second Sunday of Easter
Acts 5:27-32
Psalm 150
Revelation 1:4-8
John 20:19-31
Third Sunday of Easter
Acts 9:1-6, (7-20)
Psalm 30
Revelation 5:11-14
John 21:1-19
Fourth Sunday of Easter
Acts 9:36-43
Psalm 23
Revelation 7:9-17
John 10:22-30
Fifth Sunday of Easter
Acts 11:1-18

Psalm 148
Revelation 21:1-6
John 13:31-35
Sixth Sunday of Easter
Acts 16:9-15
Psalm 67
Revelation 21:10, 22–22:5
John 14:23-29
The Ascension of the Lord
Acts 1:1-11
Psalm 47
Ephesians 1:15-23
Luke 24:44-53
Seventh Sunday of Easter
Acts 16:16-34
Psalm 97
Revelation 22:12-14, 16-17, 20-21
John 17:20-26
Day of Pentecost
Acts 2:1-21
Psalm 104:24-34, 35b
Romans 8:14-17
John 14:8-17 (25-27)

SUNDAYS AFTER PENTECOST
Trinity Sunday
Proverbs 8:1-4, 22-31
Psalm 8
Romans 5:1-5
John 16:12-15
Sunday Between May 29 and June 4
1 Kings 18:20-39
Psalm 96
Galatians 1:1-12
Luke 7:1-10
Sunday Between June 5 and 11
1 Kings 17:8-24
Psalm 146
Galatians 1:11-24
Luke 7:11-17
Sunday Between June 12 and 18
1 Kings 21:1-21a
Psalm 5:1-8
Galatians 2:15-21

Luke 7:36–8:3
Sunday Between June 19 and 25
1 Kings 19:1-15a
Psalm 42
Galatians 3:23-29
Luke 8:26-39
Sunday Between June 26 and July 2
2 Kings 2:1-2, 6-14
Psalm 77:1-2, 11-20
Galatians 5:1, 13-25
Luke 9:51-62
Sunday Between July 3 and 9
2 Kings 5:1-14
Psalm 30
Galatians 6:(1-6) 7-16
Luke 10:1-11, 16-20
Sunday Between July 10 and 16
Amos 7:7-17
Psalm 82
Colossians 1:1-14
Luke 10:25-37
Sunday Between July 17 and 23
Amos 8:1-12
Psalm 52
Colossians 1:15-28
Luke 10:38-42
Sunday Between July 24 and 30
Hosea 1:2-10
Psalm 85
Colossians 2:6-15 (16-19)
Luke 11:1-13
Sunday Between July 31 and August 6
Hosea 11:1-11
Psalm 107:1-9, 43
Colossians 3:1-11
Luke 12:13-21
Sunday Between August 7 and 13
Isaiah 1:1, 10-20
Psalm 50:1-8, 22-23
Hebrews 11:1-3, 8-16
Luke 12:32-40
Sunday Between August 14 and 20
Isaiah 5:1-7
Psalm 80:1-2, 8-19

Hebrews 11:29–12:2
Luke 12:49-56
Sunday Between August 21 and 27
Jeremiah 1:4-10
Psalm 71:1-6
Hebrews 12:18-29
Luke 13:10-17
*Sunday Between August 28
and September 3*
Jeremiah 2:4-13
Psalm 81:1, 10-16
Hebrews 13:1-8, 15-16
Luke 14:1, 7-14
Sunday Between September 4 and 10
Jeremiah 18:1-11
Psalm 139:1-6, 13-18
Philemon 1-21
Luke 14:25-33
Sunday Between September 11 and 17
Jeremiah 4:11-12, 22-28
Psalm 14
1 Timothy 1:12-17
Luke 15:1-10
Sunday Between September 18 and 24
Jeremiah 8:18–9:1
Psalm 79:1-9
1 Timothy 2:1-7
Luke 16:1-13
*Sunday Between September 25
and October 1*
Jeremiah 32:1-3a, 6-15
Psalm 91:1-6, 14-16
1 Timothy 6:6-19
Luke 16:19-31
Sunday Between October 2 and 8
Lamentations 1:1-6
Psalm 137
2 Timothy 1:1-14
Luke 17:5-10
Sunday Between October 9 and 15
Jeremiah 29:1, 4-7
Psalm 66:1-12
2 Timothy 2:8-15

Luke 17:11-19
Sunday Between October 16 and 22
Jeremiah 31:27-34
Psalm 119:97-104
2 Timothy 3:14–4:5
Luke 18:1-8
Sunday Between October 23 and 29
Joel 2:23-32
Psalm 65
2 Timothy 4:6-8, 16-18
Luke 18:9-14
*Sunday Between October 30
and November 5*
Habakkuk 1:1-4; 2:1-4
Psalm 119:137-144
2 Thessalonians 1:1-4, 11-12
Luke 19:1-10
*All Saints (November 1, or may be
used on first Sunday in November)*
Daniel 7:1-3, 15-18
Psalm 149
Ephesians 1:11-23
Luke 6:20-31
Sunday Between November 6 and 12
Haggai 1:15b–2:9
Psalm 145:1-5, 17-21
2 Thessalonians 2:1-5, 13-17
Luke 20:27-38
Sunday Between November 13 and 19
Isaiah 65:17-25
Psalm 118
2 Thessalonians 3:6-13
Luke 21:5-19
*Reign of Christ, Sunday Between
November 20 and 26*
Jeremiah 23:1-6
Luke 1:68-79
Colossians 1:11-20
Luke 23:33-43